# ELEMENTS OF MODERN
# SHIP CONSTRUCTION

## Other Works Published by: D. J. House

Seamanship Techniques (3rd Edition), 2004, Elsevier Ltd
ISBN 0750663154

Seamanship Techniques, Volume III, "The Command Companion", 2000, Butterworth/Heinemann
ISBN 0750644435

Marine Survival and Rescue Systems (2nd Edition), 1997,Witherby
ISBN 1 856091279

Navigation for Masters (3rd Edition), 2005, Witherby
ISBN 1856092712

An Introduction to Helicopter Operations at Sea – A Guide to Industry (2nd Edition), 1998, Witherby
ISBN 1856091686

Cargo Work (7th Edition) 1998, Butterworth/Heinemann
ISBN 0750665556

Anchor Practice – A Guide to Industry, 2001, Witherby
ISBN 1856092127

Marine Ferry Transports – An Operator's Guide, 2002, Witherby
ISBN 1856092313

Dry Docking and Shipboard Maintenance, 2002, Witherby
ISBN 1856092453

Marine Heavy Lift and Rigging Operations, 2005, Brown, Son & Ferguson, Ltd
ISBN 0851747205

The Seamanship Examiner, 2007, Elsevier Ltd
ISBN 075066701X

Ship Handling, 2007, Elsevier Ltd
ISBN 978-0-7506-8530-6

The Ice Navigation Manual, 2009, Witherby Seamanship International
ISBN 978-1-9053-3159-8

Also:–

Marine Technology Reference Book (Safety Chapter) edited Morgan/Butterworths

Web Site: www.djhouseonline.com

# ELEMENTS OF MODERN

# SHIP CONSTRUCTION

BY

## D. J. HOUSE

GLASGOW

BROWN, SON & FERGUSON, LTD., NAUTICAL PUBLISHERS

4–10 DARNLEY STREET

First Edition  –    –    –    –  2010

ISBN 978-0-85174-814-6

# Contents

|  | page |
|---|---|
| About the Author | vii |
| Introduction to Elements of Modern Ship Construction | viii |
| Preface | ix |
| List of Acknowledgements | x |
| List of Shipyard and Construction Abbreviations | xi |
| Shipyard Terminology | xviii |
| Ship Types | xxxiv |

**Chapter One – Marine Measurement** ........................... 1

Introduction, Lloyds Regulations pre-amble, Class of vessels & Ice Strengthening. General definitions: ship dimensions, Ship types A & B. Assignment of Load lines. Tonnage, Ships' plans, deadweight scale, docking plan, general arrangement, shell expansion. Tank measurement/Ullage. Pitch & Slip of Propellors.

**Chapter Two – The Aft End** ........................... 31

Introduction, Propellers and securings, Rudder types and terminology Sternframes. Rudder Carriers Posts and bearings, Twin propeller and Azi-pod arrangements. Stern types and general arrangements. Stern Tubes, tail end shaft and propeller types. Securing, propeller, Thrust Blocks, Rotary Vane Steering.

**Chapter Three – Bottom Structure and Engine Room Spaces** ........................... 70

Introduction, Keel construction, Duct keels, Double bottom construction, floors, longitudinals, Intercostals, turn of bilge and bilge arrangements. Engine seating, Engine room double bottom, sump areas, Tanker Double Bottoms, Bilge and Ballast pumping systems. Stabiliser systems. Tanks fins and bilge keels.

**Chapter Four – Upper/Lower Deck Structures and Hatch Construction** ........................... 90

Introduction Deck plate construction, Hatchway arrangements, coamings and covers, Deep Tank construction, Pillars, Ventilators and air pipes, Deck openings and access points, watertight doors. Athwartships and Longitudinal framing, hold construction, Decks, deck support and wood decking,

**Chapter Five – Fore End** ........................... 126

Introduction, Bow construction, Fore peak, forward arrangements and bulbous bow. Bulkheads Collision/ engine room etc., Bow rudder, and forward arrangements, chain lockers and cable fittings, Panting arrangements, stem, Bow thrust units, Anchor/Windlass and mooring fitments. Bulwarks.

**Chapter Six – Passenger and Ferry, Constructional Features** ........................... 163

Introduction, Hull openings, ferry transports, bow and stern doors. Ro-Ro ramp arrangements, Vehicle decks and door arrangements. Passenger vessel features. Shell doors, High Speed Craft categories and design. Water jets.

**Chapter Seven – Oil Gas and Chemical Tankers** ........................... 197

Introduction, oil tanker, design and features. Tank configuration and construction. Double hulls and pipelines. Inert gas systems. Gas tanks, LNG carriers, classification of chemical carriers.

**Chapter Eight – Dry Cargo Carriers – Bulk, General and Containers** ........................... 225

Bulk carrier features, side opening hatches. Dry cargo hold construction and vessel features. Derricks, masts and Cranes. Container vessels, cell structure. Pontoon hatches.

**Chapter Nine – Miscellaneous Shipboard Fittings. Life Saving Appliances** ........................... 244

Introduction – Heli-decks, Boat Davit launch systems and free fall lifeboat structures.

**Appendix – Ship Yard Practice** ........................... 257

Ship building operations, prefabrication, welding methods. Docking methods, launching methods. Materials and ship stresses.

**General Index** ........................... 329

*Author: D. J. HOUSE*

# About the Author

David House currently lectures in Nautical Studies, his main disciplines being in the subjects of Seamanship and Navigation. He has to date, published fourteen maritime texts on related topics which encompass:– "Helicopter Operations at Sea", "Anchorwork Practice", "Marine Ferry Transports" Dry Docking, as well as Navigation, Ship Handling, Cargo Work and the popular Seamanship Techniques series.

His works are drawn from a seagoing background which gave him experience on a variety of ships, engaging on many world wide trades. Coupled with a thirty year teaching and lecture period, has led to continued research into related topics. His most recent books, being "Heavy Lift & Rigging" and the " Seamanship Self Examiner" are expected to be widely accepted throughout the maritime sectors.

This latest work on "Ship Construction" provides a comprehensive overview of shipbuilding aspects that an aspiring Deck Officer would be expected to become familiar with, during his working life.

# Introduction to Elements of Modern Ship Construction

The text and contents of this work has been influenced by the Rules and Regulations for the Classification of Ships as published by Lloyds Register. These Regulations are continually under review and experience periodic amendments effecting the building and construction methods applicable to new tonnage. Additionally other Maritime Regulations have been referred to, to provide enhancement to specific construction procedures and/or specific elements of construction.

Where specialist vessels are of concern such as those designed to carry Liquefied Gases in Bulk, additional reference to the International Code for the Construction and Equipment of Ships Carrying Liquefied Gases in Bulk, or the IGC code, as it is known, should be made. Similarly, for those vessels designed to carry Chemicals in Bulk, additional reference should also be made to the International Code for the Construction and Equipment of Ships carrying dangerous Chemicals in Bulk, known as the IBC code.

The major Classification Societies have more recently approved Unified Regulations for ship construction, known as the Common Structural Rules (CSR), but these are not universal for all societies and many follow their own national regulations. Ice Classification for ships is a typical example, where the Russian Maritime Registry (RS) and Norske Veritas (DNV) have carried out considerable research in developing high structural standards.

Shipyards around the world tend to specialise in building ship types and gain experience in a known field. However, practice from one complex to another does vary with advances in new materials and technology, systems, operations and design changes. Greater use is now made of the more modern materials like aluminium, plastics and ceramics, but the dominance of steel throughout the shipbuilding industry still persists.

The future building programmes can expect construction to be carried out to a specified life span, of not less than twenty five years, while at the same time being safe and environmentally friendly. Ships so constructed should be capable of worldwide operations and be engaged within the policies of safer ships, cleaner seas, under the International Safety Management convention. Mandatory changes effecting coatings, equipment and emissions can expect to be enforced by 2012, all of which will generate changes from the way ships are built today, to the designs and methods employed in future years.

# Preface

Elements of Modern Ship Construction has been compiled for maritime students to become aware of the many changes that have occurred within the ship building industry. Many of these changes being introduced are mandatory for the protection of the marine environment.

The extended use of new materials is pushing the boundaries of marine construction. New builds are incorporating much more in the way of labour saving concepts and safer working practice for the seafarer. It is only right that the mariner keeps himself/herself abreast of new design.

Although the work in shipyards is conducted with economics in mind, the marine industry cannot afford to build irresponsibly. The modern hull must be safe in operation and those that build should be aware of the needs of those that sail. Equally, those at sea should be familiar with general ship knowledge.

It is hoped that the work will enhance and support our seafarers when engaged in their main disciplines of navigation, seamanship, stability and cargo operations.

**David J. House**                                                            **November, 2009**

# List of Acknowledgements

B + V Industrietechnik
Dubai Dry Docks U.A.E.
Fleetwood Nautical Campus of the Blackpool & Fylde College
Holland Roer Propeller
Lisnave Estaleiros Navais, S.A. (Shipyard, Setúbal, Portugal)
Lloyds Werft. Bremerhaven GmbH
Maersk Shipping
MacGregor & Co.(Naval Architects) Ltd.,
Mitsubishi Heavy Industries Ltd., Shimonoseki Shipyard & Machinery Works
MJP Waterjets Sweden
NQEA Shipyard Cairns, Australia.
Scheuerle Fahrzeugfabrik GmbH
Schilling Rudders
Smit Maritime Contractors, Europe and Smit International
Wynn Marine Limited U.K.
Imares Publications


**The author is indebted to the following for
Additional Photographic Contributions:–**

Capt. J. G. Swindlehurst
Mr. Anthony P. G. House. B/A
Mr. G. Edwards Mar/Eng. (Rtd.,)
Mr. Stuart Mooney Ch/Off (MN)
Mr. Paul Brooks Ch/Off (MN)
Mr. M. Crofts Ch/Off (MN)
Mr. K. B. Millar Master Mariner, Lect. Nautical Studies
Mr. Mark Gooderman Master Mariner. B.A. Lecturer Nautical Studies
Mr. Sydney Garrett. Master Mariner, Lecturer Nautical Studies
Mr. John Leyland. Lecturer Nautical Studies
Mr. Christopher A. Mclallion
Mr. Robert Ashcroft 2nd Officer (MN)

Miss Martel Fursden 2nd Officer (MN)


Research Assistant: Mr. A. P. G. House BA.
I.T. Consultant: Mr. C. D. House

# Shipyard and Construction Abbreviations

| | |
|---|---|
| $^\circ$A | Degrees Absolute |
| ABS | American Bureau of Shipping |
| $A_{BT}$ | Area of traverse cross section of a Bulbous Bow |
| A.C. (i) | Alternating Current |
| (ii) | Admiralty Cast |
| ACV | Air Cushion Vessel |
| AD | Anno Domini |
| $A_E$ | Expanded blade area of a Propeller |
| AFS | Anti-fouling System |
| AHV | Anchor Handling Vessel |
| AKD | Auto Kick Down |
| AMD | Advanced Multi Hull Design |
| AP | Aft Perpendicular |
| Aux | Auxiliary |
| | |
| B (i) | Representative of the ship's Centre of Buoyancy |
| (ii) | Overall Beam Width |
| B.C. | Code of Safe Working Practice for Bulk Cargoes (code) |
| BLG | Bulk Liquid and Gases |
| BM | Height of Transverse Metacenter |
| BOG | Boil Off Gas |
| BP | Between Perpendiculars |
| BS (i) | Breaking Strength |
| (ii) | British Standard |
| BT | Ballast Tank |
| BV | Bureau Veritas |
| BWM | Ballast Water Management |
| | |
| C | Coefficient |
| C$^\circ$ | Degrees Centigrade |
| CAD | Computer Aided Design |
| $C_B$ | Block Coefficient |
| $C_{BA}$ | Block Coefficient of the Aft Body |
| $C_{BD}$ | Block Coefficient based on depth |
| $C_{BF}$ | Block Coefficient of the Fore Body |
| CBT | Clean Ballast Tank |
| cc | Corrosion control |
| CCS | China Classification Society |
| CCTV | Close Circuit Television |
| CDP | Controlled Depletion Polymers |
| CEU | Car Equivalent Unit |
| CL | Centre Line |
| CM | Construction Monitoring |
| CMP | Construction Monitoring Plan |

| | |
|---|---|
| cms | Centimetres |
| CNG | Compressed Natural Gas |
| CO | Chief Officer |
| CoG | Centre of Gravity |
| CoI | Certificate of Inspection (as issued by the U.S. Coastguard) |
| COW | Crude Oil Washing system |
| $CO_2$ | Carbon Dioxide |
| COI | Certificate of Inspection (USCG) |
| COW | Crude Oil Washing System |
| CPP | Controllable Pitch Propeller |
| CRA | Corrosion Resistant Alloy |
| CRP | Contra Rotating Propellers |
| CSH | Continuous Survey Hull |
| CSM | Continuous Survey Machinery |
| CSR | Common Structural Rules |
| CSSC | China State Shipbuilding Corporation |
| CSWP | Code of Safe Working Practice |
| CWL | Constructed Waterline. |
| $C_{WP}$ | Water Plane Area Coefficient |
| | |
| D | Moulded Depth of the ship's hull (m) |
| $D_A$ | Draught Aft |
| $D_F$ | Draught Forward |
| $D_m$ | Draught Amidships |
| $D_P$ | Diameter of ship's Propeller |
| DAT | Double Acting Tanker |
| DB | Double Bottom |
| DC | Direct Current |
| DD | Dry Dock |
| Df | Draught forward |
| DFT | Dry Film Thickness |
| Dm | Draught amidships |
| DNV | Det Norske Veritas |
| DP | Dynamic Positioning |
| DSC | Dynamically Supported Craft |
| DSS | Double Sided Skins |
| DSV | Diving Support Vessel |
| DWA | Dock Water Allowance |
| dwt (DWT) | Deadweight tonnage |
| | |
| EC | European Community |
| ECR | Engine Control Room |
| FDA | Fatigue Design Assessment |
| EEBD | Emergency Escape Breathing Device |
| EFSWR | Extra Flexible Steel Wire Rope |
| EMSA | European Maritime Safety Agency |
| ESP | Enhanced Survey Programme |
| EU | European Union |
| | |
| FMA | Finnish Maritime Administration |
| FMECA | Failure Mode Effective Critical Analysis |
| FO | Fuel Oil |
| foap | Forward of Aft Perpendicular |
| FP (i) | Fixed Pitch |
| (ii) | Forward Perpendicular |
| F.Pk. | Fore Peak tank |

| | |
|---|---|
| FPSO | Floating Production Storage Offloading System |
| FPV | Fisheries Protection Vessel |
| Frd (Fwd) | Forward |
| FRP | Fibreglass Reinforced Plastic |
| FSI | Flag State Implementation |
| FSICR | Finnish-Swedish Ice Class Rules |
| FSM's | Free Surface Moments |
| FSU | Floating Storage Unit |
| FSW | Friction Stir Welding |
| FSWR | Flexible Steel Wire Rope |
| Ft | Feet |
| FW | Fresh Water |
| FWA | Fresh Water Allowance |
| | |
| G | Representative of the ship's Centre of Gravity |
| gals | Gallons |
| GHz | Giga Hertz |
| GL | Germanischer Lloyd |
| GM | Metacentric Height |
| GRP | Glass Reinforced Plastic |
| grt | Gross registered tonnage |
| GT | Gas Turbine |
| GTM | Gas Transport Module |
| GZ | Representative of the ship's "Righting lever" |
| | |
| $h_{db}$ | Height of Double Bottom |
| Hex | Hexagonal |
| HFO | Heavy Fuel Oil |
| HMS | Her Majesties Ship |
| HP | High Pressure |
| h.p. | horse power |
| HPFWW | High pressure Fresh Water Wash |
| HSC | High Speed Craft |
| HSE | Health and Safety Executive |
| HSSC | Harmonised System of Survey |
| HTS | High Tensile Steel |
| | |
| IACS | International Association of Classification Societies |
| IBC | International Code for the Construction and Equipment of Ships Carrying Dangerous Chemicals in Bulk |
| ICCP | Impressed Current Cathodic Protection |
| ICR | Intercooled and Recuperated |
| ICS | International Chamber of Shipping |
| IG | Inert Gas |
| ILLC | International Load Line Convention |
| ILO | International Labour Organisation |
| IMO | International Marine Organisation |
| IPS | Integrated Power System (Controllable podded propulsion) |
| ISM | International Safety Management (code) |
| ISO | International Organisation of Standardization |
| ISPS | International Ship and Port Security Code |
| ITF | International Transport Federation. |
| IWS | In Water Survey |
| | |
| K | Representative of the position of the Ship's Keel. |
| KB | Height of the centre of Buoyancy above the Keel |

| | |
|---|---|
| KG | That distance from the Keel to the ship's CoG. |
| Kg (kg) | Kilograms |
| KM | That distance from the Keel to the Metacentre "M" |
| kts | Knots |
| kW | Kilowatt |
| | |
| L | Representative of the ship's length |
| LBP | Length Between Perpendiculars |
| Lbs | pounds |
| LCB | Longitudinal Centre of Buoyancy |
| LCD | Liquid Crystal Display |
| LCG | Longitudinal Centre of Gravity |
| LEL | Lower Explosive Limit |
| LFL | Lower Flammable Limit |
| LISCR | Liberian International Ship Corporate Registry |
| LMC | Lloyds Machinery Certificate |
| LNG | Liquefied Natural Gas |
| LNGRV | Liquefied Natural Gas Regasification Vessel |
| LOA | Length Overall |
| LP | Low Pressure |
| LPG | Liquefied Propane Gas |
| LPH | Landing Platform Helicopters |
| LR | Lloyds Register |
| LSA | Life Saving Appliances |
| LSFO | Low Sulphur Fuel Oil |
| $L_{WT}$ | Length at Waterline (m) |
| | |
| M | Representative of the ship's Metacenter |
| M (m) | metres |
| MAIB | Marine Accident Investigation Branch |
| MARPOL | Marine Pollution convention |
| MCA | Maritime Coastguard Agency |
| MCTC | Moment to Change Trim 1 centimetre |
| MEPC | Marine Environment Protection Committee |
| MEWP | Mobile Elevator Work Platform |
| Mg | Manganese |
| MGN | Marine Guidance Notice |
| MHR | Mean Hull Roughness |
| ml | millionth |
| mm | millimetres |
| MODU | Mobile Offshore Drilling Unit |
| m.rads | metre radians |
| MSC | Marine Safety Committee (of IMO) |
| MSN | Merchant Shipping Notice |
| MT | Magnetic Testing |
| MV | Motor Vessel |
| MW | Mega Watt |
| | |
| n | Number of Decks |
| NDT | Non Destructive Testing |
| NK | Nippon Kaiji Kyokai (Japanese Register) |
| NLS | Noxious Liquid Substance |
| NVE | Night Vision Equipment |
| | |
| OBO | Oil, Bulk Ore (carrier) |
| O/S | Offshore |

| P | Port |
|---|---|
| P/A | Public Address System |
| PCC | Pure Car Carrier |
| PCM | Plasma Cutting Machine |
| PCTC | Pure Car and Truck Carrier |
| PDM | Product Data Management |
| PDS | Product Development System |
| PHA | Preliminary Hazard Analysis |
| PLNG | Pressurised Liquid Natural Gas |
| PMA | Permanent Means of Access |
| PT | Penetration Testing |
| ppm | parts per million |
| PRS | Polish Register of Shipping |
| PSC | Port State Control |
| psi | pounds per square inch |
| PVC | Polyvinyl Chloride |
| | |
| R | Radius |
| RA | Risk Assessment |
| RD | Relative Density |
| R&D | Research and Development |
| RINA | Register Italiano Navale (Classification Society Italy) |
| RMC | Refrigerated Machinery Certificate |
| RMR | Russian Maritime Register of Shipping |
| RoPax | Roll On, Roll Off + Passenger vessel |
| Ro-Ro | Roll On-Roll Off |
| RoT | Rate of Turn |
| rpm | Revolutions per minute |
| RS | Russian Maritime Register of Shipping |
| RT | Radiographic Testing |
| RVP | Reid Vapour Pressure |
| | |
| S (i) | Starboard |
| (ii) | Wetted Surface Area |
| SBT | Segregated Ballast Tank |
| SCBA | Self Contained Breathing Apparatus |
| SDA | Structural Design Assessment |
| SECA | Sulphur Emission Control Area |
| SEVs | Surface Effect Vessels |
| SFP | Structural Fire Protection |
| s.g. | Specific Gravity |
| s.h.p. | Shaft Horse Power |
| S.I. | Statutory Instrument |
| SIGTTO | The Society of International Gas Tanker Terminal Operators |
| SLS | Skid Launch System |
| SOLAS | Safety of life at Sea convention |
| SP | Special Performance |
| SPC | Self Polishing Copolymer (Anti-fouling paint) |
| SPS | Sandwich Plate System |
| SQ | Special Quality |
| SQA | Square |
| SS | Steam Ship |
| SSA | Shipbuilding and Ship Repair Association |
| STEL | Short term Exposure Limit |
| $S_h$ | Aft Sheer Height |
| $S_v$ | Forward Sheer Height |

| | |
|---|---|
| SW | Salt Water |
| SWATH | Small Waterplane Area Twin Hull |
| SWL | Safe Working Load |
| SWR | Steel Wire Rope |
| | |
| T  (i) | Propeller Thrust |
| (ii) | Tropical |
| t | Trim |
| TBT | Tributyltin |
| T/D | Tween Deck |
| TEUs | Twenty foot equivalent unit |
| T.I.G. | Tungsten Inert Gas Welding |
| Tk | Tank |
| TLV | Threshold Limit Value |
| T/M (t/m) | Tonne Metres |
| TPC | Tons per Centimetre |
| Ts | Tonnes |
| TMA | Time Weighted Average |
| TWI | The Welding Institute |
| Tx/Rx | Transmit/Receive |
| | |
| UAR | United Arab Republic |
| UEL | Upper Explosive Limit |
| UFL | Upper Flammable Limit |
| UHP | Ultra High Pressure |
| UK | United Kingdom |
| UKC | Under Keel Clearance |
| UMS | Unmanned Machinery Space |
| USA | United States of America |
| USCG | United States Coast Guard |
| ULCC | Ultra Large Crude Carrier |
| ULCS | Ultra Large Container Ship |
| ULLNGC | Ultra Large Liquid Natural Gas Carrier |
| USS | United States Ship |
| UT | Ultra Sonic Testing |
| UV | Ultra Violet light |
| | |
| V | Speed of ship in knots |
| VCDB | Volga Caspian Design Bureau |
| VCG | Vertical Centre of Gravity |
| VCR | Voith Cycloidal Rudders |
| VDR | Voyage data Recorder |
| VDU | Visual Display Unit |
| VLCC | Very Large Crude Carrier |
| VLGC | Very Large Gas Carrier |
| VOCs | Volatile Organic Compounds |
| VSP | Voith Schneider Propellers |
| VT | Visual Testing |
| | |
| W  (i) | Representative of the ship's Displacement |
| (ii) | Watts |
| (iii) | Winter |
| WAT | Wing Assisted Tri-maran |
| WBT | Water Ballast Tank |
| WED | Wake Equalizing Duct |
| WFT | Wet Film Thickness |

| | |
|---|---|
| WiG | Wing in ground |
| WJ | Water Jet |
| W/L | Water Line |
| WPC | Wave Piecing Catamaran |
| wps | Wires per Strand |
| WTO | World Trade Organisation |
| | |
| Z | Representative of the number of Propeller Blades |
| Zn | Zinc |
| | |
| $\mu$ | Permeability Factor |

# Shipyard Terminology: Plate and Construction Terms

**Active Rudder** – A powered rudder sometimes fitted with a machinery pod and propeller causing propulsion in a positive direction as the pod and rudder are caused to move as one.

**Advance** – That forward motion of the ship from the moment that the vessel commences a turn. i.e. that distance travelled by the vessel in the direction of the original course to being on a course ninety degrees away from the original.

**"A" Frame** – A support structure, to provide rigidity to the shaft of a twin propeller construction. It is shaped like a turned over "A" shape hence its name, where the propeller shaft is supported at the apex of the structure. It is often employed in conjunction with a spectacle frame with propeller shafts of length.

**Aft Peak tank** – A water tank set right aft of the vessel. It will either be a designated fresh water tank or a ballast water tank used for adjusting the ship's trim. It is usually the only tank forward of the "Collision Bulkhead" that can be pumped in or out by means of the engine room pumping systems.

**Altars** – The stepped sides of a "Graving Dock" which accommodate wale shores when placed against the ship's side in the dock.

**Anchor certificate** – A certificate issued to the ship by a Classification Society which states that the ship is fitted with tested and approved working anchors and cables.

**Anchor Shackle** – That shackle that joins the anchor to the chain cable.

**Apron** – A part of a dry dock to which the "sill" is fastened.

**Azi-Pod** – (Azimuth Thruster) A rotating, ducted propeller secured to the ship's hull below the waterline. They are usually capable of turning through 360° and providing steerage propulsion in any direction. These units may be of a retractable type or a fixed "proud" feature of the outer hull.

**Balanced Rudder** – Is a rudder which is constructed with between 25% to 30% of its plate area positioned forward of the turning axis.

**Baseline** – Is defined by that lowest line effecting the ship's build which is horizontal to the lowest (deepest) part of the construction. Usually the lowest external edge of the keel.

**Beam Knees** – Triangular steel plates secured between beams or half beams and the side frames. They tend to compensate for racking stresses and localised stresses from heavy weights.

**Beams** – These are usually in the form of; "T" bulb bars, "H" Girders or Channel bars, which are designed to stiffen and support throughout the vessels length. They compensate for water pressure, panting, dry docking and racking stresses.

**Bearing Pintle** – Described by being the lowest bearing point of the ship's rudder, when the rudder is of a type which is supported within the structure of a stern frame arrangement.

**Bitter End** – That term given to the end of the ship's anchor cable. It is often slipped in dry dock for the purpose of ranging cables on the floor of the dock for inspection. The bitter end must have a quick, easy release fitted to facilitate slipping the anchor cable in an emergency.

**Boss Plate** – That shell plate of the hull, in a position either side of the Propeller Boss.

**Bow Rudder** – A forward rudder which is fitted in the bows of the vessel in addition to the stern rudder(s). They are a feature of some specialised vessels which are either double acting fore and aft, or a feature of ships which are engaged in regularly making sternway as a means of manoeuvring.

**Breadth, Depth Ratio** – B/D This value if it becomes large will have an unfavourable effect on the ship's strength and stability. The breadth/depth ratio should vary between 1.3 and 2. If allowed to increase the deck will be flooded when the vessel is inclined.

**Breadth, Draught ratio** – The breadth/draught ratio varies usually between 2.3 and 4.5, the larger value providing greater initial stability.

**Breast Plate** – A horizontal triangular plate fitted in the bows to join the shell plate of the port and starboard sides together.

**Bulbous Bow** – A rounded bow structure designed to reduce the effect of the bow wave of the vessel by reducing wave resistance. The internal structure usually forming a forward most tank position.

**Bulkhead Deck** – Is defined as that deck up to which all the main watertight transverse bulkheads extend.

**Bulkheads** – The steel, vertical partitions found between compartments. They compensate for racking, water pressure, dry docking and heavy weight stresses. They also combat hogging, sagging and shear forces.

**Cantilever Frame** – A curved frame set between the shell plate and the underside of deck stringers. Common to container vessels as they lent towards the construction of the under deck through passageway.

**Capstan** – A vertical warping drum employed with or without a chain cable holder. Usually fitted with an underdeck motor and employed for heaving and tightening mooring ropes. The warping drum is designed with "whelps" to provide an improved holding surface for mooring ropes.

**Caulking** – A procedure used to seal the planking of wood sheathed decks to make them watertight. Plank edge joints are slightly tapered and filled with oakum and then payed with molten pitch to seal the seam.
   **NB.** The term was also employed in riveted structures where rivets were seen to be weeping. These could be made watertight by pressure, spreading of the rivet head edge, by means of a cold chisel.

**Ceiling** – A protective cover, usually of wood, which is set over the tank tops in way of the hatchway of a cargo hold aboard a general cargo vessel. Ceiling provides protection for cargo parcels against ship or cargo sweat. Depending on how it is fitted it may also assist drainage in the hold. Referred to as the tank top ceiling.

**Certificate of Registry** – A document which is issued by a government which establishes the ownership and nationality of a vessel once built.

**Chain Locker** – A compartment usually positioned forward of the collision bulkhead which is used to accommodate the volume of chain cable attached to each of the ship's anchors. Locker maintenance is usually carried out when the vessel is dry docked because the cables are normally ranged on the dock floor freeing up the space to allow inspection, cleaning and painting to take place. The locker should be treated as an enclosed space.

**Cofferdam** – The term given to a space defined between two transverse bulkheads. The bulkheads are spaced at least 1.0 metre apart and the cofferdam is designed to keep tanks and holds isolated from each other. They are employed as a form of segregation.

**Coffin Plate** – A "U" shaped plate, found between the end of the keel and the bottom of the stern frame.

**Collision Bulkhead** – An athwartships bulkhead positioned at the forepart of the vessel. As the name suggests it is meant to sustain the rest of the ship's length following an impact like when in collision. The bulkhead is stiffened and considered watertight, although it is pierced by a single pipe usually to accommodate the fore peak pumping arrangement. It would be one of the structural members that would be visually sighted when carrying out a damage assessment following a collision, to detect for cracks or similar damage, which might lead to consecutive flooding of the vessel.

**Contra-rotating Propellers** – An arrangement of two propellers positioned on coaxial shafts which are caused to rotate in opposite directions.

**Controllable Pitch Propeller (CPP)** – A propeller where the blades are individually mounted on the "boss". The angle of pitch of the blades can be mechanically changed to suit the desired speed of the vessel. A reverse pitch angle can also be achieved for providing astern movement to the vessel.

**Crop** – The action of cutting away steelwork in a shipyard is referred to as cropping.

**Cruiser Stern** – A curved, rounded stern structure, extending from the aft part of the upper deck to the upper part of the stern frame.

**Curve of Floodable length** – Is defined by a curve which at every point in its length has an ordinate which represents the length of the ship which may be flooded, with the centre of the length at that point. Assuming that such flooding will cause the vessel to sink no further than the margin line.

**Deadlight** – Steel plate covers fitted to the inside of portholes. They can be secured by screw down bolts to prevent the ingress of water in the event that the glass porthole; is broken.

**Decks** – Horizontal steel plates providing deck flooring throughout the ship's length. Decks compensate for all longitudinal and athwartships stresses and reduce the hogging, sagging, shearing and bending forces effecting the vessel.

**Deep Tank** – A steel tank arrangement generally used for the carriage of liquid/bulk cargoes or ballast water. They are often found beneath a lower tween deck of a general cargo vessel or set either side of a shaft tunnel.

**Depth "D"** – a measure in metres taken at the middle of the length "L", from the top of the keel to the top of the deck beam at the side on the uppermost continuous deck.

**Double Bottom Tanks** – The internal tanking system found at the bottom of a ship, positioned either side of the keel. Usually employed for the carriage of fuel oil, ballast water, or diesel oil. All new tanker and bulk carrier construction can expect to be of double hull construction.

**Doubling Plate** – A reinforcing plate to strengthen a deck or bulkhead plate position, when additional supporting strength is considered necessary.

**Ducting** – A fabricated steel casement set around a propeller to influence water flow to the propeller.

**Duct Keel** – The name is given to a tunnel structure which tends to run from the fore end of the engine room to the collision bulkhead. It is usually large enough to accommodate an upright walking man. Access being normally gained through a manhole cover situated at the bottom of the engine room near the fore and aft line and close to the forward engine room bulkhead. Its function is to carry pipelines through the forward length of the vessel. There is no need for an aft "duct keel" because the same function is available with the shaft tunnel arrangement. Duct keels tend to be constructed in conjunction with a "Flat Plate Keel".

**Electric Steering Gear** – An all electric steering gear system based on the principle of a wheat-stone bridge. The imbalance in the current causing an electric motor to activate and cause corrective rudder movement.

**Electro-Hydraulic Steering** – A popular steering gear system which employs electric motors to operate pumps to activate hydraulic rams to move the tiller arm and subsequently the ship's rudder.

**Emergency Steering Gear** – A secondary steering system usually found in the steering flat remote from the navigation bridge system. It must be tested by ship's personnel at least every three months.

**Escutcheon Plate** – A centre stern plate positioned across the fore and aft line in the most aft position, bearing the ship's name.

**Even Keel** – An expression which describes a ship which is without an angle of list and no excessive trim forward or aft.

**Factor of Sub-division** – Will vary inversely with the ship's length, the number of passengers and the proportion of the underwater space used for passengers and crew and the machinery space. In other words it is a factor of safety which is allowed when determining the maximum spacing of transverse watertight bulkheads, i.e. The Permissible Length.

**Fair** – The term fair or faring is a shipyard term for straightening bent or distorted steel structure. Fairingoff, is the action of removing the structure, straightening the steelwork and then replacing. Can also be used to describe the plate lines of a ship's line plans. Known as "Fairing the lines" so that the lines of the plans agree.

**Fashion Plate** – A curved extension of the side plate. It is tapered off to meet the sheer strake.

**Fish Plate** – A narrow plate which generally runs as a boundary plate in the fore and aft direction or athwartships in way of the boat deck.

**Flanging** – The practice of bending the edge of a plate or bracket at right angles. Flanging is a stiffening action and is also used to make connections to associated steel structures.

**Flettner Rotar** – A rotating cylinder motor, fitted to the fore end, leading edge of a powered rudder. It generates a fast rotational movement to the rudder when helm is applied and could possibly be compared with power steering of a car.

**Flipper Fins** – Bilge and aft end fins built as appendages to the hull, to improve water flow to the propeller. A new development recently used by the Oshima Shipbuilding company in Japan. They are meant to raise hydrodynamic efficiency and achieve less fuel consumption.

**Floating Lever** – An element of telemotor transmission that connects the control rod from the telemotor receiver causing activation of hydraulic pumps to generate rudder movement.

**Floor** – An athwartships steel member which can be either a "watertight plate floor", "solid floor", or a "bracket floor". They act in way of the ship's frames in the double bottom structure of the vessel and interconnect the "Intercostal" and "longitudinal" members. Solid floors have lightening holes cut in and these serve to reduce the overall weight of the ship (and subsequent tonnage dues) as well as providing access for tank inspection personnel.

**Fore Foot** – That area of the shell plating where the stem of a ship is joined to the keel.

**Fore Peak tank** – A water tank set under the for'cs'tle head. It is usually a designated Water Ballast Tank, used for trimming the vessel.

**Fore Stay** – A wire stay which is stretched from the fore mast structure to the fore end of the forecastle deck. It is part of the ship's standing rigging. Its construction is $6 \times 6$ wps, and usually secured and tensioned by a bottle screw (turnbuckle) fixture.

**Frames** – Probably best described as the steel ribs of the ship. They act to stiffen the shell plating of the ship's hull and resist the stresses caused by water pressure when the vessel is at sea. They also resist dry docking stresses and racking stresses.

Ships are built either transversely or longitudinally framed.

"Frame Spacing" is a term used to describe the distance between consecutive frames.

**Freeboard Deck** – Is normally considered as the uppermost complete deck exposed to weather and sea which has permanent means of closing all openings in the weather part and below, where all openings in the sides of the ship are fitted with permanent means of watertight closing.

**Ganger Length** – A short length of the ship's anchor cable which is found between the "Anchor Crown 'D' Shackle" and the first joining shackle of the cable. It may contain a swivel fitment and usually is made up of only a few links.

**Garboard Strake** – Is defined by being that first strake of the shell plate, either side and next to the keel plate.

**Guard Rails** – The ship's side railings which are found at the perimeter of decks. They may be fitted in conjunction with bulwarks or established separately. Passenger vessels may have the upper rail in wood as opposed to steel. Cargo hatch deck areas are often fitted with wire rails which can be erected or lowered as appropriate, as opposed to steel structured perimeter rails.

**Gudgeons** – Receptacles for holding rudder pintles found on a plate rudder.

**Gusset Plates** – Triangular plates often used for joining angle bar to plate steel.

**Hat Box** – A term given to a suction or filling well found in deep tank construction. It can operate as a bilge suction or allow filling operations for water ballast. The line can also be blanked off.

**Hatchways** – Deck openings usually on the main upper deck giving access to cargo holds and specialised compartments below decks.

**Hawse Pipes** – The usual position for the stowage of the ship's anchors. The hawse pipes facilitate the run of chain cable when letting go the anchor.

**Holds** – Large underdeck compartments used for the stowage of cargo and stores.

**Hopper Tanks** – Side wing tanks found in the region of the lower cargo holds of a "Bulk Carrier" type vessel.

**Hose Testing** – A testing method designed to demonstrate the tightness of structural items which are not subject to hydrostatic or leak testing, and other components which contribute to the watertight or weathertight integrity of the hull.

**Hounds Band** – A circular fitment found around the upper structure of a mast. It is fitted with lugs employed to secure the shrouds or stays.

**Hunting Gear** – A mechanical feedback linkage found within the steering gear, to allow counter helm to be applied in order to prevent over run by the ship's head, when helm has been applied.

**Ice Knife** – A fitment required by ice classed vessels of the 1AS and 1A notation, which is fitted to protect the upper edge region of the rudder head from ice pressure. Especially useful when the vessel is operating astern and backing into ice.

**Ice Light Waterline** – is that, waterline that corresponds to the lightest condition in which the ship is expected to navigate in ice.

**Ice Load Waterline** – Corresponds to the Freshwater Load Line in summer as defined by the 1966 ILLC. It is considered the deepest ice operating waterline.

**Intercostals** – A longitudinal strength member of the ship's bottom structure. It tends to tie together the athwartships floors. It is first and foremost a steel girder used in way of the plate keel as a centre line Intercostal, running from forward to aft. Side intercostals positioned either side of the centre line are aligned at a suitable distance apart to afford continuity of strength. Centre line and side intercostals are generally interspersed with secondary longitudinals but of a smaller depth size and are considered to be a lesser strength member.

**Joggle Plate** – An obsolete form of construction of the ship's hull where the shell plates are set in and out to overlap each other. Advance welding techniques have made this method obsolete in all sectors of ship building.

**Keel (Plate)** – That centre line plate that runs at right angles to the bottom plating of the ship along the vessels centre line(Centre Girder). Modern trends fit most commercial vessels with a flat plate keel of increased scantlings when compared with other shell plates The "keel" usually extends from the Aft Peak bulkhead to the Fore Peak. Not all "Keels" are plate keels.

**Keel Block** – A centre line wood block that aligns with the keel when the vessel enters dry dock. Keel blocks usually used in association with intermediate blocks and bilge blocks and also wale shores.

**Keel Rake** – Is described as the inclination of the line of the keel to the horizontal.

**Keelson** – Historically the keelson was a long structural feature set inside the ship directly over the keel. Now they are seen as fore and aft, interior strength members in the form of fore and aft girders, positioned either side of the keel position and referred to as "side keelson".

**Kort Nozzle** – Trade name used to describe an enclosed, ducted propeller, used as a main line propulsion system or as a supporting thruster. They rotate through 360° and can provide steerage and directional movement to the vessel. Usually fitted to single screw tugs and trawlers.

**Lapped joint** – A join between plates where they are overlapped and welded.

**Launch Cradle** – A built structure on the groundways or on a launchway to hold and launch a finished ship's hull after building. It is constructed from sliding ways and/or timbers together with hull supports known as poppets.

**Launch Ways** – Also called inclusive with ground ways. It is a shipbuilding term applicable to a building slipway, which refers to the building blocks and timbers that hold the ship during construction and upon which the vessel will be launched. The groundways are built up between the lines of the building blocks.

**Leak Testing** – Is an air or other medium test carried out to demonstrate the tightness of a structure.

**Length The Rule length "L"** – is that distance in metres measured at the summer load waterline from the forward side of the stem to the aft side of the rudder post (or to the centre of the rudder stock if there is no rudder post).

**Length, Breadth ratio** – The ratio of the length to the breadth of a ship L/B, can differ considerably depending on the type of vessel. Passenger ship (6-8), Cargo vessel (5-7) A large value favours speed, but is unfavourable for manoeuvring.

**Length, Depth ratio** – The ratio of length to depth tend to vary between 10 to 15, and is relative to the determination of freeboard.

**Lightening Holes** – These are round or oval holes punched into floors and intercostals to lighten the structure of non-watertight plates, so increasing payload and allow access into tank areas.

**Limbers** – Coverings over the bilge bays at the bottom of the cargo compartments. Old tonnage usually had portable "limber boards" manufactured in timber. More modern tonnage usually has hinged steel plates which can be lifted to permit inspection of bilge areas.

**Leaching** – A term used in the marine industry in connection with the extraction of material from a solid. Frequently expressed concerning paint, where the water action causes harmful elements to be removed from the coating and may cause pollution.

**Longitudinals** – *see Intercostals.*

**Manhole** – A cutaway in a deck or bulkhead to permit the access of personnel. They are constructed with a studded arrangement that can be bolted shut against a rubber gasket so achieving a water tight seal.

**Margin Line** – (Margin of Safety Line) Established by the "Bulkheads Committee" of 1914, which recommended a 3 inch line of safety below the top of the "bulkhead deck", measured at the ship's side. Agreed by the SOLAS convention 1929.

**Margin Plate** – A longitudinal plate which passes alongside the extreme ends of the floors in way of the "turn of the bilge". The construction which provides a watertight end plate, situated either side of the vessel, to the "Double Bottom" tank system.

**Measurement Treaty** – The measurement of seagoing ships is arranged in accord with the Certificate of Registry Act 1982. Part of this Act is the International Treaty on the measurement of ships established by the IMO conference of 1969 and is applicable to ships of 24 m or more in length, effective from July 1994.

**Meirform bow** – A streamlined shaped bow which supports a bulbous rather than a conventional forefoot shape.

**Minimum Bow Height** – A statement of minimum bow height forms part the ship's stability criteria. It is the height of the deck at the forward perpendicular to the top of the forecastle or to the top of the upper most deck if no forecastle is fitted as measured from the summer loadline. It must never be less than that value quoted by the loadline regulations applicable to that vessel.

**Mud Box** – Is that space contained at the bottom of the anchor chain locker. It is usually covered by wooden gratings and accommodates mud and waste residues from the anchor cable following the anchor being heaved in. The mud box is rarely accessible accept in a dry dock situation when cables have been ranged on the floor of the dock and this presents an ideal opportunity to clean and paint the space.

**Non-Return Valves** – A valve in pipeline systems which allows the passage of fluid one way only and prevents a backwards flow. Common to cargo hold bilge lines.

**Oxter Plate** – An "S" shaped, shell plate, found around the stern quarters of the vessel at that point where the body of the ship falls away towards the boss plate.

**Panama Lead** – A pipe lead set into a bulwark, usually strengthened by a doubling plate, or a supported reinforced free standing lead, designed to accommodate moorings. They are found on the mooring decks at the fore and aft ends of the vessel.

**Panting Beams** – Athwartships steel members found in the forepart of the vessel, abaft the stem, and forward of the collision bulkhead. They are intended to brace the ship's side plating in the area of the bow to reduce the in/out movement of the plates as increased pressure is brought to bear by the depth of sea water effecting the hull when the ship is pitching.

**Panting Stringers** – Horizontal steel plates which interconnect the "Panting Beams" found at the ship's sides, in the fore part of the vessel.

**Passenger Ship** – Is defined as a ship which carries more than twelve (12) passengers.

**Pillars** – Found extensively in general cargo vessels for upper and intermediate deck support. They compensate for stresses caused by heavy weights, racking, dry docking, and water pressure stresses.

**Pintle** – An old term which was applied to plate rudders where Gudgeons and Pintles, secured the rudder plate aft of the rudder post. Modern rudder construction has superseded this system. The one remaining pintle in modern construction is the bearing pintle set into the "sole piece" of the stern frame to accept the weight of the rudder.

**Plate Floor** – An athwartships constructional member of the vessel, found in the double bottoms. The floors are positioned from the centreline outwards to the margin plate.

**Plate Rudder** – An old fashioned rudder and the fore runner to modern designs of today. The plate rudder has 100% of its area abaft the rudder post. These types of rudders can still be seen on canal barges and smaller coastal/inland water ways traffic, sometimes accompanied by rod and chain steering gear.

**Plummer Block** – A support and alignment bearing for the propeller shaft. It is usually situated between the thrust block and the tail end shaft where a long propeller shaft is employed.

**Pod Propulsion Unit** – A rotate-able engine unit employed to drive and steer the ship. It is a modern compact unit which eliminates the need for propeller shafts from the main engine drive.

**Propeller Boss** – That centre area of a propeller that is designed to accept the taper of the tail end shaft. It is internally bored to accept the shaped end and key locking of the shaft, to ensure that the propeller is secured. The "boss plate" is that plated area of the hull in line with the propeller boss, on either side.

**Propeller Hub** – A central covering that is found in the middle of the propeller designed to cover the locking propeller nut securing to the tail end shaft. Often referred to as a fair weather cone.

**Propeller Shaft** – That rotational shaft, driven from a main engine source which causes the propeller to rotate. Multiple screw vessels will have a multiple propeller shaft arrangement. With the advent of "pod propulsion units" many ships have been able to dispense with propeller shafts.

**Quadrant Steering** – A steering system that employed a steel quadrant incorporating a tiller arm, "keyed" to the rudder stock. The quadrant itself was geared to a worm and screw gearing which was effectively turned by the helmsman causing the rudder to move. These system are still found in some older tonnage, but in the main they have been superseded by hydraulic ram systems.

**Reaction Fins** – Steel plates set in "ducting" in a position forward of the propeller in order to deflect water flow more favourably to the propeller blades.

**Reserve Buoyancy** – Is defined by the difference between the volume of the hull between the waterline and the freeboard deck. It approximates to the actual displacement and that which the vessel would have if she was submerged to the freeboard deck.

**Rise of Floor** – An angular measurement taken next to the keel which indicates that angle between the base line of the top edge of the keel and the bottom shell plating.

**Rising line** – A curved line on the ship's line diagram (shell expansion plan), by which a designer determines the height of the ends of floor timbers through the ship's length (applicable Sailing Ship design).

**Rivet Structure** – An old fashioned method of constructing ships by joining steel plate by use of inserting hot rivets. The method has been superseded by welding methods.

The forerunners to riveted structure was by "treenails" for securing wood planking in the early days of ship building. This was subsequently overtaken by the use of iron spikes which became the forerunner to rivets. (Treenails and spikes now being obsolete.)

**Rotary Vane Steering** – A steering gear which employs jets of hydraulic oil at high pressure, to turn a bladed stator which is "keyed" to the rudder post. As the stator is turned so is the rudder. Movement in the opposite direction is achieved by reversing the oil flow direction.

**Rubbing Strake** – An extending strake at either side of the ship above the waterline which acts as protection for the side plate when the vessel is drawing alongside docks or piers. It may go by other names, rubrail, rubbing fender etc.

**Rudder Blade** – That flat surface area of the rudder (plate).

**Rudder Carrier** – Internal support set about the rudder post for accommodating the weight of the rudder construction. Often incorporates a stuffing box arrangement with a rudder post guide to prevent water ingress as the post passes through the hull.

**Rudder Horn** – A feature to some ships with certain types of hanging rudders e.g. "Mariner Rudders". It is an extended build from the hull which carries the bearing surface for the main rudder bearing.

**Rudder Indicator** – A bridge display unit which provides visual feedback of the movement of the rudder.

**Rudder Post** – That member that supports the position and weight of the rudder. The post passes through the hull via a watertight gland arrangement and is allowed to rotate in order to angle the rudder (also Rudderstock).

**Rudder Stock** – The centre of the turning axis of the rudder. The diameter of the rudder stock will vary depending on the type, size and weight of the rudder. Dimensions being established by Lloyds Rules and regulations for the Classification of Ships.

**Rudder Stops** – Small projections on the rudder stock and on the stern post which make contact when the rudder is at its maximum angle.

**Rudder Trunk** – That compartment that the "rudder post" passes through the ship's hull, from the steering arrangement in the steering flat, to the rudder itself.

**Sacrificial Anodes** – A method of corrosion reduction employed for many years on steel hulled vessels where dissimilar metals or different grades of steel are employed, e.g. around the stern plates and the propeller.

The use of sacrificial anodes served to reduce corrosive activity on the hull impressing a current flow to cause direct corrosion towards resistant anodes. They were usually made of zinc or other similar metal.

**Sandwich Plate System (SPS)** – A modern building method which employs two thin steel end plates with a polyurethane elastomer core. It is light and can be used as an overlay in new build or repair work.

**Scantlings** – A term used to describe the measurements of steel sections used in ship construction. A full scantling ship, is one which is constructed to the highest strength requirements of the Classification Society.

**NB.** This term was originally applied to the size of "lintels" in wood built ships.

**Scarph** – A type of joint employed for thick or block structures. Used extensively in wood build ships.

**Schilling Rudder** – A high lift, (high performance) rudder designed for vessels of any size. It may be fitted as a single rudder or in the form of a twin arrangement, (known as a VecTwin Monovec spade, or Schilling Mariner, semi-spade).

This is a single piece construction which can provide a reduced turning circle to either side.

**Schottel Rudder, Propeller steering unit** – A combined propulsion and steering unit manufactured by Schottel-Werft in Germany. The unit provides a specially designed propeller which turns through 360° providing propulsion and steerage in any direction.

**Seams** – Joints, of a long weld, as with longer side plates.

**Sea Trials** – That period after building that the ship's systems and operations are tested and assessed in a sea-going environment before handing the vessel over to new owners.

**Semi-Balanced Rudder** – this is a rudder which is constructed with usually less than 20% of its blade area positioned forward of the turning axis.

**Shaft Rake** – Propeller shaft centre lines are usually raked downwards compared to the building baseline and permits the engines to be located higher in the vessel. In multi-screw vessels, shaft lines tend to be raked in the horizontal and in the vertical, in a downward and outward directions. Shaft rake angles are referenced against the ship's centre line and the baseline.

**Shaft Tunnel** – That space which lies in the fore and aft line which accommodates the propeller shaft. This space is usually fitted with a side walk way to allow inspection of the propeller shaft, bearings, and any stuffing box or water tight glands where the shaft passes through the hull.

**Sheer** – The upward rise of the ship's deck from the amidships position towards the bow and the stern. The sheer to the deck assists deck drainage when the vessel is experiencing bad weather.

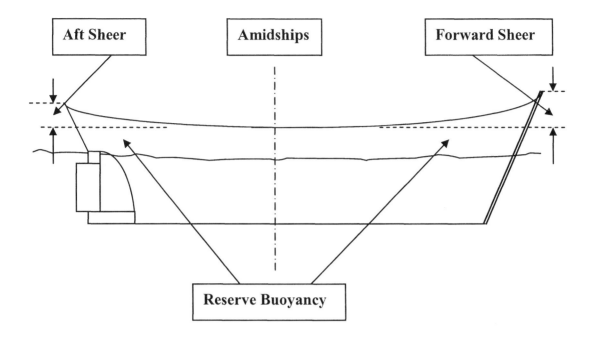

**Sheer Correction** – A sheer correction is made to increase the freeboard when a vessel has less than standard sheer. Where a vessel has more than standard sheer the freeboard may be decreased.

**Sheer Strake** – This is the uppermost strake of ship's plate beneath the ship's gunwale and in a position which is usually adjacent to the uppermost continuous deck It is one of the ship's plates that is provided with additional thickness for continuity of strength.

**Shell Plating** – The steel sides of the vessel are constructed from a series of steel plates referred to as the "shell plating". The shell plates compensate for all stresses incurred by the vessel including localised stresses, e.g. "Shell Doors".

**Shrouds** – Wire supports fitted to either side of a mast structure. The are usually rigged in pairs to port and starboard and form part of the ship's standing rigging (see also "swifter").

**Side Scuttle** – The correct name for a porthole. See also "deadlight".

**Skeg** – A narrow vertical member of the hull, found in the after part of the ship. It is more prominent in vessels fitted with twin propellers and is meant to enhance course keeping capability of the vessel by increasing the vertical lateral area. It is usually the first area of contact with the blocks when the ship is dry docked. Twin screw ships may also be constructed with a twin skeg design.

**Sole Piece** – The name given to the lowest part of the "Stern Frame" which extends from right aft to the keel plate. When a vessel grounds, because more often than not the vessel is trimmed by the stern, the sole piece is most likely to make first contact with the ground, resulting in a broken sole piece. In the event of damage to the sole piece the vessel may dry dock. This would probably be one of the rare occasions that the vessel might be docked stern first as opposed to bow first, which is the norm.

**Spade Rudder** – A hanging rudder design with a coupling at the upper edge of the rudder and supported within the hull. It takes its name from the shape being comparable to that of a "spade".

**Spar Ceiling** – Wooden cargo battens which cover the steel frames of a general cargo vessel to prevent cargo coming into contact with the steelwork and so preventing cargo sweat.

**Spectacle Frame** – A special support frame set in way of the twin propeller shafts of a twin screw vessel. The frame is found at the after part of the vessel in way of the fine lines of the ship.

**Spider band** – A circular fitment found at the head of a derrick. The function of the spider is to permit the securing of the slewing guys, topping lift and the lifting purchase.

**Spurling Pipes** – Vertical tubes designed to carry the anchor cable from the upper deck down to the lower chain locker. (Warships: Navel Pipes)

**Stabilizers** – A general term used to describe a system that will dampen down the rolling motion of a vessel when in a seaway. Two main systems tend to be the most popular,
(a) Tank (flume) systems. (b) Fin systems operating with either fixed or retractable systems.
   Additionally bilge keels tend to act to reduce the roll motion of a vessel.

**Stealer Plate** – An "L" shaped plate found generally at the extremities of the vessel where deck stringers or hull plates are reduced from a double width to a single width.

**Steering Flat** – A compartment found directly over the rudder which allows access for the rudder stock. Its function is to contain the ship's steering motors and the hydraulic rams moving the tiller. Alternatively it would contain the Rotary Vane Steering Unit, or other steering gear system, for moving the tiller and rudder.

**Stem Rake** – That inclination of the stem line to the vertical.

**Stern Frame** – That supporting structure at the after end of the ship, which provides rigidity and strength to the rotating propeller and the "Rudder Stock".

**Stern Tube** – A bearing tube found in the aft part of the vessel which allows the passage of the propeller shaft through the shell plate into the hull. They fulfil the function of lubrication to the rotating shaft and also provide a water tight entry into the hull.

**Stocks** – A term which describe the building blocks, shores and timbers on which a ship rests on the building ways.

**Strake** – A term which describes a continuous row of steel plate, e.g. Garboard Strake, Sheer strake.

**Strength Deck** – Also known as the uppermost continuous deck or the superstructure deck.

**Stringer Plate-(Deck Stringer)** – A plate which covers the top flanges of athwartships frames or other vertical tier of beams. Used as deck plate stringers as the most prominent example. Use of the stringer tends to vary with location, e.g. Bilge stringer.

**Structural Testing** – This is a hydrostatic test carried out to demonstrate the tightness of the tanks and the structural adequacy of the design. Where practical limitations prevail and hydrostatic testing is not feasible, hydro pneumatic testing may be carried out instead. Testing, tends to fall into two categories, namely non-destructive testing and testing to destruction.

**Struts** – Supporting steel work positioned to provide stiffening and support between the propeller shafts and the stern quarters of the outer hull.

**Stuffing Box** – The term is given to a gland connection where the tail shaft or rudder post pass through the hull. The packing inside the gland can be compressed tight, to ensure a watertight seal. It is a common task when in dry-dock for the packing to be renewed.

**Summer Loadline** – That horizontal mark on the ship's side that passes through the centre of the disc. It indicates the waterline level that must not be exceeded and when the ship is loaded correctly for passage through seawater in the summer loadline zone.

**Superstructure** – A decked structure extending to either side of the vessel, situated above the freeboard deck.

**Superstructure Correction** – Vessel fitted with enclosed superstructures which add to their reserve buoyancy and as such may qualify for a reduced value of freeboard.

**Suspended Rudder** – A balanced or semi-balanced rudder which is hung on a rudder post located bearing and not supported by upper and lower bearing pintle or conventional stern frame structure.

**Swifter** – The name given to a single shroud. Most shrouds are seized together in pairs. Where three shrouds are employed obviously one will be left the swifter. Also used to describe a rope that passed through the perimeter of capstan bars on manually operated capstans of sailing vessels (now considered obsolete).

**Tabernacle** – A bracket arrangement constructed to support the heel of a mast or heavy derrick.

**Tail End Shaft** – That part of the propeller shaft which is positioned most aft and accommodates the ship's propeller. It is usually tapered and the propeller is "keyed" into position. The "propeller hub" would be turned onto the shaft end. This is an important inspection area when in dry dock because it is piercing the watertight integrity of the hull. As such, it is often fitted with a stuffing box or an alternative water tight lining system to reduce the possibility of water ingress. It would be usual practice to renew packing or lining of the arrangement once the shaft has been removed in dock.

**Tandem Propellers** – A double propeller arrangement on the same single shaft. (Not to be confused with contra-rotating propellers.)

**Tank Side Bracket** – An interconnecting plate found between the margin plate and the frames. Its function is to strengthen the connection at the turn of the bilge in way of the double bottom construction.

**Tank Tops** – Tank tops are the covering deck plates over the double bottom structure and are found at the bottom of the ship's holds. They are often covered by a protective wood shield known as the "ceiling" which had a tendency to protect the plates from heavy duty cargoes being landed either intentionally or accidentally.

**Telemotor** – A popular transmission system from the remote position of the navigation bridge to the steering flat to effectively cause the steering gear to activate and move the rudder. Transmission being from the ship's steering wheel to the telemotor receiver.

**Thrust Bearing** – A bearing secured to the ship's body that receives the thrust of the propeller shaft through a thrust collar.

**Thrust Block** – That part of the ship that receives the thrust of the propeller via the thrust bearing. Thrust bearing and thrust block may be incorporated together.

**Thrust Surface** – The aft driving surface of a propeller blade that thrusts the water backwards. It may have other names such as driving face or driving surface.

**Tiller** – That structure which is usually keyed to the rudder stock which is allowed to be pushed from one side to another by hydraulic rams, causing the stock to rotate and the rudder to move from port to starboard. It was the initial way of moving the early rudders in ancient sailing craft, being manually operated by being pulled and pushed from side to side. Still extensively employed in small craft.

**Tonnage Deck** – The second complete deck of a ship upwards from the keel, may be used in tonnage measurement of the vessel.

**Torsion Box** – A feature to container ships. It is a constructional feature in way of the deck stringer and the topsides area of wing tanks positioned either side. Alternatively they may be fitted to single skin side constructed vessels. They are usually longitudinally framed inclusive of the upper deck region. They act to resist torsional deformation down the length of the ship.

**Torsion Meter** – A measuring device for measuring the torsional stress's incurred by an extended long element, like a propeller shaft.

**Transfer** – Defined by the distance that a vessel will travel, perpendicular to the fore and aft line, at the commencement of the turn. The total transfer movement lasts from the start of the turn of the vessel, until its completion. The defining limits being known as the transfer of the vessel, in a turning circle, calibrated against the ships change of heading and is usually noted at 90° and 180°.

**Transom** – A descriptive term for a type of squared stern construction. It can also be used to describe the stern framework or the floor and beams in way of the stern region, above the propeller.

**Transverse Thrust** – This is an additional property derived from a rotating propeller which causes the ship's head or stern to pay off, when moving ahead or astern respectively. It is more prominent when operating astern propulsion and can be used in a positive manner by ship handlers when manoeuvring their vessels.

**Tread** – A term which describes the length of the ship's keel.

**Triatic Stay** – (obsolete) A stay that stretched between the fore and aft masts. It has now been superseded with a signal stay used for suspending signal flag halyards.

**Truck** – A circular fitment situated at the top of a mast head. It may include a lightening conductor and is often the highest position aboard the vessel.

**Tunnel** – A section casing which extends from the engine room to right aft which covers the shaft line of the propeller shaft. The entrance from the engine room is usually fitted with a watertight door. Most tunnel arrangements also provide a walkway and an emergency escape route to the upper deck.

**Turning Circle** – The turning capability of a vessel is normally determined by a vessel on sea trials. Turning circles are meant to supply the necessary data on the advance and transfer of the vessel when conducting a hard over turn to either port or starboard. The turning of the manoeuvre is noted, together with relevant statistics on the values of how quick and how tightly the vessel would turn in routine and emergency operations. Turning manoeuvres are influenced by the type of vessel, the weather prevailing during the tests, motive power, draught and trim of the vessel and whether she is even keel or listed over.

**Type "A" Ship** – A ship designed to carry liquid cargoes with a high degree of sub-division. If it is also greater than 150 m in length it must remain afloat after the flooding of any single empty compartment.

**Type "B" Ship** – Any ship which is not a "Type A" ship. It will have a greater freeboard than a Type A, ship with a lesser degree of sub-division.

**Type "B-60" Ship** – Any type of "B" ship over 100 m in length, with steel weathertight hatch covers. It must remain afloat after the flooding of a single compartment where ($\mu = 95\%$) at the summer draught. The freeboard reduced by 60% of the freeboard tabular values for "A" ~ "B".

**Type "B-100" Ship** – Any type of "B-60" ship over 100 m in length with steel hatch covers which are "Watertight". The access to the engine room from the deck must be protected by a deck housing and the vessel would have open rails, not bulwarks for 50% of the length. It must remain afloat after the flooding of any two fore & aft, adjacent compartments ($\mu = 95\%$) at summer draught.
The freeboard reduced by 100% of the freeboard tabular values for "A" ~ "B".

**Voith Schneider Propulsion** – This is a cycloidal propeller device which can act in a passive mode like a rudder while still provide propulsion to the vessel. It is used extensively in the tug market but is also being seen in ferry type vessels.

**Wale Shores** – Wood side shores that support a narrow beam vessel when on keel blocks in dry dock. Wale shores are positioned from the ship's sides to the dock side altars.

**Watertight** – A closing appliance to an opening is considered watertight if it is designed to prevent the passage of water in either direction under a head of water for which the surrounding structure is designed.
**NB.** Generally, all openings below the freeboard deck in the outer shell/envelope (and in the main bulkheads) are to be fitted with permanent means of watertight closing.

**Watertight Gland** – The underwater hull of the vessel is pieced to accept the rudder stock and the propeller shaft. These positions are usually made with watertight glands being placed around the respective shaft, commonly known as "stuffing boxes". There are many variations available on the commercial market but a popular type is filled with a packing material that can be tightened inside the gland to press against the shaft, generating a watertight sea.

**Weathertight** – A closing appliance, to an opening, is considered as weathertight, if it is designed to prevent the passage of water into the ship's hull in any weather condition when seas are shipped on board.

**Windlass** – A mooring winch used extensively for heaving in and lowering the ship's anchor cable. It may be centre line fitted or operated as a split windlasses to accommodate port and starboard anchors.

**Windlass Bed** – Steel bed plate secured to the fore mooring deck of a vessel to accommodate the windlass.

**Windlass Brakes** – Band or disc brakes designed to control the movement of the anchor chain cable. These would normally be thoroughly inspected during the period of dry docking and brake linings would be renewed if required.

**Diagrammatic Terminology**

*Conventional Ship Design – General/Bulk Cargo Vessel*

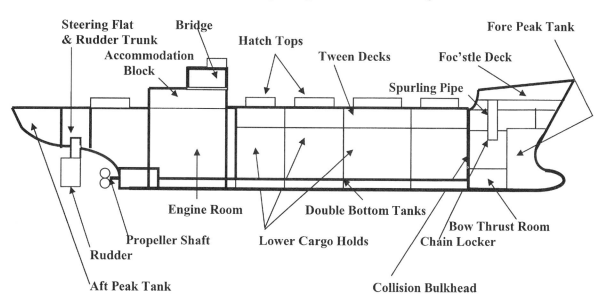

**Athwartships – Half Profile**

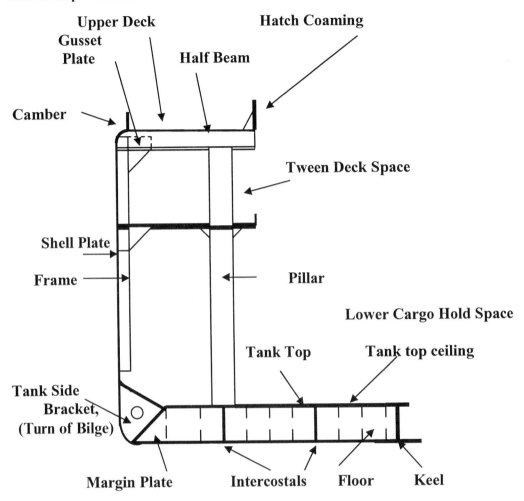

**Plate Location and Association**

**Plate Terms**

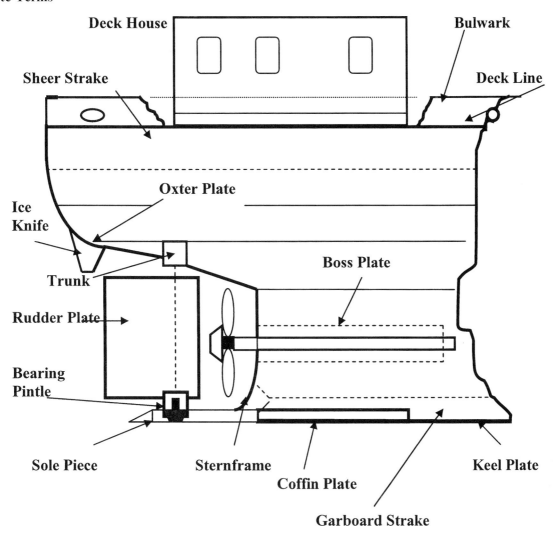

# Ship Types

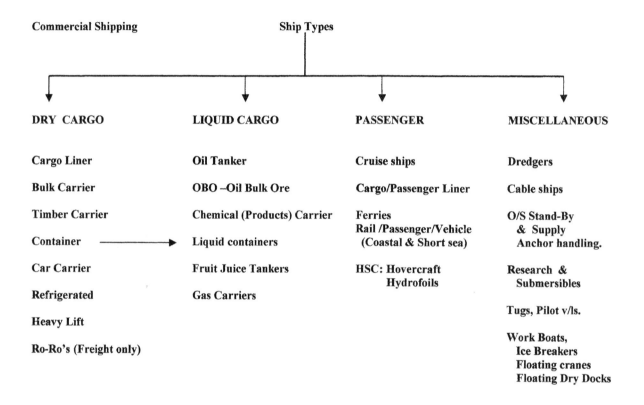

Commercial Shipping                                                Ship Types

| DRY CARGO | LIQUID CARGO | PASSENGER | MISCELLANEOUS |
|---|---|---|---|
| Cargo Liner | Oil Tanker | Cruise ships | Dredgers |
| Bulk Carrier | OBO –Oil Bulk Ore | Cargo/Passenger Liner | Cable ships |
| Timber Carrier | Chemical (Products) Carrier | Ferries<br>Rail /Passenger/Vehicle<br>(Coastal & Short sea) | O/S Stand-By<br>& Supply<br>Anchor handling. |
| Container ⟶ | Liquid containers | | |
| Car Carrier | Fruit Juice Tankers | HSC: Hovercraft<br>Hydrofoils | Research &<br>Submersibles |
| Refrigerated | Gas Carriers | | Tugs, Pilot v/ls. |
| Heavy Lift | | | Work Boats,<br>Ice Breakers<br>Floating cranes<br>Floating Dry Docks |
| Ro-Ro's (Freight only) | | | |

Specialist: Fishing v/ls, Factory ships, Auxiliaries for warships, Light vessels. Sail Training, Harbour craft, Tenders & bunker barges, Oil Recovery vessels, Emergency Support and Salvage craft.

CHAPTER ONE

# Marine Measurement

## Introduction

Today's ships are being constructed in all corners of the globe, with the largest builders located in Japan and South Korea at the present time. The expansion of China would seem to indicate that the Chinese Shipbuilding Industry will become one if not the most influential to the Industry by 2010. This would seem like poetic justice, if we consider that the early voyages of discovery were invariably carried out by the Chinese and not the Europeans as history would have us believe.

Today, different markets are demanding a different style of ship. Ferries are no longer the lethargic transport but dominate the passenger sector with High Speed Craft. While at the same time Bulk Carriers over 300,000 dwt have become the norm. LNG and LPG vessels are being constructed to meet the expected demand for 250 ships by 2010. Sizes are variable being constructed from carriage of 60,000 m³ upto 200,000 m³, gross tonnages averaging about 100,000 tonnes with deadweight averaging 75,000. The obstacles of capacity and size being continually leapfrogged.

Greater market demands, with increased competition have sharpened the ship building industry in a manner which could not possibly have been conceived a century ago.

Container ships breaking the 10,000 teu barrier and Ro-Ro vessels dominating the dry cargo sector, while at the same time passenger ships expand in a seemingly endless cruise market.

Shipyard practice had to change. Prefabrication techniques flourished, new products like aluminium and plastics became alternatives to steels. Riveted construction gave way to welded structures, joggled plating became a thing of the past and the flush sides of the new ships produced less friction and provided a reduced fuel burn for the new ship owners.

The cost of steel and labour, generated new approaches to shipbuilding. Conventional, attitudes and labour intensive tasks were re-thought for the better, easier and more cheaper ways were sort, without losing the quality required. Classification Societies raised their standards inline with the demands of the SOLAS, MARPOL, and STCW conventions, and in keeping with a consensus to protect the environment from the harmful effects of shipping. Bad practice would put the non quality shipbuilders out of business. Consequently, the quality build today, includes the double hull tanker and bulk carrier. Improved engines, built to suit a cleaner environment coupled with reduced fuel burn for improved speed. Shipboard protective systems for ballast treatment, garbage retention, and clean water discharge, being standard requirements all providing safer ships. of tomorrow. Such changes occurring inside the Lloyds Regulations or equivalent, where the ship sizes can be defined and manufactured within acceptable safety margins.

## Marine Measurement Reference

Conversion Equivalents of common units in use within the Ship Construction Industries.

| Imperial/Metric | | Mass/Weight | | |
|---|---|---|---|---|
| 1 pound (lb) | = | 0.4536 kilograms (kg) | | |
| 1 ton | = | 1,016.05 kg | = | 2,240 lbs |
| 1 tonne | = | 1,000 kg | = | 0.985 ton |
| 1 short ton | = | 907.1 kg | = | 2,000 lbs |
| | | 1 kg | = | 2.205 lbs |
| | | 1 tonne | = | 2,205 lbs |

**Fluid:—**

| | | |
|---|---|---|
| 1 pint (pt) | = | 0.568 Litre (lt.) |
| 1 quart | = | 1.13648 lt. |
| 1 gallon (gal) | = | 4.5469 lt. |
| 1 gal U.S. | = | 3.7853 lt. |

| | | |
|---|---|---|
| 1 lt. | = | 1.7599 pts |
| 1 lt. | = | 0.220 gals |
| 10 lt. | = | 2.19981 gals |
| 1 tonne of Sea Water | = | 1 m$^3$ (approximately) |
| 1 Cubic Metre | = | 35.314 ft$^3$ |

| | | |
|---|---|---|
| 1 Barrel (imperial) | = | 36,000 imp/gals |
| 1 Barrel (U.S.) | = | 42,000 U.S./gals |

**Miscellaneous Nautical Length and Distance:-**

| | | | | |
|---|---|---|---|---|
| 1 Fathom | = | 1.829 metres (m) | = | 6.0 feet (ft) |
| 1 Nautical mile (10 cable) | = | 1,852 m | = | 6,080 ft |
| 1 Cable | = | 1/10th of a mile | = | 600 ft |
| 1 Shackle (Anchor Cable) | = | 27.5 m | = | 90 ft or 15 fathoms |

**Power:—**

| | | |
|---|---|---|
| 1 Horse power | = | 745.7 Watts (W) |
| 1 metric horsepower | = | 735.499 W |

| | | |
|---|---|---|
| 1,000 W | = | 1 kilowatt |
| 1 atmosphere | = | 14.7 lbs/inch$^2$ |

**Heat Energy:—**

| | | | | |
|---|---|---|---|---|
| 1 therm | = | 100,000 British Thermal Unit | = | $1.055 \times 10^8$ J |
| 1 calorie | = | 4.187 J | | |

**Pre-amble**

The following text is based on the Lloyds Register, Rules and Regulations for the Classification of Ships (January 1995). Although this first chapter is concerned with marine measurement and a basic knowledge of ship form, it is meant to provide the reader with a level of underpinning awareness, prior to delving into the complex areas of Merchant Ship Construction.

**Classification of Ships**

| Class | Description of Ships in this Class |
|---|---|
| Class 1 | Passenger ships engaged on voyages, any of which are long international voyages. |
| Class II | Passenger ships engaged only on short international voyages. |
| Class II(A) | Passenger ships engaged on voyages of any kind other than International voyages which are not: ships of class III to VI(A) or new ships of Class A, B, C or D. |
| Class III | Passenger ships engaged only on voyages in the course of which they are at no time more than 70 miles by sea from their point of departure and not more than 18 miles from the coast of the United Kingdom and which are at sea only in favourable weather during restricted periods. |

| | |
|---|---|
| Class IV | Passenger ships engaged only on voyages in category A, B, C or D waters. |
| Class V | Passenger ships engaged only on voyages in category A, B or C waters. |
| Class VI | Passenger ships engaged only on voyages with not more than 250 passengers on board, to sea or in category A, B, C or D waters, in all cases in favourable weather and during restricted periods, in the course of which the ships are at no time more than 15 miles, exclusive of any category A, B, C or D waters, from their point of departure nor more than 3 miles from land. |
| Class VI(A) | Passenger ships carrying not more than 50 passengers for a distance of not more than 6 miles on voyages to or from isolated communities on the islands or coast of the United Kingdom and which do not proceed for a distance of more than 3 miles from land. |
| Class VII | Ships (other than ships of Classes I, VII(A), VII(T), XI, and engaged on voyages of which are long international voyages. |
| Class VII(A) | Ships employed as fish processing or canning factory ships, and ships engaged in the carriage of persons employed in the fish process or canning industries. |
| Class VII(T) | Tankers engaged on voyages any of which are short international voyages. |
| Class VIII | Ships (other than ships of Classes II, VIII(T), IX, and XII) engaged only on short international voyages. |
| Class VIII(T) | Tankers engaged on voyages any of which are short international voyages. |
| Class VIII(A) | Ships (other than ships of Classes II(A) to VI(A) inclusive, VIII(A)(T), IX, IX(A), IX(A)(T), XI, and XII) engaged only on voyages which are not international voyages. |
| Class VIII(A)(T) | Tankers engaged only on voyages which are not international voyages. |
| Class IX | Tugs and tenders (other than ships of Classes II, II(A), III, VI and VI(A) which proceed to sea but are engaged on long international voyages. |
| Class IX(A) | Ships (other than ships of Classes IV to VI inclusive) which do not proceed to sea. |
| Class IX(A)(T) | Tankers which do not proceed to sea. |
| Class XI | Sailing ships (other than fishing vessels and ships of Class XII) which proceed to sea. |
| Class XII | Pleasure vessels of 13.7 metres in length or over. |
| **Class A** | Passenger ships engaged only on domestic voyages other than ships of Class B, C or D. |
| **Class B** | Passenger ships engaged only on domestic voyages in the course or which they are at no time more than 20 miles from the line of the coast where shipwrecked persons can land, corresponding to the medium tide height. |
| **Class C** | Passenger ships engaged only on domestic voyages in sea areas where The probability of significant wave heights exceeding 2.5 metres is less than 10% over a one year period for all year round operation, or over a specific restricted period of the year of operation exclusively in such period, in the course of which they are at no time more than 15 miles from a place of refuge, nor more than 5 miles from the line of the coast where shipwrecked persons can land, corresponding to the medium tide height. |

**Class D**                Passenger ships engaged only on domestic voyages in sea areas where the
                           probability of significant wave heights exceeding 1.5 metres is less than 10%
                           over a one year period for all year round operation, or over a specific
                           restricted period of the year for operation exclusively in such period, in course
                           of which they are at no time more than 6 miles from a place of refuge, nor
                           more than 3 miles from the line of the coast where shipwrecked persons can
                           land, corresponding to the medium tide height.

**Chemical Tankers**

For ships carrying dangerous chemicals in bulk IMO have an established code for the construction
and equipment:—

**Ship Type I** – Is for those products which must have preventative measures to prevent the escape
of such cargo due to its high level of toxicity or where the release of such cargo would have
widespread impact and present an environmental hazard or additionally those products that react
with water. A maximum tank size of $1,250\,m^3$ must be employed.

**Ship Type II** – Is for those products which require some preventive measures to preclude the escape
of such product with hazards listed similar to "Type I" but to a lesser extent. A maximum tank
size of $3,000\,m^3$ may be employed.

**Ship Type III** – Is for the least hazardous of products which may still have a toxic or reactionary
properties.
   Such vessels must counter the hazards of fire, toxicity, reactivity and not pollute the air or water.
They are subject to Initial and Periodic (Renewal) Surveys. Annual surveys $+/-$ 3 months and
Intermediate Surveys at 2½ years $+/-$ 6 months.

**Ship Survivability** – These ships must be constructed to remain afloat in a condition of equilibrium
after assumed damage. In the final flooded condition the curve of Statical Stability is to have a
range of 20° beyond the equilibrium condition with a righting lever (GZ) of at least 100 mm, with
an angle of heel not exceeding 15°.

**Ice Classification and Respective Ice Strengthening**

Ships may be given a special features notation where the vessel is expected to trade in either first
year ice conditions or in multi-year ice conditions. Where ships are intending to navigate in the
Canadian Arctic they must also comply with the Canadian Arctic Shipping Pollution Prevention
Regulations of Canada, established 1978. Lloyds register is authorized to issue Arctic Pollution
Prevention Certificates.

**General Ice Classes Notations**
(Lloyds register and equivalent for Canada and Finish/Swedish Authorities)

| Lloyds Register | Canadian | Finish-Swedish |
|:---:|:---:|:---:|
| 1AS | Type A | 1A Super |
| 1A | Type B | 1A |
| 1B | Type C | 1B |
| 1C | Type D | 1C |
| 1D | Type D | II* (*Ice-Due Class II can also be assigned to 100A1 ships which are not ice strengthened). |
| 100A1 | Type E | |

**Ice Class AS** – With the exception of the engine output requirements are identical to those of Ice Class 1AS.

Ships strengthened in accord with the requirements of Ice Class AS are not intended to operate in the northern part of the Baltic in winter.

**Ice Class A** – With the exception of the engine output requirements, the remaining requirements for Ice Class A are identical to those of Ice Class 1A. Ice Class A, are not intended for operations in the northern part of the Baltic in the winter season.

**Ice Class 1D** – This strengthening is for ships intended to navigate in light first year ice conditions in areas other than the Northern Baltic. The standard of strengthening is equivalent to that of Ice Class 1C but only the requirements for the strengthening of the forward region, the rudder and steering arrangements apply.

**Baltic Ice Classes**

**Ice Class 1AS** – This strengthening is for ships intended to navigate in first year ice conditions equivalent to unbroken level ice with a thickness of 1.0 m.

**Ice Class 1A** – This strengthening is for ships intended to navigate in first-year ice conditions equivalent to unbroken level ice with a thickness of 0.8 m.

**Ice Class 1B** – This strengthening is for ships intended to navigate in first-year ice conditions equivalent to unbroken level ice with a thickness of 0.6 m.

**Ice Class 1C** – This strengthening is for ships intended to navigate in first-year ice conditions equivalent to unbroken level ice with a thickness of 0.4 m.

**Special Features – Ice Class Notations**

**Ice Class AC1** – The requirements for the assignment of this class are intended for ships designed to navigate in Arctic or Antarctic ice conditions equivalent to unbroken ice with a thickness of 1.0 m.

**Ice Class AC1,5** – The requirements for the assignment of this class are intended for ships designed to navigate in Arctic or Antarctic ice conditions equivalent to unbroken ice with a thickness of 1.5 m.

**Ice Class AC2** – The requirements for this assignment of this class are intended for ships designed to navigate in Arctic or Antarctic ice conditions equivalent to unbroken ice with a thickness of 2.0 m.

**Ice Class AC3** – The requirement for the assignment of this class are intended for ships designed to navigate in Arctic or Antarctic ice conditions equivalent to unbroken ice with a thickness of 3.0 m.

**Where the requirements for Section 9, of the Regulations is complied with the vessel will be eligible for the addition of the term "icebreaker" to be added to the ship notation.**

**NB. Section 9, of the Regulations, is concerned with the strengthening required for ships to operate in multi-year ice conditions.**

Ships having an Ice Class AC notation will be longitudinally framed at the uppermost continuous deck and at the bottom. They must also have a minimum engine power, which is never less than 740 kW. All vessels so assigned must also have propellers manufactured with steel or copper alloy.

**Marine Measurement Terminology**

**Aft Perpendicular (A.P.)** – A vertical through the rudder axis. It is more accurately described by a vertical measured from the after end of the rudder post, if the vessel has a rudder post.

**Air Draught** – Is defined by that vertical distance between the waterline and the highest point of the vessel. The minimum air draught should be that measured from the summer loadline mark.

**Amidships** – That point positioned midway between the aft and forward perpendiculars.

**Bale Space** – Is that cubic capacity of a cargo space where the breadth is measured from the inside of the cargo battens (Spar Ceiling) and the measured depth is from the underside of the deck beams to the tank tops (or hold ceiling, if fitted).

**Base Line** – Is defined by a line level with the top of the keel.

**Beam** – Is defined as being the widest part of the ship in the transverse or athwartship's direction.

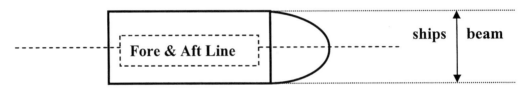

*Figure 1.1*

**Bow Height** – Is defined by that vertical distance at Freeboard, between the summer load water line to the exposed deck line, measured at the side. If the bow height is insufficient the freeboard must be increased by the amount of deficiency.

**Breadth Overall** – The maximum breadth of the vessel as measured from the outer hull on the outer starboard side to the outer hull on the Port side.

**Breaking Strength** – Defined by the stress necessary to break a material in tension or compression. The stress factor is found by testing a sample material to destruction.

**Bulkhead Deck** – The uppermost deck to which the watertight bulkheads are taken.

**Bulkhead Draught** – A term used to describe the maximum permissible mean draught for a passenger vessel to which subdivision loadlines have been assigned.

**Camber** – Is described by that athwartship's curvature of the ship's upper weather deck. This deck curvature assists drainage of any accumulated slack waters.
    It is measured by the difference from the height of the deck at the centre and the height of the deck at the ship's side.

**Coefficient of Fineness (Cw)** (of the water plane area) – That ratio of the Waterplane area to the area of a rectangle having the same extreme length and breadth. **"Block Coefficient" (Cb) of fineness for displacement** is applied in a similar manner using volume criteria instead of area.

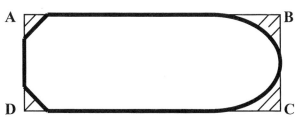

*Figure 1.2*

$$Cw = \frac{\text{Area of water plane}}{\text{Area of rectangle ABCD}}.$$

Some Example Block Coefficients for vessel types are as follows:—

| | |
|---|---|
| Container vessel | 0.6 to 0.75 |
| Liner/Freighter | 0.6 to 0.80 |
| Tanker | 0.8 to 0.90. |

**NB. The Prismatic Coefficient (Cp)** – Gives the ratio of the volume of the underwater body and the block formed by the area of the midship's section and the length between perpendiculars. The "Prismatic Coefficient" is effected by the resistance experienced by the underwater volume. This has a direct relationship with the power of propulsion required. (If the Cp is small then the required power can be small.)

**Construction Water Line (CWL)** – That water line which is used to determine the dimensions of the ship's components used in its construction.

**Container Capacity** – For cellular container vessels. Cells available for 20 ft ISO containers, i.e. in 20 feet equivalent units (units = TEUs).

**Crippling Pressure** – A term which describes the block loading and is given by the Formula:—

$$P = 11 \left( 40 - \frac{h^2}{a^2} \right) \text{ displacement tonnes/m}^2$$

where  h represents the height of the stack of blocks
a represents the block width
MN represents Mega Newton's.

Crippling pressure will be influenced by the age and grain, moisture content and surface condition of the block. It is not usual to allow the pressure to exceed approximately 0.4 MN (40 displacement tonnes) Although the load on a stack of oak blocks may be as high as 1 MN (100 displacement tonnes) at the critical instant.

**Deadweight** – The amount that a vessel can load which will bring her down to her permissible load line. This is a constant, respective to every vessel. Measured in tonnes. It is often referred to as the cargo carrying capacity and determines the earning capacity of the vessel.

Deadweight = Maximum Displacement – Light displacement.

Deadweight amounts to the weight of cargo, stores, bunkers and water on board the vessel at any one time. Stores, bunker and water tonnages being usually known.

**Depth** –
(i) pertaining to a vessel, is the vertical distance between the keel (Base line) and the top of the deck plating of the upper most continuous deck, measured at the side of the vessel.

(ii) pertaining to a dry dock, is that vertical distance from the floor of the dock, measured to the waterline. It reflects the maximum size of vessel by draught, that the dock can accept, having taken due allowance for the overall size of keel blocks.

$$\text{Length/Depth ratio : Moulded Depth} = \frac{L}{15}$$

(see also extreme depth).

**Displacement (W)** – That weight of water that a vessel will displace while floating in either Salt or Fresh water. Hence Salt Water Displacement (measured in tons).

$$\text{Displacement(t)} = \text{Volume of water displaced (m}^3)$$
$$\times \text{ Water density (t/m}^3) \text{ by the submerged volume.}$$

**Draught** – That vertical distance from the bottom of the ship's keel to the waterline.

**Draught Survey** – A survey and calculation made to determine the ship's true mean draught.

**Extreme Beam** – That maximum beam taken over all extremities.

**Extreme Breadth** – The maximum width of the vessel, measured from the outside of the shell plating (see Breadth Overall).

**Extreme Depth** – The depth of the vessel measured at the ship's side from the upper deck edge to the lowest point of the keel.

**Extreme Draught** – Described by that measure taken from the lowest point of the keel to the summer loadline. Draught marks on the ship's hull refer to extreme draught.

**Factor of Sub-Division** – This will vary inversely with the ship's length, the number of passengers and the proportion of the underwater space used for passengers/crew and machinery space. This is effectively a safety factor which is allowed in determining the maximum spacing of transverse watertight bulkheads, i.e. the permissible length.

**Flammable Liquid** – Is a liquid having a flash point lower than 37.8°C.
  A combustible liquid is one having a flash point of 37.8°C or above, e.g. gasoline is a flammable liquid, where as kerosene is a combustible liquid.

**Flammable Range** – The limits of flammable (explosive) range, in the range between the minimum and the maximum concentrations of vapour in air which forms a flammable (explosive) mixture. Usually abbreviated to UFL (Upper flammable limit) and LFL (Lower flammable limit). These are synonymous with the upper and lower explosive limits.

**Flammability Limits** – Those conditions which define the state of fuel oxidant mixture at which application of an adequately strong external ignition source is only just capable of producing flammability in a given test apparatus.

**Flare (of the bow)** – A variable curvature of the shell plating in the forward area of the vessel. It provides greater width to the fo'c'stle head and prevents ingress of water over the ship's forward decks.

**Flash Point (of an oil)** – This is the lowest temperature at which the oil will give off vapour in quantities that when mixed with air in certain proportions are sufficient to create an explosive gas.

**Floodable length** – The maximum length of a compartment which can be flooded so as to bring a damaged vessel to float at a waterline which is tangential to the margin line.
  **NB.** In determining this length account must be taken of the permeability of the compartment.

**Fore and Aft Line** – An imaginary line which passes through the centre of the ship from stem to stern.

**Forward Perpendicular (F.P.)** – A vertical at that point of intersection of the ship's summer loadline and the stem of the vessel.

    **Freeboard** – That vertical distance from the waterline of the vessel to the top of the uppermost continuous deck plating (measured at the ship's side) (see summer loadline).

    **NB.** Mean Freeboard is the half sum of the freeboards measured on either side of the vessel respectively.

    Minimum Seasonal Freeboard is the vertical distance of the upper edge of the deckline above the seasonal load line.

**Grain Capacity** – Is that cubic capacity of a cargo space, where the length, breadth and depth are measured from the inside of the ship's shell plate, with allowances being made for the volume occupied by frames and beams.

**Gross Tonnage** – Is defined by the measurement of the total internal volume of the ship. It is equal to the under deck tonnage plus the tonnage of all other enclosed spaces above deck. It is a measure of the size of the vessel so that the vessel can be entered into a specific classification It is in the ship owners interest to keep the Gross Tonnage value as low as possible in order to keep general running costs to a minimum.

    The gross tonnage figure is used to assess manning levels, fire appliance requirements, etc., to meet regulatory standards.

**High Speed Craft** – Is a craft capable of a maximum speed in metres per second (m/s), equal to or exceeding $3.7V^{0.1667}$. Where V = displacement which corresponds to the design waterline ($m^3$).

**Inclining Experiment** – A test method to ascertain the ship's light "KG". It is carried out by giving the vessel a controlled list and monitoring the results. It is usually conducted in dry dock under calm weather conditions.

**Keel Rake** – Is defined by that angle of inclination of the line of the ship's keel away from the horizontal.

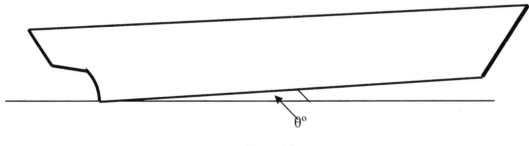

*Figure 1.3*

**Length Between Perpendiculars (LBP)** – Defined by that horizontal distance between the forward and the aft perpendiculars.

**Length on the Waterline** – Is defined by that horizontal distance between the moulded sides between the stem and the stern when the ship is at her summer load line.

**Length Overall (LOA)** – The maximum length of the vessel.

**Light Displacement** – The weight of the basic vessel, i.e. the hull, machinery, anchors, spares and boilers with water to a working level (measured in tons).

**Lloyds Length** – That length used for obtaining the scantlings where the vessel is classed with Lloyds Register. It is that same length as found between the forward and aft perpendiculars, except that it must not be less than 96% and need not be more than 97% of the extreme length on the summer loadline.

**Load Deadweight (d.w.t.)** – That total weight of cargo, stores, bunkers, etc., when the vessel is at her loaded draught (summer loadline). It is equivalent to the difference between her load displacement and her light displacement (see deadweight scale).

**Loadline** – That water line which is described by the line that the vessels makes when lying in water, coincident to the surface level. There are several waterlines, e.g. Summer Loadline, Timber loadline, Light Water line, Winter Loadline, etc., each relevant for specific circumstance.

**Long Ton** – A unit of mass weight equal to 2,240 lbs.

**Margin Line** – A line at least 76 mm below the upper surface of the "bulkhead deck", measured at the side of the vessel.

**Moulded Breadth** – The amidship's beam of the vessel measured from the inside of the shell plating.

**Moulded Dimensions** – Measurements which are obtained from the limits of the inside plating of a steel constructed vessel.

**Net Tonnage** – Is defined by the remaining tonnage value after allowing for machinery, accommodation and working spaces being deducted from the gross tonnage. (The Net Tonnage may not be less than 30% of Gross Tonnage.)
  It is a measure of the ship's carrying capacity in terms of cargo or passengers (or both).

**Oil Fuel Unit** – Is that equipment used for the preparation of oil fuel for delivery to an oil fired boiler, or equipment for delivery of heated oil to an internal combustion engine and includes any oil pressure pumps filters and heaters with oil at a pressure of not more than 1.8 bar gauge.

**Parallel Middle Body** – The middle section of the vessel about the amidship's point where the cross section remains constant in area and shape.

**Permeability** – In relation to a compartment space means the percentage of that space which lies below the margin line, which can be occupied by water.
  **NB.** Various formulae within the Ship Construction Regulations are used to determine the permeability of a particular compartment.

  Example values:  Cargo spaces = 60%, Machinery space = 85%, Passenger/crew spaces = 95%.

**Permissible Exposure Limit** – An exposure limit which is published and enforced by the Occupational Safety and Health Administration (OSHA) as a legal standard. It may be a time weighted average (TWA) exposure limit (8 hours) or a 15 minute short term exposure limit (STEL), or a ceiling limit (C).

**Permissible Length** – of a compartment, having its centre at any point in the ship's length, is determined by the product of the floodable length at that point and the factor of sub-division of the vessel

$$\text{Permissible Length} = \text{Floodable length} \times \text{Factor of sub} - \text{division.}$$

**Plimsoll Mark** – A circular mark which forms part of the permanent marking of the ship. The circle is horizontally divided and the upper edge of this dividing line is that level which is considered to indicate the minimum freeboard level permitted in salt water, summer conditions. The disc is identified by a deck line above it which indicates the position of the upper most continuous deck level.

The mark will be accompanied by a number of alternative markings, for use in waters where operational freeboards such as Tropical waters, Tropical Fresh, and for operations in Winter ice conditions. Ships which carry timber as deck cargo, will be marked with an additional specific "Timber Loadline" which allows more draught and less freeboard when satisfying certain timber loading criteria.

**Proof Load** – That tonnage value that a derrick or crane is tested to. The value is equal to the SWL + an additional% value depending on the size of the lifting gear being tested.

**Registered Breadth** – Is a measure from the outside of the shell plating in way of the widest part of the vessel. (Not necessarily the middle of the vessel.)

**Registered Depth** – Is a measure from the top of the ceiling to the top of the deck beam at a position on the centre line, at the middle of the ship's length. (Alternative: Depth of Hold.)

**Registered Length** – Is a measure from the fore part of the stem head to the after side of the stern post, or the fore side of the rudder stock if no stern post is fitted.

**Registered Ton** – Is that unit employed to determine the volume of a space.
   One registered ton is equal to 100 cu ft or 2.83 m$^3$.

**Reserve Buoyancy** – The immersed portion of the vessel, is that volume which is necessary to keep the vessel afloat. While the buoyancy contained by all other watertight, enclosed spaces above the waterline is referred to as reserve or residual buoyancy.

**Rise of Floor** – Is determined by the rise of bottom shell plating measured from the top edge of the keel plate. The rise is determined by the upward rise of the lower edges of the floors, from the keel outward to the turn of the bilge.

**Run** – Described by the length of the immersed body of the vessel, aft of the parallel middle body.

**Safe Working Load** – An acceptable working tonnage used for load bearing items of equipment. The marine industry generally uses a factor of 1/6th of the breaking strain when establishing the safe working load.

**Shackle Length** – That measure given to measuring anchor cable. One (1) shackle equals fifteen (15) fathoms or ninety (90) feet or twenty-seven-and-half metres (27.5 m).
   A ship's anchor cable will vary with the type and size of ship.

**Sheer** – Is defined by the upward turn of the ship's deck from the midship's position, towards the bow and the stern. The extreme. enclosed volumes of the ship contained between the line of sheer and the uppermost continuous deck form the vessels reserve buoyancy.

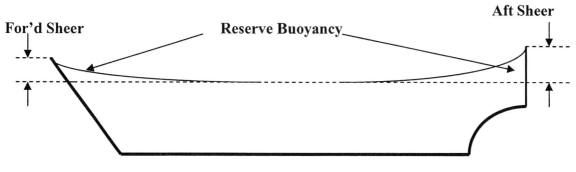

*Figure 1.4*

**Ship's Beam** – Is defined as the widest part of the ship in the transverse, athwartship's direction.

**Stem Rake** – Is defined by the angle of inclination of the stem line from the vertical.

**Stowage Factor** – This is defined as that volume occupied by unit weight of cargo. Usually expressed as cubic metres per tonne (m³/tonne) or cubic feet per tonne (ft³/tonne). It takes no account of any space that may be lost through broken stowage.

**Subdivision Factor** – The factor of subdivision varies inversely with the ship's length, the number of passengers/crew and the machinery space. In effect it is the factor of safety allowed in determining the maximum space of transverse watertight bulkheads, i.e. The permissible length.

**Subdivision Loadlines** – These are additional loadlines marked on passenger vessels to take account of the variable use of spaces for passengers and cargo. The use of spaces will effect the amount of sub-division required by the Regulations.

**Summer Load Line** – Is defined by that line of position, on the ship's side, which is established by the Load Line Regulations, corresponding to the centre mark of the loadline disc. This position is established from the mark found directly above the Plimsoll Line mark which indicates the level of the uppermost continuous deck, exposed to the weather. The "Summer Freeboard" being measured between this deck line and the centre mark of the Plimsoll (disc) Line.

The amount the ship can load for operation within the Summer Zone is determined by the Summer Loadline Mark, assuming loading in salt water and will retain sufficient reserve buoyancy.

**Tare Weight** – Is the weight of an empty container including permanently affixed ancillary equipment.

**Threshold Limit Value (TLV)** – Airborne concentrations of substances devised by the American Conference of Government Industrial Hygienists (ACGIH). Representative of conditions under which it is believed that nearly all workers may be exposed day after day with no adverse effects. There are three different types of threshold limit values and are advisory guidelines, not legal standards.

**Tonne** – Originating from the word "tun" which was a term used to describe a wine cask of capacity 252 gallons which equated to 2,240 lbs, 1 tonne (1 ton imperial) as we know it today.

**Transportation Moisture Limit** – The maximum moisture content of a cargo that may liquefy at a level which is considered safe for carriage in ships other than those ships which, because of design features of specialised fittings may carry a cargo with a moisture content over and above this limit.

**Trim** – Is the numerical difference between the forward and the stern draughts of the vessel. Most ships would be expected to trim by the stern.

**Tumblehome** – Defined by that inward curvature of the ship's side shell plates above the summer loadline.

**Ullage** – That height measurement from the surface level of a liquid, in a tank, to the underside top of the containment tank.

**Underdeck Tonnage** – Is based on the internal measurement of all the space between the tank tops to the underside of the tonnage deck.

**Underwater Body** – Is equal to the displacement minus the volumetric additions of the shell plate, the propeller(s) and the rudder.

**Vapour Pressure** – The equilibrium pressure of the saturated vapour above the liquid, expressed in bars absolute, at a specified temperature.

**Volatile Liquid** – A liquid which is so termed is one which has a tendency to evaporate quickly and has a flash point of less than 60°C.

**Waterline Length (LwL)** – The length of the vessel at the summer loadline mark.

**Structural Measurement Definition**

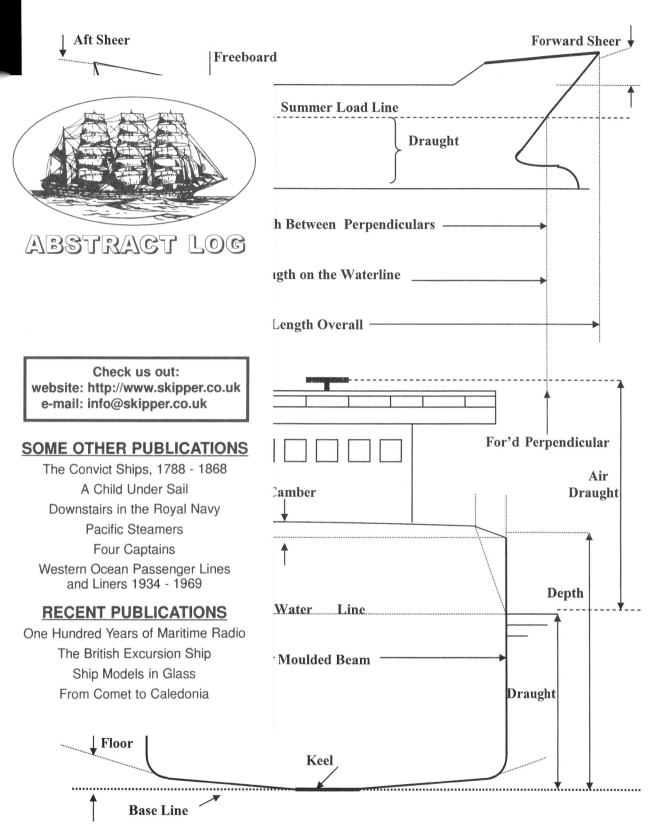

**SOME OTHER PUBLICATIONS**

The Convict Ships, 1788 - 1868

A Child Under Sail

Downstairs in the Royal Navy

Pacific Steamers

Four Captains

Western Ocean Passenger Lines
and Liners 1934 - 1969

**RECENT PUBLICATIONS**

One Hundred Years of Maritime Radio

The British Excursion Ship

Ship Models in Glass

From Comet to Caledonia

Check us out:
website: http://www.skipper.co.uk
e-mail: info@skipper.co.uk

*Figure 1.5*

**Loadline Assignment**

A ship's characteristics are taken into account when assigning the vessels loadline.

**Type "A" Ship** – Is designed to carry only bulk liquid cargoes and will have the following characteristics:—

The ship's cargo tanks will have small deck openings, which can be closed watertight by steel covers.

The overall design of the vessel will have a high degree of watertight integrity of the exposed weather deck area. As such she will have a high level of safety against flooding because of the low permeability when the cargo spaces are loaded.

When the ship is in excess of 150 m in length and has designated empty compartments when loaded at the summer loadline, the vessel should be capable of remaining afloat after the flooding of such a compartment. (Assuming permeability of the compartment is 0.95 in a prescribed position of equilibrium.)

If the vessel is over 150 m length, the machinery space is considered as a floodable compartment at an assumed permeability of 0.85.

**Type "B" Ship** – Is any ship other than a Type "A" ship.

The Type "B" ship is recognised as being more vulnerable to flooding than a type "A" vessel and as such will be assigned a greater freeboard. Although the freeboard of a Type "B" vessel may be reduced by either 60% (B-60) or 100% (B-100) of the difference between the types A and B ship's tabulated freeboards.

The above is subject to the following conditions:—

In addition to all the requirements of a Type "B" ship the vessel must be over 100 m in length and must also comply with,

(a) All hatchways must be closed by steel watertight covers.
(b) Must be capable of remaining afloat in the prescribed condition of equilibrium after the flooding of any single compartment (assumed permeability of 0.95) while floating at its summer draught.

   If the vessel is over 150 m in length then the machinery space will be regarded as a floodable compartment (assumed permeability 0.85).


**Relevant Terms – effecting the assignment of Load Lines and Watertight Integrity**

**Freeboard Deck** – Is generally considered as the uppermost continuous deck which is exposed to the weather and ingress by the sea. It must have permanent means of closure to all openings in deck areas exposed to the weather. Any openings set at the side of the vessel and below the freeboard deck must be fitted with watertight, permanent means of closure.

**Watertight** – With regard to openings, is any opening which is designed to prevent the passage of water in either direction when under a specific "head of water" for which the surrounding structure has been designed.

**Weathertight** – With regard to openings, is said to be closed weathertight, when water is not allowed to penetrate the hull or superstructure in any weather condition being experienced at sea.

**Superstructure** – Is defined as a housing structure on the vessel situated on the freeboard deck which extends from one side of the vessel to the other, or with side plating not being inboard of the shell plating, by more than 4% of the ship's beam.

**Enclosed Superstructure** – Defined as a superstructure which has enclosing bulkheads of adequate construction where any doorway openings in the bulkheads are fitted with appropriate watertight doors which comply with the regulations. Any other openings in the enclosed superstructure, either at the sides or the ends, must be fitted with efficient means of closure.

**Requirements for Sub-Division**

| Ship Type | Length (L) | Requirement for Subdivision |
|---|---|---|
| A | Less than 150 m | None |
| A | 150 m and above | To withstand the flooding of any compartment within the cargo tank length which is designed to be empty when the ship is loaded to the summer load line at an assumed permeability of 0.95.<br>The machinery space must also be treated as a floodable compartment with an assumed permeability of 0.85. |
| B | Less than 100 m | None |
| B – 60 | 100 – 225 m | To withstand flooding of any single damaged compartment within the cargo hold at an assumed permeability of 0.95. |
| B – 60 | More than 225 m | As above but the machinery space must also be treated as a floodable compartment with an assumed permeability of 0.85. |
| B – 100 | 100 – 225 m | To withstand the flooding of any two adjacent fore and aft compartments within the cargo hold at an assumed permeability of 0.95.<br>The machinery space shall be treated as a floodable compartment with permeability of 0.85. |
| B – 100 | More than 225 m | As above but the machinery space taken alone must also be treated as a floodable compartment with an assumed permeability of 0.85. |

**Freeboard Corrections**

(1) **Block Coefficient** – Where the block coefficient of a vessel is more than 0.68 the freeboard will be increased.

(2) **Correction for Flush Deck vessels** – Type "B" vessels of 100 m or less with superstructures less than 35% of the ship's length have their freeboards increased.

(3) **Depth Correction—**

Where the depth is less than $\dfrac{\text{Length}}{15}$ freeboard will be increased.

If the depth is more than $\dfrac{\text{Length}}{15}$ freeboard may be decreased depending on the position of the superstructures.

(4) **Superstructure Correction** – Because an enclosed superstructure is an addition to the reserve buoyancy the vessel will be entitled to a reduction in freeboard.

(5) **Sheer Correction** – A vessel is assumed to have a value of sheer caused by the freeboard deck curving upwards from the amidship's position towards the vessel extremities.

Where a vessel is constructed with less than standard sheer the freeboard will be increased.

Where a vessel has more than standard sheer the freeboard might be decreased depending on the positions and length of superstructures.

### Conditions of Assignment of Freeboard

1. The construction of the vessel must be such that her structural strength will be sufficient for the freeboard assigned. The design and construction should be such that the stability of the ship, in all conditions of loading, is sufficient for the freeboard assigned.
2. The superstructures end bulkheads should be sufficiently constructed. Any door openings in bulkheads, being fitted with a sill.
3. Where hatchways are closed by portable covers with tarpaulins, the hatch coamings must be of a specified height whether on an exposed freeboard or superstructure deck.
4. Hatchways, where closed by weather tight steel covers must have similar height of coamings (as in "3"), however, such height may be reduced or omitted altogether if the safety of the ship is not impaired. The strength of these covers must be specified together with the means of securing.
5. Machinery space openings must be enclosed by framed casings with steel doors allowing access. Door sills of specified height, in accord with the position on deck must be fitted. The funnel fiddly and ventilator coamings, on exposed decks must be as high above the deck as is reasonable.
6. Other openings in the freeboard and superstructure decks like manholes and flush scuttles must be closed by substantial weather tight covers. Other openings must be protected by enclosed superstructures or deck houses. (These must have steel doors and sills as stated.)
7. Ventilators must be fitted with steel coamings to the specified height, according to position. These would be provided with weather tight closing appliances, unless over a specified height.
8. Air pipes must have a specified height according to position and must be provided with means of closing.
9. Cargo ports and other side openings if below the freeboard deck, must be watertight in order to maintain structural and water tight integrity. The lower edge of openings must not be lower than the deepest loadline.
10. Scuppers, inlets and discharges below superstructure decks must be fitted with non-return valves and positive closing means from above the freeboard deck. In engine rooms which are manned, inlets and discharges may be locally controlled.
11. Side scuttles below the superstructure deck must be fitted with hinged watertight, internal deadlights.
12. Freeing ports must be sufficient for the area as determined by formula. Bulwark openings are to be protected by bars. Where shutters are fitted these should be prevented from jamming.
13. Guard rails and bulwarks of a minimum height are to be in place for the protection of the crew, on all exposed freeboard and superstructure decks. Rails must have a specified spacing and satisfactory means of allowing crew movement from accommodation to working spaces must be in place.

### Loadlines and Ships' Marks

Following construction of the vessel it will be surveyed and assigned a freeboard by an Assigning Authority. The ship will also be permanently marked with the draught marks, the Plimsoll Line, the deck line mark and the ship's official name and number. A subsequent "Carving Note" will then be issued.

The various loadlines are shown and they are assigned to the vessel following a Loadline Survey by an Assigning Authority, e.g. Lloyds Register.

**Loadline Marks**                                    **(Starboard Side shown)**
                                                      **(Loadline forward of disc)**

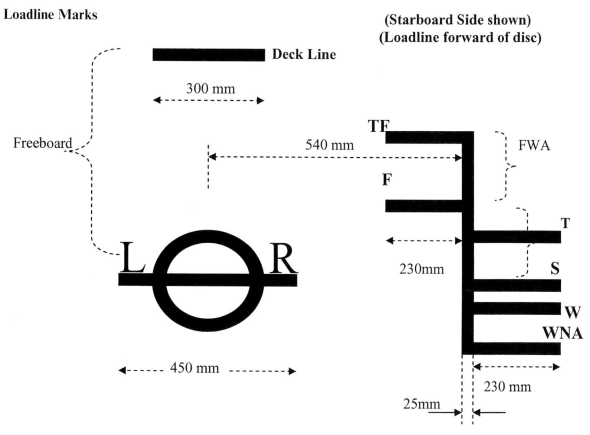

*Figure 1.6*

All lines are 25 mm in thickness.

LR    = Lloyds Register
TF    = Tropical Fresh
T     = Tropical
F     = Fresh
S     = Summer
W    = Winter
WNA = Winter North Atlantic
FWA = Fresh Water Allowance.

Should the ship carry a Lumber Loadline, this would be positioned aft of the Plimsoll Mark and identity marks would be prefixed with an "L", e.g. LTF = Lumber Tropical Fresh

"S"      The Summer loadline mark is calculated from the Load Line Rules and is dependant on many factors including the ship's length, type of vessel and the number of superstructures, the amount of sheer, minimum bow height and so on.
"W"    The Winter mark is 1/48th of the summer load draught below "S".
"T"     The Tropical mark is 1/48th of the summer load draught above "S".
"F"     The Fresh mark is an equal amount of $\triangle/4T$ millimetres above "S", where $\triangle$ represents the displacement in metric tons at the summer load draught and T represents the metric tons per centimetre immersion at the above.
        In any case where the displacement cannot be ascertained F is the same level as T.
TF     The Tropical Fresh mark, relative to "T" is found in the same manner as that of "F" relative to "S".
WNA   The Winter North Atlantic mark is employed by vessels not exceeding 100 metres in length when in certain areas of the North Atlantic Ocean, during the winter period. When it is assigned it is positioned 50 mm below the Winter "W" mark.

## International Loadline Certificate

The loadline certificate is valid for a period of five (5) years and may be extended by 3 months. The certificate is issued by the MCA or a Classification Society, under the Merchant Shipping (Load Line) Rules, which came into force in July 1968.

The validity is subject to periodic and annual inspection +/− 3 months of the anniversary date.

The certificate could be cancelled if the ship ceases to comply with the regulations,

Or if the strength of the vessel is reduced, or if incorrect information is used to calculate the freeboards, or if the periodic endorsements are wrong.

## Load Line Survey – Preparations

It is general practice that the ship's Chief Officer would prepare the vessel for the assignment of a loadline and the conduct of the loadline survey. The ship's planned maintenance schedule would be expected to cover all preparations and maintenance checks prior to the survey being conducted, in accord with the ship's "Load Line Record". This form would provide all the particulars and conditions required for the load line survey. Chief Officers would therefore benefit considerably by becoming familiar with its content and start preparations in ample time, well ahead of the survey date.

The objective of the survey is to ensure that the uppermost continuous deck can be totally sealed to prevent water ingress into the inner compartments.

The following checks and inspections would need to be conducted prior to survey:—

1. All cargo hatch covers and all access hatches into cargo holds are watertight and that securing devices such as cleats and wedges are working correctly.
2. All access points to the machinery space from exposed decks are inspected and seals are seen to be intact to retain watertight integrity.
3. All air pipes must be fitted with permanently attached means of closing. Such closing devices must be satisfactory in there operation of sealing the pipe.
4. All access openings at the ends of enclosed compartments are in good condition and that cleating arrangements, dogs, hinges and clamping facilities are free in operation and well greased. Hard rubber packing should be inspected for cracking and deterioration, so as to provide water tight seals.
5. All non-return valves associated with overboard discharges should be inspected to ensure satisfactory operation.
6. Any side scuttles (portholes) below the freeboard deck or to enclosed superstructures must be fitted with internal deadlights with rubber seals. Such seals must be inspected for possible deterioration. All dogs and cleats must be capable of effectively closing the port and providing a watertight seal.
7. The ship's bulwarks and guard rails must be in a satisfactory condition and free of corrosion.
8. All freeing ports must have hinges to flaps and shutters greased and with free movement.
9. All ventilators must be fitted with efficient weather closing devices.
10. Any manholes must be capable of being closed and made watertight.
11. Where lifelines are required to be fitted these should be rigged and sighted to be in good condition.
12. The loadline marks, plimsoll line, draught marks and freeboard deck line should be painted.

\* Ships with wooden hatch covers where tarpaulins are used, must have a minimum of two tarpaulin covers and each section of wooden hatches must be fitted with a steel locking bar arrangement. Wood hatch covers must be in good condition and any portable beams must be fitted with efficient securing.

At the time of the survey, the ship's particulars and all stability criteria should be available for inspection by the surveyor. Such documentation must show correct loading and ballasting procedures. The previous Loadline Certificate and the Loadline Record must be available for the surveyors inspection.

Shipboard resources, by way of manpower, ladders, lighting, should be kept readily available as also the keys to all compartments that may give rise to inspection.

## Timber Loadlines – Requirements for Assigning Freeboard

**Pre-amble** – Timber deck cargo is considered as deck cargo which consists of timber in any form. The major concern with such an exposed cargo in a seagoing environment is that the deck cargo may experience considerable water absorption during the sea passage causing the upper deck area to bear increased weight.

Such added weight could detrimentally effect the positive stability of the vessel and adequate allowance for such an eventuality is taken into account when assigning a suitable freeboard.

The vessel so assigned will have a forecastle of not less than the standard height of an enclosed superstructure and be of a length not less than 0.7 L (where "L" represents the ship's Length).

Where a ship is less than 100 metres in length, it must be fitted with a poop deck or a raised quarter deck, having a deck house or steel hood fitted to a height not less than the standard height of an enclosed superstructure.

The construction of the vessel will include double bottom tanks over the amidship's half length which will have satisfactory watertight longitudinal sub-division. It must also be fitted with permanent bulwarks to a height of at least 1 metre, specially stiffened on the upper edge and supported by bulwark stays secured to the deck. Alternatively, guard rails and stanchions also of 1 metre height and of especially strong construction.

Timber deck cargoes must be stowed to avoid excessive point loading and distributed having due regard to the deck strength and supporting structure of the vessel. The stowage being made with due regard to the following:—

(a) the vertical distribution of the deck cargo.
(b) the wind moments that the vessel can expect to experience during the course of the voyage.
(c) the losses of weight the ship will experience due to the consumption of fuel, stores and water during the course of the voyage.
(d) the possible increases in the ship's weight and/or its deck cargo due to the absorption of water or ice accretion.

The stowage must not interfere with the navigation of the vessel or impair the watertight or weathertight integrity of the ship's construction. Accesses should not be obstructed to any of the working compartments or crews quarters which are necessary to the normal working of the ship.

**NB.** The maximum height of timber deck cargo within a winter seasonal zone, during the winter period, must not exceed above the weather deck more than one third of the ship's extreme breadth.

Adequate protection for the crew must be provided in the form of guard rails or lifelines if the vessel is without a safe passage on or under the ship's deck.

Securing of such cargo must be such as to prevent movement of the cargo in the worse of sea conditions, which may be normally expected.

## Timber Loadlines

Certain vessels are assigned Timber Freeboards when they meet certain additional conditions. One of these conditions must be that the vessel must have a forecastle of at least 0.07 extent of the ship's length and of not less than a standard height (1.8 m for a vessel 75 m long or less in length and 2.3 m for a vessel 125 m or more in length, with intermediate heights for intermediate lengths. A poop deck or raised quarter deck is also required if the length of the vessel is less than 100 m.

(Starboard Side shown timber loadline aft of disc.)

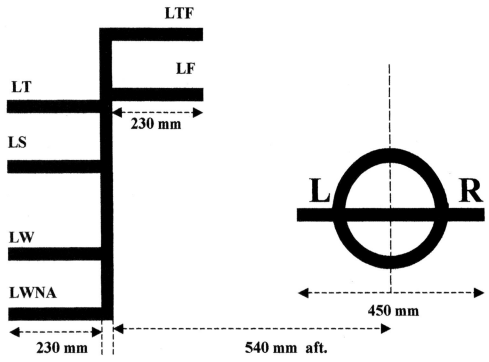

All lines 25 mm wide.                    *Figure 1.7*

The letters denoting the assigning authority LR should be approximately 115 mm in height and 75 mm in width.

LS is derived from the appropriate tables contained in the Load Line Rules.

LW is one thirty-sixth (1/36th) of the summer timber load draught below LS.

LT is one forty-eighth (1/48th) of the summer timber load draught above LS.

LF and LTF are both calculated in a similar way to F and TF except that the displacement used in the formula is that of the vessel at her summer timber load draught. If this cannot be ascertained these marks will be one forty-eighth (1/48th) of LS draught above LS and LT respectively.

LWNA is at the same level as the WNA mark.


**Tonnage**

All ships constructed on or after 8th July, 1982 are measured in accordance with the IMO 1969 International Conference on Tonnage Measurement. Existing ships built prior to this date were allowed to retain their existing tonnage if the owner so desired, for a period of 12 years. All ships must now comply with the 1969 Convention from 18th July, 1994.

**Gross Tonnage (GT)** – Defined as that measurement of the internal capacity of the ship. The Gross Tonnage value is determined by the formula:—

$$GT = K_1V$$

when $K_1 = 0.2 + 0.02\,Log_{10}\,V$,

$V$ = total volume of all enclosed spaces measured in cubic metres.

**Net Tonnage (NT)** – Is that measurement which is intended to indicate the working/earning capacity of the vessel. Port and harbour dues are based on the gross and net tonnage figures.

Net Tonnage for Passenger Ships, carrying more than 13 passengers is determined by the formula:—

$$NT = K_2V_C\left(\frac{4d}{3D}\right)^2 + K_3\left(N_1 + \frac{N_2}{10}\right).$$

Net Tonnage for other vessels:—

$$NT = K_2 V_C \left(\frac{4d}{3D}\right)^2$$

where

$V_C$ = total volume of cargo spaces in cubic metres.

d = moulded draught at midships in metres (summer loadline draught or deepest subdivision load line in passenger vessels).

D = Moulded depth in metres amidships.

$K_2 = 0.2 + 0.02 \log_{10} V_C$.

$K_3 = 1.25 \dfrac{(GT + 10,000)}{10,000}$.

$N_1$ = Number of passengers in cabins with not more than 8 berths.

$N_2$ = Number of other passengers.

NT is not to be taken as less than 0.30 GT. The factor $\left(\frac{4d}{3D}\right)^2$ is not taken to be greater than unity.

The expression $K_2 V_C \left(\frac{4d}{3D}\right)^2$ is not to be taken as less than 0.25 GT.

## Suez and Panama Canal Tonnages

Charges are imposed on vessels which transit the Suez and Panama Canals. These charges are based on the "Net Tonnage" of the vessel as determined by the regulations of the Suez and Panamanian, Tonnage Authorities. The calculation for the Panama Canal Universal Measurement is based on the 1969 Tonnage Convention and is obtained from the total volume of the ship's enclosed spaces plus the maximum volume capacity of any containers that may be carried on or above the upper deck.

## Compensated Tonnage

A system which was introduced to provide a degree of fairness when considering the output of various national shipbuilding activities. Previously output was based on "Gross Tonnage" but the building procedure for say Passenger Liners, was far more complex than say for a bulk carrier.

In 1968 the Association of European Shipbuilders devised a table of coefficients for each ship type to compensate for the anomaly, which involved the gross tonnage of the vessel being multiplied by the appropriate factor. The values produced gave a more realistic and fairer appreciation regarding a countries new build tonnage output.

## Compensated Tonnage Coefficients (Examples)

| Ship Type | Deadweight Tonnage | Coefficient |
|---|---|---|
| Cargo Vessel | + 5,000 tonnes dwt | 1.0 |
| Tanker | 30,000 to 50,000 tonnes dwt<br>Over 250,000 tonnes dwt | 0.5<br>0.3 |
| Bulk Carrier | 30,000 to 50,000 tonnes dwt<br>Over 100,000 tonnes dwt | 0.5<br>0.4 |
| Reefer Vessels | | 2.0 |
| Gas and Chemical Carriers | | 2.2 |
| Passenger vessels | | 3.0 |

## Ship's Plans and Respective Documentation

**Deadweight Scale** – The deadweight is the difference between the load displacement upto the minimum freeboard and the lightweight displacement. It is generally taken as the ship's carrying capacity or earning capability. A table of draughts and corresponding deadweights is compiled as part of the ship's stability documentation and presented in the form of a scale for ease of use by ship's cargo officers.

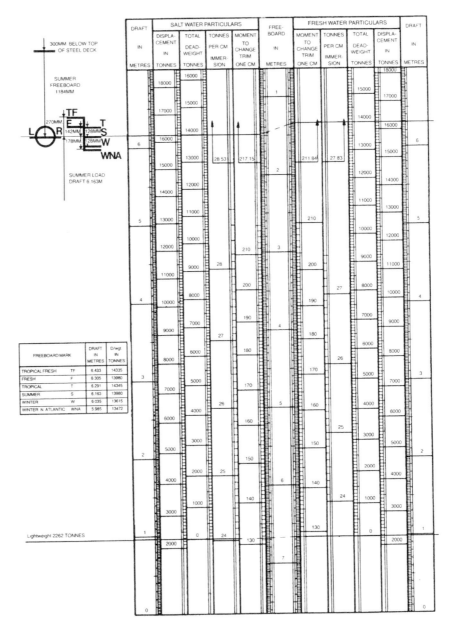

*Figure 1.8*

Once cargo has been loaded the ship's draughts would normally be ascertained and it would be the Chief Officers practice to employ the Deadweight Scale (part of the ship's Stability documentation) to ascertain the ship's final displacement.

The known figures of fuel, stores and fresh water can then be applied to provide a check against total cargo loaded.

**Docking Plan** – A ship's outline plan which depicts the essential elements that would be required by the dry dock authorities in order to dock the vessel. The positions of the block arrangements are shown together with any appendages from the ship's hull that could be obstructive to a safe docking operation, e.g. Bilge keels, stabilisers, azipod thrusters, bulbous bow, etc.,

   **NB.** The plug plan may be incorporated into the docking plan.

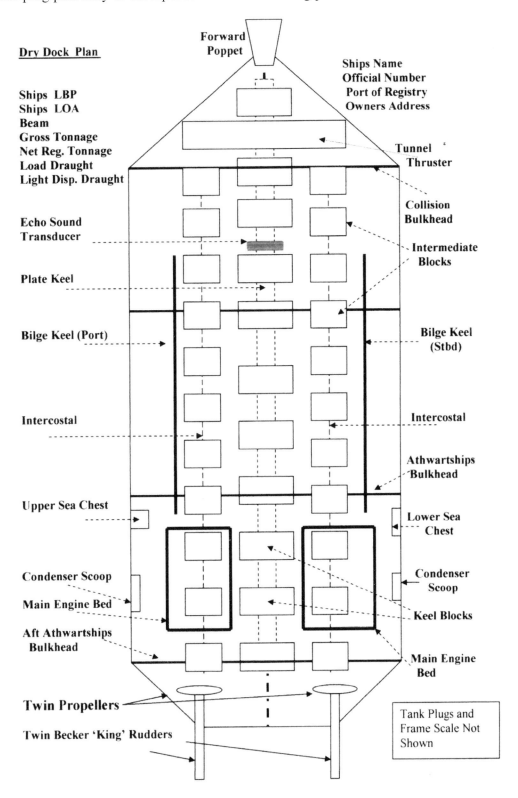

*Figure 1.9*

**Fire Fighting Arrangement** – A ship's plan which shows all the fire fighting equipment and systems which are installed on the vessel. A separate plan of any total flooding system may be miniaturised within the main plan. It is normal practice to have a more detailed, larger scale plan for any fixed total flooding operations like Carbon Dioxide, or sprinkler systems.

**General Arrangement Plan** – Shows all spaces and compartments as laid to the design of the vessel. It includes all cargo and working spaces, tank areas, machinery spaces, storerooms, accommodation areas and void spaces.

**General Particulars of the Vessel** – Considered as part of the ship's stability information and would include the ship's number, owners name and address, moulded dimensions, displacement and deadweight, together with gross and net tonnages.

**Hydrostatic Curves** – Stability curves usually set against a scale of variable draughts used for extracting stability information such as:—

displacement (moulded and extreme) MCTC, Centre of Floatation (F), Centre of Buoyancy (B) from base (KB), The Metacentre (M) from base (KM).

**Manoeuvring Criteria** – Following sea trials of a new ship, manoeuvring data respective of the stopping distance, turning circles, performance capability, etc.,would normally be given to the ship's owners.

**Plug Plan** – A ship's plan which depicts the bottom tanks and the positions of the drain plugs. This may form part of the docking plan.

**Rigging Plan** – A plan which denotes the positions, safe working loads and arcs of operation of all the ship's lifting appliances. This may incorporate the load density figures permitted for maximum deck loading in compartments.

**Shell Expansion Plan** – A plan which depicts the hull shape and identifies the shell plate and framing of the vessel. Strakes being identified by letter from the keel upwards, towards the sheer strake. Plates being cross numbered from aft to forward (sometimes referred to as a line plan). They are used extensively when a ship has received side or bottom damage to her hull.

**Stability Data** – For operational purpose the ship will also need essential stability information like, the Statical Stability Curve and damage stability notes.

### Pitch Angle of Propellers

**Pitch** – Is defined as the axial distance moved by the propeller in one revolution, through a solid medium.

### Measurement of Pitch

Most modern shipyards would establish the pitch of a propeller by the use of an instrument known as a "Pitchometer". However, if this was not available the pitch can be ascertained in dry dock from the exposed propeller.

Position the propeller blade in the horizontal position and place a weighted cord over the blades.

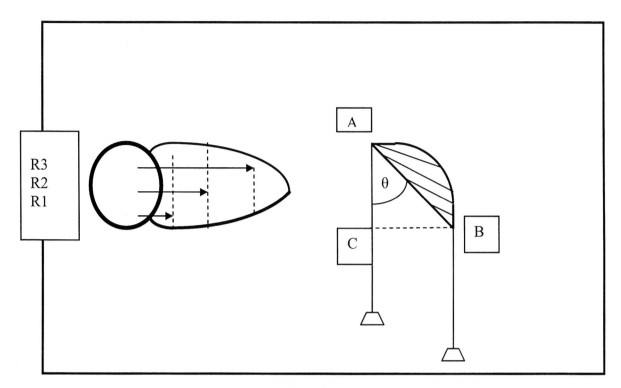

*Figure 1.10*

At different Radi R1, R2, & R3, measure the distances AC and BC as well as R1, R2 and R3.
The tangent of the pitch angle is then $\dfrac{BC}{AC}$.

Therefore Pitch $= 2\pi R \, Tan \, \theta$

$$= \frac{2\pi \times R \times BC}{AC}.$$

**Example to Calculate Pitch Angle of a Propeller**

In a four bladed propeller of constant varying pitch the following readings are obtained.

| Pitch Angle | Radi |
|:---:|:---:|
| 40° | 0.5 m |
| 25° | 1.0 m |
| 20° | 1.5 m |

Calculate the mean pitch of the blades.

Pitch of propeller $= 2\pi R \, Tan \, \theta$

At radi 0.5 $\quad = 2\pi R \times 0.5 \times Tan \, 40° \; = 2.636$
At radi 1.0 $\quad = 2\pi R \times 1.0 \times Tan \, 25° \; = 2.929$
At radi 1.5 $\quad = 2\pi R \times 1.5 \times Tan \, 20° \; = 3.430$
$$\overline{3)8.995}$$

Mean Pitch (Average) $= 2.998$ metres.

**Examples of Propeller Slip**

**Real Slip** – Occurs as a result of physical conditions existing between the propeller and the water in which it is immersed. It should only be positive.

**Apparent Slip** – Is concerned with the same factors but in addition the effects of current and/or wind are taken into account. This may be positive or negative.

**Propeller Slip›**

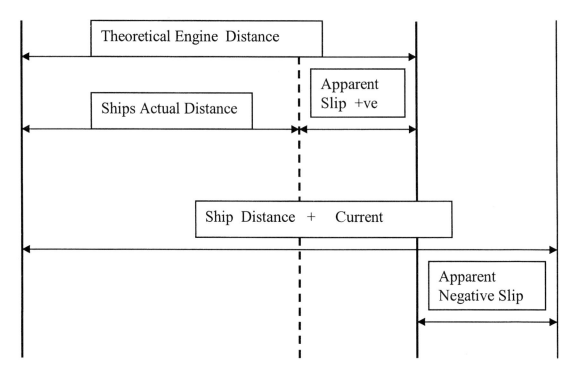

*Figure 1.11*

$$\% \; Slip = \frac{Engine \; Distance - Ship's \; Distance}{Engine \; Distance}$$

(may also be expressed using engine speed and ship's speed as opposed to distances).

**Worked Example in Propeller Pitch and Slip**
**(using pitch from previous example)**

A four bladed propeller of constantly varying pitch has the following criteria:—

RPM = 104, ship's speed = 10.3 knots

| Pitch Angle | Radi |
|:---:|:---:|
| 40° | 0.5 m |
| 25° | 1.0 m |
| 20° | 1.5 m |

Find the % Slip.

---

Pitch of the Propeller $= 2\pi R \ Tan \ \theta$

at radi  0.5 m  $= 2\pi \times 0.5 \times Tan \ 40° = 2.636$

at radi  1.0 m  $= 2\pi \times 1.0 \times Tan \ 25° = 2.929$

at radi  1.5 m  $= 2\pi \times 1.5 \times Tan \ 20° = 3.430$

$$3\overline{)8.995}$$

Therefore Mean (average) Pitch $= 2.998 \ m$

Slip $= \dfrac{\text{Propeller Speed} - \text{Ship's Speed}}{\text{Propeller Speed}}$

Propeller Speed $= \dfrac{\text{Pitch} \times \text{RPM} \times 60}{1,852}$

$= \dfrac{2.998 \times 104 \times 60}{1,852}$

$= 10.1 \ \text{kts.}$

Slip $= \dfrac{10.1 - 10.3}{10.1} \times 100$

$= -1.98\%.$

## Example of Propeller Slip

Calculate the slip incurred by a vessel when given the RPM $= 125$.

And the pitch of the propeller is 6.0 m.

The ship's run from Noon to Noon ship's mean time covers 540 nautical miles.

Clocks are advanced 30 minutes during the day's run

% Slip $= \dfrac{\text{Engine Speed} - \text{Ship's Speed}}{\text{Engine Speed}}$

Ship's speed $= \dfrac{\text{Distance}}{\text{Time}} = \dfrac{540}{23.5} = 22.96 \ \text{kts.}$

Propeller (Engine) Speed $= \dfrac{\text{Pitch} \times \text{RPM} \times 60}{1,852}$

$= \dfrac{6 \times 125 \times 60}{1,852}$

$= 24.3 \ \text{kts.}$

Slip $= \dfrac{24.3 - 22.96}{24.3} \times 100$

$= +5.5\%.$

## Measurement of Liquid Cargoes

The volume of oil in a tank is ascertained by measuring the distance from a fixed point on the deck to the surface of the oil. The distance is known as the "ullage" and is usually measured by means of a plastic tape. A set of tables is supplied to every ship, which indicate for each cargo compartment, the volume of liquid corresponding to a range of ullage measurements. The ullage opening is usually set as near as possible to the centre of the tank so that for a fixed volume of oil, the ullage is not appreciably effected by conditions of trim and list. If a favourable siting is not possible then the effects of list and trim should be allowed for.

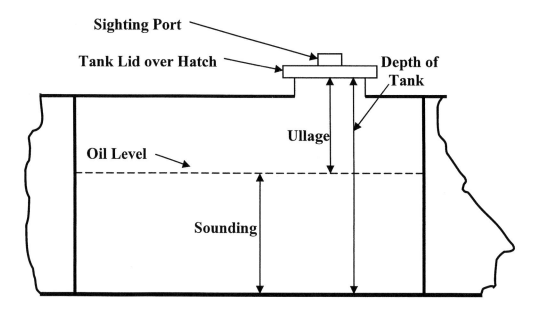

*Figure 1.12*

The important measure of oil is weight and this must be calculated from the volume of oil in each tank. Weight in tonnes is quickly found by multiplying the volume of oil in cubic metres by the relative density of the oil. This density is a fraction and may be taken out of petroleum tables when the relative density of the oil is known.

**Example**

To find the weight of $125\,\text{m}^3$ of oil at a Relative Density of 0.98
Density of oil $= 0.98\ \text{t}/\text{m}^3$
Weight of oil            $=$ volume $\times$ density
                              $= 125\,\text{m}^3 \times 0.98$ tonnes
                              $= 122.5$ tonnes.

Oil expands when heated and its Relative Density (RD) therefore decreases with a rise in temperature. In order that the weight may be calculated accurately, it is important that when ullages are taken the RD of the oil should also be known.

This may be measured directly, by means of a hydrometer.

The RD of a particular oil may be calculated if the temperature of the oil is taken. The change of RD due to a change of one degree in temperature is known as the RD coefficient. This lies between 0.0003 and 0.0005 for most grades of oil and may be used to calculate the RD of an oil at any measured temperature if the RD at some standard temperature is known.

**Examples**

A certain oil has a RD of 0.75 @ 16°C
Its expansion coefficient is 0.00027/°C
Calculate its RD at 26°C.
Temperature difference $= 26°C - 16°C = 10°C$
Change in RD          $= 10 \times 0.00027$
                           $= 0.0027$
RD @ 16°C            $= 0.75$
RD @ 26°C            $= 0.7473$

An oil has a RD 0.75 @ 60°F
Its expansion coefficient is 0.00048/°F
Calculate its RD at 80°F
Temperature difference $= 80°F - 60°F = 20°F$
Change in RD             $= 20 \times 0.00048$
                         $= 0.0096$
RD @ 60°F                $= 0.75$
RD @ 80°F                $= 0.7404.$

**Tank Measurement and Ullaging**
**Use of the Whessoe Tank Gauge**

The function of the gauge is to register the ullage of the tank at any given time, in particular when the liquid level in the tank is changing during the loading and discharge periods. The gauge is designed to record the readings not only at the top deck level of the tank but also remotely at a central cargo control room. A transmitter being fitted on the head of the gauge for just this purpose.

The unit is totally enclosed and various models manufactured are suitable for use aboard not only oil tankers, but chemical and gas carriers also.

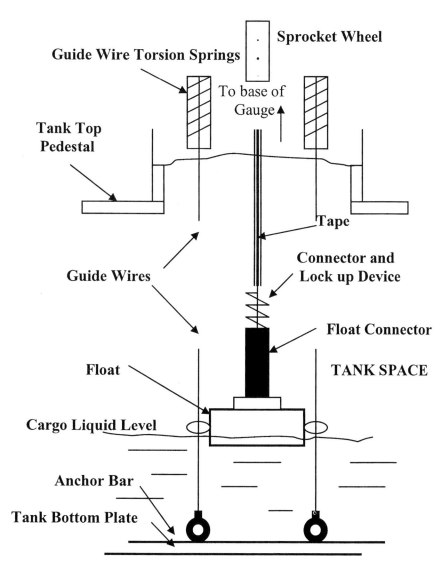

*Figure 1.13*

Inside the gauge housing is a calibrated ullage tape, perforated to pass over a sprocket wheel and guided to a spring loaded tape-drum. The tape extends into the tank and is secured to a float of critical weight. As the liquid rises or falls, the tape is drawn into or extracted out from the drum at the gauge head.

The tape-drum being spring loaded, provides a constant tension on the tape, regardless of the amount of tape paid out. A counter window for display is fitted into the gauge head, allows the ullage to be read on site at the top of the tank.

### Tank Measurement – Radar System

This is a totally enclosed measuring system which can only be employed if the tank is fully inerted. Systems are generally fitted with oxygen sensor and temperature sensor switches, so if the atmosphere in the tank is hot or flammable the radar will not function.

The main unit of the system is fitted on the deck with an inserted cable tube into the tank holding a transducer. Cable then carries the signal to a control unit in the cargo control room where the signal is converted to give a digital read-out for each tank monitored.

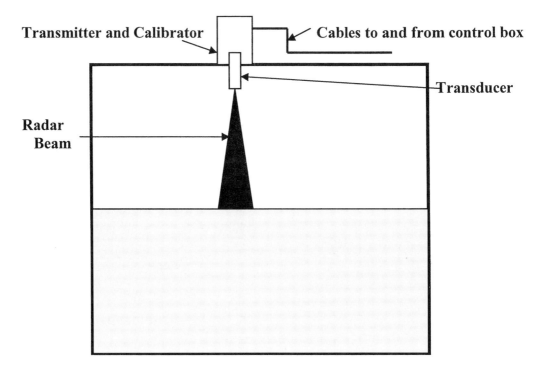

*Figure 1.14*

The transducer would be fitted as close to the centre of the tank area as was possible. Such siting tends to eliminate errors due to trim and list.

# CHAPTER TWO

# Aft End Structures

## Introduction

The forward end of a vessel is generally the more prominent, but the Aft end of a ship, is most certainly the business end. That area where the hull is pierced by the stern tube (s). That end that drives the vessel with single or multiple propellers. The end that controls the movements of the ship with its rudder(s) and contains the steering mechanism. It is one of the most complex areas of ship construction and an area that has many variations in this modern age.

Many new concepts in steering and propulsion have taken place over the last twenty years. Pod propulsion units have increased in popularity, while ducting around propellers is no longer unusual. Fixed pitch propeller units although still dominant, are operating alongside ever increasing designs of Controllable Pitch Propellers (CPP). Multiple propeller builds have increased with the corresponding expansion in the passenger and ferry trades, with water jets encroaching more and more into high speed craft operations.

The aft end is an area that encompasses many specific topics and not limited to propeller shafts, stern tubes, rudder posts and carriers, special rudder types, and not least special shell plating like the boss plate, stealer plates, the oxter, the coffin, the garboard and sheer strakes are all interrelated in the stern area.

Special ships, like the anchor handling vessel, the dynamically positioned offshore supply vessels, tugs, survey vessels or cable laying ships tend to have speciality features like the 360° controllable thruster, specific stern anchor arrangements, mooring leads and fittings, etc., While the Roll On, Roll Off vessels require unique stern arrangements, to accommodate the stern door and/or ramp feature, the reader should note, that these can be found in the special ship section on pages 172-175.

## Rudders and Fitments

### The Construction of Rudders

The majority of rudders are constructed in pre-fabricated steel, built about an internal webbed structure. The webs act to provide vertical and horizontal stiffening to the whole construction. Depending on the type of fitting arrangement, whether it is for a "hanging (suspended) rudder" or for the more conventional style, mounted to a stern frame arrangement, will obviously influence the design of securing.

The rudder movement about the turning axis is achieved by rotation of the stock on a bearing. In the case of the suspended style of rudder this bearing will be established inside the rudder blade area, immediately below the rudder carrier and in line with the axis. Such a design would incorporate an inspection plate, welded to the rudder blade to cover and protect the internal bearing. This inspection plate would normally be easily removed in dry dock, when the bearing is due for survey.

The more conventional Balanced or Semi-Balanced Rudders would be hung in position in association with a stern frame structure. This would have a lower heel, pintle bearing inset into the sole piece of the stern frame and in line with the turning axis of the Rudder Stock.

Virtually all fabricated rudders are fitted with a drain hole and plug arrangement. They are usually protection coated both inside and out to resist corrosion effects, some may be fitted with an internal foam filler for added anti corrosive provision. Once established the rudder would be tested when completely submerged under a head of water of 2.45 metres above the upper edge of the rudder.

## Steering Gear Systems

All steering gears must be fitted with a locking or brake arrangement to permit the rudder to be maintained in a stationary position, when necessary. Some protection to relieve shock from the action of heavy seas must also be incorporated in all power operated steering gears. Where hydraulic steering gears are employed without shock absorbing protection, relief valves are usually included in the design.

The peak horse power developed by a steering gear system is derived from the product of the maximum torque (T) usually assumed at the hard over position, when the ship is travelling at full speed, and the maximum speed (S) in seconds, of the rudder movement.

Steering gears must be fitted with limiting cut outs, to become effective at a smaller helm angle, than those stipulated for the rudder. In general they must have the ability to place the rudder hard over in 28 seconds, when one of the power units is out of action.

## The Rudder Stock

The rudder stock is of a variable diameter which is established on the size of the rudder and the torque that it is expected to experience. It is manufactured in cast or forged steel.

The rudder stock is normally carried inside a "rudder trunk", positioned above the stern frame, but below the steering flat space. The trunk is constructed in such a manner that it may not be watertight at the lower end, but would have a water tight gland fitted at the upper inboard end. Once the stock is positioned and the rudder hung and movement tested, the trunk is usually closed up by a welded seal as a final action.

In passenger vessels where the diameter of the rudder stock exceeds 230 mm, an alternative steering position, remote from the navigation bridge is to be provided.

## Bearing Pintle

This bearing pintle is found at the base of the rudder and accepts the full weight of the rudder. This lower bearing is in line with the turning axis and established into the sole piece of the stern frame. Depending on the type of rudder the weight may be shared between the bearing pintle and any suspended bearing inside the rudder or by the rudder carrier as the stock passes through the hull. In the event that the bearing pintle experiences excessive wear, the rudder bearing could expect to take more weight than for what it was originally intended.

## Rudder Terminology

### Balanced Rudder

A "Balanced Rudder" is one that is constructed with a large area 25% to 30%, of the rudder blade situated in a position forward of the turning axis. The old fashioned first rudders* from the sailing ship era, were secured by a gudgeon and pintle arrangement to the aft end of a stern post, having no area forward of the turning axis. This was seen as a totally unbalanced rudder system, and has all but become obsolete, except on small barges and inland waterway traffic.

The introduction of a balanced rudder effectively reduced the torque, bringing the centre of lateral pressure closer to the turning axis, effective to both Balanced and Semi – Balanced Rudders. This balancing effect reduced the stress on the rudder stock and the steering mechanics.

### Semi-Balanced Rudder

A Semi-Balanced Rudder is one which has a small area of the rudder blade, usually less than 20%, positioned forward of the turning axis. These are probably the more popular of the modern designs for today's shipping operations.

---

* Single Plate rudders have been largely superseded by Double plate and balanced rudders in the construction of modern hulls.

*Figure 2.1    The upper coupling of a semi balanced rudder, seen above the waterline secured to the aft end of the ship's stern frame.*

**Rudder Flap**

The modern rudder may have an extended length by incorporating a flap, with or without a rotor being fitted to the leading edge of the rudder. Unfortunately this type of rudder tends to be expensive to fit and is accompanied by high maintenance costs, though performance gives high manoeuvrability. They are often fitted to the smaller vessel which desires high manoeuvrability because of their trade.

**Rudder Types**

**Rudders** – With so many rudder types available to the ship owner today it would be totally in appropriate to discuss one kind of rudder with possibly a "Rudder Post" and "Bearing Pintle". The fact that the majority of rudders have variations of Rudder Bearings, Rudder securing, together with different transmission methods from the steering consul, tends to make the operational needs different for each particular rudder.

Rudders are now active in nature having hydrodynamic flaps, or have power motors to provide improved positive response to steering orders. Many ships are fitted with the modern "Schilling Rudders" or the popular hanging "Becker Rudder" or the "Becker King Support" variety.

**Stern Rudder/Propeller Arrangements**

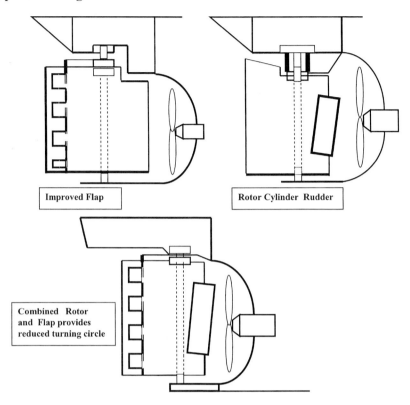

Figure 2.2

**Suspended Rudders**

*Figure 2.3  Suspended (Hanging) Flap Rudder, seen* in situ, *fitted to a twin screw vessel. The rudder is seen exposed in dry dock after it has been cleaned and coated. Sacrificial anodes have also been replaced to reduce the corrosive effects anticipated in this area of dissimilar metals.*

## Suspended Rudder – Stern Arrangement

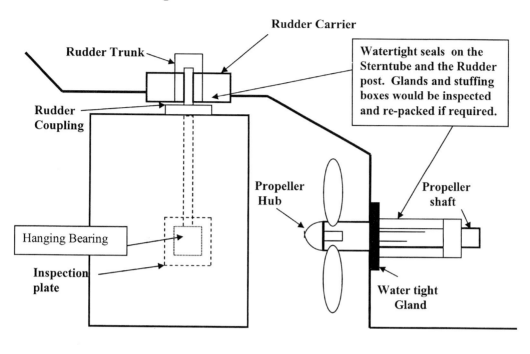

Rudder Carrier

Rudder Trunk

Watertight seals on the Sterntube and the Rudder post. Glands and stuffing boxes would be inspected and re-packed if required.

Rudder Coupling

Propeller Hub

Propeller shaft

Hanging Bearing

Inspection plate

Water tight Gland

Hanging /Suspended Rudders

*Figure 2.4*

## Stern General Arrangements

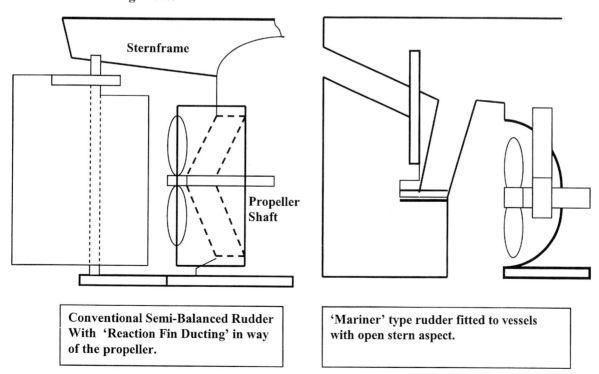

Sternframe

Propeller Shaft

Conventional Semi-Balanced Rudder With 'Reaction Fin Ducting' in way of the propeller.

'Mariner' type rudder fitted to vessels with open stern aspect.

*Figure 2.5*

## Rudder Detail

The rudder (s) is the means of steering the vessel by generating a turning action.

The area of the rudder being approximately 1/60th to 1/70th of the ship's length × its breadth. The ratio of Depth of rudder, to Width of rudder (Aspect Ratio) varies between ship types.

Examples:—

Tankers = 1.7
Ro-Ro's = 2.2.

Balanced Rudders will have an area greater than 25% forward of the turning axis.

Un-balanced Rudders will have 100% area aft of the turning axis (Plate Rudder)* Semi-balanced Rudder will have a small part of the area forward of the turning axis.

## Rudder Construction

Basic rudder construction is by steel plate sides welded internally to a webbed framework. The more modern rudder can expect to be double plated and streamlined.

Every rudder is pressure tested to a head of 2.45 m to prove watertight integrity before being fitted.

They are fitted with a coupling plate to secure to a flat palm and a lifting point to permit securing and also allow removal. Drain holes are also featured.

## The Mariner Rudder

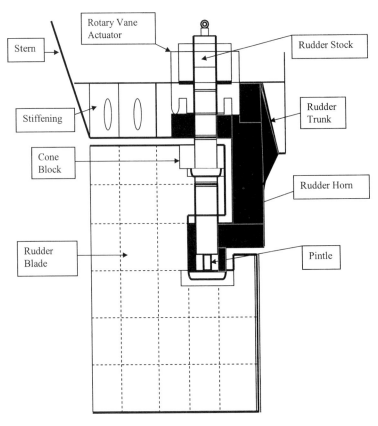

*Figure 2.6*

---

* Plate rudders are virtually obsolete except in small craft and barge construction.

**Parts of Example Rudder Construction**
(Flap Rudder type)

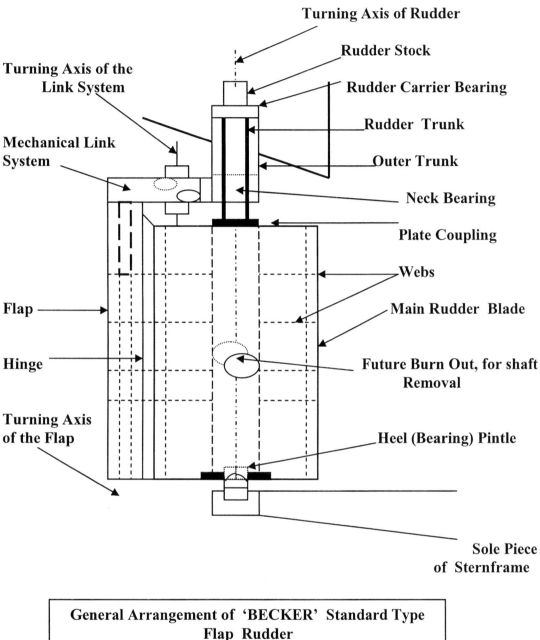

Turning Axis of Rudder

Rudder Stock

Turning Axis of the Link System

Rudder Carrier Bearing

Rudder Trunk

Mechanical Link System

Outer Trunk

Neck Bearing

Plate Coupling

Webs

Flap

Main Rudder Blade

Hinge

Future Burn Out, for shaft Removal

Turning Axis of the Flap

Heel (Bearing) Pintle

Sole Piece of Sternframe

| General Arrangement of 'BECKER' Standard Type Flap Rudder |
|---|

*Figure 2.7*

**Becker King Support Rudder**

These rudders are connected with the ship's hull by means of a rudder trunk which is a cantilever design with an inside bore for location of the rudder stock.

The end part of the rudder trunk is provided with an inside bearing for mounting the rudder blade. The exposed, lower part of the rudder stock, is fixed to the rudder body for input of the torque.

**Becker King Support Rudder**

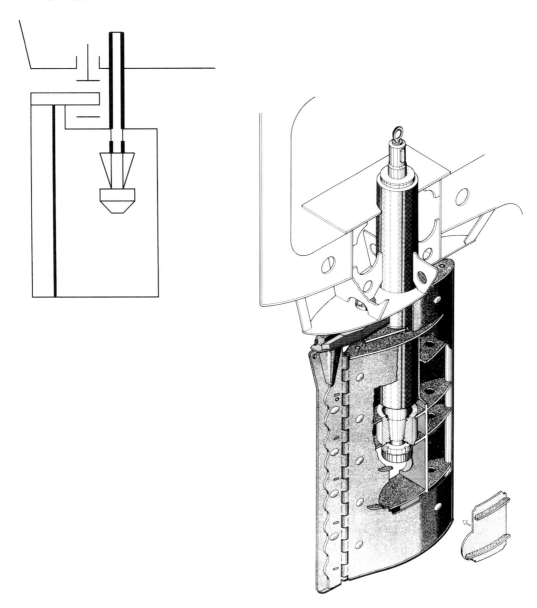

*Figure 2.8*

**Schilling Rudders**

With the advance of rotors and flaps the turning circle of vessels were able to be considerably reduced. With the introduction of the schilling rudder a further major reduction of the turning circle was achieved.

This particular design is a single piece construction with no moving parts. It has a hydrodynamic shape fitted with end plates which help to extract slipstream rotational energy. The trailing wedge reduces yaw to provide excellent course stability according to the manufacturers.

When operational, the 70° to 75° helm position, takes the full slipstream from the propeller and diverts it at right angles to the hull, eliminating the need for stern thrusters. An ideal property for berthing operations, giving a sideways movement to the vessel.

The rudder design may be a fully hung spade, or a simplex type and balance being at about 40%. Sizes of rudders vary, but the positioning should take account of the recommended distance between the trailing edge of the propeller and the stern of the vessel, to equal 1½ × the propeller diameter.

Rudder movement is achieved by steering motors supplied by reputable manufactures although several fittings have employed rotary vane steering gear with extremely responsive results. Torque effecting the stock being similar to conventional rudder design.

## Twin Schilling Rudders

This system of twin schilling rudders operated by rotary vane steering is expected to provide improved course stability over and above a conventional rudder. From the point of view of the ship handler a single joystick control provides comparatively easy manoeuvring, the ship moving in the direction of the joystick movement. The propulsive thrust being proportional to how far the stick is pushed from the "hover" position.

Again there are no moving parts underwater, so providing reduced maintenance and less wear and tear compared to conventional rudders. A further advantage is that with the rudders in the clam shell position, the stopping distance of the vessel is greatly reduced and the heading is still retained. The arrangement tends to work well with bow thrust in opposition at the fore end giving the vessel an extremely tight turning circle practically within its own length.

If the turning circle of the vessel with a Vec Twin Rudders arrangement is considered, the rapid speed reduction caused by the large rudder angles (65°/70°) would expect to result in reduced angles of heel. Also because the speed is reduced so is the "advance" and the "transfer" values of the vessel in the turn. This subsequently provides a tighter turning ability than say a conventional vessel.

## Twin Shilling Rudder – Manoeuvring Configurations

## ARRANGEMENT OF VECTWIN RUDDERS

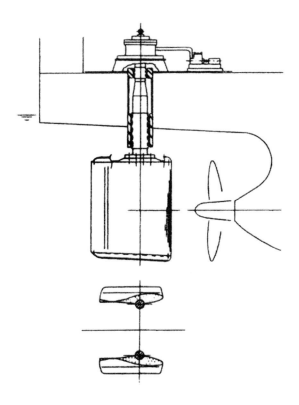

*Figure 2.9*

## TYPICAL RUDDER ANGLES FOR BASIC MANOEUVRES

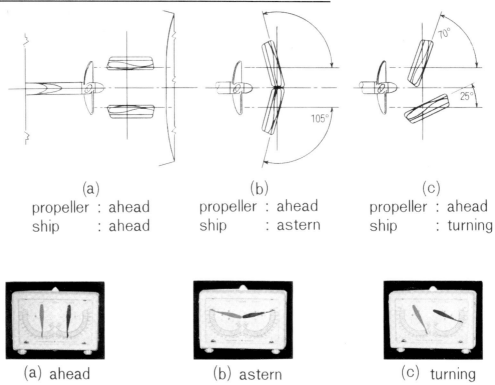

(a)
propeller : ahead
ship     : ahead

(b)
propeller : ahead
ship     : astern

(c)
propeller : ahead
ship     : turning

(a) ahead        (b) astern        (c) turning

*Figure 2.10*

**Schilling Rudder**

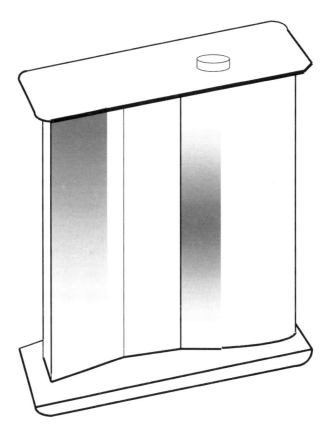

*Figure 2.11    Schilling, high lift, high performance rudder.*

**Stern Arrangement with Reaction Fin and Propeller Ducting**

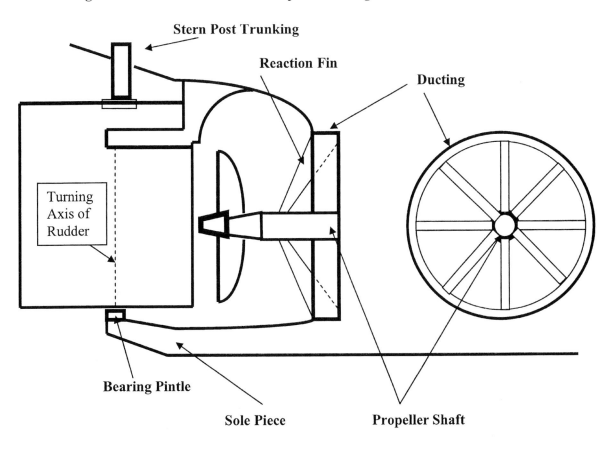

**Ducting**

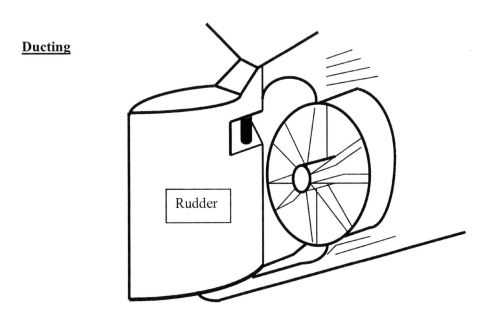

**(Propeller not included for clarity).**

*Figure 2.12*

**Ducting and Rudder Arrangement**

*Figure 2.13   Example of propeller ducting structured in conjunction with the "Flap Rudder" arrangement of a twin screw vessel. (Starboard side only displayed.) The stern features shown, also illustrate the draught marks, sacrificial anodes in the underwater area of the ducting, rudder and propeller region. The propeller shaft is seen extended and strut supported from the hull. The vessel shown also displays twin stern thrust tunnel units, noticeable behind the propeller shaft.*

**Arguments for Ducted Propellers**

If the ducted propeller is compared with the open propeller, several distinctive aspects are noticed. The most influential. probably being the enhanced speeds gained of upto about 0.6 knots. This can clearly be translated to a fuel burn/power saving over an example voyage. Such a saving could justify the initial expense of fitting the ducting arrangement at the building stage.

Experience has also shown that ducting may reduce vibration effects, particularly where cavitation is a feature. In comparison with an open propeller, vessel vibration about the stern and the "thrust block" is noted as being suppressed by the installation of ducting. The reduced vibration effects may be as a result of the reduced overall size of the propeller where ducting is employed, as compared to a larger propeller in open design where ducting is not present. An exception to the norm would be where a vessel is lightship or in ballast when excessive vibration (nearly twice the normal levels) can expect to be experienced. When the vessel is deep laden and fitted with ducting, such a vessel benefits from reduced vibration effects. Assuming the ship is gainfully employed with continuous cargoes ducted propellers would seem to be a favourable addition.

Obviously with smaller propellers being used in construction (including the spare) production costs are reduced. However, this reduction would be offset by the cost of installing the duct itself. In practice, if a vessel suffers damage in the propeller region, the duct itself may suffer damage.

This may be seen to afford some protection to the propeller and the duct could be repaired by regular shipyard methods. Where as a damaged propeller would need to be drawn and possibly recast.

Ducted propellers would seem to be economically viable to the ship owner. However, corrosion on such an additional fitment, below the waterline must also be considered in the economic equation. It would also seem to be better to fit at the new build stage than to retro-fit ducting to an existing vessel. Retro-fitting is more labour intensive and therefore some thought should be given at the design stage as to the needs of the trade and the voyage plans.

## Sternframe

The conventional vessel fitted with cruiser or transom stern, usually incorporates a stern frame construction. The purpose of which is to support the bearings for the rudder and the propeller shaft with the weight of the propeller itself. It also provides an ideal landing for the shell plate as well as giving strength to the aft part, when taking blocks in dry dock.

The sternframe can be "cast", "forged" or of a fabricated construction. The size will extend to upto about three frame spaces in length and is often notched joined, to the coffin plate and to the garboard strakes either side of the keel. One of the main benefits of the sternframe is to absorb vibration stresses brought on by the propeller activity. This benefit is further enhanced by running the rudder post into the hull and connected to a transverse floor.

The forward part of the sternframe constitutes the sternpost of the vessel and this tends to extend into the hull being connected to a deep floor. This additional securing provides further reduced vibration effects. The lower part of the frame is called the "Sole Piece" and as this is usually the deepest part of the vessel during operation, it is that area which is most susceptible to damage from grounding. It also accommodates the lower bearing support to the rudder which in the event of damage could seriously effect the ship's steering ability.

Plate landings are with the Boss Plate, in way of the propeller boss and the "Oxter Plate". This is a double curvature plate below the transom floor which runs into the foreside of the sternpost. Stealer plates are also a feature, often employed in this region, as the fine lines of the ship bring the shell plating together at the vessels extremities.

**Sternframe with Balanced Rudder Arrangement**

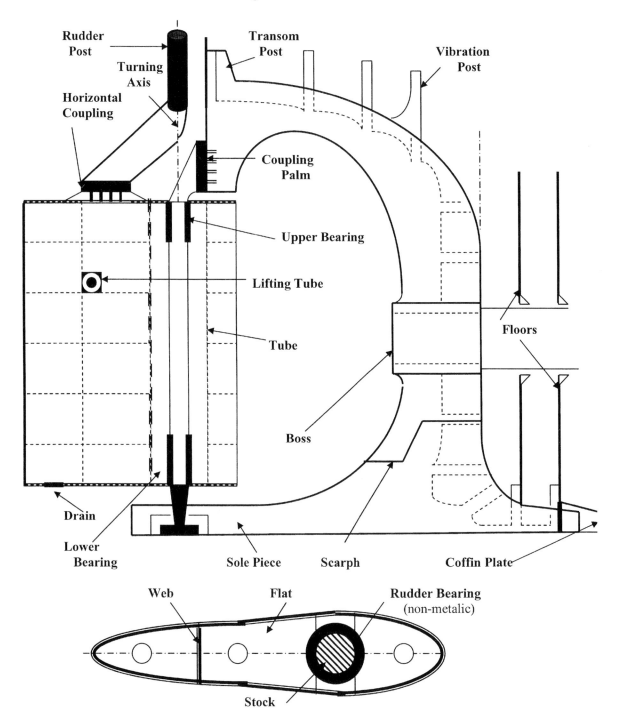

*Figure 2.14*

**Rudder Carriers**

There are two main types of "Rudder Carriers":—

(a) Combination type which has an integral watertight gland.
(b) Separate gland and carrier:—
  (i) A water tight gland is fitted where the rudder stock enters the rudder trunk. The access to the greater length of the stock removes the need to include a watertight rudder carrier because it reduces the unsupported length of the stock.
  (ii) Where the carrier is in two sections the upper part is keyed to the stock to allow them to turn together. Direct weight of the rudder assembly being transferred to the rudder carrier via a shoulder casting which forms part of the stock forging. Alternatively a collar arrangement is fitted between the tiller and the carrier itself.

Bearing surfaces can be flat or of a conical design, while the lower part of the carrier is bolted into a heavy insert plate in the deck.

In either case the duties of the ship's engineers are meant to cover the regular maintenance with watertight glands and ensure that packing of the gland is tightened down at regular intervals. Repacking of the glands normally take place during the ship's dry dock periods where packing material is renewed if required.

Some seepage on gland seals is not unusual and can generally be controlled by tightening of the nuts in a symmetrical, even manner.

**Rudder Stock Constructional Features**

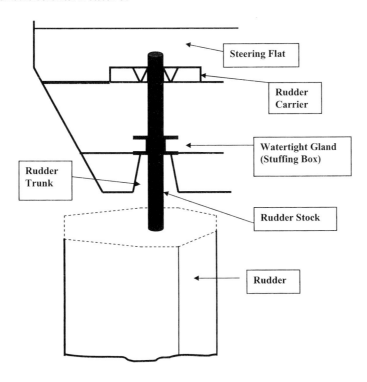

*Figure 2.15*

The above arrangement shows a separate rudder carrier and watertight gland at the inner end of the rudder trunk. The weight of the rudder and stock being carried by the carrier positioned in the steering flat.

Other systems employ a combined carrier and watertight gland as depicted in Diagram 2.16. The type and weight of rudder influences the arrangement for the various systems of rudder carrier available. All arrangements, however, must have a water tight seal as the rudder stock passes through the outer hull.

**The Rudder Carrier**

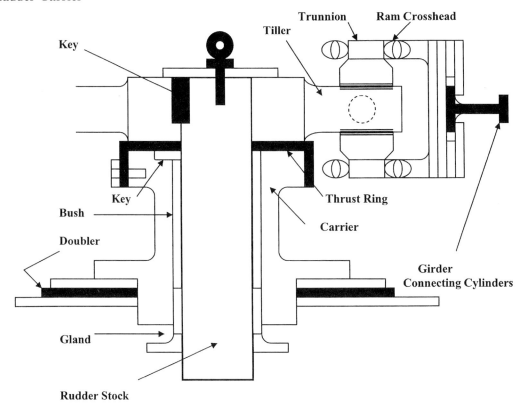

*Figure 2.16*

**Watertight Gland – (Stuffing Box)**

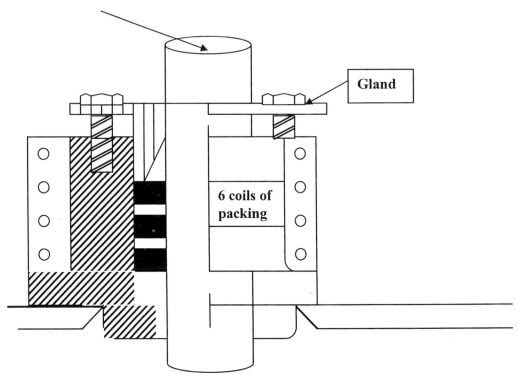

*Figure 2.17*

The Gland is regularly inspected through the watch keeping system on a daily basis. The engineers would normally tighten up on the holding bolts to squeeze the packing tighter against the stock to maintain the watertight integrity.

It would be normal practice to inspect and repack the gland during scheduled dry dock periods. Once the Gland is opened up the surveyor would be expected to sight and inspect the inner surfaces for any corrosion effects.

## Rudder Stock Seals

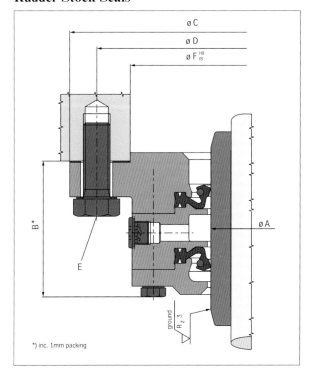

*Figure 2.18   Lower seal*

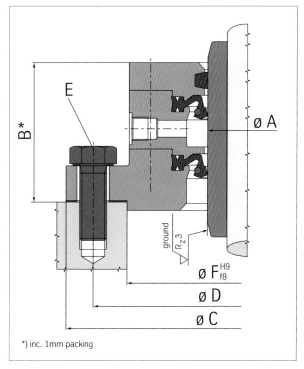

*Figure 2.19   Upper seal*

## Rudder Pintles and Bearings

The type of bearings employed depend mainly on the type of rudder being used. Earlier construction used bronze liners and lignum vitae bearings but these have generally been replaced by the use of stainless steel liners and stainless steel bushes. Bushes are usually spiral grooved to aid lubrication.

Semi-balanced rudders have both a top and bottom pintle arrangement for the purpose of anchoring the rudder. The top pintle is a lock securing, construction to prevent the rudder from lifting. While the bottom pintle is a bearing point, with its lower edge resting on a hard disk in the event that the rudder carrier fails. Lubrication to upper and lower pintle's is usually provided by sea water.

## Locking Pintle

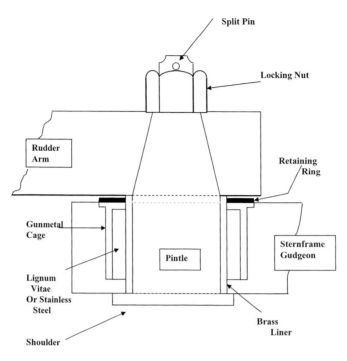

*Figure 2.20*

## Lower Bearing Pintle

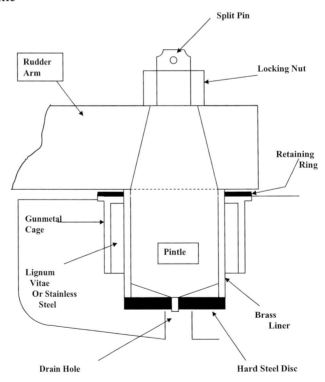

*Figure 2.21*

Rudder pintles are usually tapered and manufactured with a stainless steel liner in a water lubricated bearing. The bearing material usually being a synthetic product in tufnol or other laminated plastic. Although oil lubricated bearings are possible they are not in common use.

**Twin Propeller Options**

*Figure 2.22   Twin Controllable Pitch Propellers (CPP's), each fitted with ducting and flap rudders designed either side of a single skeg stern structure. The vessel is also fitted with twin stern thrusters set forward of the propellers, on the centre line above the keel. Extensive use of sacrificial anodes has been used to reduce corrosion effects in the stern area due to the construction in dissimilar metals namely with tail end shafts, bronze propellers and the steelwork of the rudders and hull.*

**Twin Propellers, Twin Rudder Arrangement**

*Figure 2.23   The twin screw, twin hanging rudder arrangement as seen on the Fisheries Protection vessel "Sulisker" in Dry Dock. A "bolster bar" is seen in position at the edge of the "boot topping" and the topsides paint covering, on the port quarter. The propeller shafts are supported by external hull struts, bearing the draught markings. The rudder plates are both fitted with sacrificial anodes either side.*

## Twin Screw Support

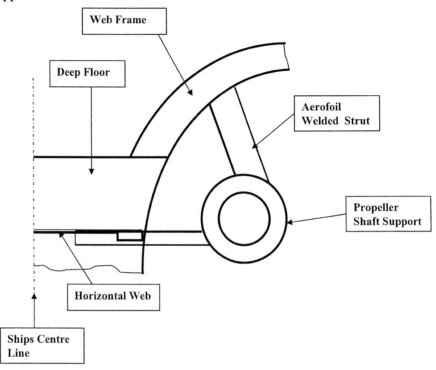

*Figure 2.24  "A" Bracket, strutted support used in the construction of twin screw vessels. The struts are usually of an aerofoil section to reduce drag effects on the ship's speed. They are positioned either side of the centre, to support the twin shafts.*

## Supporting Structure for Propeller Shafts

*Figure 2.25  Supporting struts seen reinforcing the propeller shaft to the hull of a twin screw vessel. The struts are welded directly to the outer stern tube section and onto the outer shell plate of the hull. Propellers shafts and rudders are further protected by a "bolster bar" seen in position secured to the shell off the starboard quarter.*

**Twin Propeller – Boss Plating Arrangement**

*Figure 2.26 The tail shaft arrangement of the starboard propeller, showing the extension from the hull and boss plating of the outer hull. The vertical support strut to the outer shaft is seen vertically over the propeller.*

**Internal Support for Twin Propeller Shafts**

**The Cast Spectacle Frame**

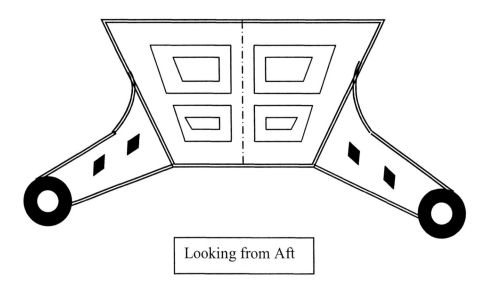

Looking from Aft

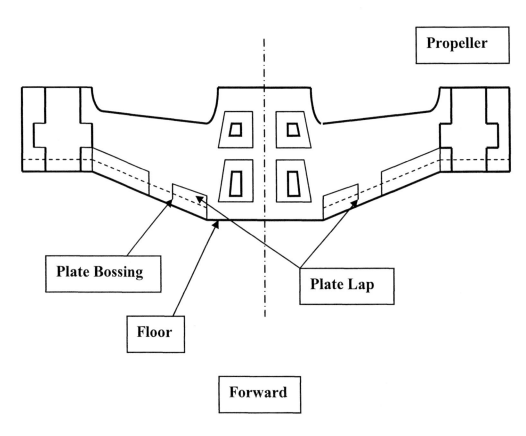

Propeller

Plate Bossing

Plate Lap

Floor

Forward

*Figure 2.27*

## Pod Propulsion Units

*Figure 2.28   The aft end of a twin pod propeller vessel seen exposed in a Dry Dock. Each Pod unit carries an underside fin, and they are set either side of a centre line "skeg".*

Pod machinery units have removed the necessity for shaft drive tunnels and consequently have provided vessels with greater space to increase pay load capacity. They are popular with passenger cruise type vessels where a saving in machinery space can be utilised to increase passenger cabin volume.

From the point of view of maintenance, pod machinery units can be removed and replaced, generally quite quickly. This reduces losses in earning capacity, caused by being off charter and incurred costs for replacement tonnage, often required to sustain designated route schedules.

## Machinery "Pod" Propulsion
(Pod Propulsion Units)

Several recent cruise ships have moved towards "Pod propulsion units" as a means of main power and the more recent buildings in the ferry sector reflect the potential use of "Pod Technology" for many different size of vessel of the future. The compactness of the "pod" and the associated benefits to passenger/ferry operations would seem to offer distinct advantages to ship handlers, operators and passengers alike.

Some of the possible advantages from this system would be in the form of:—

1.   Low noise levels and low vibration within the vessel.
2.   Fuel efficiency with reduced emissions.
3.   Good manoeuvering characteristics and tighter turning circle as when compared with a similar ship operating with standard shaft lines and rudders.

4. Reduced space occupied by bulky machinery making increased availability for additional freight or passenger accommodation.
5. Simpler maintenance operations for service or malfunction. (Pods are easy to remove/and replace.)

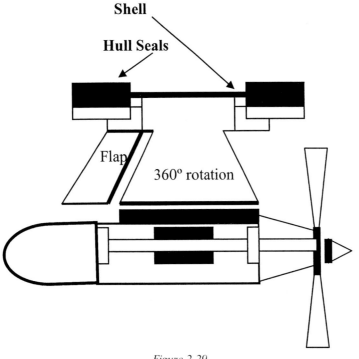

*Figure 2.29*

Machinery pods are usually fitted to the hull form via an installation block.

Each vessel having customised units to satisfy the hydrodynamics and the propulsion parameters. Propeller size and the rpm would also need to reflect the propulsion requirements to the generator size with electric "Azipod Units".

The direction of the shaft line is acquired from a hydraulic steering unit giving the versatility of directional thrust to port and starboard as well as ahead or astern.

For extremely high speed steering a 360° rotation pulling pod with a rudder flap has been designed.

Control means is provided by flap movement with the complete "Pod" turning.

Pod propulsion systems provide the action of pulling, rather than pushing the vessel through the water. A typical twin propeller pod configuration would consist of three main diesel generators driving an electric motor to each propeller, with full bridge control transmission. Power ranges start from about 5 MW upto 38 MW dependant on selected rpm. (Adequate built in redundancy is accounted for by providing 3 generators for only two propellers.)

It is reported that ship handling is easier, turning circles are comparatively tighter than vessels fitted with conventional rudders and example speeds of 25 knots ahead, 17 knots astern and 5 knots sideways provides excellent harbour manoeuvring. Varieties of pod designs are rapidly entering the commercial market supported by associated new ideas to improve fuel efficiency and provide better performance. Many are water cooled eliminating the need for complex air cooled systems, while the Siemans-Schottel Propulsion (SSP) system has propellers at each end of the pod rotating in the same direction.

Rotable "Pods" provide directional movement to the hull, without the use of attached rudders. The thrust being directed in line with the axis of the pod. Sideways motion from the stern position being possible by main engine propulsion systems, effecting directional change, similar to bow thrust units in the fore part.

**Azipod Thruster Construction**

Many types of vessels are now being fitted with steerable, thruster units, known as "azipods". They operate as rotable thrusters providing not only main propulsion but also steerage to the vessel. They are usually fitted as a multiple feature and are usually ducted but not always. They tend to give high manoeuvrability to a vessel, especially when featured as an addition to main propellers. They are extensively employed with vessels which operate with "Dynamic Positioning".

*Figure 2.30 A ducted azipod, featured on the outer hull, port side, of a twin rudder/twin propeller vessel. Sacrificial anodes are seen on the outer ducting. Some types of Azipods are retractable and may be fitted with CPP.*

## Propeller Shafts and Bearings

*Figure 2.31 A new propeller shaft bearing, seen prior to fitting at the B and V Industrietechnik plant, Hamburg Germany. The structure of bearings vary between manufacturers and may feature ceramics in modern design.*

**Stern tubes** – An item of major concern to both shipboard and dock personnel. Tail end shafts are regularly drawn for inspection, which necessitates the Sterntube becoming exposed. The bushes and the watertight seals become exposed, revealing any damage or corrosion effects which might directly influence satisfactory propulsion operations. Surveyors, naturally would expect to sight this area and take keen interest in the overall condition of fitments pertinent to the propeller shaft rotation. This operation would usually entail removal of any Rope-Guard, the measuring of any wear-down and the repacking of the stern gland.

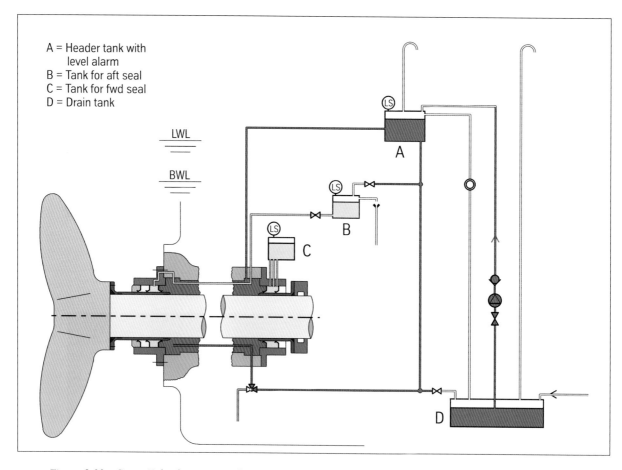

A = Header tank with
        level alarm
B = Tank for aft seal
C = Tank for fwd seal
D = Drain tank

LWL

BWL

*Figure 2.32    Stern Tube four ring, Lubrication System. This seal incorporates a third seal ring which faces the stern tube and may be run as a spare ring, to be run with or without load on the liner. Other systems operate where the oil pressure is slightly lower than that of the sea water, thus achieving a leak proof seal arrangement.*

**Stern Tube Sealing Arrangements**

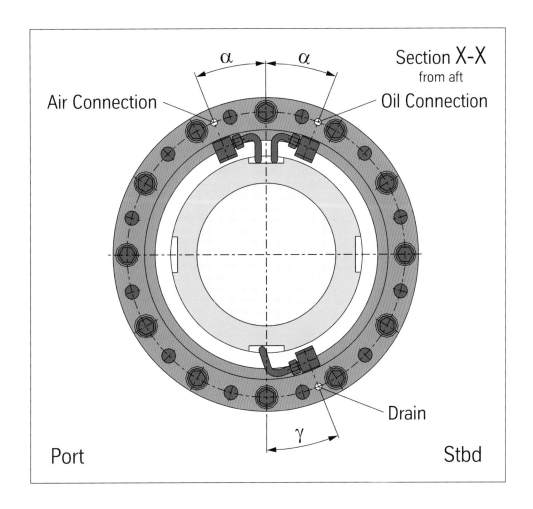

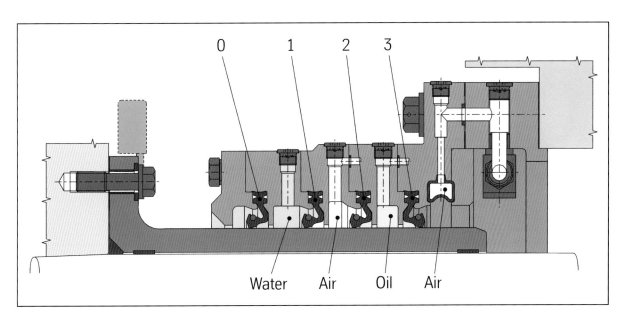

*Figure 2.33*

## Stern Tube Criteria

The function of the stern tube is to provide a bearing for the tail end shaft. It is usually made in cast iron. Stern tubes are lubricated by either a water lubrication system or an oil lubricated system.

The older form of tube was water lubricated and inserted from forward to aft. The forward end of the tube was then bolted and secured to the after peak bulkhead via a water tight gland (stuffing box). While the aft end of the tube was threaded and a large external nut was fitted, securing the tube to the stern frame. A keeper plate was welded to the nut to prevent the nut slacking down inadvertently.

The tube was then lubricated by sea water entering the tube by the aft end. The water being stopped from entering into the shaft tunnel by the watertight gland at the fore end. The tail end shaft was supported originally by a hard wood known as lignum vitae, but this tended to be dated by a laminated plastic like "Tufnol" set into a brass bush at the aft end of the tube.

Oil lubricated stern tubes had a oil tight gland at each end of the tube. This prevented foreign bodies like sand or grit entering the tube and causing wear down on the bearing surfaces. The tube itself was bushed in a soft white metal which replaced the brass bush and bearing strips of the water lubricated systems.

Modern construction incorporates the stern tube, built into the structure and are not usually removable. Twin screw arrangements support the shafts by a spectacle frame or by "A" brackets or a combination of both.

## Stern Tube Profile

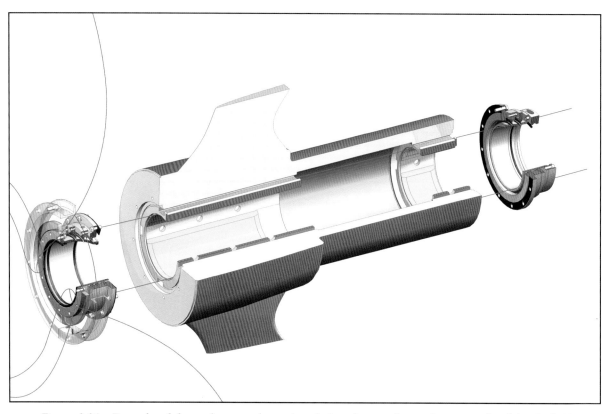

*Figure 2.34   Example of forward stern tube seal and the aft propeller seal systems fitted by B & V Industrietechnik, in Germany. Liners for shaft bearings are now often manufactured in ceramic materials.*

## Propellers

Marine propellers vary considerably across the fixed pitch (FPP) and the controllable pitch(CPP) ranges. They differ not only in the number of blades employed per unit but also in the substance of manufacture. Many being constructed in a bronze alloy, like Manganese bronze or Cunial bronze, probably being the most popular and best known casting material. Other copper based alloys are widely used because they offer strength and ductility. Since the late 1950's, higher strength nickel-aluminium bronze has been employed in their manufacture. More recently, propellers have been manufactured in stainless steel particularly where ships are destined for Arctic operations.

Propellers may have a multiple number of blades and many modern designs use upto seven blades. (Three bladed propellers generally stopped being used on commercial vessels in the 1940's) The choice of blade numbers, tend to reflect consideration of vibration effects. The greater number of blades, seemingly reduce the exciting forces about the propeller. Blade minimum thickness is designated by classification society regulations.

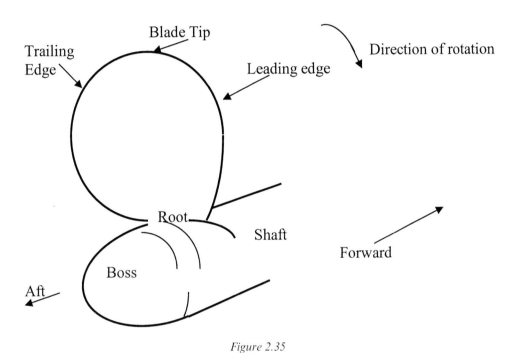

*Figure 2.35*

Many studies have been undertaken to establish the maximum output possible from the optimum shaped blades used in modern day propulsion systems. Manufactures consider durability and reliability required of the propeller unit, while the ship's Master and owners look to the efficiency and the operational aspects of specific units.

It is also considered an advantage if the material of manufacture is capable of being welded. In the event of damage, then repairing the unit becomes a possibility.

Propellers are closely associated with the ship's main propulsion systems and most manufacturers supply their product with respective shaft(s), bearings and seals, very often in partnership with engine manufactures. As the integrated propulsion Package (IPP) they may also be fitted alongside thruster units and/or jet nozzles, depending on the size and type of vessel.

Propellers are designed to produce maximum efficiency from the engine at the most economical fuel burn. However, the propeller itself gives rise to some drag effect and will experience transverse thrust as a side effect. A degree of cavitation on the forward side of the blades can also be expected. Such effects continually reduce the propellers effectiveness and have associated side effects like generating excessive vibration and noise.

The rotation of the propeller and the generation of cavitation leads to a vortex being created in the region of the blade tips. This influences the slip value and hence the speed of the vessel. This action could also cause damage through "pitting" which could also effect propeller performance.

Disc Area (of a propeller) is defined by the area of the circle that passes through the tips of the blades and is found by the formula:—

$$\frac{\pi D^2}{4}$$ where "D" represents the propeller diameter.

In general, the larger the propeller diameter, the greater its efficiency. So designs of the hull form, tend to accommodate the largest propeller that is practical, while at the same time provide adequate clearances from the baseline of the ship's build. The more usual clearance being between about 15 cms to 30 cms with open water sterns or enclosed stern apertures. Adequate clearances between the propeller and the hull have the tendency to reduce vibration effects to this aft region of the build.

Where twin propellers are engaged and support shaft struts are used, clearances tend to differ to suit the hull lines. Clearances being usually in the range of 0.2D to 0.4D from blade tip to hull lines.

There are now many different types of propeller systems in operation. The right hand fixed blade propeller is still common but developments in Controllable Pitch Propellers, contra rotating propellers, Multi-blade propeller systems, propeller sets, pod propulsion units, Kort nozzle systems and Azipod systems, have all taken market share in both commercial and warship construction. Active rudders with propeller attached are also an added feature while Voith Schneider Propellers (VSP) have made advances with the Voith Cycloidal Rudder working in conjunction with cycloidal propulsion.

**Propeller Rake**

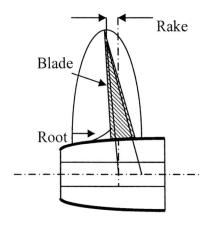

Propeller rake is defined as that distance at the blade tip between the generating line and the perpendicular to the propeller axis that meets the generating line at the propeller axis.

Rake Angle of a propeller is the angle measured from the plane perpendicular to the shaft centreline to the tangent to the generating line at a specified radius.

*Figure 2.36*

**Factors of Propellers**

**Single Fixed Pitch Propeller**

Fixed pitch propeller(s) are subject to drag effects and slip, when the vessel is moving through the water. Being usually constructed in a dissimilar metal to the steelwork of the hull they are subject to pitting and corrosion effects necessitating in most cases the use of sacrificial anodes about the rudder propeller area. These anodes can themselves also generate some frictional resistance.

In the event of damage to one of the blades of the propeller, it would become necessary to replace the whole propeller. (unless the material of manufacture is weld able) Changing a propeller is expensive and will usually require the vessel to enter dry dock.

**NB.** Historically smaller vessels could and have been known to change a propeller while alongside, with the assistance of shore side cranes and excessive forward trim.

## Nozzle Propellers

When operating at high speed, these propellers experience a reduced value of slip but when at slow speed, under heavy load, may experience increased values of slip. They also experience erosion on the inside edge of the nozzle and at the blade tips, usually due to cavitation and vortex effects. The nozzle itself tends to be a protective and tends to prevent debris hitting the actual propeller blades.

These propellers are used extensively in tunnel bow thrusters, stern thruster units, set into the skeg and in azi-pods. Ducted propellers are considered as a similar disposition. Any such fittings are prone to damage and corrosion over time.

*Figure 2.37   A rotable "Nozzle Propeller" seen exposed in dry dock prior to the hull being cleaned. These can provide main propulsion for ahead or astern, but are often used as versatile thruster units through 360°.*

## Controllable Pitch Propellers (CPP's)

These are more expensive to fit than fixed pitch propellers, especially if they are to be fitted retrospective to the building stage. They are subject to more maintenance but have distinct advantages over and above fixed pitch blades.

If a blade is damaged, it can be removed comparably quickly and replaced by a spare blade (Usually carried by the ship itself). The whole propeller does not need to be replaced. The CPP is also cost effective, in that with a constant rotating shaft, shaft alternators can be used for electrical power generation, without having to resort to the use of additional generators. Additional, auxiliary generator sets, require expensive auxiliary fuel, a necessity with fixed pitch propellers.

The benefits to the ship handlers from CPP over FPP are immediate bridge response to ship control, without having to go through engineers to obtain manoeuvring controls. However, the controllable propellers still generate an element of drag effect, especially at zero pitch and they are also subject to similar corrosion as the fixed pitch propellers, for the same reasons. They are generally subject to reduced slip values.

*Figure 2.38   A Controllable Pitch Propeller (CPP) of a twin screw vessel seen exposed in dry dock prior to cleaning and polishing.*

**Controllable Pitch Propeller Operation**

Although there are many manufacturers of CPP's the majority conform to a basic design of having a shaft within a shaft. The outer main rotating shaft having the blades connected, with an inner lateral moving shaft, generating a pitch angle to the propeller blades.

The inner shaft is moved in a fore and aft direction by means of hydraulics and the aft end is secured to a "spider". Individual blade links, fit to the spider and to the circumference of each circular blade base. As the lateral movement of the shaft is caused, the blades are turned to a calibrated angle of pitch.

The forward end of the inner shaft is acted on like a piston, which generates the lateral movement. The amount of movement is a direct influence from the desired value of pitch (speed required by the operator). A typical control set, with twin controllable pitch propellers, will have twin operating handles on the navigation bridge. As the handles are pushed forward positive pitch is put on the blades by increasing movement to the piston. When the operational handles are pulled backwards, the pressure to the piston is put on, in the opposite direction, causing a negative pitch to be applied. (Effectively causing an astern movement.)

Where the operating handles are set at a neutral position of zero pitch, the rotating shaft remains turning, but no forward or astern pitch is on the blades. Hence the ship remains stationary without having to stop and restart engines. The system should be treated with operational respect because it can generate "creep effect" a condition when operators think they have zero pitch, when in fact a fraction of pitch is left on and goes unnoticed. Particularly dangerous if alongside on tension winches, the vessel could pull herself ahead or astern unintentionally. To prevent such an occurrence the operating handle sequence, is often fitted with a locking sleeve at the zero pitch control, to ensure that the blades are actually at zero and not carrying any pitch angle.

The benefits of the CPP have already been mentioned, in that shaft alternators can be employed with the constant rotating shaft, saving auxiliary fuel costs, direct ship control is more effective and damaged blades can easily be replaced. An additional asset is that as the ship can be stopped, without stopping the engine, less air is required to restart the plant. This means that a smaller air capacity is required, causing less weight and less occupying space, which can be better employed towards the earning capacity of the vessel.

Overall, the CPP has considerable advantages over and above the fixed pitch propeller not least providing some ships with the unnecessary need for expensive tug use, in and out of harbour. The main disadvantage being the initial cost of installation of such a system and its ongoing maintenance.

## Controllable Pitch Propellers (CPP)

With a controllable pitch propeller, all the blades are separate and fitted independently to the central hub of the propeller fitted to the end of the rotational shaft. These blades are bolted to the flush faces of the hub (the number of faces equals the number of blades). Once each blade is bolted into position the heads of the bolts are braced by welded straps to prevent unwanted movement.

One of the many advantages of the Controllable Pitch Propeller is that in the event that a blade becomes damaged, it can easily be removed by ship's engineers and a new blade (usually carried as ship's spares) can become a fitted replacement.

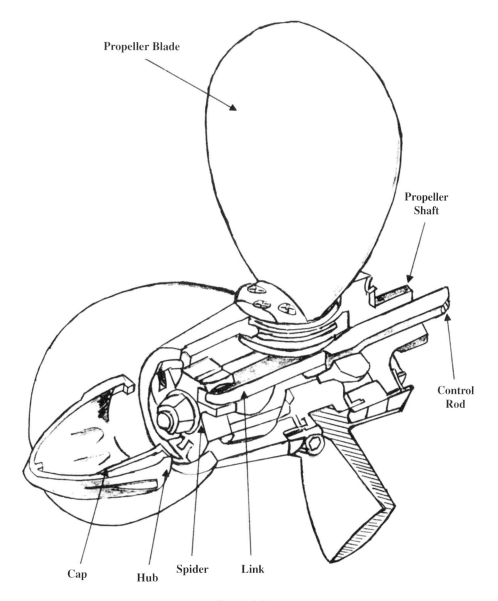

*Figure 2.39*

## Propeller Connections

Propellers are usually fitted to a tapered "tail-end" shaft. The propeller being *keyed to the shaft so preventing the propeller just slipping around the end. A large nut is then fitted over, with a locking plate to secure the propeller to the shaft. Where the propeller is a right hand turning, the nut would be a left hand thread to prevent any slackening off while the shaft is turning. (Vice versa for left hand turning propellers.)

## Propeller Securing (Conventional Fixed Pitch)

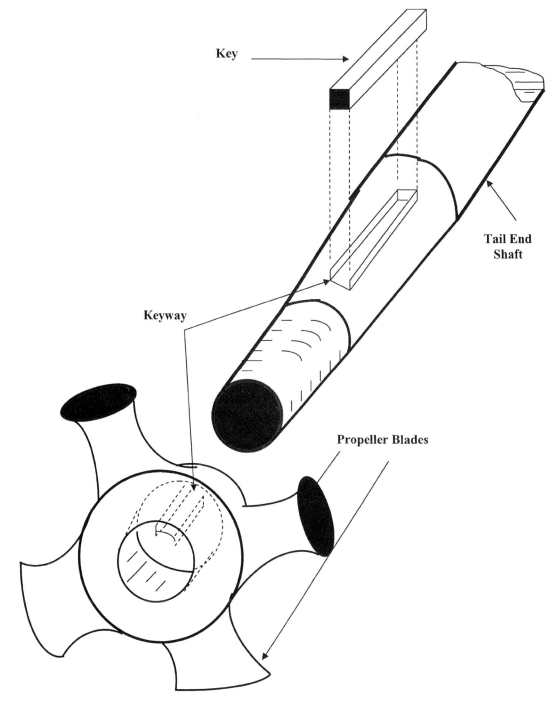

Key

Tail End
Shaft

Keyway

Propeller Blades

*Figure 2.40*

## Keyless (propeller) Connections

An alternative securing method is achieved by a "Pilgrim Nut". This uses hydraulic pressure to force the propeller onto the tail end shaft in such a hard manner that a key becomes unnecessary. The hardness of the fit, prevents the propeller slipping on the shaft.

## Propeller Removal

The removal of the propeller is not an unusual action and is a recognised practice when the ship is in dry dock. The weight of the propeller is taken up by chain purchases. The "hub" capping and the large nut are removed, together with any locking device.

The propeller is then eased backwards off the tail end shaft.

The operation may cause suspension lugs to be temporary welded to the ship's hull over and above the position of the propeller to allow the chain blocks and purchase lifting gear to be suspended and take the propeller weight as it slides aft of the shaft.

*Figure 2.41  A propeller is seen being removed inside a repair dry dock. Scaffolding is erected around and under the stern area. Purpose lugs are welded on to the underside of the hull above and aft of the propeller. These lugs are temporary fixtures and established to hang off chain blocks and lifting tackles to aid the propeller removal from the tail end shaft. This operation in some circumstances entails removing the rudder first, prior to removing the propeller.*

**Propeller Shaft Arrangement (contra-rotating propellers)**

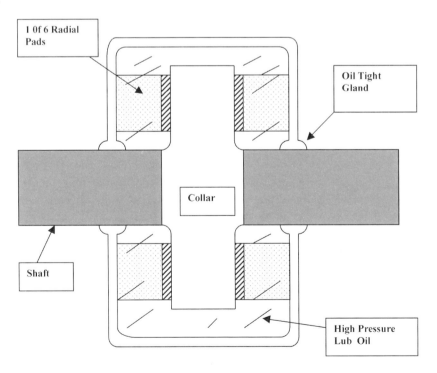

Seals

Outer propeller
Shaft

CR Gearing

Intermediate
Shaft

Thrust
Block

CR Seal

CR Thrust
Bearing

Radial Bearing

Steady
Bearing

CR Radial
Bearing

Inner Propeller
Shaft

Geislinger
Coupling

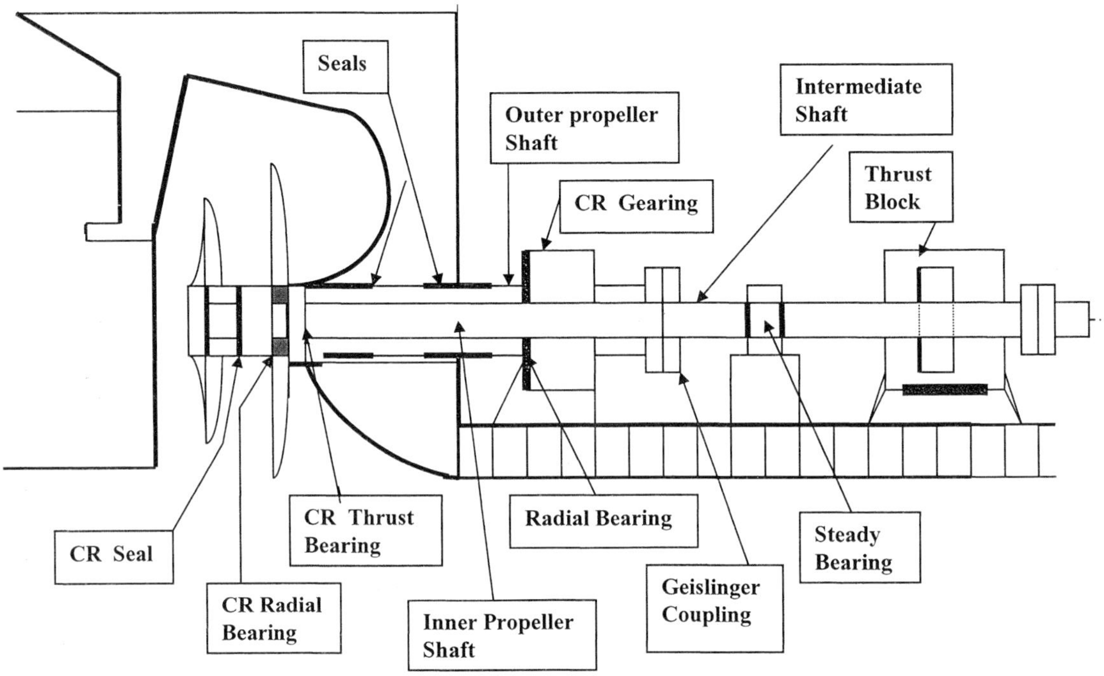

*Figure 2.42*

**Contra-rotating Propellers**

The title reflects two propellers arranged in tandem on coaxial shafts, rotating in opposing directions. Higher efficiency with this arrangement is anticipated.

**Thrust Block**

1 0f 6 Radial
Pads

Oil Tight
Gland

Collar

Shaft

High Pressure
Lub Oil

*Figure 2.43*

The thrust from the propeller is transmitted to the hull by a single collar mounted integral with the shaft. Situated either side of the collar are six (6) thrust pads (total 12 × 6 either side.) A thrust in excess of 40 tonnes is capable of being accepted by the thrust pads.

The thrust action and the rotational property of the collar causes the pads to tilt slightly so that the leading edge of the pad is clear of the collar surface. This allows lubricating oil to enter the leading edge of the pad and forms a high pressure oil wedge preventing any metallic contact between the collar and the pads.

Thrust developed is measured in thrust metres from which power available for driving the shaft is calculated.

**Shaft Line Support**

*Figure 2.44   Propeller shaft line, supported by "Plummer Block" positioned on steel support structure. The "U" cutaway in the support reduces overall weight and permits underside inspection of the bearing and the shaft.*

**Rotary Vane Steering – Stiffening Arrangement**

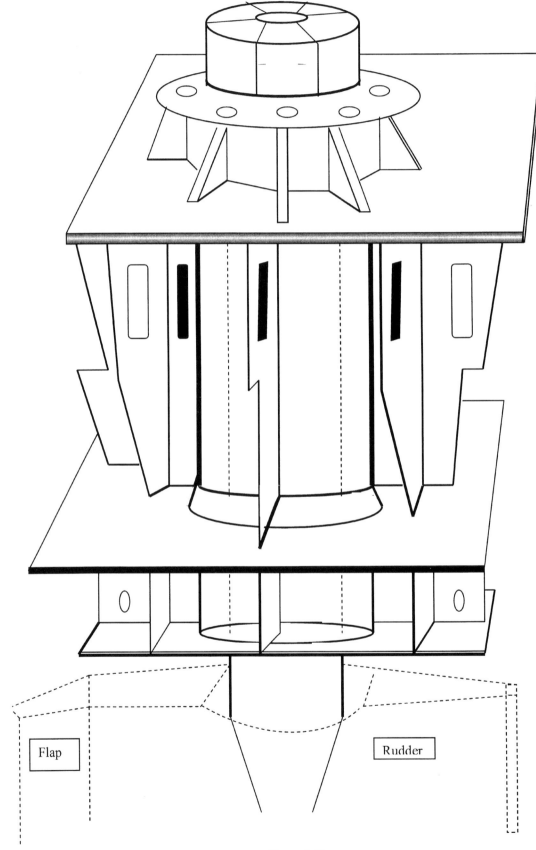

Flap

Rudder

*Figure 2.45*

## Rotary Vane Steering

Rotary Vane steering is a compact steering unit which is situated on top of the rudder stock. A rotor is "keyed" onto the stock and the whole is encased by a steel casing known as a "stator". The concept allows follow up and non follow-up modes to operate with either electric or hydraulic transmission systems.

Model variations allow rudder angles of $2 \times 35°$, or $2 \times 60°$ with options of upto $90°$. The system tends to act as a self-lubricating, rudder carrier as well as generating the turning movement to the rudder. This is achieved by oil being delivered, under pressure to one side of the blades of the rotor. With the rotor being "keyed" to the rudder stock, when the rotor is caused to turn so does the stock.

Clearly the direction of turn will be effected by the direction of the pressurised oil effecting the rotor blades. Therefore in theory the rotor and stock can turn only one way, namely in the direction of the pressurised oil. However, if the directional flow of the oil is reversed, by reversing the rotation of the oil pump, then the rotor will also be caused to turn in the opposite direction. This pump reversal from one direction to another provides the necessary directional oil flow to cause movement to port and starboard.

The oil under pressure is kept contained within the unit by the stator. The stator is dynamically sealed and is leak free, providing generally an effective, alternative steering mechanism within the created pressure chambers.

## Rotary Vane Steering Unit

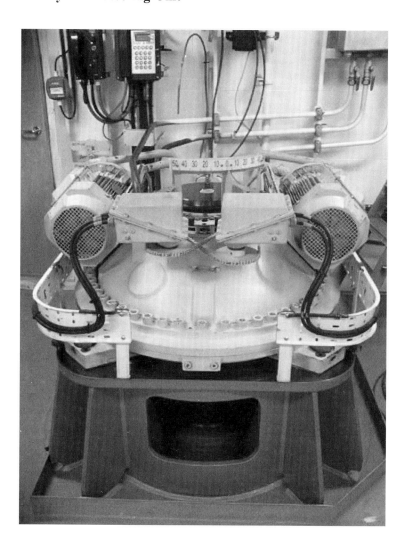

*Figure 2.46    An example of the stator case mounting for a rotaey vane steering gear, situated directly over the rudder stock.*

# CHAPTER THREE

# Ship's Bottom Structure

## Introduction

The building used to start with the laying of the keel. This longitudinal member is still one of the most critical components but with ships of excessive length, and vessels being constructed by prefabrication methods, the keel is no longer the first component always laid.

Many older ships, and certainly the wooden sailing ships had the keel laid first and the hull was then built up around the added timbers (frames) to form the hull. Modern ship building with the use of computers, has changed the order of events. Now sectional prefabricated elements are constructed with the view to assembly at a later stage and often in a different place. Multi corporations are now often involved in joint build ventures with one company constructing one section of a vessel while another is involved in the construction of a secondary section. Sometimes at separate sites.

The recent changes in legislation which requires all tankers to be of a double hull construction will clearly be influential on building methods and of course the costs of future construction. Neither will this stop at tankers as "Bulk Carriers" will also be expected to follow suit with similar double skin construction. These changes are seen as making the vessels more environmentally acceptable as well as reducing the risk of direct pollution following impact from collision or grounding.

Double bottom construction has been around since Brunel's third vessel, the "Great Eastern" (1858). Its benefits being experienced by many vessels which unfortunately have grounded at one time or another. The structure though basically based on the same principals incorporates both bracket and solid floors, with either athwartships or longitudinal framing options.

Engine room double bottom structures are specific to accommodate the increased loading from the weight of the machinery and these should be given particular attention, as specialised components. Other pertinent areas of concern in the ship's bottom structure is the type of keel fitted to the ship. Whether a plate keel, or a duct keel and if bilge keels are a feature.

The bottom area of the ship is generally only sighted during dry dock periods, yet it is clearly one of the most high risk, exposed areas of the ship's plating, during the ship's life. The underwater volume is continuously at risk from corrosion, impact or fouling, and every opportunity to inspect the bottom should be taken by ship's personnel.

**Bar Keels** are to have a cross sectional area "A" derived by the formula:—

$$A = (1.8L - 16)\,cm^2.$$

The thickness (t) derived by the formula:—

$$t = (0.6L + 8)\,mm.$$

**Plate Keels** – The breadth (b) of a plate keel is found from the formula 70B mm (where "B" = Breadth of Vessel) but need not exceed 1,800 mm and must be not less than 750 mm.

## Flat Plate Keel Construction

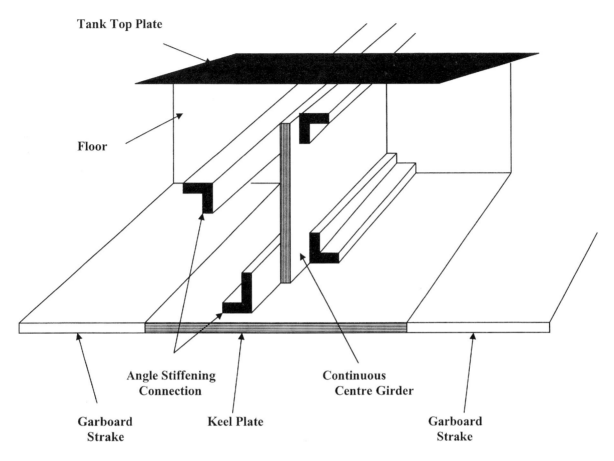

**Tank Top Plate**

**Floor**

**Angle Stiffening
Connection**

**Continuous
Centre Girder**

**Garboard
Strake**

**Keel Plate**

**Garboard
Strake**

*Figure 3.1    Plate Keel, welded connection in way of floor. Angle bar stiffening is an option to just welded joints and is not always used, especially in vessels which have longitudinal framing.*

The thickness (t) of a plate keel is found from the formula $t = (t_1 + 2)\,mm$, where $t_1$ is as the location in table 1.5.2 of the Rules and Regulations for the Classification of Ships. Using the spacing in way of the keel plate "t" is to be taken not less than the adjacent bottom shell thickness.

## Laying the Keel

The majority of the large shipyards have changed from the old style of laying the keel first and building upwards. Modular building with major advances in prefabrication have generally superseded this method of build. However, some of the smaller yards still continue to build from the keel up and it is still traditional to "lay the keel" for a new build. In this day and age it would be more realistic to recognise when steelwork is first cut, to provide indication that building has actually commenced.

*Figure 3.2   The "plate keel" of a large bulk carrier is laid and the bottom shell plate is seen constructed on the launchways. The double bottom construction is being added to the longitudinally framed vessel.*

**Duct Keel Arrangement.**

**In way of Double Bottom**

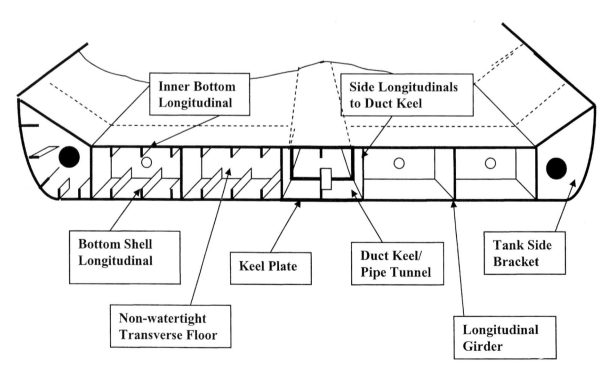

*Figure 3.3*

**Duct keels** are not common to all vessels but where they are fitted will extend from the forward end of the engine room bulkhead right forward to the collision bulkhead. They carry pipelines and cable leads lengthwise through the bottom of the ship's structure and the structure itself provides longitudinal strength.

Entrance into the duct keel is by watertight manholes, usually from the engine room and the duct is large enough to act as a passage way to allow personnel to move right forward. Maximum width of a duct keel structure being so that the sides are not spaced more than 2.0 metres apart. The tank top and keel plate members must be strengthened by stiffening to provide continuity of strength. Stiffening in the transverse direction must be suitably aligned with the floors.

**NB.** Where the duct keel is adjacent to double bottom tanks which are interconnected with side tanks or cofferdams the stiffening must be in accord with the requirements for "Deep Tanks" (Ref. 9.2.1 of the Rules and Regulations for the Classification of Ships).

## Double Bottom Arrangements

### Plate Floor

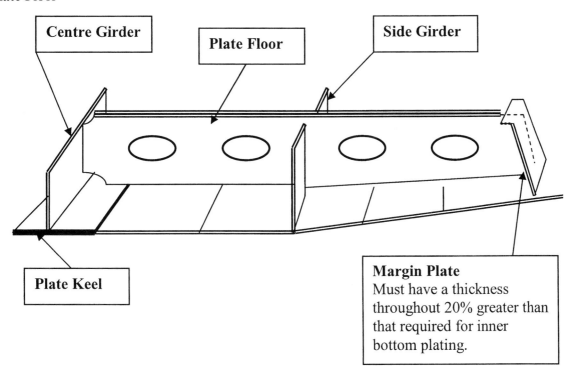

**Centre Girder**

**Plate Floor**

**Side Girder**

**Plate Keel**

**Margin Plate**
Must have a thickness throughout 20% greater than that required for inner bottom plating.

*Figure 3.4*

**Plate Floors** – in longitudinally framed ships are to be fitted under bulkheads and elsewhere at a spacing not exceeding 3.8 m.

In transversely framed vessels. Plate floors must be fitted under bulkheads and elsewhere at a spacing not exceeding 3.0 m.

**NB.** Adequate access must be provided to all parts of a double bottom structure. The size of openings for manholes should in general not exceed 50% of the double bottom depth, unless edge support reinforcing is provided.

### Double Bottom Arrangements

Cellular Double Bottoms (CDB's) are now constructed in the majority of ships because of the new double hull legislation. They provide a series of shallow tanks where the tank tops form the upper boundary and the inner part of the shell plate forms the tank bottom. The tanks themselves are divided into cells by athwartship's floors and fore and aft girders which also add extensive stiffening to the lower construction.

Double Bottoms have distinct advantages in that ballasting can take place simply and quickly by the filling or emptying of the tanks. Added security to the ship is also achieved, should the tank be damaged or holed, sea water is prevented from entering the body of the vessel. Where the construction is such that the centre girder acts as a watertight divide, any list on the vessel can be easily corrected. In addition further storage is gained for the carriage of fresh water or oil fuel supplies.

**Margin plates** – Form the tank sides and run in a fore and aft direction for the length of the double bottom tanking system. These margin plates are normally fitted perpendicular to the bilge strake and are flanged to provide a connection for the tank top plating. Margin plates are watertight and are not pieced by frames or other structural members.

**Tank Tops** – Cover the double bottom structure and run in a fore and aft direction. Watertight bulkheads divide compartments and these are stopped at its upper surface. then continued to extend in the form of a watertight floor inside the tank system. Tank top plate forms a common connection between all the transverse floors within the tanks. Increased scantlings are used in way of engine room and boiler room double bottom systems.

**Floors** – These are vertical transverse plates which connect the bottom plating to the underside of the tank tops. Watertight floors are found at the tank ends and in way of compartment bulkheads so fixed as to extend the bulkhead down to the bottom plating. Intermediate floors have lightening holes and drain holes cut into them and this acts to allow liquid free flow and reduces overall ship's weight. An alternative to a solid plate floor, is a bracket floor, which is a transverse bracket fitment between the centre girder and tank side margin plate.

**Bracket Floor**

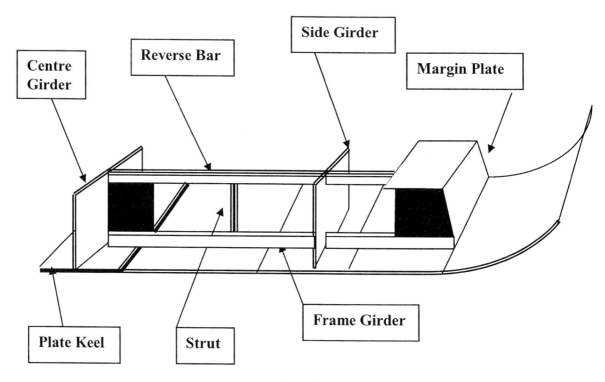

*Figure 3.5*

Bracket Floors, where fitted must not have an unsupported span exceeding 2.5 m. The breadth of the brackets attaching the frames and the reverse frames to the centre girder and margin plate must be three-quarters of the depth of the centre girder.

The brackets are to have the same thickness as the plate floors.

## Double Bottom in way of the Turn of the Bilge

### Flush Inner Bottom

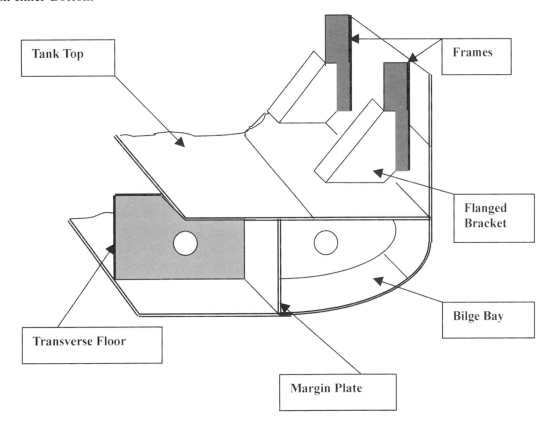

Tank Top

Frames

Flanged Bracket

Transverse Floor

Bilge Bay

Margin Plate

*Figure 3.6*

Most modern tonnage is now being constructed with flush inner bottoms. This type, as opposed to the conventional double bottom structure at the turn of the bilge, lends to easier cargo handling and stowage. Flush deck finish also favours the use of fork lift trucks and the stowage of palletized cargoes, package timber and such.

The bilge bays run fore and aft each side of the hold, with the bilge suctions positioned in the aft most bay. As vessels normally trim by the stern the suctions are positioned aft to gain the best advantage from incline to provide effective drainage.

**Double Bottom – Conventional Vessel (Break Bulk, General Cargo)**

*Figure 3.7*

Conventional turn of the bilge construction is favoured by cargo vessels with break bulk capability. They tend to have a strong tank side bracket joint which is not much favoured to fork lift trucks, pallets or packaged timber cargoes. The turn of the bilge causing considerable broken stowage and prevents large case or bale goods being stowed tightly.

**Double Bottom and Hopper Tank Arrangement**

*Figure 3.8   The double bottom arrangement of a large "Bulk Carrier" seen under construction following the keel being laid. The side hopper tanks are under construction down the length of the double bottom section. One of the holds transverse bulkheads is seen in the vertical in a background position.*

**Engine Room Bottom Plate Construction**

*Figure 3.9    The bottom plate arrangement of a twin screw new build vessel. Twin engine bed mountings and sump wells are identified either side of the fore and aft line, as viewed from an aft position. The assembly has been manufactured in sections, blasted and is being systematically coated. It will be lifted into a final assembly position with the bow and midship's sections respectively, in a conveyor belt style of build on the building slip.*

**Engine Room Double Bottom Floors**

**Aft Floor**

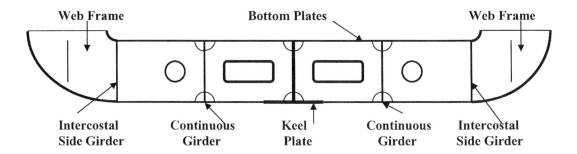

**Engine Room Floor – In way of Sump and Twin Engine Seating**

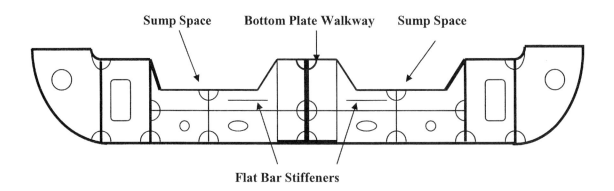

**Forward End of Engine Room Double Bottom**

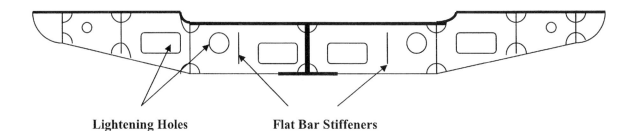

*Figure 3.10*

**Engine Seatings**

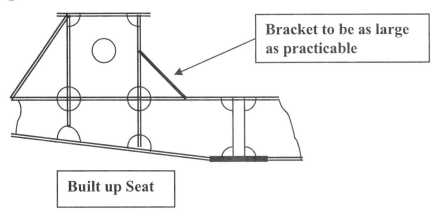

**Bracket to be as large as practicable**

**Built up Seat**

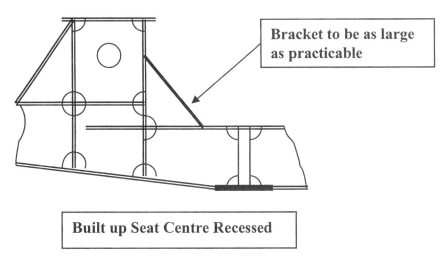

**Bracket to be as large as practicable**

**Built up Seat Centre Recessed**

*Figure 3.11*

Engine seatings are to be designed, so that they distribute the forces from the engine as uniformly as possible into the supporting structure. Longitudinal members supporting the seating should be arranged to line in with double bottom girders and transverse stiffening should be arranged to line up with floors.

Main engines and thrust bearings are to be adequately secured to the hull structure by seatings of adequate scantlings to resist various gravitational, thrust, torque, dynamic and vibratory forces which may effect them.

*Figure 3.12    (above) Undercover module construction, ongoing in way of No 3. Double Bottom of a vessel. Note that the construction takes place in the reverse position with the keel and outer shell plating being fitted last.*

*(below) A floor under construction in way of No 4. Double Bottom Tank. Modules once completed are assembled on the building slip.*

## Tanker Double Bottom Structure

New legislation now requires that all new tanker vessels are constructed with a double bottom structure. The experience of building double bottoms has been around since the building of Brunel's Great Eastern in 1858. The fact that the ship's have become larger the corresponding size of the double bottom tanks has been forced to increase accordingly.

*Figure 3.13  Tankers "Double Bottom" (section) of a longitudinally framed vessel seen on a mobile platform ready for transport to the assembly line of a new build. The full size of this cross section module can be appreciated by the view shown in Fig. 7.8 (Tanker chapter) page 204.*

## Passenger Vessel – Bottom Tank Disposition

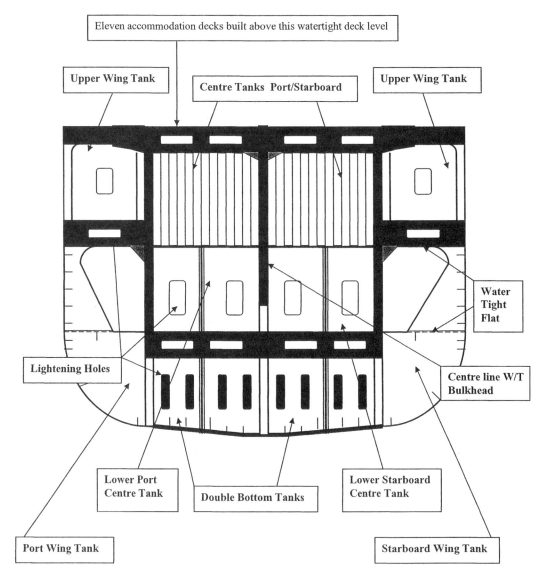

Eleven accommodation decks built above this watertight deck level

Upper Wing Tank

Centre Tanks  Port/Starboard

Upper Wing Tank

Water Tight Flat

Lightening Holes

Centre line W/T Bulkhead

Lower Port Centre Tank

Double Bottom Tanks

Lower Starboard Centre Tank

Port Wing Tank

Starboard Wing Tank

*Figure 3.14*

The tank disposition is designated for fresh water and water ballast. Additional tanks fore and aft would also be designated ballast trimming tanks. The double bottom tanks are retained for fuel oil. Earlier designs sometimes incorporated forward deep tanks.

**Transom Stern and Parallel Body**

*Figure 3.15   The transom stern and ten deck levels seen above the lowest mooring deck level of the passenger vessel "MSC Sinfonia". The lines of the ship's "Parallel Body" about the amidship's position are clearly defined as seen down the Port Side. The disposition of the ship's tanks would be located below the mooring deck level and below the water line.*

**Bilge and Ballast Piping Arrangement**

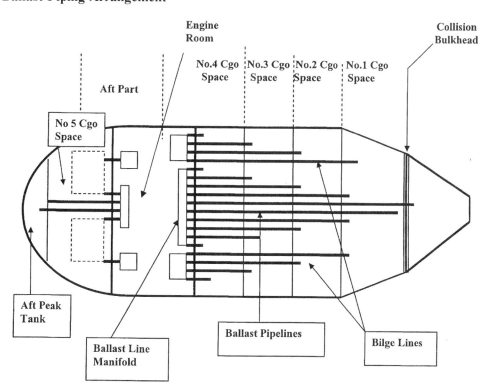

*Figure 3.16   The ship's Engine Room would contain Bilge and Ballast pumps and be Connected to a manifold and valve chest arrangement. Only one line is allowed by regulations to pierce the "Collision Bulkhead" giving rise to the reason why the chain locker is usually emptied by a hand pump or an eductor.*

The construction regulations require that all cargo vessels must be able to pump out, any watertight compartment when the vessel has an adverse list of upto 5°. Statutory requirements require that piping arrangements must be capable of draining the bilges, ballasting the vessel, providing general service facilities and in the case of tankers provide for liquid cargoes (load & discharge). Additionally tankers must also provide tank washing and inert gas piping arrangements.

Passenger vessels must also comply in their ability to pump out any watertight compartment or watertight section following damage, notwithstanding practical considerations.

## Pumping and Bilge Suctions

The bilge piping arrangement must include two bilge suction pumps in the machinery space of the vessel.

They must have the capability of operation when the vessel carries an adverse list and one of the pumps must be via the main bilge line while the other must be powered from an independent power driven pump.

The machinery space must also be fitted with one emergency bilge suction capable of being connected to:—

(a) the main circulating water pump, for the condenser in steam ships.

Or

(b) the main cooling water pump in motor ships.

## Bilge Suction Arrangements

Bilge suctions are positioned at the aft end of cargo spaces and are pipeline connected via the valve chest to the pumps in the machinery space. The aft position of the bilge suctions assists the drainage of bilge water because most ships trim by the stern and this allows the accumulation of water in aft bilge bays, where the suctions are placed.

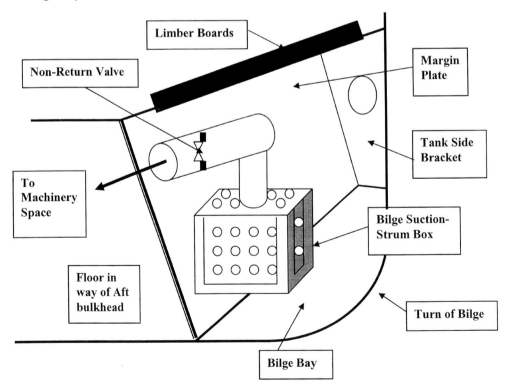

*Figure 3.17*

**Engine Room Deployment – Bilge Pumping Systems**

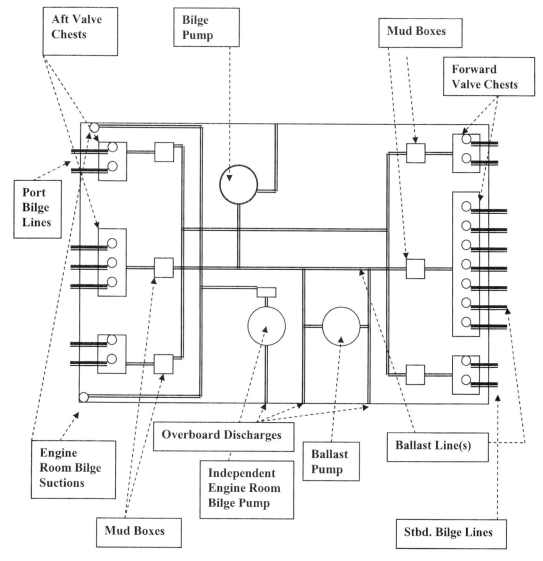

*Figure 3.18   Cargo Vessel Engine Room Bilge Pumping Arrangement.*

In the case of Passenger vessels the power driven bilge pumps should be in separate watertight compartments so that all three would not be compromised in the event of flooding damage from the same action.

Passenger ships which are longer than 91.5 metres must have one of the pumps serviceable at all times and have the pumps distributed so that in the event of an incident that not all the pumps would be out of action at the same time, considering reasonable damage.

**Stabilisation Systems**

**Anti-Roll Stabiliser Units/Bilge keels and appendages**

The main features of the folding active fins, apart from the fin unit itself, is the electric control system and the hydraulic pumping arrangement which causes the fin to be housed and deployed to the needs of the ship. The design is usually with low maintenance cost in mind and the supporting shaft of the fin is not exposed to sea water. They may or may not, be fitted with articulated flaps, depending on the type of stabilisers fitted and the size and type of vessel they are employed with.

Non-folding type, fin stabilisers are usually mounted on shafts fitted with pre-stressed roller bearings. They will also be fitted with electronic control systems and will usually incorporate a zero angle locking fitment. Clearly the position of such units must be displayed on the dry dock plan and the appendages brought to the attention of the dry dock manager prior to vessels entering into a dock. Block settings must be such to accommodate the fin units and where non folding units are known to be a feature diver inspection would confirm clearances from the docking blocks.

Similar clearances are noted for bilge keels and fixed, non active fin units fitted to some vessels. Some of the new ferry designs now operate with hydrofoil type fin appendages and these may be of a fixed or retractable design. The docking process, must take account of all such external hull features when the vessel takes the blocks, in order to avoid incurring expensive damage claims. To this end divers are being employed more and more by dock authorities.

**Fixed Stabiliser Fins**

*Figure 3.19    Non-Retractable stabiliser fins seen exposed in dry dock, at approximately one third of the ship's length (from aft).*

## Control of Active Fin Stabilisers

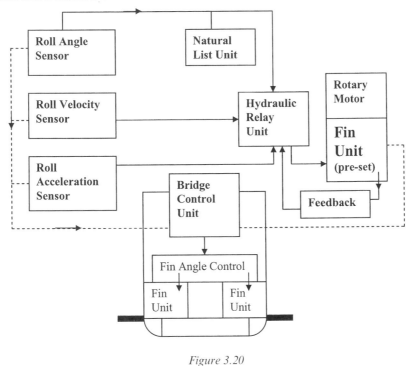

*Figure 3.20*

Roll sensors for the angle, velocity and acceleration are effected by the use of gyroscopes to obtain measured values for comparison.

## Fin Stabilisers

*Figure 3.21  Port side stabiliser fin seen in situ, exposed in dry dock from the hull of the "Wind Surf". The ship's hull received surface preparations while in Lisnave, Hydro-Lift dry dock. Coatings applied to the below waterline surfaces including the bilge keels and stabiliser fins.*

**Stabilising Folding Fin Unit**

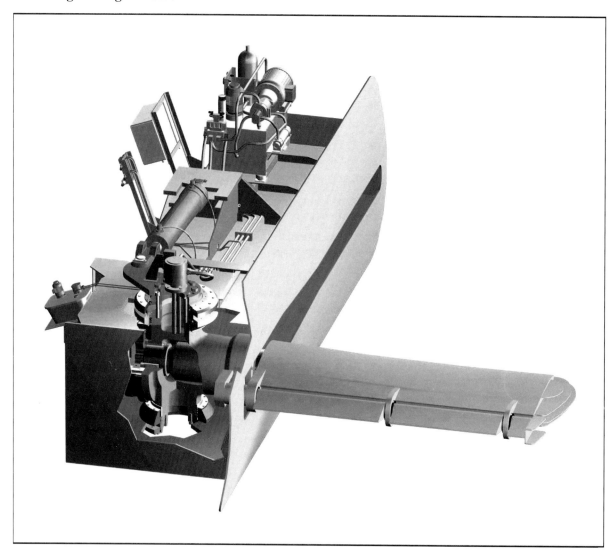

*Figure 3.22*

**Bilge Keels**

Bilge keels tend to vary with the overall length of the vessel. The shorter the vessel the more chance of the keel being a single continuous bulb angle section, welded to the external hull, in a position just above the turn of the bilge area. Where as in the longer larger vessel the bilge keel is often positioned in two or three sections.

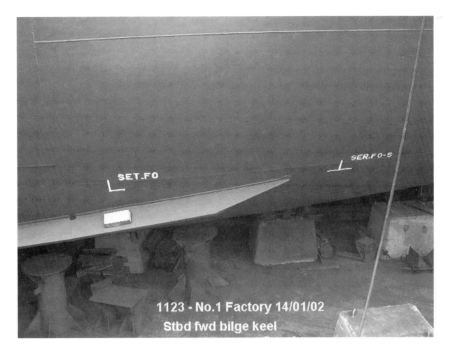

*Figure 3.23  The end of a bilge keel section seen welded to the outer hull in the region of the turn of the bilge.*

## Bilge Keels

The regulations recommend that vessels intending to navigate in severe ice conditions are not fitted with bilge keels in the forward 0.3L. When constructed they should be connected to a continuous ground bar where the minimum thickness of the ground bar is to be equal to the thickness of the bilge strake or 14 mm whichever is the lesser. The ground bar is connected to the shell by a continuous fillet weld and the bilge keel is then welded to the ground bar.

The ends of bilge keels are to be tapered or rounded. The taper of the ends being to a gradual ratio of at least three to one (3:1). The end of the actual bilge keel web is to be between 50 mm and 100 mm from the end of the ground bar. In vessels over 65 m in length holes are to be drilled in the bilge keel butt welds.

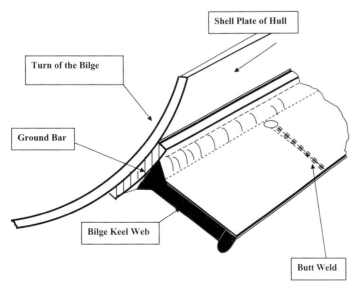

*Figure 3.24*

# CHAPTER FOUR

# Deck and Hatch Constructions

## Introduction

The main deck is without doubt one of the most if not the most important steel member of the vessel. It is the uppermost continuous deck. That deck which provides for the water tight integrity of the ship and also that one which contains the largest openings, by way of cargo hatchways.

Access points into accommodation and down below to cargo holds are all generally established on the main deck. These openings as such need also to have watertight seals, similar to the bow and stern ramps of Ro-Ro vessels. The main deck as the working deck is the foundation for Mast houses, pump rooms, ventilation opening, crane housings, mast and derrick support structures, as well as being that base to generally accept the lower edge of the bridge front.

Associated decks like the boat deck or the "poop deck" and the bridge deck are all functional serving decks with variations on construction suitable to the respective tasks. However, for area, these must be considered as secondary to the welded deck stringers that form the ship's main deck. They are required to be hard wearing and must be well maintained to retain the desire value of water tight integrity.

Depending on the type of ship, will reflect the type and style of deck fittings from cleats and ring bolts, to the type of hatch coamings and covers. In the case of tankers, the size and securing of pipelines, tank lids and manifolds. Such specialised vessels will have cofferdams strategically placed while the container vessel will cater to the cell guides for its box cargoes.

Deck areas have by their very being, taken the beatings of the weather, through out maritime history. It is therefore becoming that considerable attention is given to the construction and detail of this essential element and its fittings.

## Decks

A ship's deck is considered as that horizontal platform which causes an enclosure of the hull form. They are positioned at different levels throughout the vessel and are usually described by the function that they perform, i.e. the uppermost continuous deck, being that deck level that is the highest which is fitted from stem to stern. The same deck may also be termed the "weather deck" because of its overall exposure to the weather, if it is one and the same. Another term employed is known as the "bulkhead deck", being that deck level that the athwartship's bulkheads extend too, very often being the same weather deck.

A further example being the "boat deck" where the ship's lifeboats are stowed. Multi decked ships are those vessels being constructed with several decks above the keel and upwards to the height of the upper bridge deck, e.g. Passenger Ships. Not all decks are continuous over the ship's length and many are stayed at the bridge front position, or some other interval.

In virtually every case they are stiffened from the underside and carry effective drainage by way of scupper arrangements to allow water to be shed. Many passenger vessels tend to operate with wood sheathed decks, but the majority of deck constructions are of a steel base with a paint or composition coating.

Conventional cargo vessels were built with tween-decks an intermediate deck level between the tank tops of the cellular double bottom and the uppermost continuous weather deck. Ships having a deep tank design being operated with an upper and lower tween decks arrangement.

Historically, the old sailing ships were built with wood planks, edge butted together, over supporting beams. With the advent of steel ships, deck plates, or deck stringers as they have become known, form the working deck platforms. They are strong and support superstructures like accommodation blocks and hatch openings. Where weight bearing elements are established, increased scantlings are the order of the day and or doubling plates to provide additional strength.

Current building tends to employ, two dimensional and three dimensional blocks to develop prefabricated units. Deck and shell sections are an example of two dimensional building sections, where as tank systems are generally considered as three dimensional units.

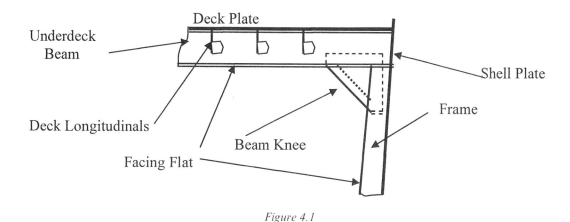

*Figure 4.1*

## Main Deck Construction

Most ship types have main weather decks constructed in steel and fitted with underdeck "H" support girders and half girders where appropriate. Stringer plates may have a painted or a composition surface. In either case each coating is designed to prevent corrosion while at the same time provide a suitable working surface for crew and/or passengers.

Specialised vessels like container vessels, often operating in the dual mode of Load On, Load Off (Lo-Lo) with a Roll On, Roll Off (Ro, Ro) facility beneath the upper deck, may have additional container securing fittings.

*Figure 4.2    The upper Container Deck, of the "Baltic Eider" seen with container location base plates for use with container stacking cone fitments.*

## Main Deck – Hatch way Connection

General cargo ships and bulk carrier type vessels are usually built with large hatch way openings to permit cargo handling access and discharge. These wide open spaces, are clearly seen as potential weak areas in the ship's continuity of strength. The steel hatch covers, when in place, provide some athwartship's rigidity. However, the fact remains that deck coverage with a large hatch access cutaway, weakens the overall deck strength. The continuous run of beam support girders is interrupted and very often is reduced to half or quarter length alternatives in way of the hatch.

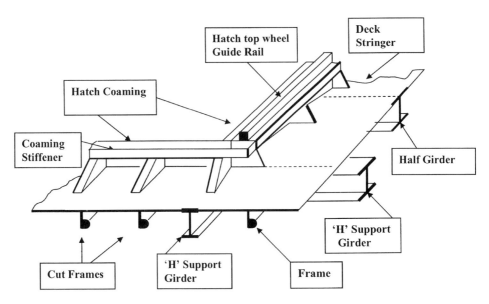

*Figure 4.3*

## Open Hatchways

*Figure 4.4   Open hatchway, seen with pontoon hatch covers stacked in the amidship's position. The stacked hatch covers are achieved by use of a miniature mobile travelling gantry which manoeuvres along the track ways, up and down the length of the hatch. (Mobile gantry not shown.)*

## Hatchway Construction

With any opening in way of steel work the result will be an overall weakening of the structure. In the case of hatchways, which are probably the largest of openings in the upper deck structure, it is essential that continuity of strength is retained through out the ship's length.

This is achieved by curved cutaways at the hatch corners so reducing the possibility of shearing cracks being generated as with a right angled cut. These are then supported by doubling plates to each corner to provide added strength in way of the more vulnerable corner areas.

Clearly access by way of the hatchway is a fundamental requirement while at the same time it is necessary to reinforce the surrounding deck area. This is achieved by employing the basic principle of athwartships, half beams positioned underdeck between the hatch coaming line and the ship's side. While longitudinal strengthening is achieved by the positioning of underdeck longitudinals to pass either side of the hatchway. Shortened longitudinals being situated at the hatch ends, complete the surrounding underdeck strengthening.

Where a tween deck or single hold vessel is considered, any intermediate decking would be additionally supported by corner pillars from the tank tops in the lower hold to the underside of the tween deck. Pillars would generally be secured by flanged gusset plates to the undersides of the deck plate.

The outer hull, in way of the hatch, is strengthened by athwartship's framing or longitudinal framing on a ship so structured. Where athwartship's framing is used the half beams are positioned at every fourth frame position. Bulkheads at the hatch ends can be either flush or of the corrugated type. Greater strength is found in the corrugated bulkheads and these are favoured by bulk carriers.

Strength members in the vicinity of the hatchway surround are usually of an "H" cross section, or a channel "U" (sideways) cross section. Scantlings being appropriate to satisfy the Survey Authority. Deck stringers cover the whole support structure and establish the upper deck plating area as we know it. Deck plating. by way of stringers are seam welded through the ship's length. Stealer Plates being employed at the fore and aft ends where the fine lines of the ship tend to join (see page 122).

**Hatchway Strengthening (Plan View)**

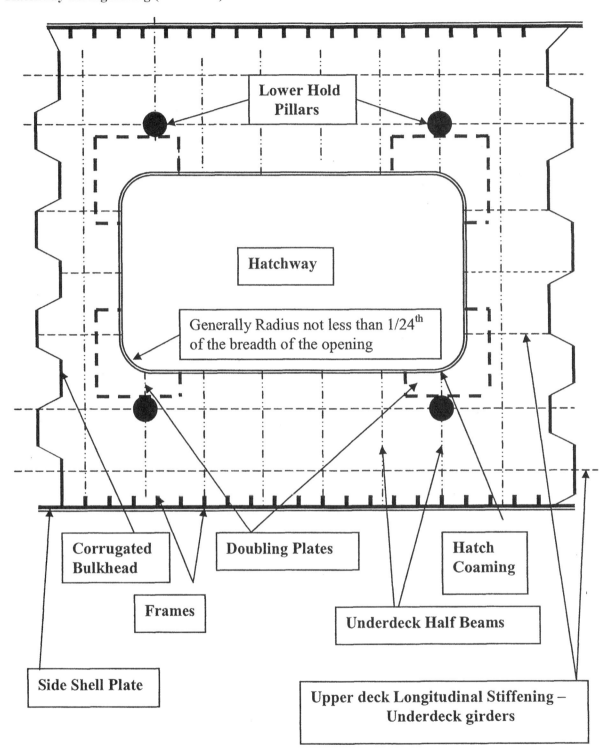

*Figure 4.5*

**Hatch Corner Construction (Upper Deck Level)**

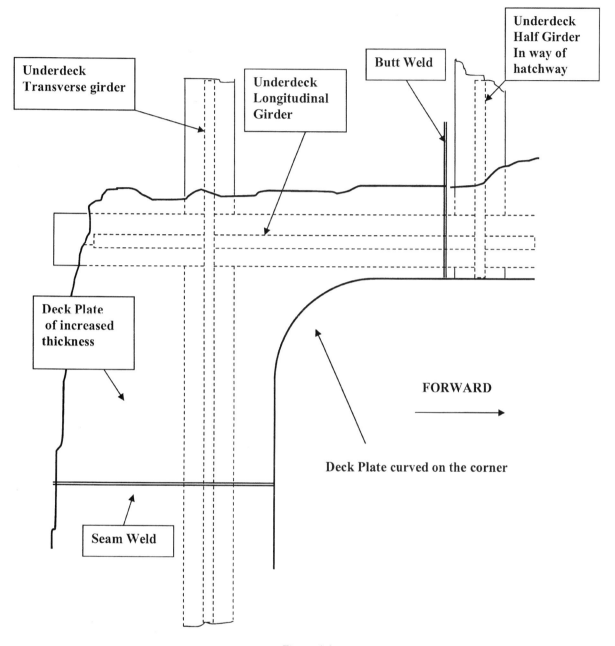

*Figure 4.6*

Deck plates, in way of hatch way corners, are virtually always cut away on the round. This tends to act in a preventive manner to sheer forces and provides some resistance to damage from cracking in the athwartships and longitudinal directions.

   (The principle employed is similar to stopping a developed crack from extending by drilling at the base of the crack.)

**Hatch Coaming Structure**

**For Rolltite hatch covers**

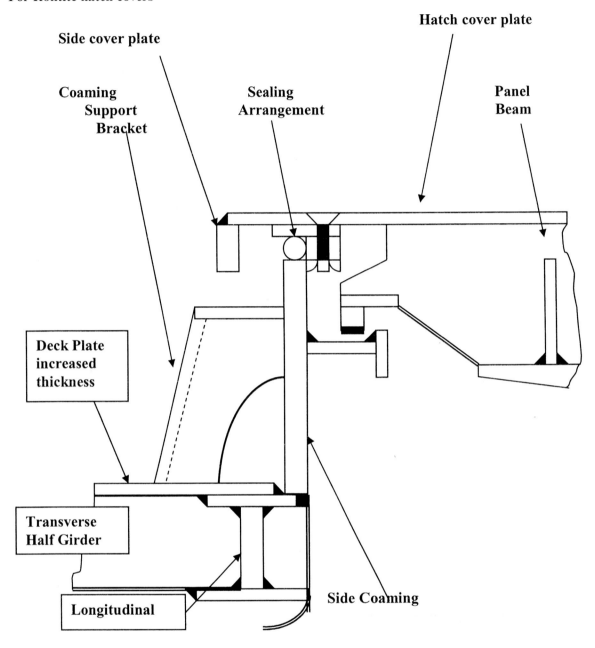

*Figure 4.7    Transverse part section through hatch side coaming in way of sealing arrangement.*

**Hatchway Covers**

These were previously constructed in wood slab form as hatch boards, then covered by secured tarpaulins. Security was then established by the use of locking bars to ensure the openings remained closed against the weather and pilferage. Modern construction has long been employing steel hatch covers of various types, providing a faster closure and opening procedure with improved ship's strength and better security.

The mode of operation is usually mechanical or electro-hydraulic to open and close the hatch sections. Alternative pontoon hatches popular with container vessels are positioned by a lift on, lift off process and can be easily stacked in stowage, when working cargo holds. The hatch tops must all be watertight and this fact is continually monitored by surveyors when conducting loadline surveys. Sealing is usually achieved by hard rubber packing being compressed by the sheer weight of hatch sections (upto approximately, 40 tonnes) combined with either hydraulic pressure or mechanical cleating or a combination of these.

**MacGregor – Single Pull Type**

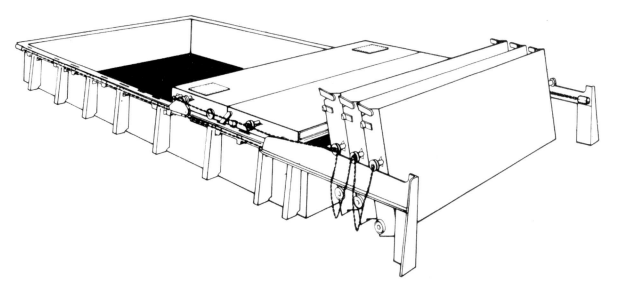

*Figure 4.8*

**Pontoon Type**

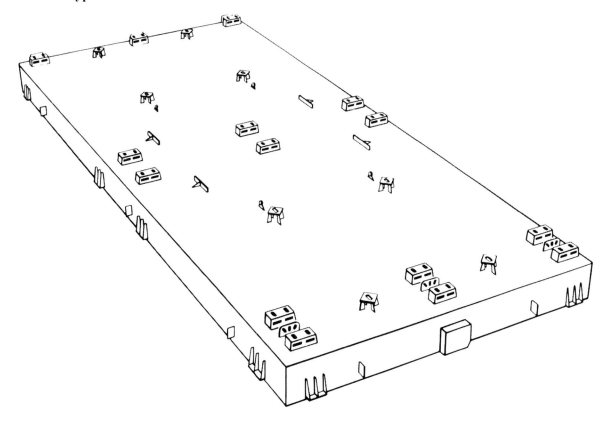

*Figure 4.9*

**Direct Pull (MacGregor) Weatherdeck Hatch Cover Arrangement**

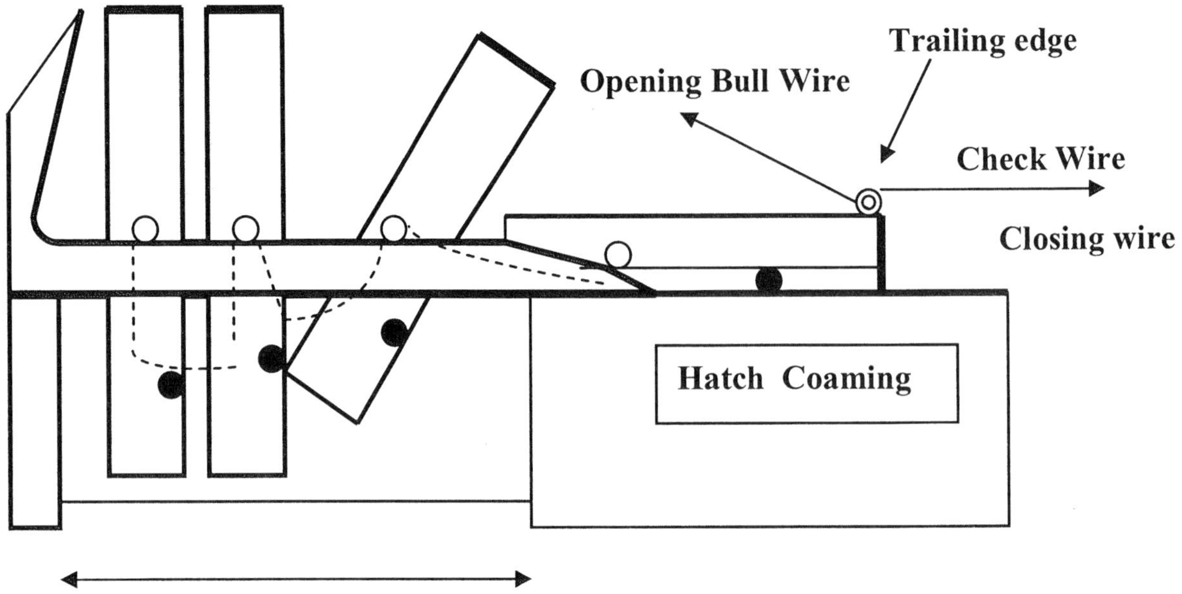

*Figure 4.10*

**Stowage Bay for Hatch Top Sections**

- ● Eccentric wheels lowered to track by manual levers or hydraulics.
- ○ Stowage Bay wheels with interconnecting chain.

Raising and lowering of the eccentric wheels by use of portable hand operated jacks or hand levers.

**Operation**

All hatch top wedges and side locking cleats must be removed and the tracks should be seen to be clear. The Bull wire and check wire would be shackled to the securing lug of the trailing edge of the hatch top.

**NB.** The bull wire and check wire change function depending on whether opening or closing the hatch cover.

The eccentric wheels are turned down and the "stowage bay" is sighted to be clear.

The locking pins at the end of the hatch would be removed as the weight is taken on the Bull Wire prior to opening the hatch.

Once the hatch lids are open and stowed vertical into the stowage bay, the sections would be locked into the vertical position by Lock bars or clamps, to prevent accidental roll back.

## Steel Hatch Covers

*Figure 4.11 Two small coastal dry cargo vessels lie port side to the berth. The vessel in the back ground is seen with the hydraulic "M" type covers in the closed up position, while the vessel with mini-gantry operated stackable pontoon covers is seen in the foreground with the amidship's section of hatches in the open position.*

## Hatch Coaming

*Figure 4.12 Hatch Coaming structure designed to support rolling steel hatch covers. Also configured to accommodate maximum deck container capacity with container reception pedestals welded into the coaming at appropriate lengths. Additionally, a 35 tonne SWL, hydraulic crane, is shown elevated on the port side between hatch tops.*

Hatch coamings have experienced many changes over the years, mainly because of the dominance of varied steel hatch cover types. Coaming support brackets have seen increased scantlings, in order to support the heavier weight of the steel covers. Also different designs, like side opening covers as opposed to fore and aft opening methods required accommodating tracks and pedestals to be incorporated into the overall designs.

### Steel Hatch Cover Construction Requirements

Hatch coamings must be substantially built and have a bearing surface for the hatch cover of not less than 65 mm. They must be constructed in mild steel or equivalent material providing the required stiffness and strength of mild steel. They must provide a weathertight seal when secured. Securing being made by use of gaskets and clamping devices. Such devices being spaced not more than 600 mm apart and be not more than 150 mm from the hatch corners.

The coaming shall be at a height above the deck of 600 mm (Position 1) or 450 mm (Position 2). The coaming size may be reduced if the safety of the ship is not impaired in the worst sea or weather conditions likely to be encountered by the ship when in service.

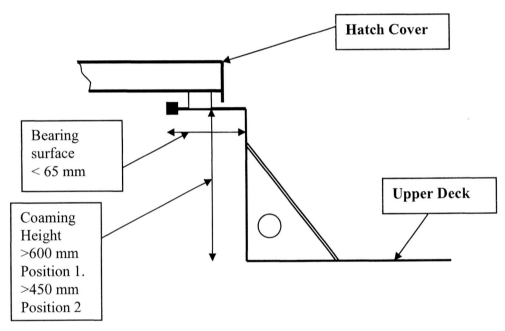

*Figure 4.13*

Mild steel forming the plating of the top of the cover shall be of a thickness not less than 1% of the spacing of the stiffeners or 6 mm whichever is the greater.

**Pontoon Hatch Covers** – Must be designed to limit the deflection and be of equivalent strength and stiffness as covers constructed in mild steel.

### Hatch Coaming

Hydraulic folding, hatch opening, showing the lead section lifting the trailing panel. The weight of the coaming structure supports the weight of the hatch tops and provides guidance to track rollers. Typical hatch top panels weigh upto about 5 tonnes each. Coaming supports shown cut-away to allow the through passage of pipelines passing fore and aft along the outer length of the hatch coaming length.

Hatch top cleating arrangements may be manual or automatic cleat securing methods.

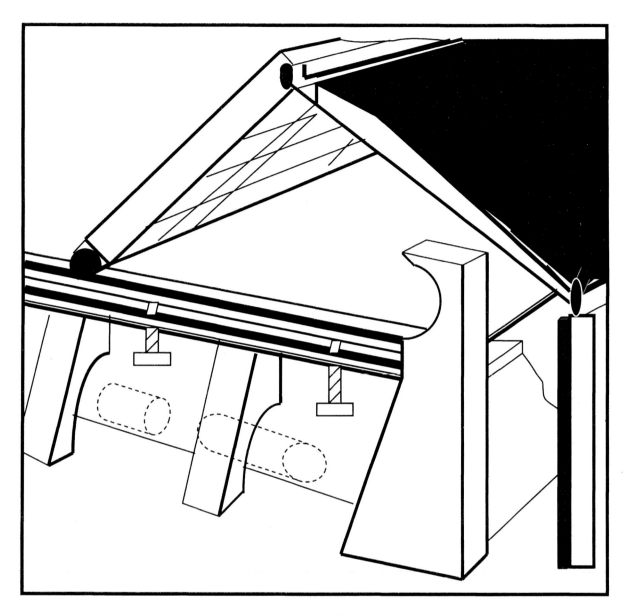

*Figure 4.14*

## Hatch Top Loading

Hatch top construction must be of sufficient strength to withstand an assumed load as per the table below:—

| Ship's Length (L) | Assumed Load per square metre | |
|---|---|---|
| | Hatchway in Position 1 | Hatchway in Position 2 |
| 24 metres | 1 tonne | 0.75 tonnes |
| 100 metres or over | 1.75 tonnes | 1.30 tonnes |
| Over 24 metres but less than 100 metres | To be ascertained by linear interpolation | |
| | | |

The design of the cover must be such, as to limit the deflection to not more than 0.0028 times the span under the assumed load, as specified in the above table, to the respective hatch cover.

Where hatch covers are constructed in other than mild steel the strength and stiffness of the cover must be equivalent of a mild steel cover.

## Pontoon Hatch Covers

*Figure 4.15   Pontoon hatch top covers being lifted and stacked to one end or the other of the hatchway by a mini track mounted, gantry crane. Slab pontoon covers are also a feature of some container vessels, where the pontoons are removed by the shoreside container gantry cranes of the container terminal.*

## Tween Deck Flush fitting Folding Hatch Covers

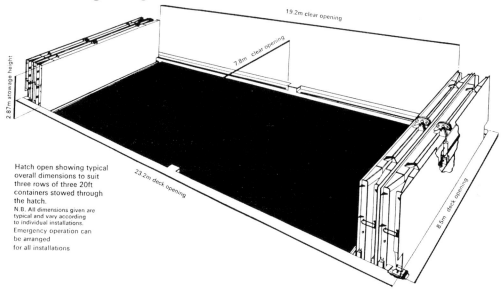

*Figure 4.16*

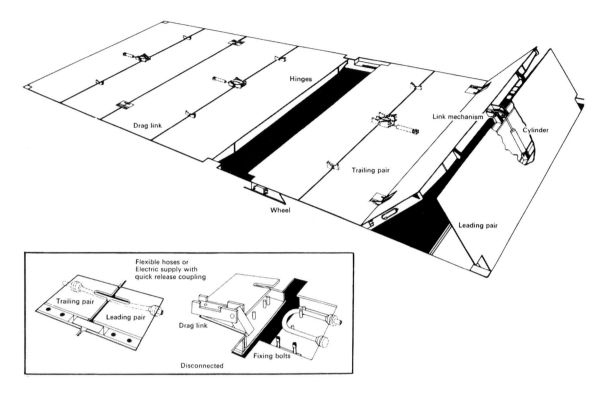

*Figure 4.17*

## Hatchways

*Figure 4.18    A typical upper deck hatchway built to accommodate steel hatch covers is seen with the roller wheel trackways positioned either side to carry single pull chain. McGregor hatches. The hatch is seen with flush end bulkheads and athwartship's framed sides.*

**Weather Deck Openings**

Closing arrangements for deck openings and not maintaining the same, is an infringement of the Loadline Rules. Deck openings will be identified as being in either Positions 1 or 2, which will effect those vulnerable areas of the vessel:

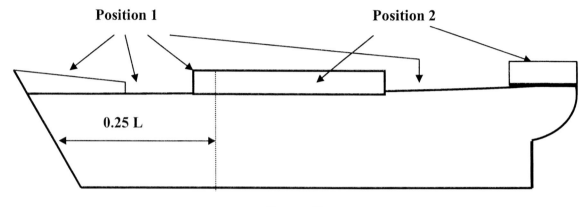

*Figure 4.19*

**Position "1"** – Is defined by being on the superstructure deck in the forward quarter length of the vessel and/or on the weather deck.

**Position "2"** – Is defined by being on the superstructure decks of the vessel abaft of the forward quarter length.

End bulkheads in superstructures on or at the weather deck level are considered extremely vulnerable to excessive volumes of sea water. They must therefore be of strong construction with efficient means of closing from both the inside and the outside directions.

**Deep Tank Structure and Use**

Many vessels are fitted with "Deep Tanks" employed as ballast tanks or for the carriage of specialised liquid cargoes such as:—

Vegetable Oils, i.e. Coconut oil, Bean Oil, Cotton Seed Oil, Linseed Oil, Palm Oil or Mineral Oils. Other cargoes include "Tallow" or bulk commodities like grain. Molasses, or Latex. The specialisation of such cargoes often require rigid temperature control of the cargo and to this end most cargo deep tanks are fitted with "Heating coils" which may or may not be blanked off as the circumstances dictate.

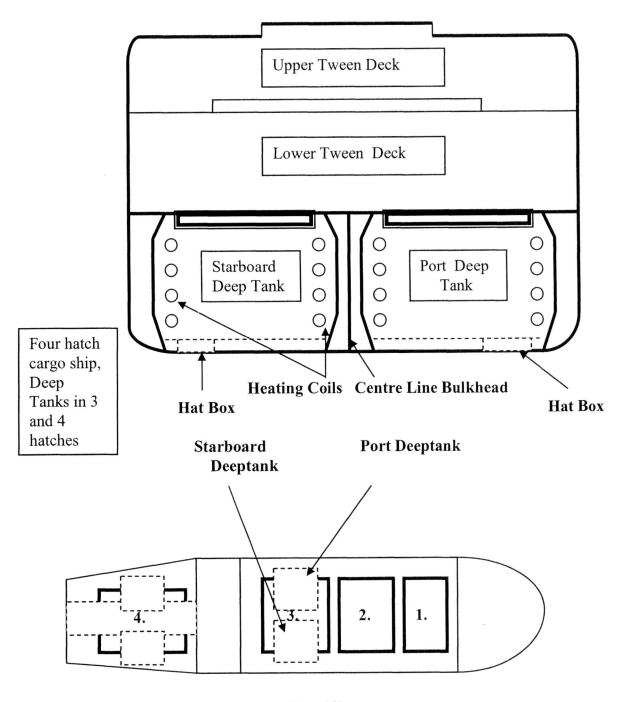

*Figure 4.20*

**NB.** Some vessels with a shaft tunnel may be fitted with additional deep tanks aft, in a position either side of the shaft tunnel, but these are not common.

**Deep Tank Construction**

Deep tanks are usually constructed in pairs either side of the centre line bulkhead. Each will have its own pumping arrangement via a hat box outlet. Tank lids being secured by screw sown bolts around the lid perimeter onto a hard rubber packing seal.

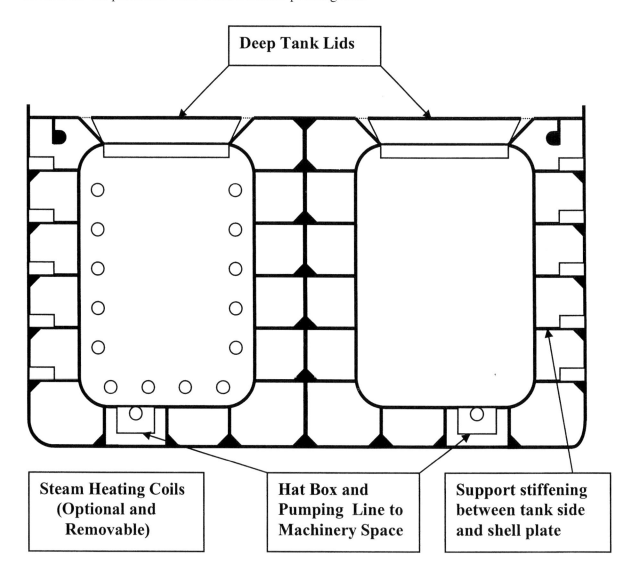

*Figure 4.21*

Deep tank arrangements may be fitted with heating coils (usually steam) but these may be blanked off and removed to provide greater capacity. Similarly the hat box lines may be blanked off, as when carrying a grain cargo for example.

**Pillar Construction**

**Head of welded pillar**

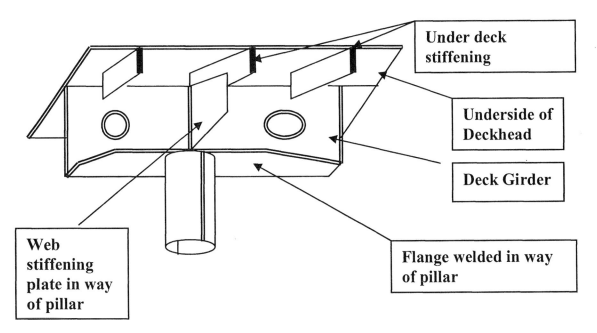

Under deck stiffening

Underside of Deckhead

Deck Girder

Web stiffening plate in way of pillar

Flange welded in way of pillar

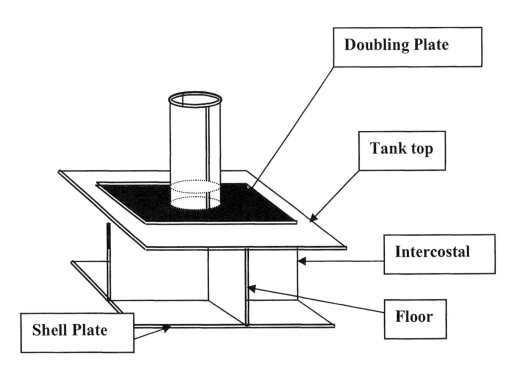

Doubling Plate

Tank top

Intercostal

Floor

Shell Plate

**Foot of welded pillar**

*Figure 4.22*

### Alternative Pillar Supports

Not all decks are supported by pillars of conventional structure. Some Ro-Ro vessels which have wide open vehicle decks often require underdeck support members between the main under cover vehicle deck and upper open decks.

The use of "H" girders as pillar support, is not unusual. They tend to be aligned with the vehicle lanes to facilitate ease of loading of the mobile units. They can be flush fitting to decks or bracket supported where added weight may be experienced.

*Figure 4.23   The enclosed maindeck of a High Speed Ferry seen with "H" girder pillar supports through the length of the deck. The right hand corner shows a fixed vehicle ranp supported by the pillars either side. The pillars are bracket supported at deck level and knee supports are positioned to accommodate the angle of the ramp. The deckhead structure shown, is in aluminium, left unpainted to, effectively reduce overall weight.*

### Structure of Pillars

The structure of tubular and hollow square pillars are to be attached at their heads to plates supported by efficient brackets to transmit the load effectively. Doubling plates or insert plates must be fitted to the inner bottom and to the deck under the heels of such large pillars. The head and heel plates of pillars must be attached by continuous welding methods.

Pillars should be fitted in the same vertical line wherever possible. Where pillars are expected to take eccentric loads, they must be strengthened for any additional bending moment that may be imposed upon them.

Pillars would be generally positioned to fit over the intersections of floors and girders in the double bottoms. However, where pillars are not directly above such intersections, then partial floors and intercostals are to be fitted as necessary to support the pillars.

**NB.** Manholes are not to be cut into floors or girders which lie below the heel of a pillar.

**Cowl Ventilators**

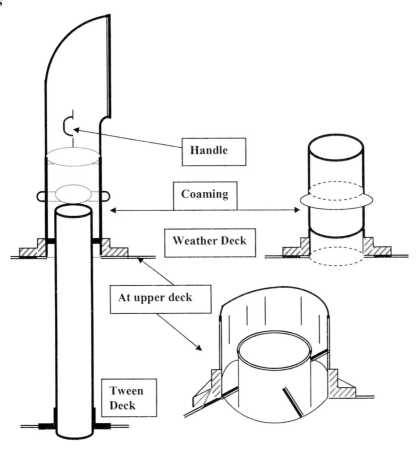

*Figure 4.24*

The upper cowl can be removed in the event of bad weather and the ventilation aperture can be sealed by a plug and cover system. This may be in the form of a mechanical internal flap arrangement that can seal the aperture in the event of fire, to eliminate oxygen.

Normal use is to trim (turn) the cowls into, or back to, the wind direction, in order to permit the required air flow to cargo or working compartments below decks.

Accommodation deck houses are usually fitted with "Torpedo Ventilators" which allow forced draft into compartments.

**Torpedo Ventilator**

*Figure 4.25*

**Mushroom Ventilator**

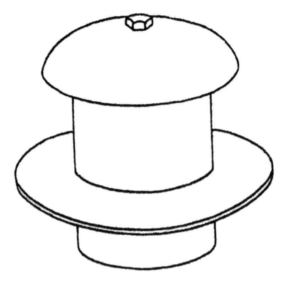

*Figure 4.26*

Mushroom ventilators to provide ventilation to below deck compartments.

**Ventilators**

Every ventilator on an exposed freeboard, raised quarter deck, or exposed superstructure deck, which is forward of a point located a quarter of the ship's length from the forward perpendicular (Position 1):— must have a coaming of 900 mm above the deck.

The height of the coaming may be 760 mm, if the ventilator is on exposed superstructure decks which are situated abaft a position which is a quarter of the ship's length from the forward perpendicular (Position 2). Where ventilators are situated in a position that they would be especially exposed to weather and sea, the height of the coaming's must be increased to such a height as will provide adequate protection, having regard to this exposed position. Coamings must be made of steel or equivalent material.

Ventilators in "Position 1", which extend more than 4.5 metres above the deck and ventilators in "Position 2" extending more than 2.3 metres above the deck need not be fitted with a closing device, unless a closing device is considered necessary.

Battery room ventilators need not have a closing device fitted.

**Access Hatches**

Many compartments like cargo hatches are fitted with separate access positions often referred to as "Booby Hatches" However, upper decks often accommodate escape hatches from shaft tunnels and similar working compartments.

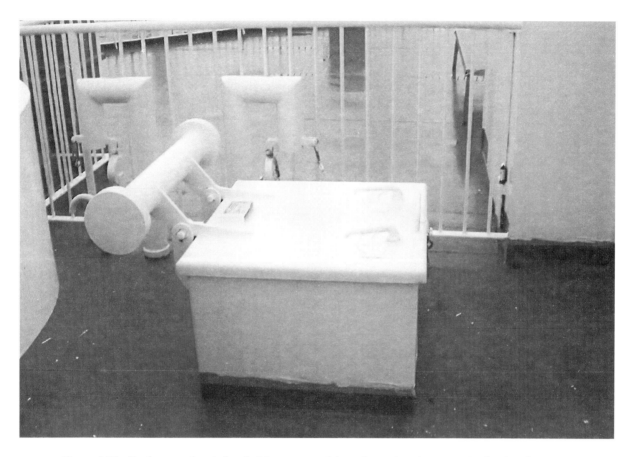

*Figure 4.27   Deck access hatch fitted with counter weight and securing cleats, seen in the closed position.*

## Air Pipes

Air pipes from tanks which extend above the freeboard deck must be of substantial construction and must be fitted with efficient means of closing off and making weathertight. Where the air pipe is exposed over the freeboard deck, the opening of said pipe must be situated at least 760 mm above the deck.

If the deck is a superstructure deck, or if the superstructure is less than standard height, then the opening of the air pipe must be at least 450 mm.

The heights given above may be reduced if the working of the ship would be unreasonably impaired or where the closing arrangement ensures that the lower height is adequately compensated for.

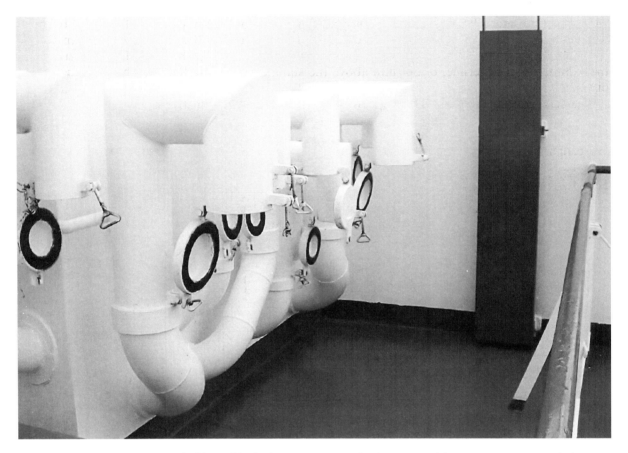

*Figure 4.28   Gooseneck Air Pipes with closing arrangements in the open position, seen on an upper deck. The screw cleating of the closing plates and the hard rubber seals should be inspected and maintained under the ship's planned maintenance system.*

### Deck Openings

Any deck opening other than a hatchway, machinery space opening, scuttle or manhole:—

Any deck opening, if it is positioned in way of the freeboard deck, must be protected by an enclosed superstructure or by a deck house or companionway of equivalent strength and weather tightness, as an enclosed structure.

Alternatively, if situated in an exposed deck position, over an enclosed superstructure in providing access to that superstructure, or on top of a deck house on the freeboard deck and providing access below that deck, must be protected by a deckhouse or companionway fitted with weather tight doors.

If the opening is in an exposed position on deck, above the deck of an enclosed superstructure and giving access to a compartment within that superstructure, it must be protected by efficient deckhouse or companionway fitted with weather tight doors, or protected to a lesser extent, taking account of its position.

### Doors

Each door into a superstructure, deckhouse or other enclosed superstructure associated with a machinery space steel casing, must have a sill to a height of 600 mm if in position 1, or 380 mm, if in a position 2.

### Side Scuttles

Every side scuttle fitted to a space which is below the freeboard deck, or within an enclosed superstructure must be fitted with a hinged deadlight so that it can be effectively be made watertight. Side scuttles must not be fitted in a position where its sill is below a line drawn parallel to the freeboard deck at the side and having its lowest point 2.5% of the breadth of the ship above the summer load waterline, or 500 mm above the summer load waterline, whichever is the greater distance.

The glass contained within the scuttle must be of substantial construction.

**Watertight Doors**

**Rear View**

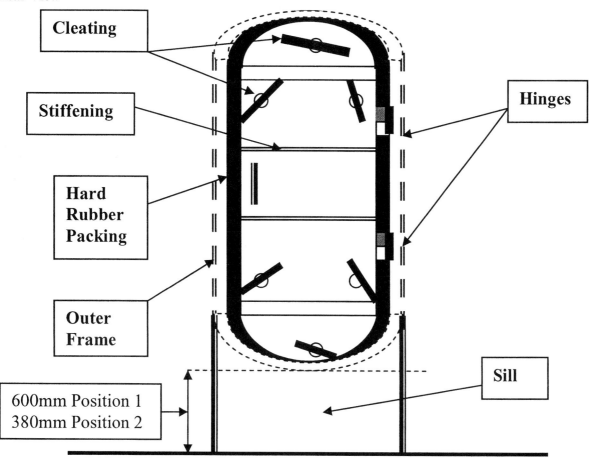

*Figure 4.29   Manually cleated water tight door set into bulkheads. The sill is designed to prevent water ingress at deck level. Regular maintenance is required on this type of door. The cleats require lubrication and the hard rubber packing must be watched for quality deterioration.*

Such doors are generally fitted as outer accommodation access points from the main deck area. They are heavy in construction and the cleating when in place creates a pressure seal against the hard rubber packing. When employed they are often employed with an inner second doorway providing access into alleyways.

**Door Sills** – May be increased on type "A", Type (B 60) or Type (B-100) vessels, if the loadline calculation reflect an increase in freeboard is necessary.

**NB.** These vessels are not allowed to have direct access from the freeboard deck into the machinery space through exposed casings. They must be fitted with an additional watertight door access from a companionway.

**Hydraulic Control of Water Tight Doors**

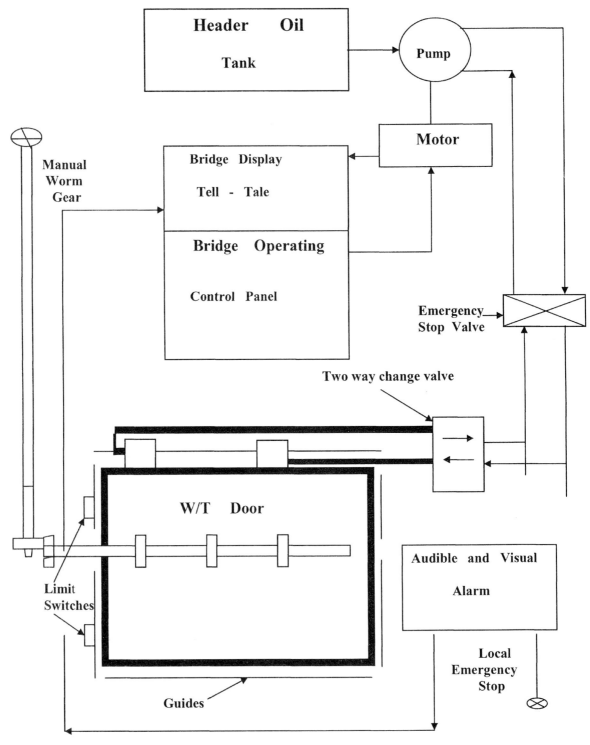

*Figure 4.30*

**Regulations effecting Watertight Doors**

Watertight doors tend to divide and protect shipboard compartments in an emergency especially where flooding is a potential threat. They are meant to reduce the ingress of water and also prevent the passage of smoke. To be effective these doors must be:—

(1) Provided by indicators showing whether the door is open or closed.
(2) Each power operated, sliding watertight door, must be provided with an individual manual operating mechanism. It must be possible to open and close the door by hand from either side of the door itself and also from a remote position above the bulkhead deck. This remote position must be furnished with an indicator to ensure that the door is fully closed.
(3) Watertight doors must be capable of operation when the vessel is listed to 15°.
(4) A tell tale arrangement must be provided on the navigational bridge to show whether the doors are open or closed.
(5) Each watertight door must have an operating and maintenance manual. Clear instructions on the use of the door must be posted at all control stations. These instructions must include procedures to prevent injury to persons.

The ship's plans would reflect the positions of watertight doors and respective control stations. Where a vessel is constructed with a shaft tunnel, this would normally be fitted with an overhead worm and screw or hydraulically operated downward sliding door.

Closing devices would also be listed and form part of the Safety Equipment – Record of Inspection. Watertight doors, aboard passenger vessels and passenger ferries must be operated and tested each week. A record of testing being entered in the Official Log Book.

**Deck Access Doorways**

Figure 4.31 Steel weather deck door used for access into the Emergency Generator Room. Access from a wooden deck above the boat deck of a passenger vessel. This is only a double cleated door and would not provide an all round water seal. Passenger vessels have a security concern and such a room is fitted with a hasp and padlock arrangement, as well as a mortice key lock fitting. A ventilation lattice is seen to the right of the access door.

### Companionways (Deck To Deck)

Usually fitted with side rails steel companionways allow access to upper and lower deck levels of accommodation blocks. Passenger vessels will normally have gate access at the top and lower levels of a companionway to restrict use by non-authorised persons. They are usually well illuminated at both ends and the stairway treads are given a non-slip surface to provide accident prevention. They may be constructed with open or enclosed steps and should be kept clear of obstructions to allow easy use, when the vessel is at sea.

*Figure 4.32   Companionway seen aboard a passenger/vehicle ferry provides access from a lower deck level to a higher deck. Guarded by side rails and bulkhead hand rail for personal security when the vessel is in a seaway.*

### Engine Room Escape Hatches

*Figure 4.33   Regulations require a secondary means of escape from engine room high risk areas. Such systems may operate via the propeller shaft tunnel if fitted, or from a secondary area of the machinery space. The escapes are water tight and lead to an exposed deck area. The two shown are from the P & O Ro-Pax Ferry, "European Ambassador" and are fitted with external counter weights to ease opening, with a four cleat arrangement and lift handle.*

**Framing**

**Welded, Inverted Angle**            **Web Frame**

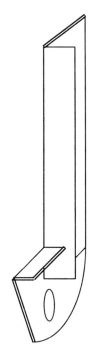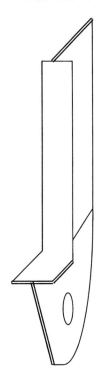

*Figure 4.34*

**Welded and Scalloped Bulb Bar**

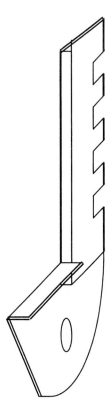

*Figure 4.35*

**Cantilever Frame (Athwartships)**

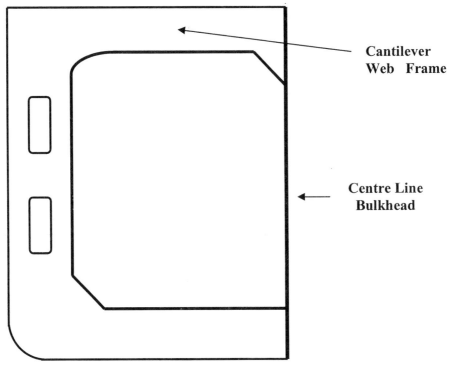

*Figure 4.36*

**Knee Bracket and Frame Connections**

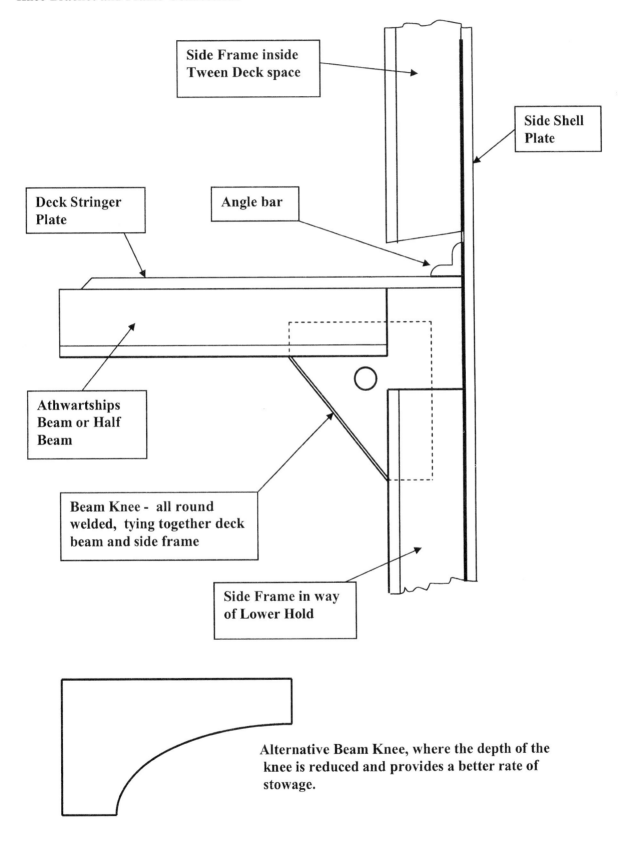

Side Frame inside Tween Deck space

Side Shell Plate

Deck Stringer Plate

Angle bar

Athwartships Beam or Half Beam

Beam Knee - all round welded, tying together deck beam and side frame

Side Frame in way of Lower Hold

Alternative Beam Knee, where the depth of the knee is reduced and provides a better rate of stowage.

*Figure 4.37*

**Longitudinal Side Framing**

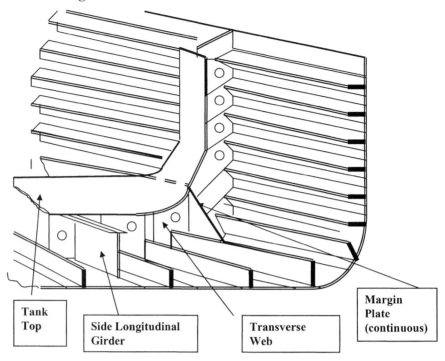

| Tank<br>Top | Side Longitudinal<br>Girder | Transverse<br>Web | Margin<br>Plate<br>(continuous) |
|---|---|---|---|

*Figure 4.38    Side shell with longitudinal framing in way of the turn of the bilge. (* Margin Plate may be angled or vertical and runs from the collision bulkhead to right aft in the cargo holds. The diagram shows the plate cropped short for clarity.)*

**Longitudinal Framing**

*Figure 4.39    An example of side longitudinal framing seen on the internal bulkheads of a vehicle deck, aboard a Ro-Ro vessel. Side support "T" girders seen in the vertical supporting the deck head and upper deck stringers.*

## Side Framing – Bulk Carrier

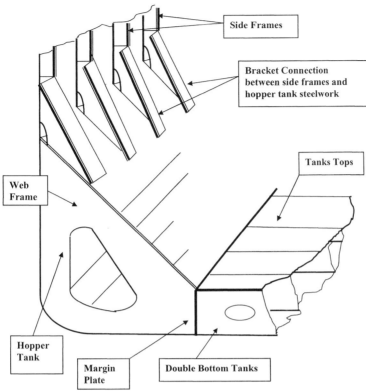

*Figure 4.40*

## Transverse Underdeck Support

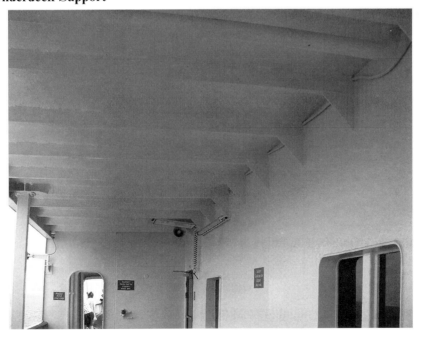

*Figure 4.41 Deck support and stiffening is achieved by various methods including pillars, athwartship's beams, half beams and in way of transverse bulkheads. The above view shows the main deck alleyway positioned either side of the superstructure. The underside of the boat deck is seen supported by athwartship's deckhead framing welded between a fore and aft bulkhead and the ship's side. The transverse frame support exists from the aft end of the boat deck to the forward athwartship's bulkhead, in each alleyway. Each frame connection is with a bracket to the fore and aft bulkhead and a butt connection to the ship's side shell plate.*

**The Stealer Plate Use**

**(In way of the bow deck plating)**

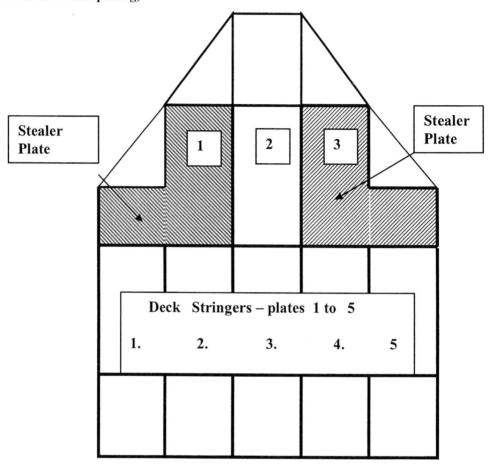

*Figure 4.42   Stealer "L" shaped plates, employed at the port and starboard sides of the fore end of the vessel where the fine lines of the ship come together.*

Stealer plates act as a reducing plate and in the example shown they are seen to have reduced the number of deck stringers from 5 across the beam, to 3 in the region of the bow area. A similar practice can be employed aft, or with the side shell plates, or bulkheads where the area is tapered in a reduction.

**Wooden Deck Construction**

Wood sheathed decks are invariably found on the passenger ships, generally of an older build. The more modern passenger vessel has moved more to composition type surfaces which provide a more spongy, rubber surface effect. Wooden decks are considered expensive in modern ship building and new commissions tend to avoid them if possible.

Wood decks are not restricted to just the passenger type vessels, some cargo ships and especially the cargo/passenger types still favour wood boat decks. However, the maintenance on wood decks is labour intensive and is a distinct dis-advantage especially in non-passenger vessels. Caustic soda, deck scrubbers and sand, have all been historically used, to keep wood decks clean. They also require "caulking" from time to time with hot pitch.

*Figure 4.43   Passenger main deck connection to the "Bridge Front" with wooden deck construction. Cut away alley entrance is seen without weather door fitting and the bridge front connection is seen as a riveted connection. Also shown is the side bulwark with welded stiffeners and flanged support brackets, a wood taff rail is set along the length of the bulwark on this older build of vessel.*

**Wood Decks**

Wood decks are constructed from planking laid directly onto the steel beams where no steel decking is fitted. The wood planks being bolted to each beam. They are caulked in a similar manner to "sheathed decks" to ensure water tight integrity.

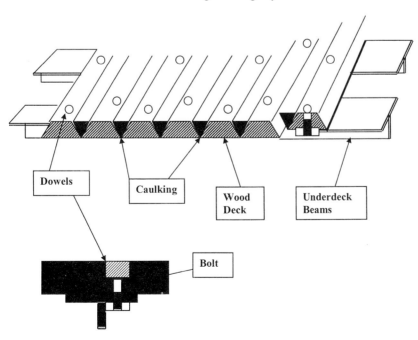

*Figure 4.44*

### Wood Plank Securing

The wood planking usually in "pine" is secured by bolts through the under deck girders. They are similarly caulked as described with wood sheathed decks to provide water tightness.

Wood dowels are used to cover the bolts and provide a satisfactory finish, to the deck.

### Sheathed Wooden Decks

Wooden decks can be of a "sheathed" variety where a steel deck is seen as undesirable as with passenger ships. Sheathed wood decks are expensive to install and maintain and have given way to special plastic composition surfaces instead.

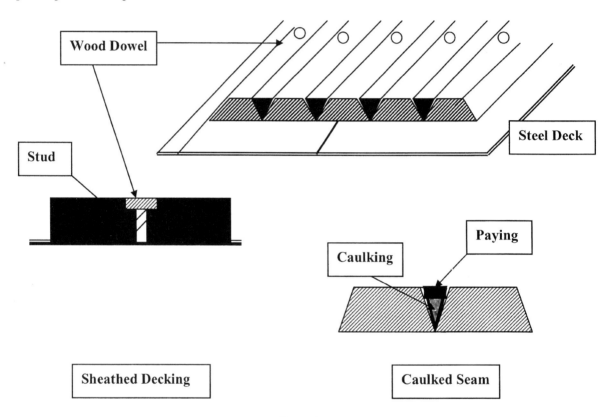

*Figure 4.45*

### Caulking

Caulking is a procedure employed between wood planks to make the deck watertight. Plank edges are tapered and oakum or corking cotton is forced between the taper edges, being hard pressed by a "Caulking Tool". The upper part of the join is then "payed" by running in molten pitch over the packed oakum.

## Wooden Sheathed Decks

*Figure 4.46    The Boat/Disembarkation deck of a passenger vessel. The steel bed plate of the deck is seen hard to the side shell forming a scupper way between the outside bulwark and the wood decking. Maintenance on wooden decks tends to be tedious with deck scrubbers employed with sand and or holy stones when time permits.*

# CHAPTER FIVE

# The Fore End Structure

## Introduction

The prominent end of the vessel is without doubt the bow section. When sighted, it is the dominant lead of the vessel and will generally provide the first impression to an observer. It is the part of the vessel that bears the ship's name that can lead to expectation, like with the Queen Mary 2nd.

The bow section takes the brunt of the waves when at sea and so must be strongly constructed. While the flare of the bow can accentuate like the curves of the beautiful lady. It can be striking, but it must also accommodate the forward business of the ship. It must have mooring capacity, it must accommodate necessary working spaces, including the foc'stle stores and the chain locker. It carries the security of the collision bulkhead and the extreme length, trimming tanks of the fore-peak. It is the tell tale of what the ship is.

Many bow sections are now fitted with the "Bulbous Bow" in conjunction with a part stem bar. The "soft nose" option stem bar, designed to give under impact from collision. The older design of "solid bar stem" being generally superseded. Modernisation has encroached dramatically into the fore end structure with the incorporation of the "Bow Visor" (found in Chapter 6) with the integrated vehicle ramp and/or bow door.

Additional features like bow thruster units (Tunnel types) have become an operational requirement of many ship types and the inclusion of these, has by the very size of the thruster unit, changed the design of the fore part. Anchor arrangements from centre line windlass, have moved in favour of split, port and starboard cable lifters. This tends to allow greater vehicle deck space. Broad beam ships have also moved in favour of the separate windlass, giving more accessible deck space in the fore part.

The forward end of the vessel, has always been considered the most senior part, next to the bridge. It must emanate strength and has been perceived not only as a working area but an area of dominance where ship handling has been concerned. Once the bow was secured the rest of the ship followed. The changes over the years have not been cruel, in fact the innovations of the 21st century, have gone some way to advance ship construction, to its current standing. The bow section has progressed with advances in technology and stands as a prominent standard reflecting the quality of today's ship building expertise.

## Stem Bar and Fore End

The construction of the ship's stem varies with build and ship type. The most common consists of a solid round bar extended from the keel plate to the lower water line. A curved stem plate then extends from the lower water line to the main deck, stiffened by breast hooks.

The fore end assembly on a conventional vessel may be considered to extend from the stem, right forward, to the collision bulkhead aft. Any panting arrangement, chain locker, peak tanks or bulbous bow formation, will be integrated into the construction.

**Bow Section (Conventional Ship) Side Elevation**

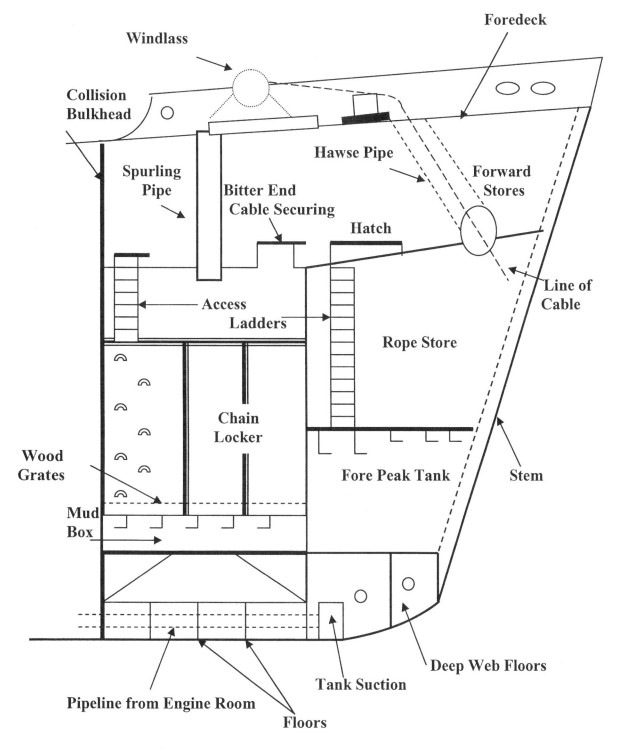

*Figure 5.1*

**NB.** Chain Locker is pumped out by a manual hand pump or by means of an eductor, depending on the draught of the vessel.

**Cross Section of the Forward End Viewed forward of Collision Bulkhead**

**(Conventional Vessel Centre Line Windlass)**

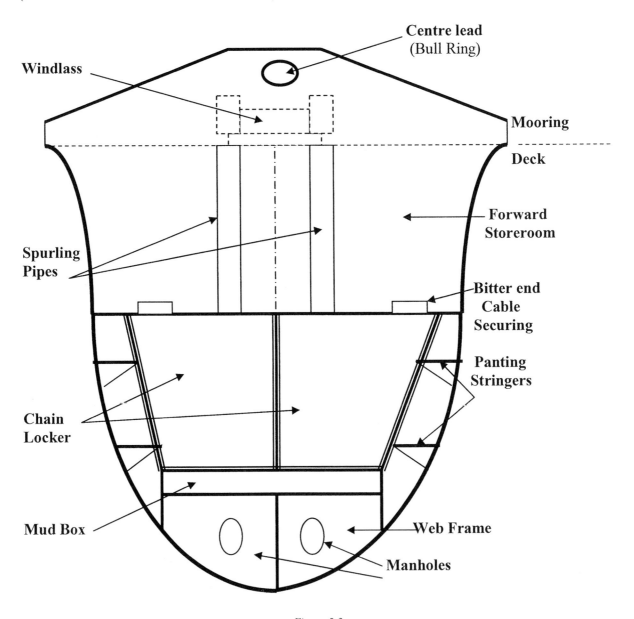

*Figure 5.2*

**Bow Shape**

With the advent of the "bulbous bow" and reduced level of water resistance advocated, various bow shapes have entered the commercial shipping arena. One such development has come from the Society of naval Architects of Japan with an Ax-Bow, shape. Comparison between the conventional shape to an ax-bow shape is shown:—

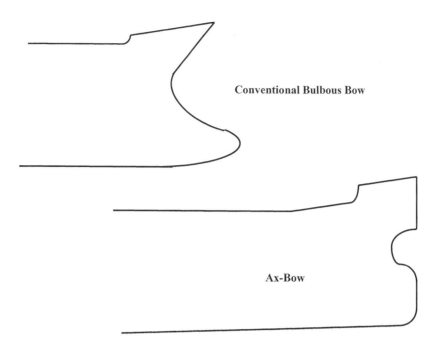

Conventional Bulbous Bow

Ax-Bow

*Figure 5.3*

Where as the bulbous bow is expected to reduce resistance below the surface, the ax-bow shape, is anticipated to reduce resistance at the surface level.

**Conventional Bow Arrangement**

*Figure 5.4    Fork end of the "Apollon Hellas" showing the forward mooring station with centre line windlass in a position forward of the bridge front.*

## X Bow Concept

One of the latest innovations in bow construction is the X-Bow from "Ulstein Design" of Norway. This unusual approach to bow design where the inverted bow shape is being used is in offshore vessels like; anchor handling, emergency response and "Research Ships".

It is anticipated that this shape of bow will enhance transit speeds in rough sea conditions, head seas as well as in calm water conditions because of low angles of entry and the increased length of waterline when compared with a stem rake of a conventional bow shape.

## X Bow Profile

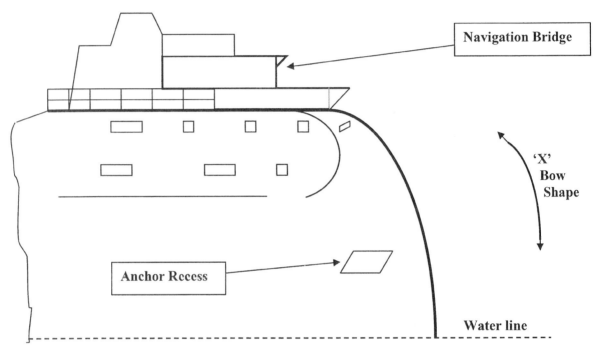

*Figure 5.5*

The new bow form has been constructed at the Barreras Shipyard at Vigo, in Spain and changes the entire form of the fore end. With hull form extending from the waterline upto the bridge deck provides greater internal volume and increasing comfort for crew members. Vessel motions are improved with less vibration from wave impact.

## The Bulbous Bow

The fitting of a bulbous bow has arguments for and against. However, the need for an optimum high speed tends to lend to fitting ships with the bulb as opposed to a conventional bow structure. The purpose of the bulbous bow is meant to reduce the resistance to the water flow around the hull form. The theory behind this, is that the bow wave is reduced by the rounded form and the maximum water resistance, generally assumed to be at the bow position, can be reduced.

They are more popular with the higher speed vessels with large block coefficients, which are not usually engaged in ice regions. The bulb of the bow increases the wetted surface area of the hull and therefore the overall hull resistance must assumed to be decreased. The trade off with reduced bow wave resistance, compared to overall hull resistance, seems to have won the argument, depending on the trade, operational cruising speed and the comparison of fuel burn, against the conventional bow construction.

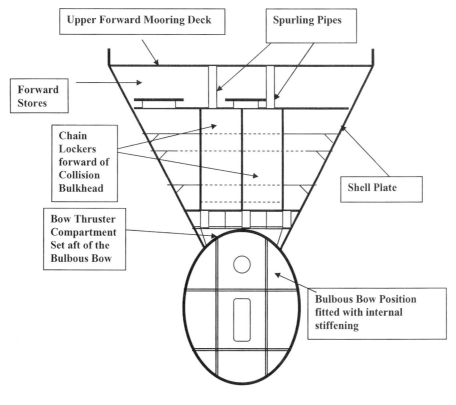

*Figure 5.6*

Forward construction in way of the Collision Bulkhead on a vessel type with Bulbous Bow structure. The bow thrust compartment is set aft of the bulb connection position.

## Bulbous Bow Structure

*Figure 5.7   Prominent Bulbous Bow seen exposed in dry dock. The outline of the bulb can be seen against the fine lines of the hull. A variety of bulbous bow shapes are dominant throughout the marine industry.*

## Bulbous Bow Shapes

The shape, design and overall size of the bulb tends to vary and they are now common to virtually all types of vessel. It is often employed as an additional ballast tank and can be used for enhancing trim and increasing the draught when in heavy weather. Alternatively, it may be left as a void space. It is always susceptible to contact damage from floating obstructions and warrants close inspection during docking periods.

*Figure 5.8    The bulbous bow shape of the the Tanker "Guadalupe Victoria II" as seen exposed in the Lisnave, Hydro-lift, dry dock. The bulbous bow symbol is seen on the hull between the draught marks and the ranged anchor cable.*

## Collision Bulkhead

The "Collision Bulkhead" is a watertight bulkhead designed to limit the flooding of the vessel in the event of collision. The transverse bulkhead is stiffened throughout its length and depth and is usually interconnected by the panting stringers, arranged forward of the bulkhead. The Anchor Chain lockers are positioned just forward of the Collision Bulkhead and secured against the panting stringers.

*Figure 5.9  The stiffened Collision Bulkhead of a new build bulk carrier. The bow section shows the aft part of the four "panting stringers" welded into position, forward of the bulkhead. The bow section being in the early days of construction.*

## The Collision Bulkhead

The Collision bulkhead will be watertight to the height of the freeboard deck* and has two main functions:—

(1) To protect the remainder of the vessel from flooding in the event of damage to the bow region.
(2) To prevent the vessel taking on an excessive forward trim should the forepeak become bilged.

It is a watertight bulkhead which is placed not less than 5% of the length of the ship, or 10 metres whichever is the least, abaft the forward perpendicular. Exception to this is by permission of the certifying authority and then it should not be more than 8% of the ship's length. It can only be pieced once below the freeboard deck and this would be for the purpose of ballasting the fore peak tank. The pipe line must be fitted with a deck operated isolation valve at the position of the bulkhead.

Collision bulkhead plate, must be 12% thicker than other bulkheads in the vessel.

Specific regulations apply to Ro-Ro vessels which are constructed with Bow Visor and an internal vehicle ramp, which may require the fitting of an additional collision bulkhead.

---

\* In every ship which is provided with a long forward superstructure the collision bulkhead will be extended to the deck above the freeboard deck.

**Table use for the Position of the Collision Bulkhead Non Passenger Ships**

| Arrangement | Length $L_{L1}$ In metres | Distance of Collision Bulkhead Aft of fore end of $L_{L1}$ | |
|---|---|---|---|
| | | Minimum | Maximum |
| (a) | $\leq 200$ | $0.05\ L_L$ | $0.08\ L_L$ |
| | $> 200$ | 10 | $0.08\ L_L$ |
| (b) | $\leq 200$ | $0.05\ L_L - f_1$ | $0.08\ L_L - f_1$ |
| | $> 200$ | $10 - f_2$ | $0.08\ L_L - f_2$ |

<u>**Symbols and Definitions**</u>

$f_1 = \dfrac{G}{2}$ or $0.015 L_L$, whichever is the lesser

$f_1 = \dfrac{G}{2}$ or 3 m, whichever is the lesser

$G$ = projection of bulbous bow forward of fore end of $L_{L1}$, In metres.

$L_{L1}$ is as defined in Chapter 1, 6.1.

Arrangement (a) A ship that has no part of its underwater body extending forward of the fore end of $L_L$.

Arrangement (b) A ship with part of its underwater body extending forward of the fore end of $L_L$ (e.g. Bulbous Bow).

**NB.** The position of the collision bulkhead for Passenger vessels employs a similar but different table. Reference should be made to the Rules and Regulations for the Classification of Ships, Part 3, Chapter 3 (Table 3.4.3).

**Rule length L** – Is the distance, in metres, on the summer load waterline from the forward side of the stem to the after side of the rudder post or to the centre of the rudder stock if there is no rudder post.

$L_L$ – A load line length to be taken as 96% of the total length on the waterline at 85% of the least moulded depth measured from the top of the keel, or as the length from the fore side of the stem to the axis of the rudder stock on the waterline, if that is greater.

## The Construction of Bulkheads

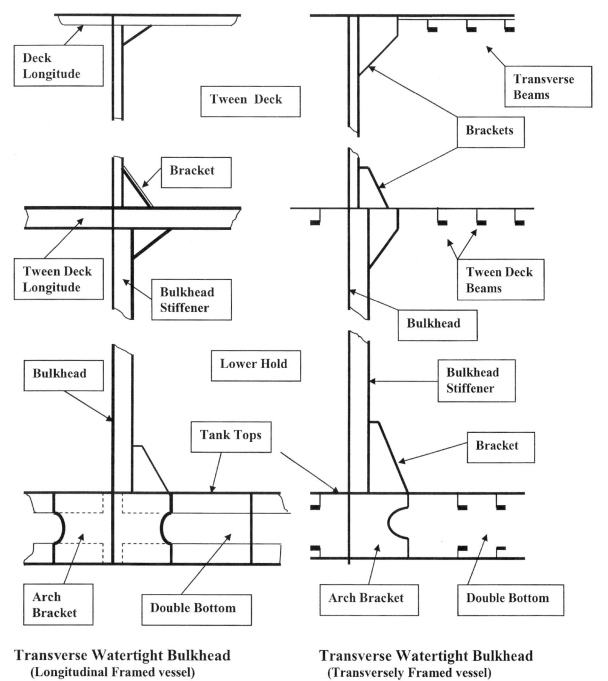

Deck Longitude

Tween Deck

Transverse Beams

Brackets

Bracket

Tween Deck Longitude

Bulkhead Stiffener

Tween Deck Beams

Bulkhead

Bulkhead

Lower Hold

Bulkhead Stiffener

Tank Tops

Bracket

Arch Bracket

Double Bottom

Arch Bracket

Double Bottom

**Transverse Watertight Bulkhead**
(Longitudinal Framed vessel)

**Transverse Watertight Bulkhead**
(Transversely Framed vessel)

*Figure 5.10*

## Bulkhead Height

The collision bulkhead is normally to extend to the uppermost continuous deck, or in the case of ships with combined bridge/forecastle or a long superstructure which includes a forecastle, then to the superstructure deck.

In vessels fitted with more than one complete superstructure deck the collision bulkhead may be terminated at the deck next above the freeboard deck.

**NB.** Where the collision bulkhead extends above the freeboard deck, the extension need only be to a weathertight standard.

**The After Peak Bulkhead**

All ships are to be constructed with an after peak bulkhead which will generally enclose the sterntube and rudder trunk, inside a watertight compartment.

In twin screw arrangements where the "bossing" ends forward of the aft peak bulkhead, then the stern tubes are to be enclosed in suitable watertight spaces inside or aft of the shaft tunnels.

In passenger ships the sterntubes are to be enclosed in watertight spaces of moderate volume. The stern gland is to be situated in a watertight shaft tunnel or other watertight space separate from the stern tube compartment, and of such a volume that if flooded by leakage through the stern gland, the margin line would not be submerged.

The aft peak bulkhead may terminate at the first deck above the load waterline, provided that this deck is made watertight to the stern or to the watertight transom floor. In passenger ships the aft peak bulkhead is to extend watertight to the bulkhead deck. It may be stepped below the bulkhead deck provided the degree of safety of the ship with regard to watertight subdivision is not impaired.

**Corrugated Bulkheads**

Where corrugated bulkhead are used, the angle of corrugation is to be not less than 40°. If they are employed as transverse bulkheads they must provide adequate resistance to compressive forces in the form of horizontal stringers or equivalent. Where a transverse horizontally corrugated bulkhead is used the span of the corrugations should generally not exceed 5.0 m.

Adequate support must be provided to corrugations in way of flanges or the abutting of corrugations. Where both transverse and longitudinal bulkheads are seen to intersect, the arrangement at intersections must facilitate attachment and maintain continuity.

Where corrugated bulkheads are on "stools" these must have a suitable end connection. Where stools are not provided to corrugated bulkheads they must be supported at deck level and inner bottom at both flanges.

**Engine Room Bulkheads**

The machinery space as probably the most important space of the vessel and must be enclosed as a watertight compartment. To this end watertight bulkheads must separate the engine room from other compartments. If the engine room is situated aft, the Aft Peak Bulkhead could form one of the bulkheads, otherwise a machinery space will have two, one forward one aft. These bulkheads would have increased scantlings and the double bottom tanks in way of the engine room will have increased depth to the floors to provide increased strength to accept the additional weight of heavy machinery.

**Construction and Stiffening of Plane Bulkheads**

Plate thickness of bulkheads will vary from the top at about 7 mm to the bottom at about 12 mm. The bulkhead must be stiffened with angle bars in the vertical direction spaced at about 750 mm apart.

**NB.** Tanker and bulk carrier must have substantially thicker bulkheads by virtue of their initial design and expected trade as compared with general cargo vessels.

**Regulations for Bulkheads**

The basis for having a bulkhead in position is to separate one space from another.* Its function is to provide watertight integrity for a space in order to restrict flooding. It is meant to provide sub-division of spaces for cargo, fuel, ballast and the machinery space.

---

* Bulk carriers and chemical tankers are often fitted with corrugated end bulkheads to cargo compartments.

Additionally it will provide support and transverse strength. Longitudinal bulkheads provide strength longitudinally. Bulkheads support deck plating, contain fluids and reduce free surface effects.

Legislation in force stipulates minimum requirements to provide basic protection for crew and passengers in the structure of bulkheads.

(a) The machinery space must be enclosed inside a watertight compartment.
(b) A collision bulkhead must be fitted in the forward position.
(c) A bulkhead must be fitted aft, termed the "Aft Peak Bulkhead".
(d) Transverse watertight bulkheads must be fitted. The number and size are dependant by the strength and watertight sub-division that is required for the vessel.

### Testing of Watertight Bulkheads

In every ship longitudinal and transverse bulkheads must be constructed to withstand the pressure due to the maximum head of water which it might have to sustain.

Watertight compartments will be tested by flooding or by a hose test conducted at the most advance stage of the fitting out of the vessel, or by other means approved by the authority to establish the water tightness of the bulkheads. The forepeak, double bottoms, duct keels, and inner skins shall be tested by flooding as previously stated.

Tanks intended to hold liquids and which form part of the subdivision, must be tested by flooding with water to a head which corresponds to the deepest subdivision loadline or to two thirds of the depth from the top of the keel to the freeboard deck, whichever is the greater. In no case must the test head, be less than 0.9 metres, above the top of the tank.

### Bow Section fitted with Bulbous Bow

*Figure 5.11   Large Bulk Carrier nearing build completion but still on building blocks, seen fitted with a bulbous bow in the shadow of the shipyard crane.*

**Bow Rudder Arrangement**

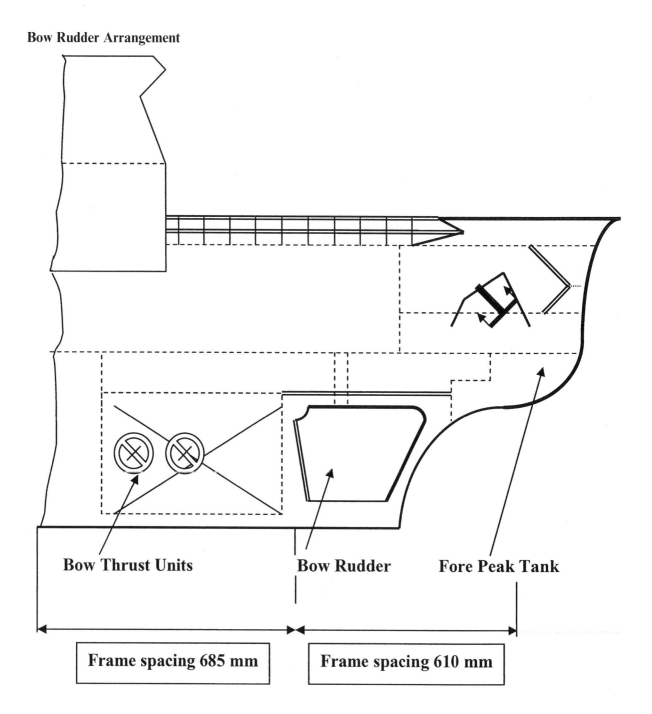

**Bow Thrust Units**         **Bow Rudder**      **Fore Peak Tank**

| Frame spacing 685 mm | Frame spacing 610 mm |

*Figure 5.12*

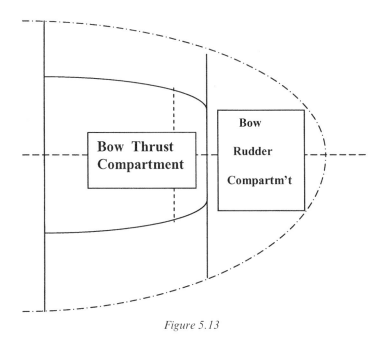

*Figure 5.13*

## Bow Rudders

The bow rudder is a specialist feature and generally not a common fitting other than to ferries and similar vessels that have a need to navigate stern first on a regular basis. Its effectiveness comes from the main propellers right aft, which send the wash of water right forward passing under the keel of the ship.

The bow form is shaped to accommodate the structure of the bow rudder and frame spacing is reduced in the structural area to provide added strength to accept the rudder activity. The pivot point of the vessel will have a tendency to move towards the bow region to a position of about $\frac{1}{3}$L, measured from the forward perpendicular, when navigating with astern propulsion. The position of the rudder in conjunction with the new position of the pivot point of the vessel, will usually achieve maximum effect from the arrangement.

**NB.** The pivot point of a conventional vessel, when moving ahead could expect to be approximately 0.25 of the ship's length from the forward position.

**½ Bow Section (Internal) structure of High Speed Ferry Craft**

**(Aluminium/Steel Support Construction)**

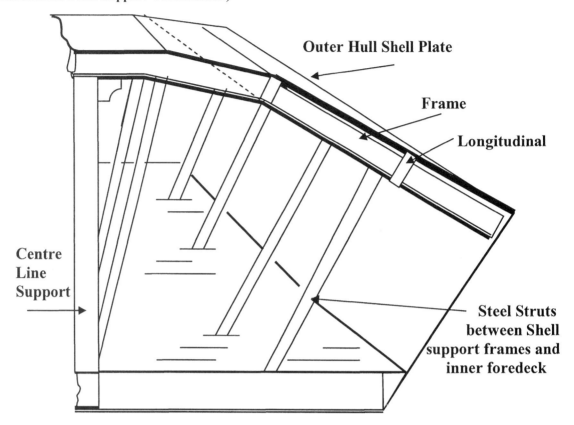

*Figure 5.14    Internal arrangement leading to the Forward mooring Deck of a High Speed Ferry.*

**Split Windlass Arrangement**

**(seen from port side)**

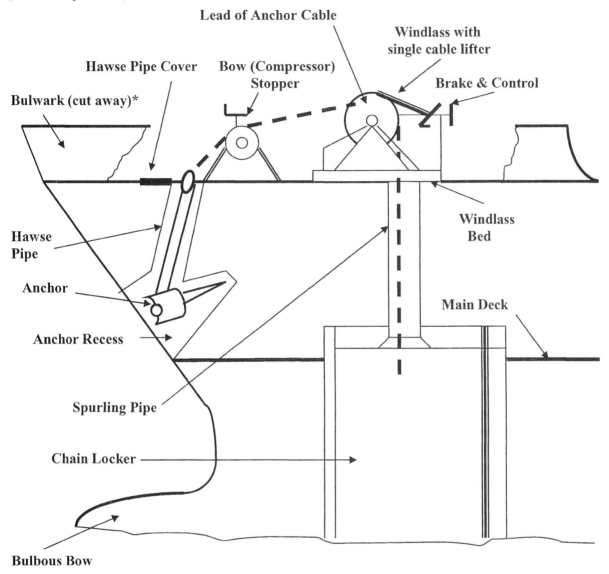

*Figure 5.15*

The horizontal deck distance between the windlass Gypsy and the hawse pipe is short and by necessity the hawse pipe accommodating the anchor is nearly vertical Many vessels are currently being constructed with either protruding anchor beds to clear the bulbous bow region when operating, or alternatively, where the flare of the bow is wide, recessing the anchor bed into the hull, as shown above.

Roll On, Roll Off vessels, fitted with a "Bow Visor" will generally have the Hawse Pipe and separate anchor lockers set back, aft to allow the operation of the hydraulic rams of the bow visor.

* Bulwark cut away for clarity.

**Windlass Braking System**

**The Band Brake**

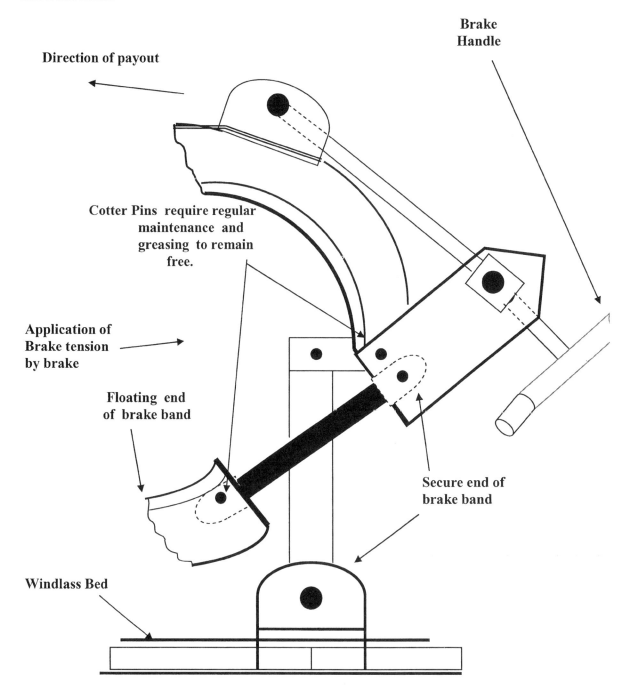

**Brake Handle**

**Direction of payout**

**Cotter Pins  require regular maintenance  and greasing  to remain free.**

**Application of Brake tension by brake**

**Floating  end of  brake band**

**Secure end of brake band**

**Windlass Bed**

*Figure 5.16*

**Separate (Split) Windlass Arrangement**

*Figure 5.17 The "Ganger" length of the chain cable is seen passing over the "Gypsy" of the starboard windlass, the brake handles on both the gypsy and the powered mooring rope drum are seen in the foreground. (A similar arrangement is mirrored on the Port Side) The screw turning handle of the bow stopper/ compressor securing the cable is seen prominent just above where the cable is shackled to the anchor.*

Virtually all mooring winches now incorporate either a tension winch or powered mooring rope drum, together with a warping drum at the extremity. These tend to be made operational by means of a central axle to which each drum is geared.

**Split Windlass Construction**

The use of split separate windlass arrangements, is now far more common than the single centre line, single axle type windlass. The main reason for this, is that generally speaking, ships are bigger and being constructed with the wider beam. Such wide beam vessels lend more easily to the separate port and starboard windlass operations. Additionally, specialist vessels like ferry's with "bow visors", require the windlass arrangement to be set further aft to allow the operation of bow doors/cargo ramps, etc., while at the same time permitting the working of anchors and cables. Clearly the construction arrangement of such a vessel favours separate windlass's to port and starboard.

*Figure 5.18   The Starboard windlass arrangement showing the short cable run from the "Gypsy" over the "Guillotine Bow Stopper" with a sharp vertical cable descent into the "Hawse Pipe" The cable water wash valve is seen on deck on the inboard side. The brake handle is seen sloping backwards towards the operators position.*

## Hawse Pipe Construction

Hawse pipes are constructed in tubular steel section having a diameter which is nine times the diameter of the chain cable it is meant to carry. The shank of the ship's anchor is stowed inside the hawse pipe and the arms and flukes of the anchor are either left exposed on the outer hull or housed in an anchor recess position. The extremities of the hawse pipe are fitted with castings in order to accept the robust treatment expected by handling anchors and cables.

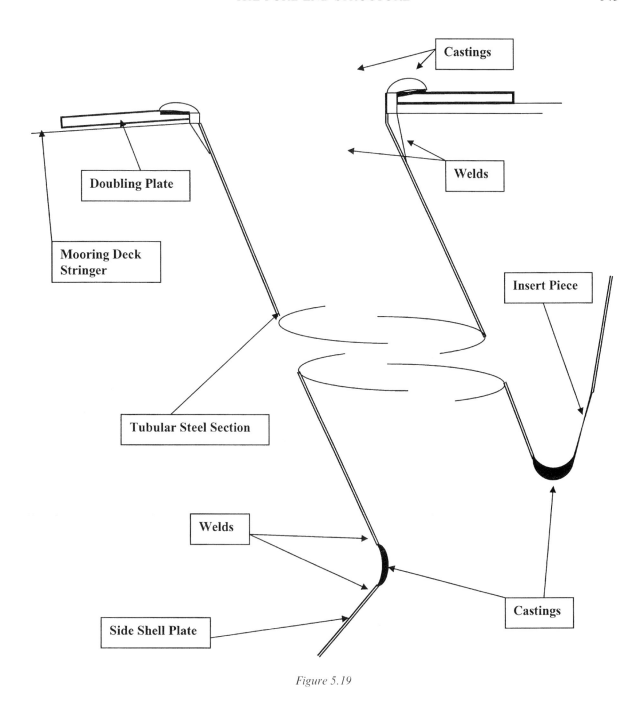

*Figure 5.19*

## Hawse Pipe – Constructional Features

A "hawse pipe" is constructed of an ample size to accommodate the smooth running of the cable and to this end the angle away from the perpendicular (conventional vessel) will be approximately forty (40) degrees. This will differ considerably with vessels operating with split windlass as opposed to a centre line windlass, and the downward fall angle would also be influenced by the horizontal deck space available between the windlass position and the bow.

The diameter of the pipe is usually based on the size of chain cable which is intended for operation within the pipe. As a guide 10 times the diameter for 25 mm chain, or 7.5 times the diameter of 100 mm chain would provide some indication of constructional size. Such a diameter would provide adequate space for messengers additional to the cable itself.

The extremities of the hawse pipe, at deck level and at the shell plate are strengthened by doubling plates. Modern vessels would have a welded structure, where as older tonnage had the hawse pipe flanges secured by counter sunk bolts into the underdeck frames. The length of the pipe varied but most constructions were of such a length as to allow the anchor crown "D" shackle to be within thirty centimetres of the deck opening.

Most hawse pipes of Merchant vessels are fitted with sliding covers, some also carry a chain roller at the deck edge to improve the run of the cable. Some warships are also fitted with helmets (hoods) over both hawse pipes and "Navel Pipes" (spurling pipes MN) to prevent water ingress into chain lockers and onto upper deck spaces, but these are somewhat dated.

## Chain Locker

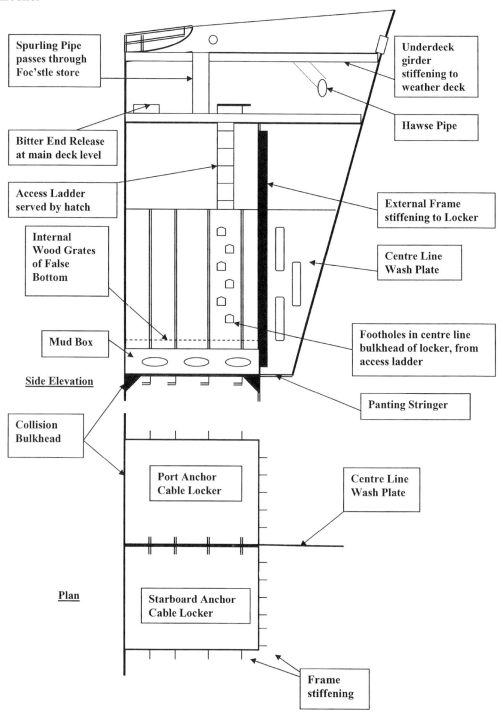

*Figure 5.20*

**Centre Line Chain Locker**

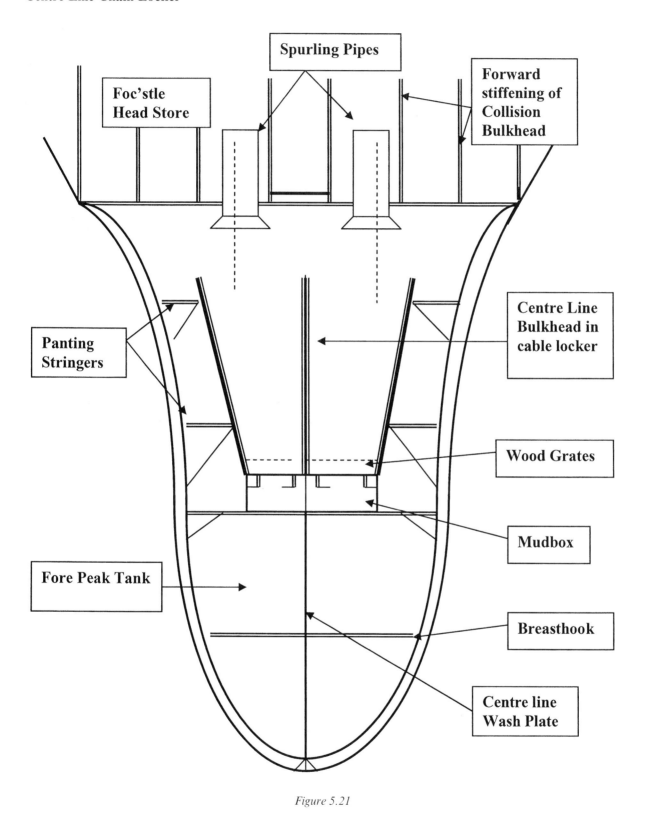

*Figure 5.21*

Aspect of Chain Lockers for single cable locker situated on the centre line forward of the collision bulkhead.

## Constructional Features – Chain Locker

The conventional, commercial vessel will generally have the "Chain Locker" positioned forward of the "Collision Bulkhead". Depending on whether the ship is equipped with separate cable lifters or a centre line "windlass" the design will influence the separation between Port and Starboard lockers. All modern vessels will also be designed with a self stowing locker for each anchor chain.

**NB.** Older tonnage previously employed crew members to stow the chain inside each locker when weighing anchor.*

Most common cable lockers are separated by a centre line bulkhead with footholds leading to an access ladder and upper deck access hatch. This provided the means of entering either Port or Starboard lockers from the upper store rooms in the fo'c'stle head. The cables themselves led from the mooring deck, via "spurling pipes" (RN – Navel Pipes) through the fo'c'stle stores to open into each of the chain stowage areas.

At the base of each locker is a "Mud Box" covered by wooden grates to allow sediment to clear from the chain and drop into this save all area. Periodically the space is pumped out, by either a manual hand pump, or an educator system. Regulations only allow the Collision Bulkhead to be pieced once and this allocation is normally left for the more frequently operated fore peak tank. It is for this reason that a hand pump is often employed for use with the chain locker on smaller tonnage, while the educator is employed for the larger vessels.

The locker area would also accommodate the slip/securing arrangement for the bitter end of the cable and this is now more frequently found external to the locker itself, with the end, open link, passing through either a side bulkhead of the locker or passing up through the deck head into the stores area.

All chain lockers have their bulkheads suitably stiffened on the outside by framing and are incorporated as an integral part of the fore end construction of the vessel. The space does not normally equal the breadth of the ship and will often be set inboard on either side in way of the panting arrangement of the fore end. Virtually all maintenance regarding the chain locker is considered in dry dock as it is one of the few occasions that the locker can be emptied by ranging cables on the bottom of the dock.

* Non self stowing lockers required the cable to be stowed in flakes to prevent a chain "pile-up" inside the locker. The problem of this was that if the pile toppled while the vessel was at sea, the cable invariably buried itself and could not be guaranteed to run free when the anchor was next required.
** Historically the early steam boats had the same problem and they often used to lash the cables together underneath the "Spurling Pipes". This served two purposes (1) it prevented the bight of cable being buried and (2) it stopped the cables banging together and allowed the men in the "cable tier" to get some sleep if the vessel was in a seaway. The crew being accommodated away from the officers.

## Chain Lockers

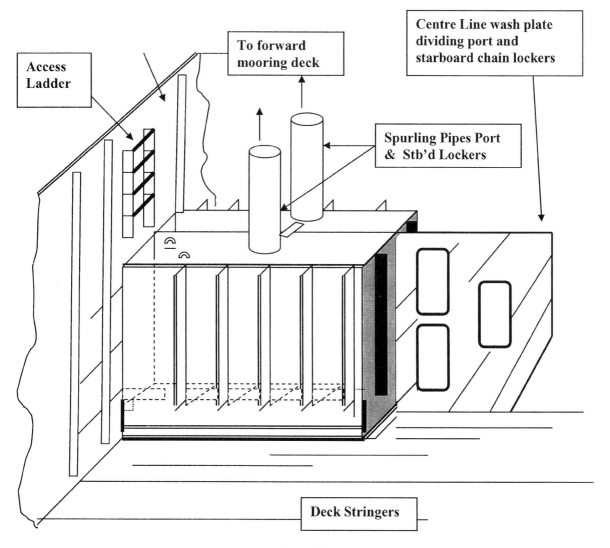

Figure 5.22

## Securing the "Bitter End"

Current regulations require that chain cable can be slipped from a position external to the locker and the bitter end attachment is achieved by a tapered draw bolt system or other similar slip.

This version is seen where the cable passes through the side bulkhead of the chain locker.

* Decking over the chain lockers has been omitted for clarity.

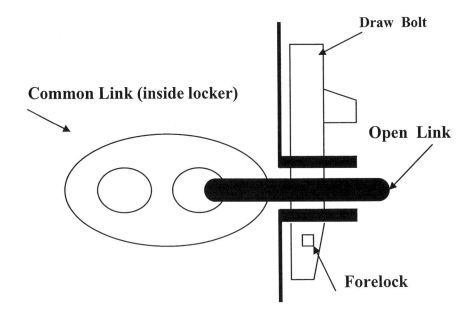

*Figure 5.23   Releasing the draw bolts of the bitter ends inside the securing hatch on an upper deck.*

## Bow Thrust Units

Considerable changes in thrusters have taken place over the last decade. The advances in "Pod Propulsion Units" being a direct follow on from azi-pod 360° rotating thrust units of the 1980's. Tunnel thrusters have probably been the most popular of all thruster units installed and continue to be widely installed in new tonnage, especially in the "Ferry Sector".

Smaller craft have tended to employ retractable thrusters because of draught limitations on the coastal trades. While supply boats operating in the offshore sector have been constructed with dual activity in mind as supply craft and ice breakers. Ducting around appendage thruster propellers, being removed from these craft because of the prospects of accumulating ice formations. Directional propellers being capable of operating with equal efficiency in Baltic ice conditions, without the duct surround.

*Figure 5.24   Twin "Tunnel Bow Thrust Units" seen protected by steel grating arrangements to protect the propeller blades from damage by debris which might be encountered in the water in the region of the bow. Floating debris at surface level is unlikely to cause operational problems but submerged articles at a similar level to the submerged units have been known to cause damage in the past. Tunnel thrusters normally operate on a 50% or 100% thrust power effect and are often used in conjunction with twin CPP's to provide tight turning manoeuvres for ferry vessels especially inside port and harbour confines.*

**Example Lubricating Oil System to Tunnel Thruster Arrangement**

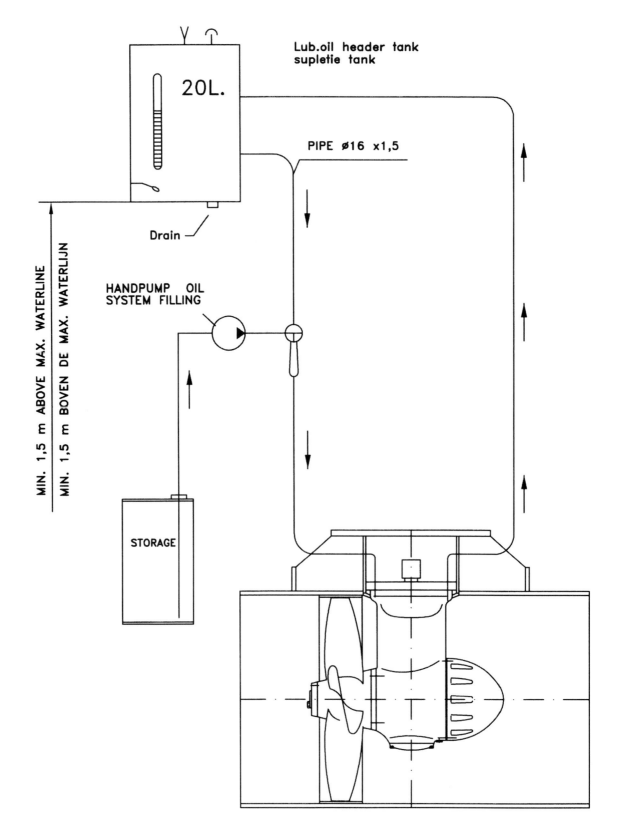

*Figure 5.25*

## Fore End Structure in way of Tunnel Bow Thrust Unit

*Figure 5.26   Fore End structure in way of a tunnel Bow Thrust Unit. The mid compartment would allow access to the machinery for shipboard personnel. (Seen reversed in a shipyard prior to assembly in a new build.)*

## Constructional Notes "Bow Thrust Units"

Thruster units generate exceptional vibration in the associated support area of the unit. To this end, increased stiffening is a standard feature of installation. Vertical stiffening with horizontal brackets to the tunnel itself. Reinforced pipe flanges provide further rigidity to the tunnel. Increased scantlings to the interconnecting steelwork is considered standard practice.

Dry dock survey periods tend to provide an ideal time for the inspection of thruster units. Surveyors would be particular to check the surrounding steelwork and supporting members for any cracking or deterioration in the area of welded seams effecting the tunnel unit. Blade clearances would also be an item of concern during such an inspection.

**Retractable Thruster**

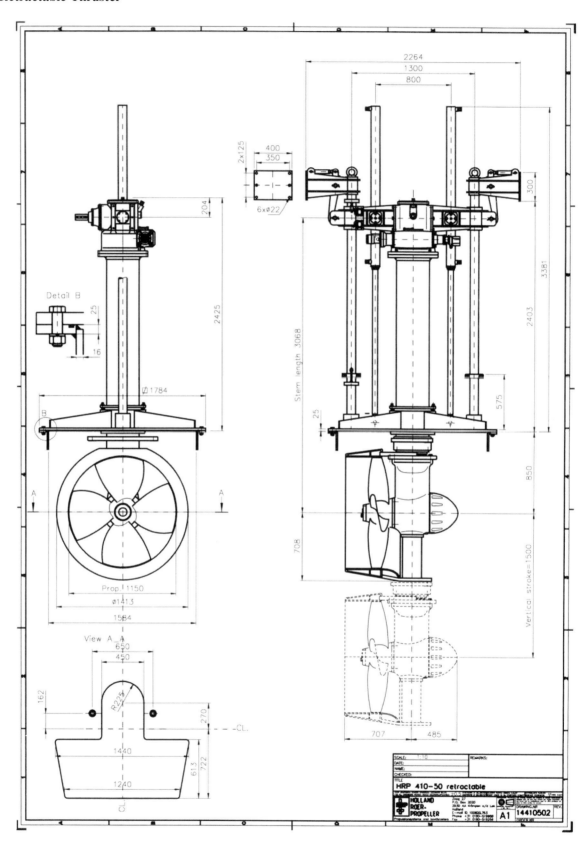

*Figure 5.27*

### Construction features to combat: Fore End Stresses

### Panting

When the vessel is moving ahead, through a seaway, the fore end can expect to experience a pitching motion as the bow section rises and then falls back with the encounter of the waves and any swell effecting the ship's progress. The shell plate, in the region of the bow, will go through an inward and outward movement,(known as panting) due to the changing pressures at different depths. The variations in water pressure will fluctuate as the immersed section is lifted clear of the water surface. The panting movement being compensated for, by construction features at the building stage. Conventional tonnage countered these pressures by fitting a "Panting Arrangement" forward of the Collision bulkhead.

### Panting Arrangement (over 15% ship's length)

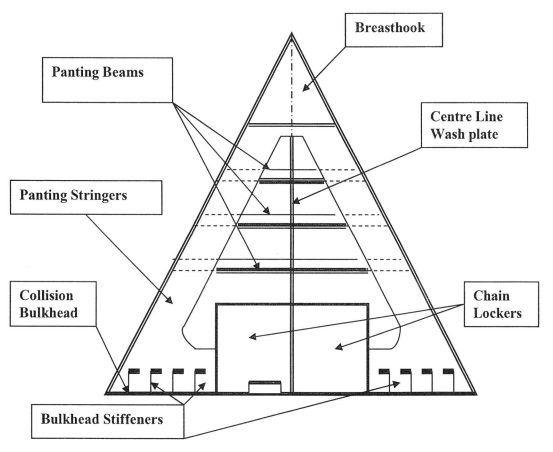

*Figure 5.28*

This arrangement consisted of "panting stringers" secured to the shell plate and interconnected by "panting beams". These beams being positioned at intervals not exceeding 2 metres apart at alternative frame spacing intervals. The alternative frames being fitted with interspersed brackets connected to those frames without beams.

An alternative construction to this is employed with perforated flats which are stiffened to suit the build. These flats are spaced at no more than 2.5 metre intervals apart. While in order to maintain continuity of strength, side stringers are fitted aft of the collision bulkhead, at the same levels as the panting stringers. Where and if the side plating is of an increased thickness, these stringers may be omitted.

It should be realised that similar pressures and stresses can expect to occur at the after end, abaft of the after peak bulkhead, as the stern of the vessel moves in opposition to the movement of the bow. Similar stiffening as with the fore end, may be included aft of the aft peak bulkhead, at intervals of up to 2.5 metres apart.

## Pounding

A stress that occurs to the fore end, bottom structure, forward and abaft of the collision bulkhead position. It is caused by heavy and violent pitching of the vessel when in a seaway.

Pounding can expect to be experienced in a region of 25% to 30% of the ship's length as measured from aft of the Forward perpendicular. The actual percentage depending on the ship's block coefficient. The area is provided with additional stiffening to counter the effects of pounding. Where the ballast draught is small the bottom plate size is increased. Where a vessel is longitudinally framed, solid plate floors would be fitted at no more than 2.1 metres apart and the bottom longitudinals are fitted closer together.

Where a ship is framed transversely, solid plate floors are fitted at every frame space within the pounding region. Additionally, intercostal side girders need to be fitted at intervals not more than 2.2 metres apart with half height intercostals fitted in between.

**NB.** Frame spacing tends to be progressively reduced towards the fore end and into the pounding region. The ship experiences pounding by slamming into the water surface when pitching steeply. Most ships can expect this during its working life and surveyors look for damage to floors and intercostals in the fore region when carrying out inspections.

## Forward Mooring Deck

The forward mooring deck of the vessel is often raised as a fo'c'stle deck. (Taken from the early shipbuilding days when vessels of the 14th/15th centuries were constructed with a fore castle and aft castle, at respective ends of the ship.)

The modern passenger vessel or specialised merchant vessel like a Ro-Ro, with numerous deck levels, has moved away from fo'c'stle deck construction by running a deck through the length of the vessel. The deck space if exposed, is heavily strengthened by underdeck beams to support the weight of mooring equipment like the windlass, anchor activity, bollards and weight bearing leads.

The perimeter of the deck area is bordered by supported bulwarks and/or a combination of rails. These are additionally strengthened in the way of a variety of roller fairleads and/or "Panama Leads" to accommodate mooring ropes (see Figure 5.29).

## Mooring Leads

Roller leads are free standing and generally are not powered in any way. They rotate on a centre spindle arrangement with the friction generated by the mooring rope or wire as it is heaved from the warping drums of the windlass or docking winches. they require regular maintenance by way of oiling and greasing as per the planned maintenance of the vessel.

Rollers can also be found in a raised positioned at the level of the gunwale capping. Where this method is employed, the fall of the deck aft, to the windlass, would provide a better lead. The bulwark would have increased stiffening and probably be structured with increased scantlings (see Figure 5.30).

*Figure 5.29 The exposed forward mooring deck of a passenger vessel sided by supported bulwarks running to side rails. Extensive roller fairleads, international roller leads and "Panama Leads" with "old men" pedestal rollers positioned to provide suitable mooring options to permit working the split windlass arrangement.*

*Figure 5.30 Triple roller lead, set into a cut away from the solid bulwark below the gunwale. International Roller lead set aft into the bulwark supported by a pedestal single roller lead fitted with an anti-jump guard. (Colloquially referred to as an "Old man" lead.) Two sets of bollards (Bitts) are positioned strategically to the leads to accommodate transfer of moorings from the warping drums of the windlass (not shown).*

**Mooring Equipment**

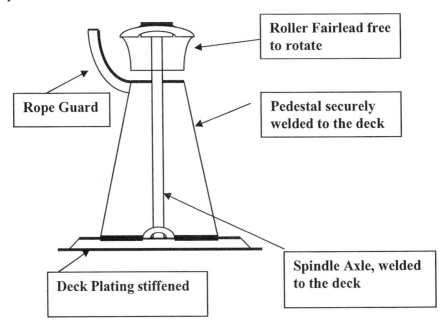

Roller Fairlead free to rotate

Rope Guard

Pedestal securely welded to the deck

Spindle Axle, welded to the deck

Deck Plating stiffened

**Pedestal Roller Fairlead welded to deck area aft of windlass.**

*Figure 5.31*

**International Roller Fairlead**

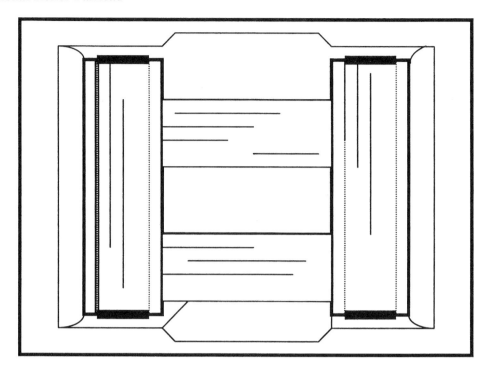

*Figure 5.32    International Roller Fairlead set at the Stern between two "Panama (pipe) leads".*

**Specialist Mooring Leads**

*Figure 5.33   Bow situated "Panama (pipe) Leads" seen right forward in the bow region of a tanker vessel. The leads are back supported by AKD Chain Stoppers to take the combined chain/moorings from the Floating Production Storage and Offloading system (FPSO).*

Panama Leads commonly referred to as "pipe leads" are usually set into solid bulwarks with or without a doubling plate reinforcement. They are always well stiffened by angle bar support.

They are favoured by seaman the world over in preference to open roller leads where the possible jumping of the mooring can occur, when under tension. They often form the centre lead in the bows, known as a "bullring" and may be fitted with a company badge or emblem which can be removed for centre lead activity if and when required. Also employed for the compulsory, emergency towing lead, which is a stipulated requirement for tankers.

**Panama Leads**

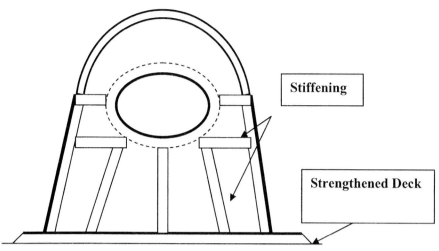

Stiffening

Strengthened Deck

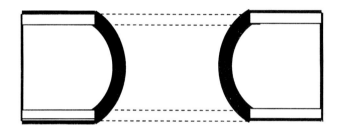

*Figure 5.34*

## Bollards (Bitts)

The term "Bollard" is usually applied to quayside mooring posts. The term "bitts" tends to refer to a double post, bollard set as mounted on the deck of virtually all ocean going vessels. The securing of "bitts" to the deck, is more often achieved by a welded structure but alternative methods have been employed in the past.

The posts themselves will be manufactured in cast steel or more commonly strengthened tubular steel. They are normally fitted with lugs and/or lips to the upper edge of the post to prevent the moorings jumping from the posts when under tension.

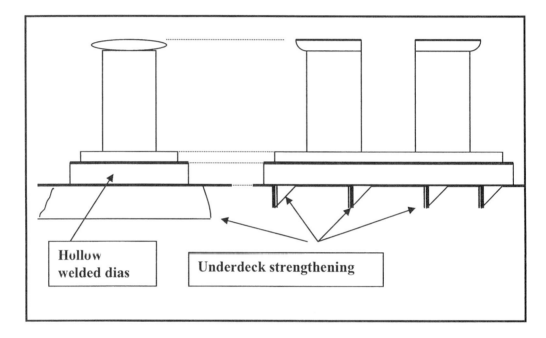

Hollow welded dias

Underdeck strengthening

*Figure 5.35   Example ship board bollard posts. Double bitts are usually fitted with stopper deck ring bolts.*

# CHAPTER SIX

# Shipboard Constructional Features: Ferries, Passenger Vessels and High Speed Craft

## Introduction

Every ship, at its time of building, will incorporate the technology of the day and in so doing will adopt its own special features. Many of these features are common to other vessels, i.e. Hull openings, bridge fronts, multiple decks, cargo doors, etc.

This chapter has been included within the text, to provide extensive examples of specific constructional items that lend directly to Ro-Ro, Ro-Pax and Passenger Vessels. The new SOLAS requirements will influence new build and ship design of the future to incorporate the concept of safe return to port and safe areas to effectively reduce casualty thresholds. These changes are expected to come into force by 2010 and have already started to be generated in new builds.

The new concepts are being incorporated to ensure passengers and crew in the event of an accident, to be sustained in habitable conditions, for the time it takes either to evacuate or reach a port of refuge. Redundant propulsion, steering systems and power supplies, are meant to be included to cover against equipment failure. Additionally, "vertical fire safety zones" need to be established to protect passengers and crew to permit movement towards a safe haven.

The aim of the text has been to bring forward those special features that the mariner and shipyard personnel could be expected to be reasonably familiar with. Some ships have specific identifying features, like a Ro-Ro ferry which could expect to be fitted with a stern door and vehicle ramp. The need for vertical fire protected zones for the future may be a difficult concept to accommodate, with the car deck of some existing Ro-Ro designs.

Specific elements can of course be expected to change with the passing of time, as new technology and new concepts come into being. Specific trades influence the style and operation and the build of designated vessels. However, trade patterns tend to be somewhat flexible, causing change and modifications to be ongoing within this vast industry of shipping. The need for safer ships and cleaner seas is paramount within the build, as well as being the main driving force within all sectors of the maritime world.

## Hull Openings

There are now many ships specifically designed with openings into the hull other than the conventional hatchways of the dry cargo ship. Ro-Ro vessels are nearly all fitted with stern ramp openings and often incorporate a bow visor to provide drive through capability. Car carriers incorporating quarter angled vehicle ramps, as well as amidship's side ramps tend to provide double hull openings for drive on cargo units. While some of the more modern dry cargo vessels operate with side loading facilities for paper products, handled by elevators and fork lift, truck stowage systems.

Passenger vessels and similar high sided Ro-Ro ships are usually provided with shell door access points for gangway use and/or marine pilot reception. In virtually all these examples of hull openings, hydraulics tend to be the main mode of operation and sealing, to ensure water tight integrity.

Hull openings are virtually all monitored by CCTV and seal protected by tell-tale light indicators, usually established on the navigation bridge. Since the lessons of the Herald of Free Enterprise, it is essential that hull openings like stern ramps, bow visors and shell doors are reported and observed in the closed position, prior to the vessel departing the berth and putting to sea.

Positive seals are achieved against hard rubber packing set around openings and closure is doubly increased, by cleating arrangements being left under a level of positive hydraulic pressure, once the access is closed. Limit switches are incorporated in the structures to activate the tell tale systems and cameras provide visual coverage to bridge mounted monitors to show open or closed status to the bridge conning position.

Opening and closure of apertures is nearly always achieved by mechanical or hydraulic means, or a combination of both. Perimeter locking cleating, once the ramp or door is in the stowed position, is affected by hydraulics being left on positive pressure. Lifting or lowering of large heavy ramps, tends to be controlled by winch and purchase wires, with preventer chains incorporated to provide a maximum extended outreach angle. Other systems operate with hydraulic rams positioned either side of the door or ramp. Such operations would expect to include a fail safe in the event of oil pressure failure, the ramp would be held and not allowed to collapse.

Some of the more specialised items are detailed as follows:—

## The Ferry Transport

The Ro-Ro principle and the many vessel types associated with this sector of the industry, caused major upset amongst dock labour in the development years. The conventional stevedores, saw Ro-Ro traffic the same as containerisation, as just another means of reducing employment. While the ship owners saw quicker ship turn rounds, together with reduced port costs. Harbour Authorities were also to gain from additional freight movement, without having to install major amenities like the Gantry Cranes as required for containers.

Ro-Ro ferry activity has provided the door to door freight service and benefits to many communities, not least boosting the tourist industry. Ferries have also been seen to act in several global conflicts and provide strategic support to the military, most notably in the Falklands War of 1982. They continue to boost economic developments in ship building, chartering, employment and all aspects of commerce. It is a sector of shipping which seems to expand continually beyond its own boundaries on a regular basis and continues to thrive on development and expansion.

**General Arrangement Modern Ro-Ro Ferry (Freight only or Ro-Pax)**
**1,900 metres Lane Length**

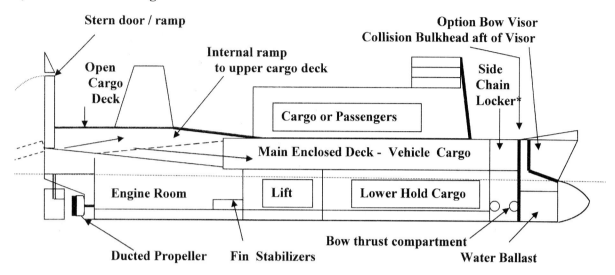

*Figure 6.1*

Open deck stowage of Ro-Ro Cargo either side of the engine room smoke stack.

Chain locker at the ship's sides either side of the fore and aft line to facilitate the operation of separate port and starboard windlass operations.

Bow visor option to permit drive through capability and is not always featured.

Lift to lower cargo hold may be mechanical or electro/hydraulic operation.

All cargo ramps are fitted with wheel tread, anti-skid, steel grips.

Usually twin suspended rudders with twin CPP propellers and twin bow thrust.

**The Roll On-Roll Off (Ro-Pax) Ferry**

**Design Cross section**

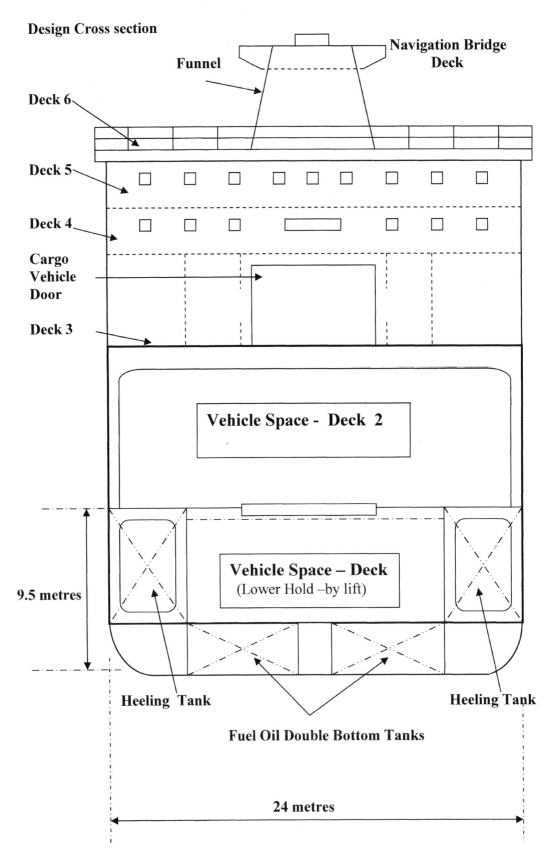

*Figure 6.2*

## Vehicle Decks and Superstructure of the Modern Ferry

## The Bow Visor for Ro-Ro Ships

*Figure 6.3   The bow visor arrangement of the "Jupiter" (since renamed) seen in the open position. Such doors are normally coupled with a stern door/ramp permitting drive through capability without having to turn vehicles or use reverse discharging discharge methods.*

## Bow Doors

Bow doors must be fitted above the freeboard deck. They are found in a watertight recess forward of the "collision bulkhead" and above the deepest waterline. If the bow door leads to a long forward, enclosed superstructure, it must also be fitted with an inner door. Some arrangements where a sloping vehicle ramp is incorporated above the freeboard deck, this ramp will form part of the collision bulkhead. The inner ramp in such an arrangement can be omitted, if the ramp is weathertight over its complete length and is fitted in accord with regulations concerning collision bulkheads.

Bow doors must be fitted with arrangements that ensure watertight sealing and provide protection for inner doors. Where an inner door forms part of the collision bulkhead then this door must be watertight over the full height of the cargo space and arranged with fixed sealing supports on the aft side.

Bow doors with inner doors must be arranged so that the bow door cannot cause structural damage to the inner door or the collision bulkhead in case of damage to, or the detachment of, the bow door. Should such an arrangement not be possible, a second separate inner weathertight door, must be installed in accord with the regulations.

**NB.** The requirements for inner doors are based on the assumption that vehicles and cargo are effectively secured against movement from the stowed position.

The strength of a bow door must be equivalent to the surrounding structure. Where the bow door is of a "visor" type, or a hinged opening type, these are to be adequately stiffened. Such doors must be provided with means that prevent lateral or vertical movement of the doors when closed. Adequate strength must also be incorporated into any connections, hinges or link arms to the door structure. The shell plate of the door must not be less thickness than the side shell plating with door stiffening and in no case to be less than the minimum shell plate end thickness or forecastle side thickness, as appropriate.

## Securing and Locking Devices for Bow Doors

Doors are to be fitted with a securing device to keep the door closed by preventing it from rotating about its hinges. A locking device, locks a securing device, in the closed position. The doors must be provided with adequate means of closing, securing and supporting and such elements must be commensurate with the strength of the surrounding structure. Similarly, the supporting structure in way of a bow door must be suitable for the design loads and stresses of the securing and supporting devices.

Securing devices are to be simple to operate and to be provided with interlocks in such a way that they can only be operated in correct sequence. The doors must be provided with positive locking arrangements so that they remain closed within design limitations of inclinations and vibration or other induced loads in the event of any loss of the actuating power.

**NB.** Securing devices must be approved by Lloyds Register. If they are of a hydraulic type they must comply with the Rules and Regulations for the Classification of ships.

**Inner Structure and Upper Deck Structure of Bow Visor**

*Figure 6.4   The underside of the bow visor in the open position as seen from the lower vehicle deck of a Roll On, Roll Off vessel.*

**NB.** Split windlass and anchor arrangements are set to either side and well aft so as not to interfere with the Bow Visor operation.

**Bow Visor Open/Closed Arrangement**

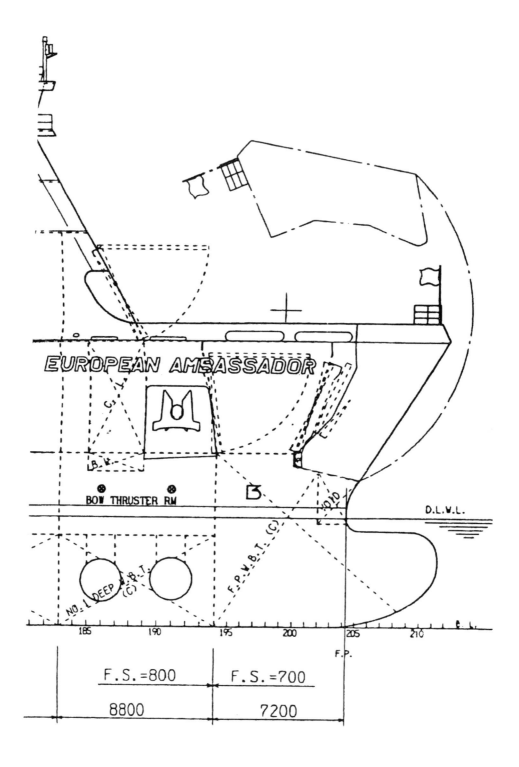

*Figure 6.5  Note the positions of the waterline well below the lower seal of the visor. Anchors are also observed set well aft to facilitate the operational working of the hydraulic rams used to close and open the inner doors and vehicle ramps.*

**Operational Features for Bow Doors**

Once opened, bow doors must be provided with mechanical means to be fixed in the open position. Such fittings must take account of the weight of the door and a minimum wind pressure of 1.5 kN/m acting on the maximum projected area when in the open position.

Where a bow door and inner door give access to vehicle decks, they must be provided with a remote control station from a position above the freeboard deck. This position must be such that the opening and closing operation can be observed by the operator or by CCTV. Means must also be provided to prevent unauthorised operation of the doors.

Operation of the doors must be provided with lights and audible alarms on the navigation bridge and on the operating panel to ensure that the doors are closed, secured and locked in their proper position. A light test facility must be included and indicator lights must be arranged so that they cannot be turned off.

Separate power supplies must be provided for the indicator/alarm system and the operational open and closing system of the door(s). Alarm sensors must be provided, being protected from water, ice formation and mechanical damage. The Bridge indicator system is to be fitted with a mode selector function Harbour/Sea Voyage, so that an audible alarm is given should the vessel leave harbour with the bow door or the inner door(s) not properly closed and locked.

A water leakage detection system with audible alarm and CCTV surveillance are to be arranged to provide an indication to the navigation bridge and to the engine control room if any leakage through the inner and bow doors occur. In the event of failure of any securing or supporting device, the system must also be built with redundancy, so that in the event of any single failure, the remaining devices are capable of withstanding reactionary forces.

**Hydraulic Operational Precautions**

Where doors are fitted with hydraulic locking/securing devices, the system is to be mechanically lockable in the closed position, so that in the event of hydraulic system failure, the securing devices will remain locked. The hydraulic system for securing and operating locking devices must be isolated from other hydraulic circuits when in the closed position.

**General Operational Features for Bow Doors**

An operating manual for bow and inner doors must be approved and provided on board the vessel. Operating procedures for the doors must be documented and displayed at appropriate places.

**Stern Door/Ramp**

*Figure 6.6    Example arrangement of the stern Door, combination ramp of a Roll On, Roll Off vessel. The main ramp being to facilitate the movement of vehicles on or off the vessel while the additional feature of a foot passenger walk way is seen extended from the port quarter.*

The ramp acts as a watertight door, being sealed by hydraulic cleating against a hard rubber surround once hoisted into the vertical stowed position. Hydraulic pressure is brought to bear to generate the seal, prior to the hydraulic pumps being switched off.

The hoist and lowering actions of the ramp are achieved by mechanical means by use of the flexible steel wire ropes led to winches on the upper vehicle mooring deck.

**Example Axle/Vehicle Loads**

Stern ramps and vehicle doors are designed to accept most types of vehicles. The following ramp examples are for a 16 m length (inclusive of the flaps) and a total width of 18.6 metres:—

Fork lift truck    :    Axle load 15.8 tonnes, over four wheels

Mafi-trailer    :    Axle load 27.5 tonnes, over four wheels
                         Bogie load 55 tonnes, two axles

Road trailer    :    Three axles (20 t – 20 t – 10 t)
                         Axle load on pneumatic tyres 20 tonnes

Tug master    :    Axle load 35 tonnes.

*Figure 6.7 The twin stern doors and ramps deployed from the Greek Ro-Pax ferry "Theofilos" seen working cargo in the port of Pireas. Personnel access is by the inshore railed gangway. The offshore access is seen in the stowed position.*

## Garage Decks

*Figure 6.8 Herring bone steel pattern on vehicle ramp designed to provide a non skid surface for large and heavy vehicles. The small edge coaming to the ramp, may or may not, be fitted with a stanchion/wire fencing arrangement.*

**Stern Ramp/Stern Door**

*Figure 6.9    The Stern Ramp of the "Baltic Eider" deployed flush with the loading berth. The hydraulic operational rams are seen inset to either side of the aperture to the internal vehicle deck.*

Internal ramps, together with stern and bow door/ramps are manufactured in steel and generally fitted with a welded "herring bone" structure. This provides a non skid surface on angled steel work to reduce the possibility of vehicles skidding and losing control. Flat deck surfaces are not usually so fitted but tend to have a flush surface with star dome securing points, positioned to suit the vehicle stowage lanes.

Ramps are load tested to accept a certified axle weight. Most articulated vehicles operate with a minimum of four axles, while 6 axles to a vehicle is not abnormal.

**Stern Ramps**

With virtually all Ro-Ro vessels where a stern door is situated, the door itself acts as the vehicle ramp. The sealing of the stern door being made watertight by hard rubber packing in association with a hydraulic and/or a mechanical cleating system. It follows that the door itself if being employed for the dual purpose of acting as a vehicle ramp must be exceptionally strong in order to accept the heavy weights of laden trailer vehicles.

To this end the construction of the stern doors are usually reinforced underside, by a systematic arrangement of "H" girders to support the vehicle surface once the door/ramp is deployed for the loading or discharging of vehicles.

*Figure 6.10   The stern door of a Roll On, Roll Off ferry seen cleated up in the seagoing position. The visible underside is noted as a series of fore and aft "H" girders with a single welded beam across the middle of the door to provide additional rigidity to the structure.*

Once deployed to the shore side link span. the stern door acts as the vehicle ramp. The ramp being deployed usually by a heavy duty wire/winch system and may have a secondary chain suspension system as an option.

*Figure 6.11   Example of cargo door, seen in the raised open position (Underside) against the deckhead of the vehicle space. Strength members ("H" girders) are seen to be aligned in both the fore and aft and athwartship's directions.*

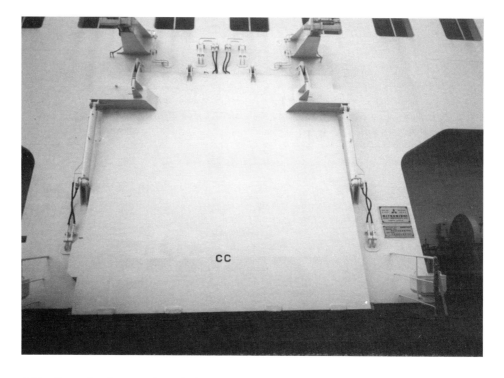

*Figure 6.12   Example of upper vehicle deck cargo door, seen in the lowered position. It is raised and lowered by means of hydraulic rams set either side. Water tight integrity is achieved by hydraulic bolts and hard rubber seal about the perimeter of the door.*

**Hydraulic Ram Operations for Inner and Outer Stern Doors**

*Figure 6.13   The inner door, seen open, against the deckhead and held in a locked position by an internal hydraulic ram arrangement on the port side. (duplicated on the starboard side – not shown). The stern ramp/ outer door seen deployed with the Hydraulic ram extended. Both inner and outer doors are hydraulically sealed onto hard rubber packing with a positive pressure. Cargo is not stowed in the space between the inner and outer doors.*

**Stern Door – Securing Arrangements**

*Figure 6.14    Hard Rubber packing and hydraulic side cleating on the Port side of the stern door of a modern Ro-Pax vessel. Additional hydraulic operated locking cleats are also fitted at the head and bottom positions of the door. Example seen just below the black hard rubber, on the recess for the upper edge of the door, when closed.*

**Car Carriers**

This type of ship is noticeable because of its exceptionally high sides and often fitted with an angled quarter, vehicle ramp in addition to an amidship's cargo ramp. Their main feature is the high number of decks, usually at least twelve (12) to accommodate the numerous vehicle cargo. Return voyages are often empty as return cargoes are difficult to come by, but some palletised cargoes may be suitable.

**Hinged Stern Slewing Ramp**

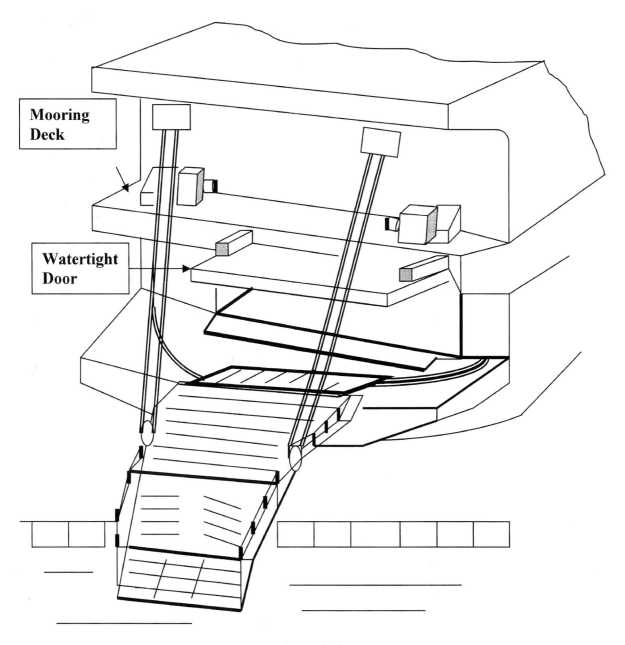

*Figure 6.15*

Slewing ramps are popular with car carriers, providing versatility in load/discharge procedures. They are often incorporated with an amidship's ramp to allow a double method of loading and/or discharge. As with other types of vehicle ramps they tend to have a herring bone, non-skid surface and are fitted with removable stanchions and fencing. Angled flaps at each end provide flush joins to deck and quay landings, provided the vessel is upright, on an even keel.

**Angled Quarter, Vehicle Ramps**

*Figure 6.16    The double hinged quarter ramp of the "Thebeland" is prepared for landing. This style of vehicle ramp is common to car carriers and some ferries and is often worked in conjunction with a beam on side ramp to increase the speed of loading and discharge of wheeled cargoes.*

**Car Carrier Construction**

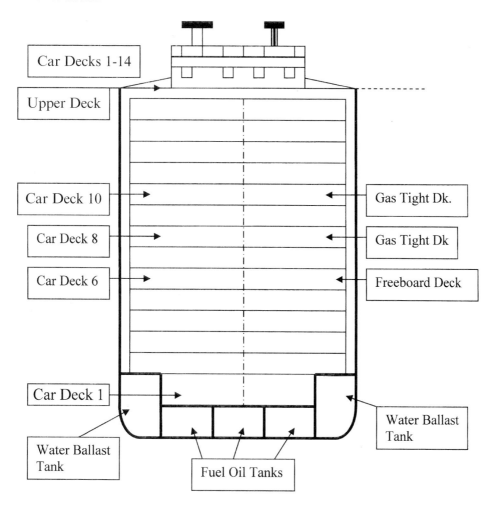

Typical Build features:—

| Gross tonnage | 60,587 gt |
|---|---|
| Draught | 9.82 m |
| Air Draught | 52.0 m |
| Length O/A | 121.08 m |
| Breadth | 32.23 m |
| Service speed | 21.0 kts |

*Figure 6.17   Panamax sized vessel. Serviced by ship to shore ramps, one at the stern (Stbd Quarter) the other midships (beam on). Also has an option to carry refrigerated cargo on decks 5, 6 and 7 instead of making the return voyage in ballast.*

**Vehicle Deck Access – Car Carriers**

*Figure 6.18    Stern access onto the vehicle deck from an angled quarter vehicle ramp. The off centre stowage recess for the hinged ramp is also featured. Mooring deck leads are sited above the vehicle access area, situated to port and starboard of the ramps position.*

**Car Carrier Profile**

*Figure 6.19    One of Neptune Lines high freeboard car carriers. Looking more like a high speed car ferry. The vessel is prominent with the ellipse of the bow shape and the bow flare set well aft from forward. The forward mooring deck and anchoring positions are seen undercover, positioned below the fore deck, similar to the modern passenger cruise vessels.*

## Passenger Vessels

**Class 1**, Passenger vessels are generally large high sided vessels with a multi deck construction. The main emphasis is on safety and they tend to have prominent boat decks with adequate survival craft to ensure the passenger complement and crew numbers are legally provided for. The very nature of the cruise market dictates that these vessels carry a large crew often in access of 600 persons, mostly engaged in the catering and service sector of the industry. The largest passenger vessel (proposed) is in the drawing and planning stage. It is expected to carry 8,000 passengers and 1,500 crew members. If it is actually built, it is anticipated to take three years.

The ships therefore require extensive accommodation blocks for both passengers and crew numbers, together with the necessary functional spaces to conduct day to day operations. Leisure facilities for the passenger contingent are extensive and will usually include, swimming pools, theatres, cinemas, casinos, lounge and bar facilities as well as restaurants, breakfast and dining areas.

On board shopping, hairdressers, photographers, etc., are all party to the make up of the larger vessel. Contracted service personnel like entertainers, sales staff, are additional personnel on board and must be accounted for. Most will carry a hospital facility together with medical staff and emergency facilities. Security staff are also prominent within the working environment.

*Figure 6.20   Extensive fitting out is required on passenger vessels. Passenger alleyways are usually carpeted and public rooms tend to require a large quantity of furniture, with many items in soft fabrics. At the same time fire resistant partitions, with non-toxic materials must provide an internally safe environment.*

**Passenger Vessels**

*Figure 6.21   Profile of the "Star Princess" Class 1, passenger cruise liner. The vessel is seen berthed starboard side to in the Port of Barcelona, Spain. Special features include the wide beam navigation bridge with supported Bridge wing structures.*

*Figure 6.22   The high transom stern arrangement of the passenger vessel is seen as a dominant feature of modern passenger vessel construction.*

## Passenger Vessel Features

*Figure 6.23    The P & O Class 1, Cruise Ship "Oriana" seen alongside, Port side to a passenger terminal berth. The ship is seen dressed overall and shows the many deck levels employed for passenger accommodation and operational working.*

## Bulwarks

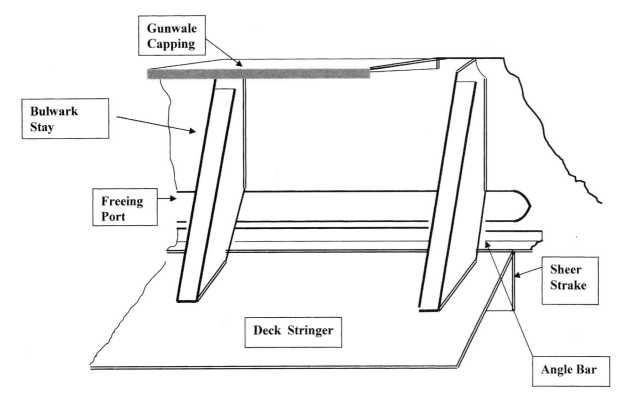

*Figure 6.24*

**Floating Bulwark**

Bulwarks can be inset with mechanical freeing ports, panama pipe leads, rigging cleats, pad eyes, etc., Where weight bearing fittings are situated they are usually fitted with backing/doubling plates and load tested.

*Figure 6.25 Bulwark situated on the starboard side of the fore deck of Cruise Passenger ship.*

**Bridge Front Construction (Port Side)**

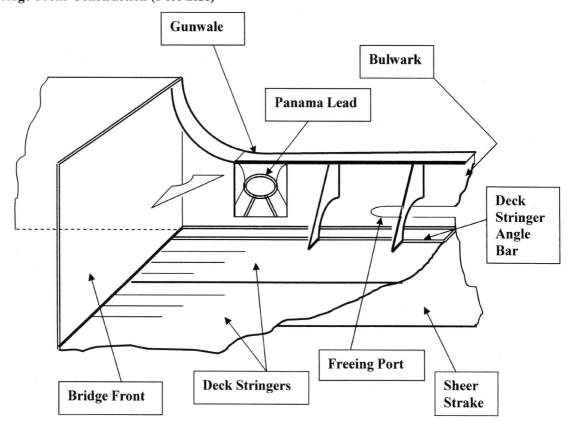

*Figure 6.26 The Connection between deck stringer and Bridge Front Bulkhead.*

**Bridge Front**

*Figure 6.27 Accommodation windows seen above a passenger observation deck, below the level of the Navigation Bridge windows. Radar mast and communication aerials seen above the Bridge deck of the passenger vessel "Van Gogh".*

Where applicable the number and disposition of bulkheads are to be arranged to suit the requirements for subdivision. Their position must take into account flood ability and damage stability and are to be in accord with the National Authority of the country, in which the ship is registered.

Bridge fronts tend to be designed to encompass the navigation deck and in particular the bridge windows. They will often incorporate maintenance platforms below the level of the bridge windows to permit access for cleaning, monitoring the wiper motors and general painting procedures or passenger observation decks. Some ships' bridge fronts are designed to accommodate side alleyway doorways, and these are usually provide with weather deck doors, providing access to the foredeck area.

**Bridge Front**

Figure 6.28     The bridge front of a Ro-Pax ferry, set above the passenger promenade deck which overlooks the forecastle head. The navigation bridge windows extend from each bridge wing.

Figure 6.29     Side view of the bridge wing of the above Ro-Pax vessel, which highlights the backward slope of the bridge front and the superstructure connections.

**Passenger Ship Profile**

*Figure 6.30    The "Queen Mary 2" seen port side to, the passenger terminal berth, in Southampton, England. The ship engages in a lifeboat drill in order to comply with the legal requirements that boats must be launched and manoeuvred in the water every three months. With the number of lifeboats carried on a Class 1, passenger vessel, holding a boat drill and launching half the ship's boats is a complex operation. The profile of the vessel reflects the size and the complement of the ship for 3,000 persons.*

**Shell Doors**

Many vessels have a need for incorporating a shell door either side of the vessel. Certainly the high sided vessels like passenger ships, car carriers, and Ro-Ro vessels. The doors themselves tend to have varied employment as with providing a gangway landing access, pilot access, or loading discharging stores. In this day and age they are invariable hydraulic in operation with hydraulic cleating in place when closed. Being outlets to the body of the main hull they will be covered by CCTV, and fitted with sensors to provide indication to the navigation bridge as to whether open or closed.

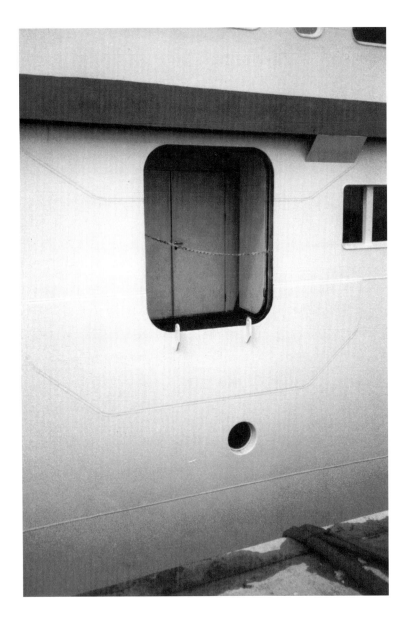

*Figure 6.31 A gangway landing position at a shell door opening set into the ship's hull. The door is in a position well above the waterline and is fitted with an inner protective doorway. Such an access provides flexibility to the safe angle of passenger gangways, and can be employed for loading or discharging stores close to quay level. A side scuttle (porthole) is featured in a position below the shell door.*

## High Speed Craft

Predominantly in the ferry sector of commercial shipping these vessels are being constructed as mono or multi hull craft in the form of Catamarans, or Tri-marans. They are generally of a light construction with aluminium or composite superstructures and fitted with powerful high speed machinery often including waterjet propulsion systems delivering normal speeds of 45-50 knots. The sector encompasses hydrofoils, wig craft, catamaran and trimaran designed hulls.

The overall size of these craft reflect the trade and the need to also carry a number of private/ passenger vehicles. Generally, freight wagons tend to operate with cargo only mono hull ferries operating out of freight terminal ports.

*Figure 6.32   Example profile of a typical Catamaran the "Sea Cat Isle of Man" which operates on the Irish Sea routes with the Isle of Man Steam Packet Company. The vessel incorporates a stern door/vehicle ramp to accommodate vehicle traffic (85 cars) as well as 432 passengers. Operational speeds of these craft tend to be in excess of 36 knots. Many being fitted with forward viewing, night vision equipment (NVE) and camera recording devices.*

### HSC Categories

The IMO, HSC code was introduced in 1994 and had mandatory implementation in 1996. Under the auspices of the code, High Speed Craft were placed into one of three categories:—

### Category "A" Craft

Is defined as any high speed passenger craft, carrying not more than 450 passengers, operating on a route where it has been demonstrated to the satisfaction of the flag or port state that there is a high probability that in the event of an evacuation at any point of the route, all passengers and crew can be rescued safely with the least of:

  (i) The time to prevent persons in survival craft from exposure causing hypothermia in the worst intended conditions.

 (ii) The time appropriate with respect to environmental conditions and geographical features of the route.

(iii) Four hours.

### Category "B" Class

Is defined as any high speed passenger craft other than a Category "A" craft, with machinery and safety systems arranged such that, in the event of damage, disabling any essential machinery and safety systems, in one compartment, the craft retains the capability to navigate safely.

### A Cargo Craft Class

Is defined as any high speed craft other than a passenger craft and which is capable of maintaining the main functions and safety systems of unaffected spaces, after damage in any one compartment on board.

## Maximum Speed Formula

Speed must be equal to, or exceed $3.7 \times$ the displacement corresponding to the design waterline in metres cubed, raised to the power of 0.1667 (metres per sec).

Applicable to most types of craft, corresponds to a volumetric Froude number greater than 0.45.

## Survey of HSC

Each craft is subject to the following surveys:—

(a) An initial survey before the craft is put in service or before the Certificate is issued for the first time.
(b) A renewal survey at intervals specified by the Administration but not exceeding 5 years (Notable exemptions where a renewal survey has taken place 3 months before the expiry date, or where the craft is not in a place of survey, a 1 month extension may be granted)
(c) A periodical survey within 3 months before or after each anniversary date of the certificate.
(d) An additional survey as the occasion arises.

## Catamaran Profile

*Figure 6.33    The fine lines of "Speedrunner 1", Aluminium and composite construction, operating as a high speed passenger ferry in the waters of the Mediterranean. Seen moored alongside in the Greek port of Piraeus.*

## Multi Hull Constructions

Many ship builders are exploring and expanding into multi-hull constructions, especially those in and around the High Speed Craft sector. Catamarans and tri-marans are typical current new builds. These vessels, often being constructed in lightweight aluminium alloys and form lines providing inherent stability with wave piecing capability.

**Amidship's Cross Section: Tri-maran (Length 120 m × 26 m Beam)**

**Custom Aluminium Light Weight Construction**

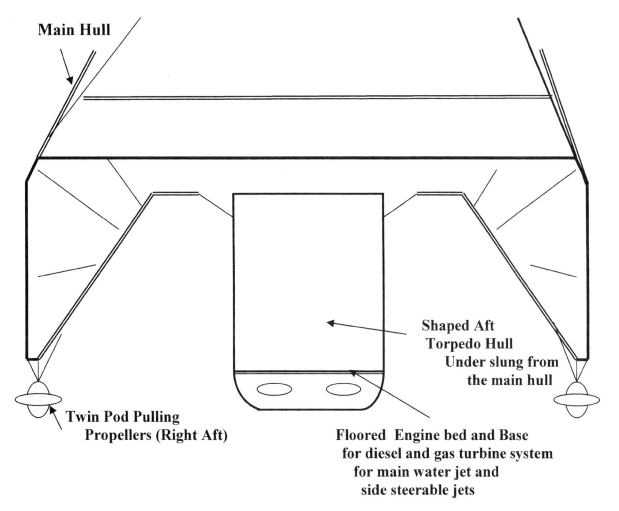

**Main Hull**

**Shaped Aft
Torpedo Hull
Under slung from
the main hull**

**Twin Pod Pulling
Propellers (Right Aft)**

**Floored  Engine bed and Base
for diesel and gas turbine system
for main water jet and
side steerable jets**

*Figure 6.34*

Tri-maran hull based on builds by Austal Ships & Rodriquez Cantieri Navali of Italy. It is powered by three propulsors, namely a central water jet and two lateral steerable jets producing a service speed of 35 knots. Its design incorporates an arrow shaped cargo deck with Ro-Ro capacity for 60 vehicles and accommodation for 450 passengers

The modern design is based on an air cavity system (ACS) that combined with a narrow centre hull producing less wave resistance and reduces hull friction because of minimum wetted surface area. Hydrodynamic efficiency is achieved by the injection of air below the underside of the hull and between the water surface. The air is contained by a steel skirt arrangement causing a glide action through the water, so reducing drag effects by between 5% to 15% while reducing fuel burn at the same time.

**Hydrofoil Construction**

*Figure 6.35    The lower hull supporting, struts set either side to the bow and quarter regions of the hull. Tyre Fender supports, are also seen either side in the shoulder and off the port quarter of a high speed hydrofoil seen at sea. Prominent bow flare is often a feature of such craft often engaged on the "plane" in excess of 45 knots.*

**Hydrofoils**

Hydrofoil craft are probably those vessels that sowed the seeds of the High Speed Craft code as we know it today. The vessels themselves were limited on size and subsequent payload which could well explain why few if any are being currently built. The principle of operation is to lift the hull onto "Foils" clear of the surface. This action removes hull friction and drag effect with the sea surface, allowing an overall increased speed.

Unfortunately, this type of craft, although fast, can be an uncomfortable ride when compared to the larger craft like the SEACATS. As such passenger comfort has dictated the style of tomorrows building. They generally carry no more than 200 passengers but an average figure would probably be more like 100-150 at speeds upto about 40 knots. They were usually operated by high speed propellers, but the later varieties are more commonly operated by "Jetfoil Propulsion" and reflect speeds of 40-50 knots.

Heavy seas can restrict operation and generate noise and vibration peculiarities. Popular areas of activity are the Mediterranean, Hong Kong, Australia and the West Coast USA, though other areas like the Caribbean have some history of hydrofoils.

The action of the hydrofoil is one of an on the "plane craft" where once the hull is riding on the foils, its displacement is virtually zero. When stopped, the hull experiences similar buoyancy and gravitational forces as any other mono hull. When operational, the speed of the vessel can be compared to an aircraft taking off using excessive power to gain altitude. In this case the faster the craft can gain speed the sooner the hull is raised onto the foils. This effectively raises the hull above the surface and removes hull friction, leaving only the foils lifting area, immersed. The buoyancy forces are so removed and hydrodynamic forces support the craft on the foils.

There are different types of foils in operation, some are fitted with "flaps" similar to aircraft wings, to facilitate control. However, they generally fall into two categories, namely:— "Fully Submerged Foils" and "Surface Piercing Foils".

**Waterjet Propulsion**

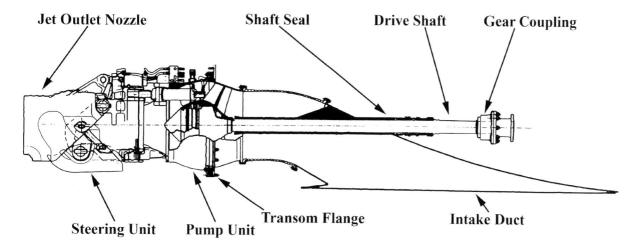

*Figure 6.36*

Many ferries are now fitted with 2, 3 or 4 waterjets in addition to main engine propulsion. The additional power and manoeuvrability achieved with these units has become widely accepted through the industry especially in the High Speed Craft sector.

Different manufacturers lend to specific designs but the advantages and features of the units are generally common. The MJP Waterjets, for example, are manufactured in stainless steel castings with intake diameters of between 450-1350 mm capable of delivering an engine brake power from 500 to 10,000 kW.

A high thrust pump unit operates on comparatively lower fuel consumption which also produces a high reverse thrust capability. They are fitted with a full electro/hydraulic control package which provides alternative steering, auto pilot, wing stations and various RPM interfaces.

Special features include a flexible drive shaft allowing $+/- 0.25°$ to take account of movement within the ship's structure when underway. Hydraulic rams provide a steering angle of $+/-30°$ in a rapid response time, while the reverse bucket mechanism is said to achieve full astern from full ahead (or vice versa) in 5 seconds. (Model MJP650)

**Waterjets – General and Operational Arrangement**

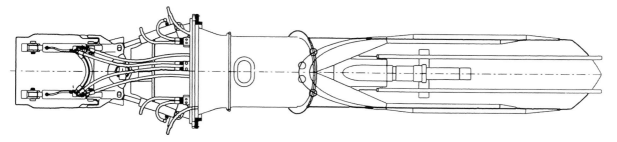

*Figure 6.37*

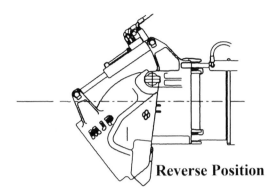

**Reverse Position**

*Figure 6.38*

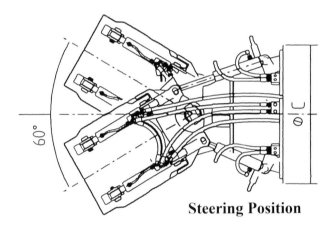

**Steering Position**

*Figure 6.39*

# CHAPTER SEVEN

# Oil, Gas and Chemical Tankers: Constructional Features

## Introduction

A great proportion of the worlds shipping is in liquid cargoes and tankers form a large percentage of commercial shipping. It would be remiss not to include details of this specific characteristic of the industry and high light key operational, on board features of these dominant ships.

With the introduction of the Common Structural Rules and the requirements to build double hull vessels this sector has experienced major change to its building programmes. Oil tanker vessels with crude oil washing, must operate with inert gas systems, while the double hulls go some way to align with the cleaner seas, safer ships requirement of the International Safety Management Systems currently exercised.

These vessels are designed with several alternative tank configurations and built with a variety of choice on pipeline systems. All constructions incorporate safety levels in the event of fire or pollution emergencies. Mooring systems can be specialised to suit the trade of loading/discharging at terminals, floating, production storage platforms, or offshore Single Buoy Moorings. The massive VLCC to the smaller shuttle tanker are all encompassed under this same umbrella of the carriage of "Liquid Cargoes".

The recent expansion in the building of Gas Carriers has enlarged this umbrella to take account of major new building for the movement of LNG and LPG. Alongside this development, the transport of chemicals in bulk, has also seen a notable increase in tonnage and has jointly enlarged this sector of the industry.

Tank designs have changed over the years and continue to be at the forefront of technology. Ice strengthening has also become a regular feature of these ships, since the potential development of the Arctic Ocean is expected to yield massive deposits of natural resources. The many facets of the offshore sector is influencing the small and larger builders within the construction industry, from anchor handling and supply to the ULCC and the smaller product carriers. All shipyards around the globe are experiencing full order books 2005-2010. The ramifications are new designs, improved systems and modernisation throughout the shipbuilding industry.

## Tanker Vessels

Tankers form a large sector of the worlds merchant fleet. They tend to come in all sizes from the massive VLCC, and ULCC down to the smaller shuttle coastal type vessel. The products they carry are varied and range from crude oil to wine, orange juice to chemicals. Various cargoes are carried at different temperatures and the vessels are equipped with ventilation and temperature control systems to suit the product.

Legislation has now made it compulsory that all oil tankers are constructed with double hull integrity to reduce the risk of pollution. They are also equipped with monitoring systems for loading and discharge together with anti-pollution equipment as standard, in order to be compliant with MARPOL requirements.

Oil tankers must specifically be fitted with an inert gas system and oil in water separators Large vessels must also be fitted with emergency towing arrangements.

*Figure 7.1    The oil tanker "Folesandros" lies alongside the oil berth in Gibraltar, while discharging cargo.*

## Oil Tanker Profile

*Figure 7.2    A large oil tanker seen in the Mediterranean Sea. Prominent features include the Bulbous Bow and all accommodation aft. An amidships crane position is used for lifting connection oil pipes aboard in way of the manifold.*

**Double Hull Tanker Design Example**

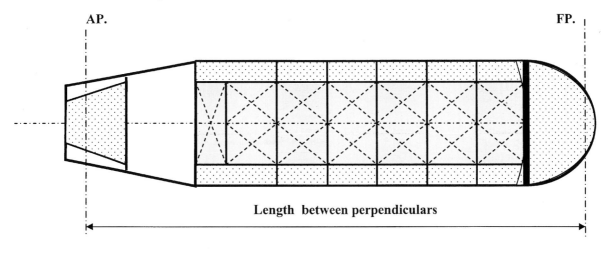

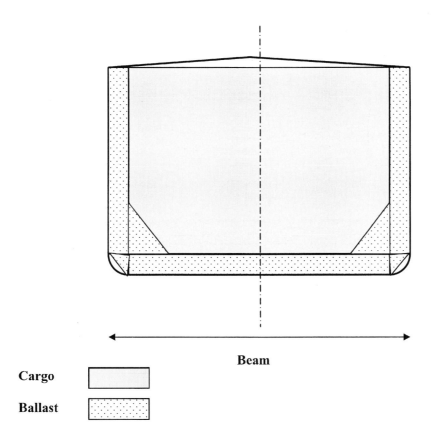

*Figure 7.3 Double hull design example for deadweight of 150,000 dwt.*

**Double Hull Tanker Configuration**

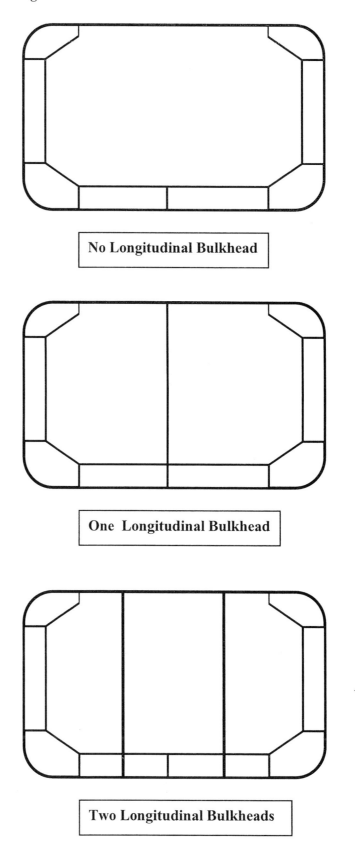

*Figure 7.4*

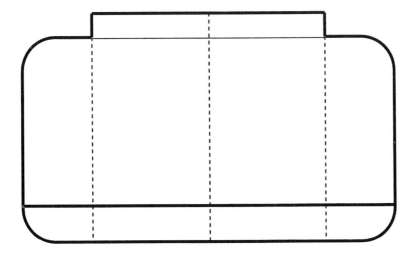

**Trunk deck in association with longitudinal bulkheads**

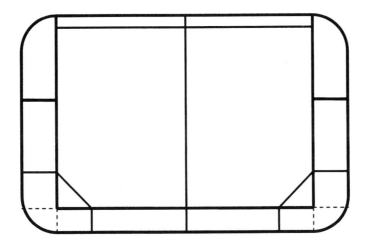

**Double deck in association with a centre line bulkhead**

*Figure 7.5*

**Structural Terminology Associated with Tanker Design**

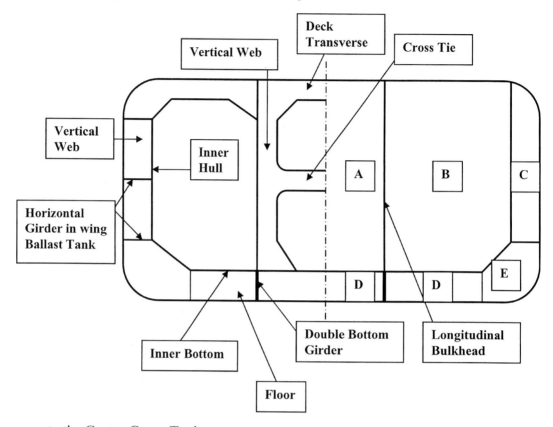

A represents the Centre Cargo Tank
B represents the Wing Cargo Tank
C represents the Wing Ballast Tank
D represents the Double Bottom Ballast Tanks
E represents the Hopper Tank.

*Figure 7.6*

**Wing Tank Alternative Construction**

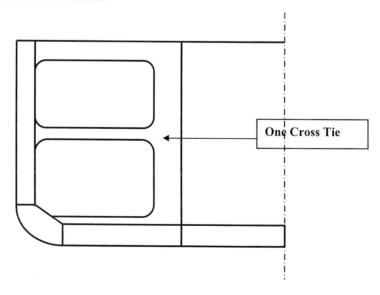

*Figure 7.7*

## Constructional Features of Tankers

Specialist vessels like tankers have specific constructional requirements and the main items are listed below for ships designed to carry crude oil and petroleum products which have a closed flash-point, not exceeding 60°C and a Reid vapour pressure below atmospheric pressure, or other liquids having a similar fire hazard. (Not applicable to chemical tankers and gas carriers)

Machinery spaces shall be positioned aft of Cargo Tanks and Slop Tanks and must be separated from them by a cofferdam, cargo pump room, oil fuel bunker tank or permanent ballast tank.

Except as otherwise specified by regulations 3, 4, and 5, accommodation spaces, control stations, cargo control rooms and service spaces must be positioned aft of cargo tanks and slop tanks, pump rooms or cofferdams, which separate the cargo tanks.

Navigation spaces may be positioned over cargo tanks and slop tanks, provided they are used only for navigation purposes and are separated from the upper deck by an open space of a height not less than two (2) metres.

Means must be provided to isolate oil spills on the upper deck from accommodation and service spaces. This must also account for stern cargo handling facilities.

The cargo tank venting system must be independent from any other ventilation arrangement, for any other compartment.

Cargo pump rooms shall be mechanically ventilated and discharges from exhaust fans must be led to a safe place over the open deck so as not to allow an accumulation of flammable vapours. The number of changes of air, per hour, shall be at least 20.

Cargo pump rooms and double hull spaces must be provided with a fixed gas detection system to include pipe ducts and cofferdams. The monitoring system for double hull spaces may be by flexible gas sampling hoses, but if not considered reliable, then such spaces must be fitted with permanent gas sampling lines.

Double hull spaces inclusive of double bottoms must be fitted with suitable connections for the supply of air. Where a vessel is fitted with an inert gas system, suitable connections must be made to supply inert gas to the double hull spaces.

Access to cofferdams, ballast tanks, cargo tanks and other spaces in the cargo area shall be direct from the open deck.

Access points through manholes, hatches or horizontal openings must be of sufficient size to permit the passage of a person wearing breathing apparatus.

**Double Hull (Athwartship's Section) of a New Build Tanker Vessel**

*Figure 7.8   Longitudinally framed section through modern tanker seen during its building stage. The completed section will then be transported by module, multi axle shipyard, mobile platform, to the assembly slipway.*

**ULCC Tanker General Perception**

*Figure 7.9   The largest man made mobile transport in the world is the "Jahre Viking", which is 564,000 dwt. Seen manoeuvring with tugs off the Dubai, Dry Dock complex. This vessel has recently been de-commissioned and is to become a floating oil storage unit.*

**Half Section of a VLCC Double Hull Tanker**

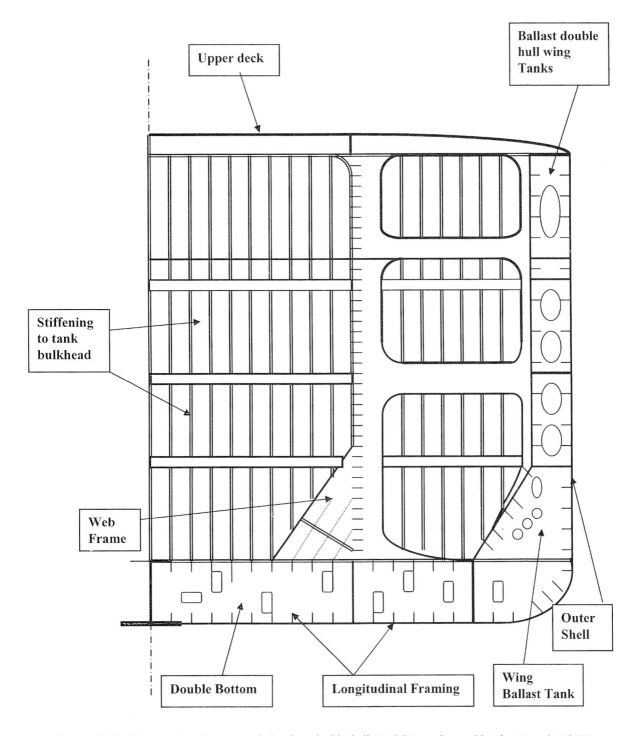

*Figure 7.10   Diagram based on one of the first double hull VLCC's in the world. The "Epoch-MkII" structure built by "Hitachi Zosen" in 1993. Section shown is in way of the amidship's section of the foredeck.*

## Additional Regulatory Requirements – Oil Tankers

Tankers must now comply with the following requirements:—

(1) Must have Cargo Pump Bearing Temperature monitoring systems in place.
(SOLAS II-2, Regulation 4, 5, 10.1)
(2) Must have Cargo Tank Pressure monitoring systems.
(SOLAS II-2, Regulation 59/IBC Code)
(3) Must have Cargo Pump Room, Gas detection/Bilge Alarm systems in place.
(SOLAS II-2, Regulation 4, 5, 10.3/4
(4) Must have Fixed Ballast/Void, Gas and H2S gas detection inside pumprooms.
(5) Must have a High Level and Overfill alarm system.
(USCG Regulation 39)

**NB.** These vessels must now also carry Emergency Escape Breathing Devices (EEBD's) placed in strategic locations, e.g. Pump Rooms. (SOLAS II-2)

Additionally they must carry portable measuring instruments for measuring oxygen and flammable vapour concentrations.

## Tanker Pipelines

There are three basic types of pipeline systems:—

(1) Direct system,
(2) Ring main system,
(3) Free flow system.

Each system has their uses and are designed to fulfil a need in a particular type of vessel.

## The Direct System

This is the simplest type of pipeline system which uses fewer valves than the others. It takes oil directly from the tank to the pump and so reduces friction. This has an effect of increasing the rate of discharge and at the same time improves the tank suction. It is cheaper to install and maintain than the ring main system because there is less pipeline length and with fewer valves less likelihood of malfunction. However, the layout is not as versatile as a ring main system and problems in the event of faulty valves or leaking pipelines could prove more difficult to circumvent. Also the washing is more difficult since there is no circular system and the washings must be flushed into the tanks.

The advantages are:

(a) It is easy to operate and less training of personnel is required.
(b) As there are fewer valves it takes less time to set up the valve system before commencing a cargo operation.
(c) Contamination is unlikely, as it is easy to isolate each section.

The dis-advantages are:

(a) It is a very inflexible system which makes it difficult to plan for a multi-port discharge.
(b) Block stowage has to be used which makes it difficult to control "trim".
(c) Carrying more than three parcels concurrently can be difficult.

**Direct Line System**

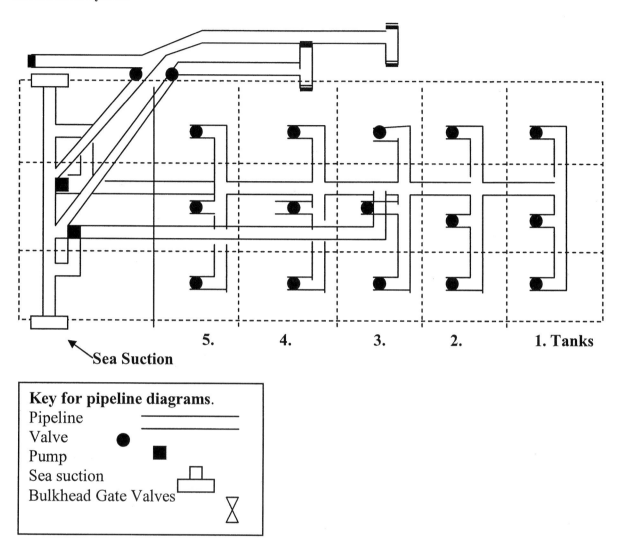

**Sea Suction**

5.     4.     3.     2.     1. **Tanks**

**Key for pipeline diagrams.**
Pipeline
Valve
Pump
Sea suction
Bulkhead Gate Valves

*Figure 7.11*

Used mainly on crude and black oil tankers where separation of oil grades is not so important.

*Figure 7.12   Direct pipe line system seen on the deck of an oil tanker while in dry dock.*

*Figure 7.13   Manifold connections for load/discharge operations. Seen on the deck of an oil tanker while in the dry dock at Lisnave, Portugal.*

## The Ring Main System

This is basically a ring from the pump room around the ship, with cross over lines at each set of tanks. There are various designs usually involving more than one ring. It is extensively employed on "Product Tankers" where the system allows many grades of cargo to be carried without contamination. This is a highly versatile system which permits several different combinations of pump and line for any particular tank.

The advantages of the system are:

(a) Cargoes can be more easily split into smaller units and placed in various parts of the ship.
(b) Line washing is more complete.
(c) A greater number of different parcels of cargo can be carried.
(d) Trim and stress can be more easily controlled.

The dis-advantages are:

(a) Because of the more complicated pipeline and valve layout, better training in cargo separation is required.
(b) Contamination is far more likely if valves are incorrectly set.
(c) Fairly low pumping rates are achieved.
(d) Costs of installation and maintenance are higher because of more pipeline and an increased number of valves.

## Ring Main System, Pump Room Aft

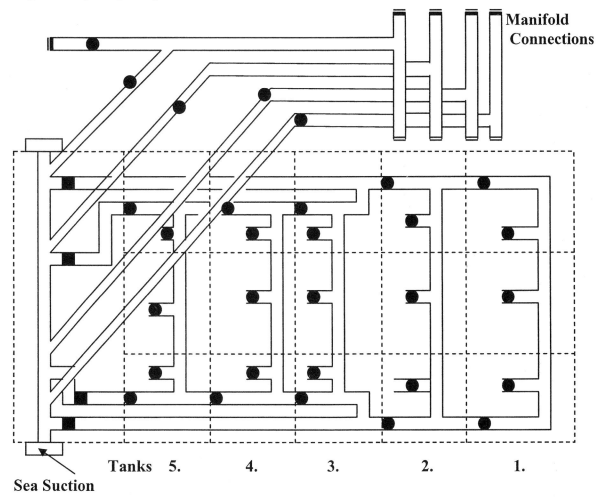

Figure 7.14

**Pipe Line and Deck Connection Example**

*Figure 7.15    An example of a branch pipe line and associated deck connections seen on board a tanker vessel. Bracket supports and over pass walk way are also seen.*

**The Free Flow System**

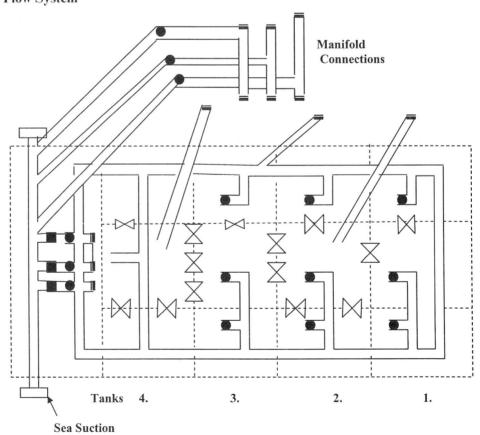

*Figure 7.16*

The "Free Flow System" employs sluice valves in the tank bulkheads rather than pipelines. With a stern trim this system can discharge all the cargo from the aftermost tank via direct lines to the pump room. The result is that a very high speed of discharge can be achieved and as such, is suitable for large crude carriers with a single grade cargo. Tank drainage is also very efficient since the bulkhead valves allow the oil to flow aft easily. There are fewer tanks with this system and it has increased numbers of sluice valves the farther aft you go. The increased number of sluices is a feature to handle the increased volume being allowed to pass from one tank to another.

The main advantage is that a very high rate of discharge is possible with few pipelines and limited losses to friction. The main dis-advantage being that overflows are possible if the cargo levels in all tanks are not carefully monitored.

## Pipeline Arrangements

*Figure 7.17    The pipeline arrangement seen on the laden BP tanker "British Reliance".*

**Inert Gas System**

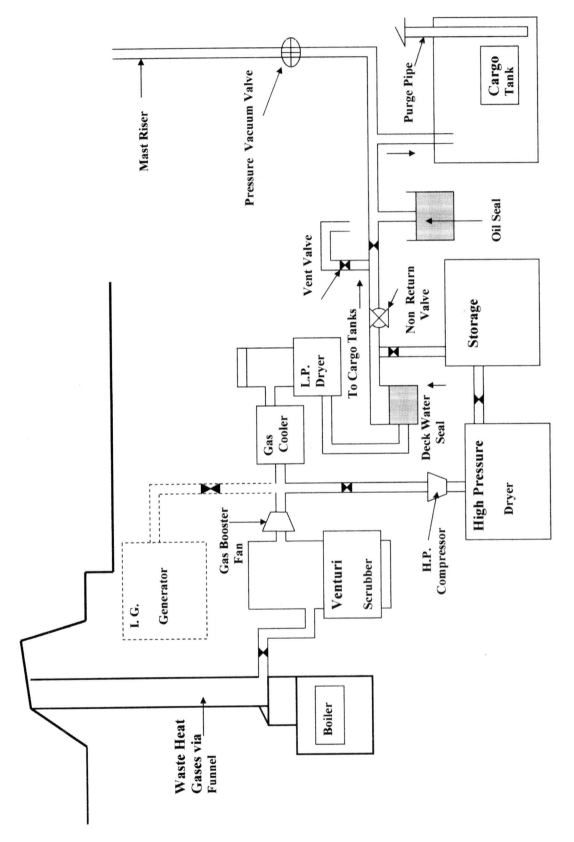

*Figure 7.18*

## Alarm Systems with Inert Gas Operations

Audible and visual alarms for the following:—

1. Low water level in the deck water seal.
2. Low water flow rate to the scrubber.
3. Scrubber water level to high.
4. High Gas temperature at the blower discharge.
5. Blower failure.
6. Low gas pressure in the supply line.
7. High gas pressure in the supply line.
8. Oxygen content to high.
9. Power failure to the gas regulating valve.

## Advantages and Disadvantages of the Inert Gas System

### Advantages
1. A safe tank atmosphere is achieved which is non-explosive.
2. It allows high pressure tank washing and reduces tank cleaning time.
3. It allows crude oil washing.
4. Reduces corrosion in tanks with an efficient scrubber in the system.
5. Improves stripping efficiency and reduces discharge time.
6. Aids the safe gas freeing of tanks.
7. It is economical to operate.
8. It forms a readily available extinguishing agent for other spaces.
9. Reduces the loss of cargo through evaporation.
10. Complies with legislation and reduces insurance premiums.

### Disadvantages
1. Additional costs for installation.
2. Maintenance costs are incurred.
3. Low visibility inside tanks.
4. With low oxygen content, tank access is denied.
5. Could lead to contamination of high grade products.
6. Moisture and sulphur content corrodes equipment.
7. An established reverse route for cargo to enter the engine room.
8. Oxygen content must be monitored and alarm sensed at all times.
9. Instrumentation failure could effect fail safe devices putting the ship at risk through the I.G. system.
10. An additional gas generator is required in the system in the absence of waste heat products from boiler flue gases.

**NB.** Instrumentation of the system to cover:—

Inert gas temperature pressure read outs and recorders.

Alarms for: Blower failure, high oxygen content alarm, high and low gas pressure alarms, high gas temperature, low sea water pressure and low level alarm in the scrubber and the deck water seal respectively.

**Deck Water Seal Operation**

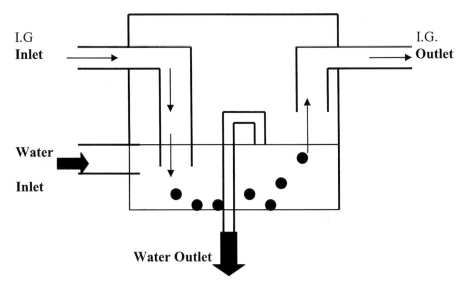

*Figure 7.19*

The water level in the seal is maintained by constant running of the sea water pump and a gooseneck drain system. Under normal I.G. pressure the inert gas will bubble through the liquid from the bottom of the I.G. inlet pipe and exit under normal operating pressure.

In the event a back pressure did develop and the water surface experienced increased pressure, this would force the water level up the I.G. inlet pipe sealing this pipe entrance and preventing hydrocarbons entering the scrubber.

**Tanker Operational Features**

*Figure 7.20   Use of the oil hose handling crane would be employed as with SBM, or floating storage unit (FSU) operations. The above view shows a floating oil pipeline which is connected to a shuttle tankers manifold once recovered via its pick up buoys. The tanker connects to the FSU by taking on board the heavy duty moorings.*

**Oil Hose Handling Crane**

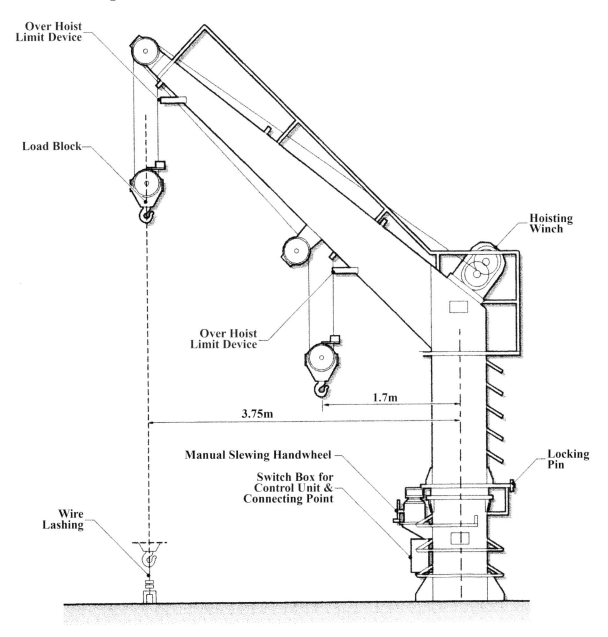

*Figure 7.21    Oil hose handling crane employed to connect pipelines to manifolds.*

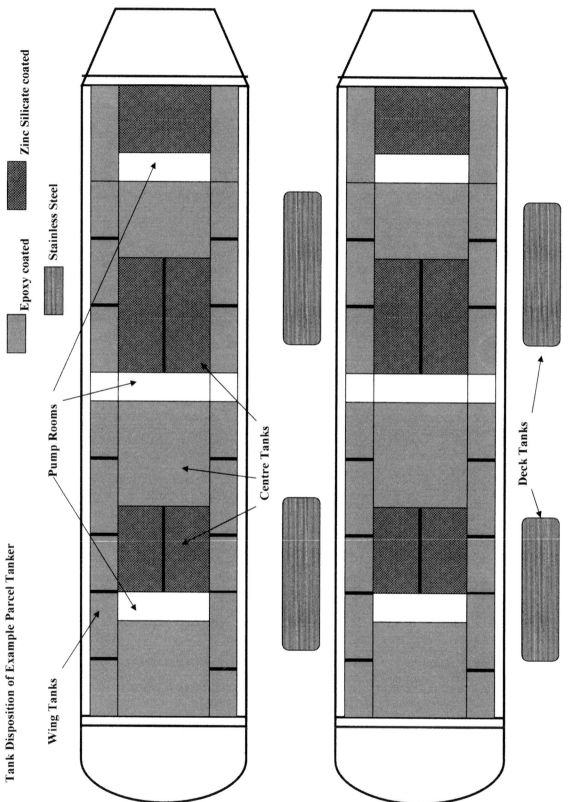

Figure 7.22

**Building for and Shipping of LNG**

There are basically two types of tank systems engaged in the transport of LNG, namely the spherical Moss tank design and the Membrane type.

**Moss Tanks**

The Moss design is a self supporting tank which is normally constructed in aluminium and is free of internal structure. They are fitted with a cylindrical, metallic, flexible expanding skirt. The skirt acts to support the tank around the mid part and is welded to the ship's hull.

Tanks are covered by an insulation and a protective coat of aluminium foil. The insulation space is fitted with gas detection monitors and is regularly purged with nitrogen. Failure in the system is unlikely and a second barrier is generally not used, although a drip tray is fitted to prevent any contact with the tank top.

**Membrane Tanks**

There are three types of membrane tanks, one is the GazTransport type, the second is the Technigaz System and the more recent one, is a combination of the first two. The build tends to employ a flexible steel membrane (approximately 1 mm thickness) as a cargo containment barrier. The membrane being supported by a total coverage of insulation attached to the double hull of the vessel. The system employs both a primary and secondary membrane. The secondary membrane being capable of containing the cargo for several days in the event of a failure of the primary membrane.

Full insulation is contained between the primary and secondary membranes and also between the secondary membrane and the ship's inner hull. Each space is fitted with gas and temperature monitors and can be purged with nitrogen.

The GazTransport system uses a primary membrane of flat panels in invar, against the Technigaz system which employs a corrugated stainless steel membrane. The CS1 system combines its construction from both these designs.

About 70% of the vessels currently under construction are of the membrane design. These vessels are comparatively, a smaller ship but having the same payload capacity as an equivalent Moss designed vessel. Under construction, the membrane vessels would use less steel and subsequently deliver a reduced air draught than the Moss tank designs. This provides cost savings in lower tonnage taxes and canal transit fees.

The LNG sector remains probably the only shipping area, still operating with steam ships. Vessels are being constructed to carry upto 250,000 $M^3$ and also being fitted with reliquefaction plants to use boil-off gas, as a means of propulsion.

## Carriage of Liquefied Natural Gas

*Figure 7.23   Two LNG vessels lie alongside each other at the Dubai Shipyard complex. The vessels are prominent by the cargo dome structures familiar to the deck. Deck fittings are clearly identified including the inspection walkways ranging from the Navigation bridge region to the forward mooring deck regions.*

## Gas Tank Construction (Based on Moss Design)

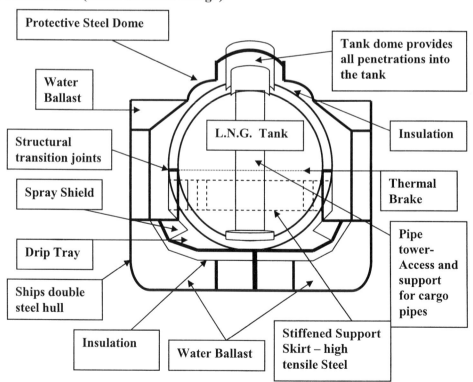

*Figure 7.24   Fully refrigerated spherical LNG tank, the protective steel dome protects the primary barrier above the upper deck. (No secondary barrier)*

**NB.** Prismatic tanks, fully refrigerated, carrying cargo at atmospheric pressure, require a primary and secondary barrier to resist undetermined design stresses. The space between the primary and the secondary barriers is known as "hold space" and is filled with inert gas to prevent a flammable atmosphere being generated, in the event of cargo leakage.

Double hull construction is required in way of all cargo tank spaces.

**Gas Carrier is defined as** – a tanker constructed or adapted and used for the carriage in bulk, of liquefied gas or certain other substances of a flammable nature as listed in Chapter 19 of the IGC.

Vessels carrying "Liquefied Gases in Bulk" are designed to meet the most stringent of regulations as per the International Code for the Construction and Equipment of Ships Carrying Liquefied Gases in Bulk, more commonly referred to as the IGC code.

Gas cargoes are carried at either fully pressurised, semi-pressurised and semi-refrigerated or fully refrigerated depending on the nature of the gas commodity being carried.

**Cargo Containment**

Containment of cargo is achieved by the use of integral tanks which form a structural part of the vessel (as with any tanker). They are usually employed for gas products where the hull structural temperature will not fall below $-10°C$. Cargo Tanks are well insulated.

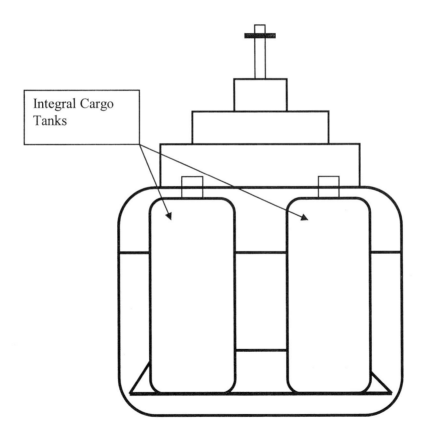

*Figure 7.25*

**LNG Gas Carrier Profile**

*Figure 7.26    The Gas Tanker Al Ashtan seen lying at anchor.*

**Corner Section of Membrane Tank Structure (Based on Technigaz System)**

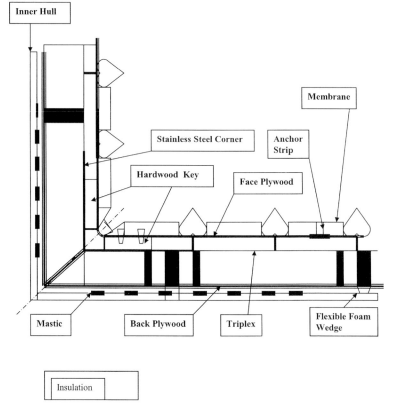

*Figure 7.27*

**Membrane Tanks**

Membrane tanks are now probably the most popular type of build of LNG carrier construction today.

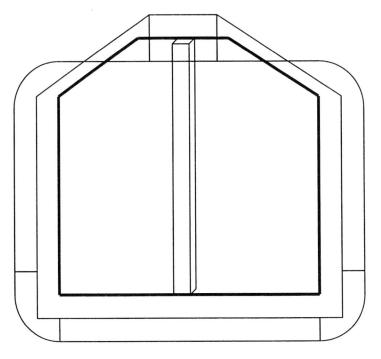

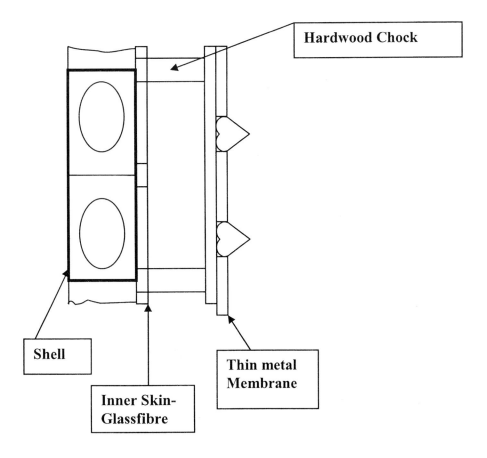

*Figure 7.28*

**Classification – Chemical Carriers**

(chapter references to the International Code for the Construction and Equipment of ships carrying Dangerous Chemicals in Bulk) (IBC)

In general ships carrying chemicals in bulk are classed into three types:—

1. **A "Type 1" ship**, is a chemical tanker intended to transport chapter 17 products with very severe environmental and safety hazards which require maximum preventive measures to preclude an escape of such cargo
    (Maximum tank size 1,250 m$^3$)

2. **A "Type 2" ship**, is a chemical tanker intended to transport chapter 17 products with appreciably severe environmental and safety hazards which require significant preventive measures to preclude an escape of such cargo.
    (Maximum tank size 3,000 m$^3$)

3. **A "Type 3" ship**, is a chemical tanker intended to transport chapter 17 products with sufficiently severe environmental and safety hazards which require a moderate degree of containment to increase survival capability in a damaged condition. Designed for the least hazardous cargoes, but these cargoes may possess some toxicity and reactivity.

Many of the cargoes carried in these ships must be considered as extremely dangerous and as such the structure of the ship's hull is considered in the light of the potential danger, which might result from damage to the transport vessel. Type III ships are similar to product tankers in that they have double hulls but have a greater sub-division requirement. Where as Types I and II ships, must have there cargo tanks located at specific distances inboard to reduce the possibility of impact load directly onto the cargo tank.

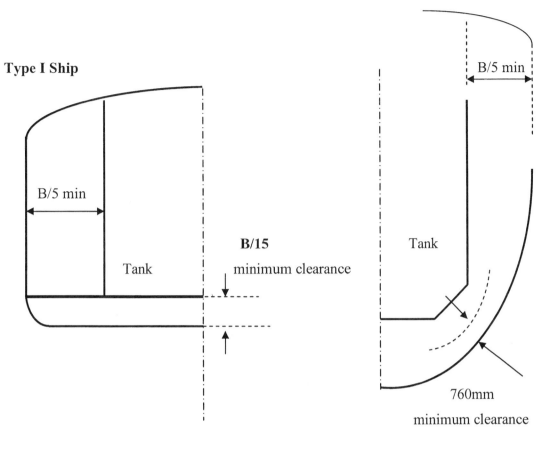

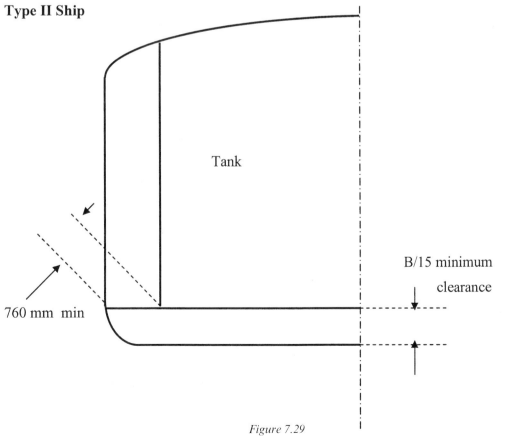

*Figure 7.29*

**Tank Plan (All Types)**

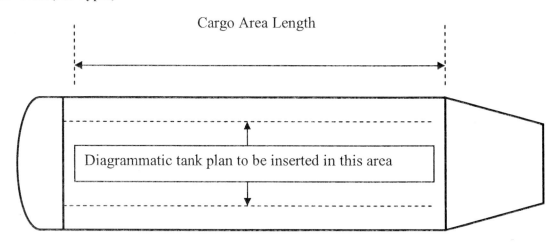

*Figure 7.30*

The tank arrangement must be attached to the International Certificate of Fitness, for the carriage of Dangerous Chemicals in Bulk.


**Parcel Tankers – Construction Features**

Ships built specifically as parcel tankers with the intention of carrying a wide variety of cargoes will generally have some tanks of "stainless steel" or tanks clad in stainless steel.

For reasons of construction and cost this means having a double skin. Mild steel tanks may similarly be built with side cofferdams and a double bottom and are usually coated in either epoxy or silicate. Chemicals of high density like "ethylene dibromide" may have specially constructed tanks or in some cases only carry partly filled cargo tanks.

Similarly, cargoes with higher vapour pressures may generate a need for tanks to be constructed to withstand higher pressures than say the conventional tanker. Particularly relevant where the boiling point of the more volatile cargoes is raised and the risk of loss is increased.

The IBC code specifies requirements for safety equipment to monitor vapour detection, fire protection, ventilation in cargo handling spaces, gauging and tank filling. Once all criteria is met the Marine Authority (MCA in the United Kingdom) will issue, on application an MCA/IMO Certificate of Fitness for the carriage of Dangerous Cargoes in Bulk.


**Vapour Lines**

In general each tank will have its own vapour line fitted with Pressure Vacuum (P/V) valves, but grouped tanks may have a common line. Since some vapours from specific cargoes are highly toxic, or flammable, the lines are led well over accommodation and are expected to release vapour as near as possible in a vertical direction. Some vessels carry provision to return vapour expelled during the loading process to the shore side tank. Examples are when the cargo is highly toxic or the chemicals react dangerously with air.


**Main Hazards Associated with Chemicals to Humans**

The substances carried in chemical tankers present certain hazards to operations of transport and to the crews of the ships. The main hazards fall into one of a combination of the following:—

   (a) Danger to health toxicity and irritant characteristics of the substance or vapour.
   (b) Water pollution aspect – human toxicity of the substance in the solution.
   (c) Reactionary activity with water or other chemicals.
   (d) Fire and/or explosion hazard.

# CHAPTER EIGHT

# Constructional Features: Bulk, General and Container Dry Cargo Vessels

## Introduction

Although the tanker element of shipping is large, it is not a stand alone sector and has the dry cargo vessels as close relations. Commodities in bulk are shipped in many forms, including cereals, coal, ore, concentrates, sugar, etc., The dry cargo sector also includes the shipping of manufactured goods which are mostly transported by containers, though some break bulk general cargo ships are still operational.

Container ships came on the back of general cargo vessels and have expanded into an enormous shipping sector providing door to door service for a variety of goods. There are few goods these days, that cannot be containerised and shipped on a designated container vessel. Even specialised fluids, like whiskey, can be transported in (liquid) tank containers. These vessels which have already broken through the 13,000 teu size, tend to trade directly between container terminals. As such they have little need for their own lifting gear, though some of the smaller transports carry their own container lifting facilities.

Dry cargo ships, sadly came along with, during and after the slave trade, when commerce saw development as part of the industrial revolution. Everything was shipped, from bagged cocoa to livestock, machine parts to confectionary, trade and shipping exploded alongside the steel world of shipbuilding.

Riveted structures carried every form of dry cargo in tween decks and in cargo holds as well as on deck. Timber and tobacco, ingots and mails were all transported by sea. Welding superseded riveting, and container ships started to dominate the dry cargo markets. So much so, that general cargo ships have become the poor relation of the dry cargo sector. Some specialization has gone some way to cushion its demise, by way of heavy lift ships, reefers and paper product carriers as successful prime examples.

Ship building for the dry cargo market has been continuous but has clearly not been on a par with the gas expansion, the passenger market development or the container increase. However, new buildings still carry regular features, such as hatch tops and coamings, mast structures and lifting gear. Ventilation systems may differ, but double bottoms stay very much double bottoms. While deck cranes are prolific, derricks are scarce, but never the less, are still to be found.

## Bulk Carriers

As with many sectors within the shipping industry, bulk carriers have experienced new trends to conform with revised and new legislation. Double hulls have become the order of the day alongside cost effectiveness. Cargoes of coal, iron ore, grain, minerals and fertilisers are all common to this type of vessel and modern cargo handling systems together with innovative building has reduced costly time in port.

Smooth cargo hold sides and self trimming designs tend to speed up turn rounds to deliver reduced voyage time. This effectually allows additional voyages to be made annually and goes some way to compensating for the reduced cargo capacity incurred because of the double hull.

New builds are required to conform to the new Common Structural Rules (CSR) being applied to double hull tankers over 150 m or more and bulk carriers. They must also comply with the

Inspection and Survey regime under the SOLAS convention and fit Hull Stress Monitoring Systems (MSC/Circ, 646 June 1994 and MGN 108 M)

**Features of the Bulk Carrier**

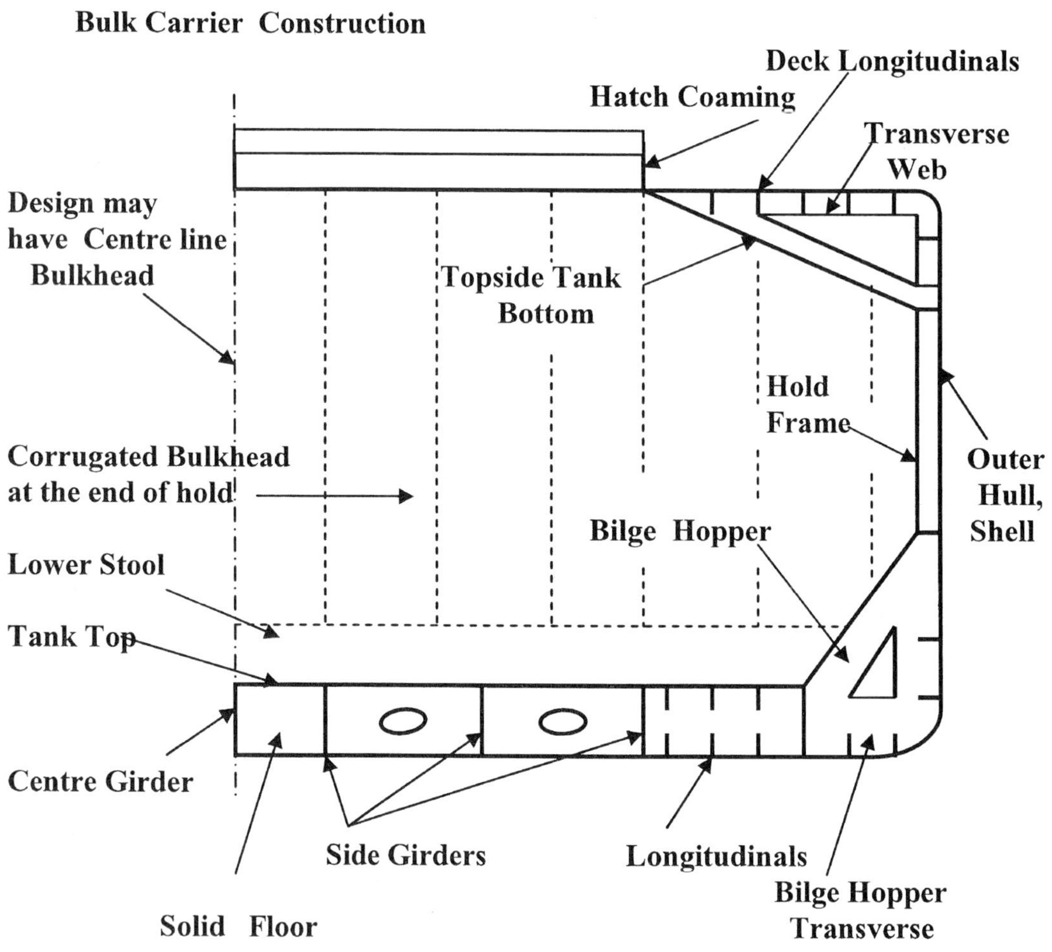

### Bulk Carrier Construction

*Figure 8.1*

**NB.** Framing on bulk carriers is designed as a longitudinal system in topside and double bottom tanks and as a transverse system at the cargo hold and side shell positions.

These ships usually have a large active ballasting role and new builds are now being constructed to incorporate *Ballast Water Treatment Plants. These systems must meet the ballast water performance standards required by the regulations delivered from the international convention for the Control and Monitoring of Ship's Ballast Water and Sediments. (Known as the BWM Convention)

**Outline of Double Hull Bulk Carrier design**

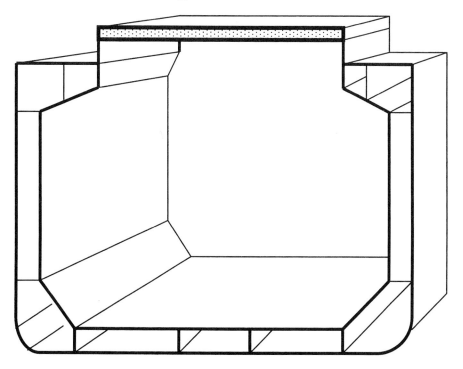

*Figure 8.2    Diamond 53, design complete double hull in way of cargo holds.*

The double hull types have inherent strength which allows flexible loading patterns, which will increase capacity for heavy load density cargoes like steel coils. The design dispenses with exposed side frames in the holds and presents a flush side and hold ceiling for cargoes. Such flush features have distinct advantages for hold cleaning and cargo working options with bulk commodities.

The double design also provides a perceived safer protection against water ingress and is therefore seen as being more environmentally friendly in comparison with the single hull types. Tank arrangements permit a large water ballast capacity, in both double bottoms and side tanks, eliminating the need to input ballast into cargo spaces, in the event of heavy weather.

**Bulk Carrier Designs and Hatch Coverings**

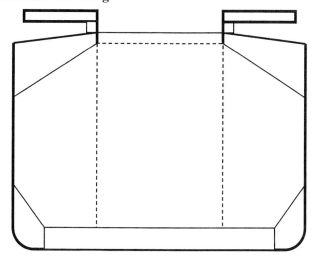

*Figure 8.3    Conventional Design – Twin side moving hatch covers.*

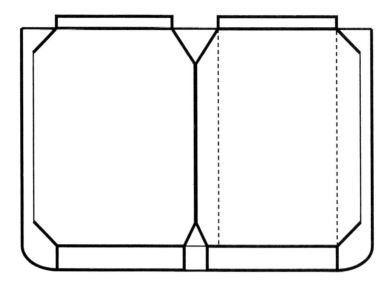

*Figure 8.4    OJ Libaek's Optimum 2000 (Capesize) Bulk Carrier Design (Twin Hatch Covers).*

## Side Opening Hatch Covers

*Figure 8.5    Bulk Carrier construction passed through many phases and included side opening hatch covers closing large holds. The covers when open being supported by a transverse trackway and stanchion arrangements. Operation being by sideways operation of chain traction and roller action.*

**Operational Mode – Side Opening or End Opening, Hatch Covers**

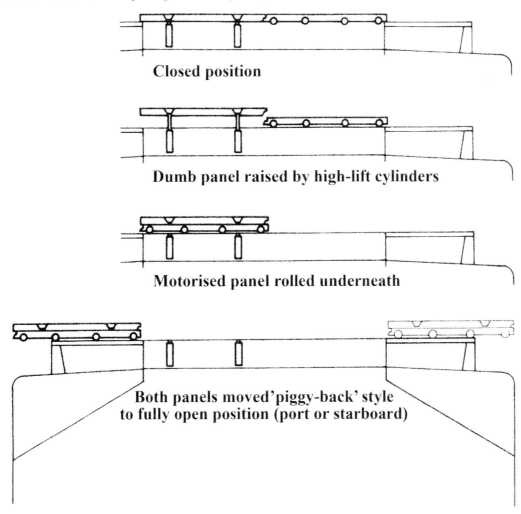

Figure 8.6    *Amidship's section showing sequence operation of side opening hatch covers. Current build, side moving hatch covers are operated by hydraulic motors in conjunction with a rack and pinion system. They are self locking and fitted with automatic cleating to rubber packed seals. Optional limit switches can be incorporated to permit remote Bridge operation.*

**Smaller Cargo Vessel – Modern Trend, Single Cargo Hold Construction**

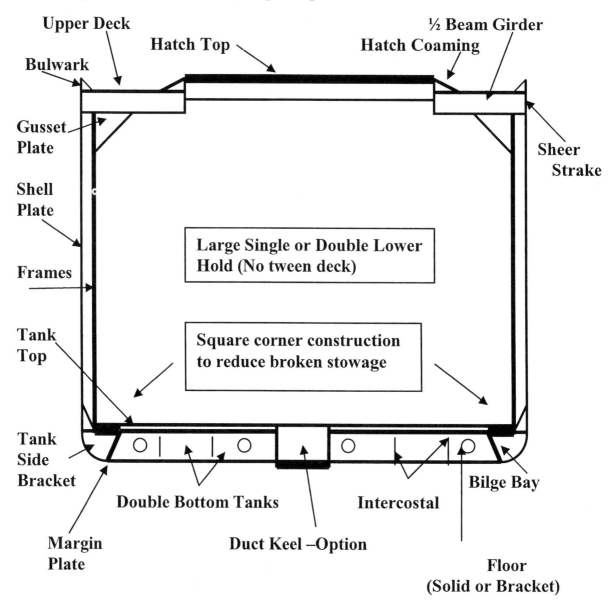

*Figure 8.7*

The more modern vessel, probably operating with cranes, may be fitted with twin hatch tops to facilitate ease of operation from both ends of a hold. While the construction of the hold tends to be spacious to accept a variety of long cargoes. Double hold space with or without temporary athwartship's bulkheads which can section the hold depending on the nature of the cargo, provide flexibility to accommodate a variety of cargo types.

Square corner construction lends to reducing broken stowage especially with containers, pallets, vehicles or case goods. They also allow better usage of fork lift truck operations within the hold itself. Flush "bilge plate access" is generally a feature of this type of design. Where steel bilge covers (previously limber boards) are countersunk into the deck so as not to obstruct cargo parcels being manoeuvred towards a tight side or corner stow.

## Conventional Dry Cargo Vessel

*Figure 8.8   Dry Cargo Vessel seen at sea in transit through the Dardanelle's. The vessel is fitted with heavy derricks for operation from "Samson Post" and fore mast structure over three hatches.*

## Hallen Derrick

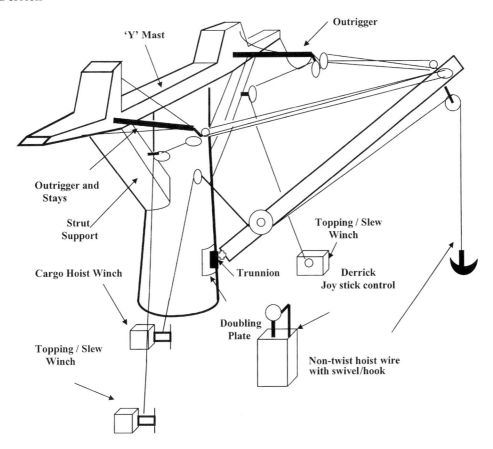

*Figure 8.9*

The "Hallen Derrick" has a similar concept to the "Velle", in that the topping lift arrangement and the slewing wires are incorporated together and secured aloft, clear of the lower deck. The outreach and slew are wide, achieved by the "T" Bar on the Velle derrick and by outriggers with the "Hallen".

Both Velle and Hallen systems are labour saving and can be operated by a single controller, operating the luffing and slewing movement together with the cargo hoist movement.

The Hallen is distinctive by the "Y" Mast structure that provides the anchor points for the wide leads. The derrick also accommodates a centre lead sheave to direct the hoist wire to the relevant winch.

### General Cargo Vessel – Profile

*Figure 8.10    Four hatch, general cargo vessel the "Lily Crown" seen with all aft accommodation. Its six hallen derricks, are all topped and supported by Samson (Goal posts), Post structures.*

### Mast Structures

Very few modern commercial ships are fitted with an old fashioned mast, as developed by the sailing ship era. The mast was initially established to take the "Yards" to spread the sails. They later accommodated aerials, lookout posts, and more recently derrick supports in the form of mast tables to secure the topping lifts.

With the advent of high bridge positions being established, lookouts no longer need to climb to a crows nest, Satellite communications has replaced the wire communication aerials and cranes have all but replaced derricks and eliminated the need for mast tables and topping lift supports. Heavy lift derricks aboard ships are now limited by greater use of crane/sheer leg barges for the occasional lift and the submersible decks of designated "Heavy Lift" vessels dominate the project cargo sector. The need to have a conventional mast structure has been virtually eliminated.

This said, the much reduced in size, radar mast, remains a dominant feature to nearly every ship of size, afloat. The tall sail training ships and some older tonnage still display a mast structure or a vessel with a specific lifting rig like the "Hallen Derrick" may need such a structure, but generally they are now somewhat limited.

Where a mast is established they are usually made of tubular steel section, shaped from a broad base to a tapered truck. Strength of the mast is specified by the Classification Society. The scantlings should be such that they can remain unstayed (e.g. "Y" structured mast), unlike the older sailing ship masts which incorporated fore and aft stays and shrouds to port and starboard.

When they are used to support derrick(s) the derrick boom is usually manufactured away from the shipyard and contracted in, to the ship owners/shipyards specification. However, it should be realised that the shipyard is responsible for the manufacture and fitting of the mast itself, generally being fitted after launch, to the standards compatible to suit all stress calculations.

Mast structures, especially with heavy derricks tend to be synonymous with tween deck structure, to provide lower deck support. The upper tapered sections of construction are usually constructed in high tensile steel providing less high weight while at the same time retaining the required strength. The lower deck levels being provided with rigidity and strength support stiffening to the mast base and the associated surround landing area. Heavy lift derricks, if employed, are often stepped in a tabernacle or pyramid roller bearing structure close too, but not actually on the mast itself. Such an arrangement requires separate calculations for the derrick heel bearing and the joint mast structure support elements, to ensure the rig is not overloaded.

Many mast constructions incorporate a "Mast House" at the weather deck position of the base. This housing structure accommodates extensive stiffening to ensure athwartship's support and deliver load through the ship's structure to the ship's bottom area. This is further enhanced by the under deck girder supports to the mast house and the hold, where fore and aft bulkheads are fitted with stiffening webs.

**Mast Structure and Support**

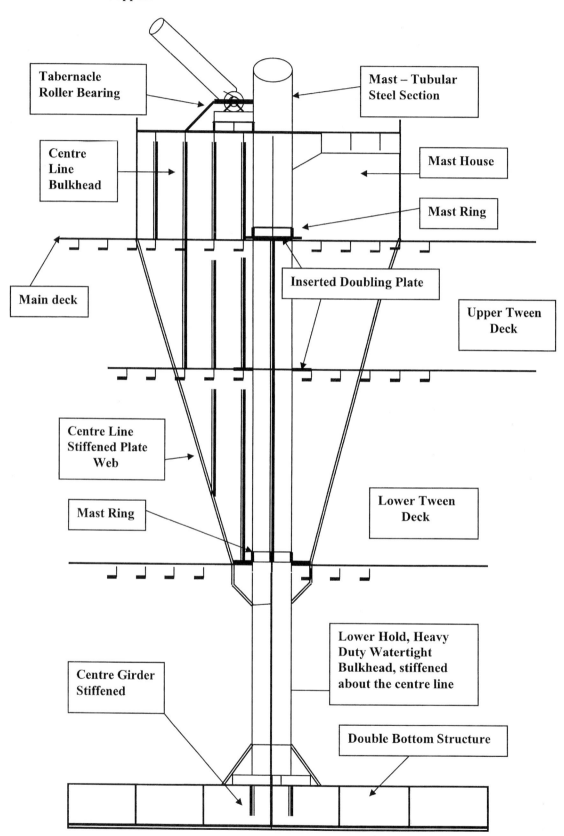

Tabernacle
Roller Bearing

Mast – Tubular
Steel Section

Centre
Line
Bulkhead

Mast House

Mast Ring

Main deck

Inserted Doubling Plate

Upper Tween
Deck

Centre Line
Stiffened Plate
Web

Lower Tween
Deck

Mast Ring

Centre Girder
Stiffened

Lower Hold, Heavy
Duty Watertight
Bulkhead, stiffened
about the centre line

Double Bottom Structure

*Figure 8.11*

## Upper Mast Support

The purpose of the lower support to the mast is to prevent horizontal movement and a mast ring is fitted. Where a mast is fitted directly to a deck, a doubling plate would normally be used or the deck area given increased thickness.

The upper part is secured by shrouds to Port and Starboard, secured to the mast "Hounds Band", designed specifically to accept shackled stays and shrouds.

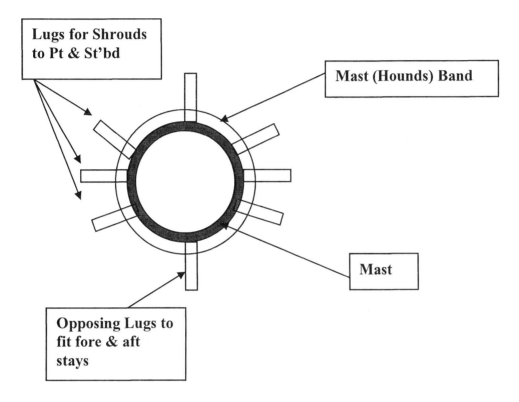

*Figure 8.12*

The early designs of conventional mast structures and their functional purpose has all but disappeared on modern tonnage and must be considered as nearly obsolete. Samson posts have remained on some general cargo vessels, still operational with derricks, but these have been dominated by deck mounted cranes. Mast structures in the main are reduced to essential radar masts which tend to accommodate scanners and communication aerials.

## Cargo Handling Lifting Appliances

*Figure 8.13    The "Y" supporting mast structure for a "Velle Derrick". The derrick is seen stowed In the crutch and the "Yoke" is seen rigged with the heavy duty bridle strops and attached to the topping lift/ slewing guy arrangement.*

*Figure 8.14    25 tonne SWL pedestal deck crane seen on the Port side of the cargo vessel "Scandia Spirit". The ship is fitted with two such Cranes, both positioned on the Port side with an outreach of 22 metres. Fitted with single wire hoist And topping lift arrangement To a tubular steel section jib.*

## The Container Vessel

The container vessels continue to grow in both size and in numbers. So much so that new builds are now approaching the current maximum of 13,000 teu. Such a size of vessel may incur draught restriction in the smaller ports. The overall structure of these enormous ships, varies considerably. Virtually all are built with deck stowage in mind and subsequently are fitted with hatch top and deck reception fittings to accommodate a container stack of upto about six (6) containers high. Such a large deck stack leads to the possibility of parametric rolling occurring and as such the modern vessel is generally equipped with fin and tank stabiliser systems. The danger of parametric rolling with a large deck container stack is that upper container units in the stack may be lost overboard.

During the loading and discharge of container units it is also imperative that the vessel is kept in the upright position. The main reason for this is that the container stowage, below decks, employs "cell guides" and if the ship is allowed to heel the gantry lifting beam would be denied access into the respective container cell. Causing a cessation of cargo operations.

*Figure 8.15    Container cell structure showing the cell guides as numbered against the bulkhead. The guides allowing the systematic slotting and stowage of containers to the relevant cells.*

**Container Hatch Covers**

*Figure 8.16   A steel pontoon hatch cover is seen being lifted clear of the container cargo hatch by the container lifting beam. The pontoon cover has a weight of approximately 40 tonnes and is fitted with container reception fittings to accept deck stow containers.*

**Container  Vessel Construction**

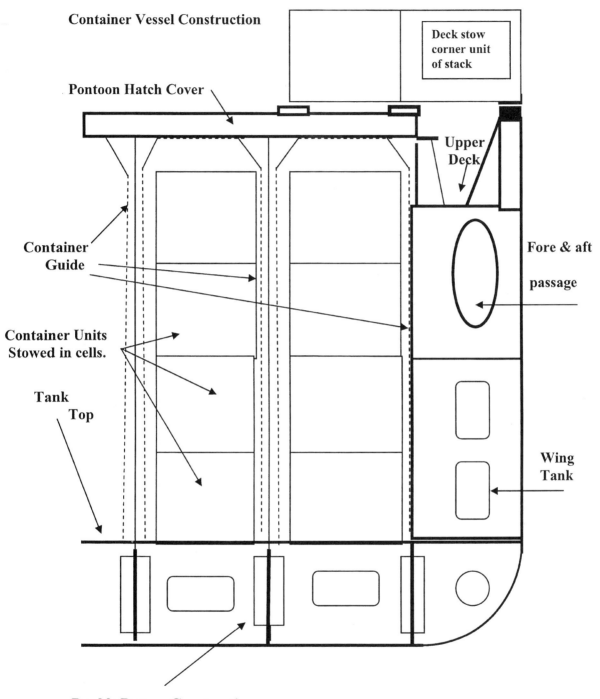

**Container Vessel Construction**

Deck stow
corner unit
of stack

**Pontoon Hatch Cover**

**Upper Deck**

**Container Guide**

Fore & aft

passage

**Container Units Stowed in cells.**

**Tank Top**

**Wing Tank**

**Double Bottom Construction**

*Figure 8.17*

**Container Pedestal Support**

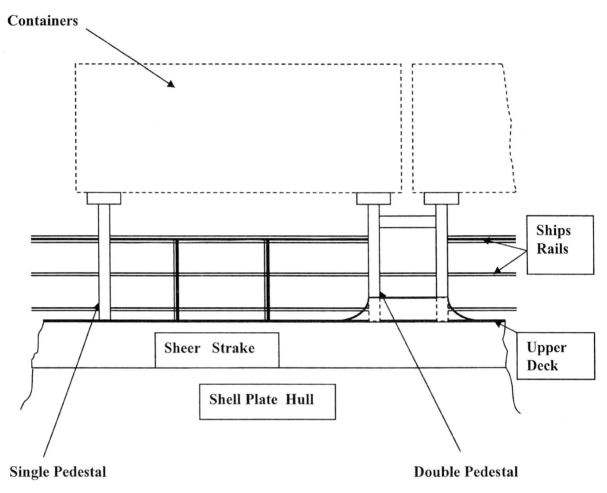

*Figure 8.18*

Where container stowage overlaps the pontoon hatch tops the ships side structure tends to incorporate pedestal supports to maximise space for container stowage. Pedestals either single or double standing are manufactured in tubular square steel cross section and stiffened at deck level.

**Container Deck Stack**

Figure 8.19    The Container vessel "Lircay" seen fully loaded. The deck stow being five high, over nearly all of the virtual ships length. Such a deck stack stowage, increases the windage that can be expected to be experienced by the vessel. Height of the container stack is not allowed to obscure the bridge watch viewing position to permit the safe navigation and progress of the vessel when making way.

**Container Ship – Profile**

*Figure 8.20    The "OOCL Shanghai" berthed alongside the container wharf in Barcelona, Spain.*

The style of the high transom stern fitted with container guides is becoming more popular as a new build. The structure giving body support to the on deck, container stack which has become a trade mark for the larger container vessels, now designed to accommodate 12,500 teu.

The vessel does not carry its own deck container cranes and relies totally on the use of shoreside terminal gantry cranes.

Another feature is the below maindeck, aft mooring station where access is gained from the fore and aft underdeck passageway.

## Container Vessel Features

*Figure 8.21    The OOCL Fortune seen in a loaded condition at sea. No shipboard gantry cranes are fitted and cargo movement is handled by terminal gantries.*

*Figure 8.22    The MSC Sintra seen alongside terminal gantry cranes working cargo. Own ships container cranes are turned outboard but would provide the flexibility to dock and work cargo in non-designated container ports.*

# CHAPTER NINE

# Miscellaneous Constructions

## Introduction

Many aspects of ship construction do not readily sit alongside any one specific section. Several on board systems, are incorporated on many different types of vessel. Life saving appliances, for example are onboard every vessel but differ considerably from one ship to another. Similarly, gangway systems, window types, and communication systems, are common to all ships, but each tends to be fitted with alternative features.

Specific items, like helicopter landing decks, though not common to all, are a regular structure to many vessels. However, underdeck strengthening with a deck space above, clear of obstructions, is often an alternative to a purpose built landing deck.

*Figure 9.1    The Heli-Deck structure seen in the forward section of an offshore support vessel as it enters the synchro-lift at Las Palmas, in Grand Canary.*

## Helicopter Landing Decks

The construction of any helicopter landing area aboard a ship, must take into account that the design must be suitable for the largest type of helicopter that it is intended to accept. Attention must also reflect the requirements of National Authorities and how the platform could effect the design and working features of the ship. The type size and weight of helicopters that are intended for their use, must be submitted with the constructional plans to the authority.

Landing areas are to be free of any projections above the level of the deck and must also incorporate a drainage system capable of draining spilt fuel. The area must have a non-slip surface and be fitted with anchoring devices. (Tie down points)

The deck area and any supporting structure must be designed with stiffening capable of withstanding permissible stresses(Given in Part 3 Chapter 9, Table 9.5.3, of the Rules and Regulations for the Classification of Ships) Landing areas must also conform to the markings and requirements as designated by the International Chamber of Shipping (ICS)

**Shipboard Bow Supported Heli-Deck**

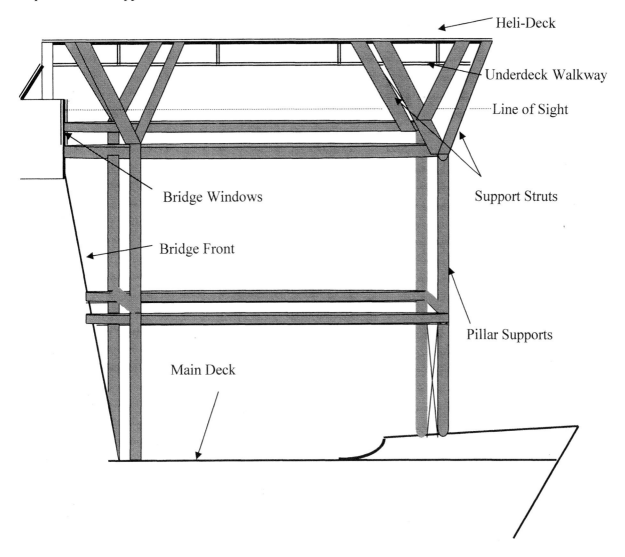

*Figure 9.2*

## Heli-Deck Profile

*Figure 9.3 Side elevation of the support structure to the forward fitted heli-deck aboard the offshore support vessel "Toisa Mariner".*

## Life Saving Appliances and Launching Devices

The lessons learned from the Titanic disaster do not allow ships to operate without a basic second line of support, namely its survival craft. The development of survival craft has experienced major changes over the last century. Wooden and alloy lifeboats have given way to fibre glass (GRP) construction. While life rafts, since the war years have gained improved equipment and become enclosed in a brushed nylon fabric. All launching devices for boats and rafts, employ gravity as a means of launching, although power recovery systems are used to recover survival craft.

Lifeboat construction has moved away from open boats and are now predominantly totally enclosed or partially enclosed emergency transports. Free fall systems, with davit launched liferafts and semi-rigid rescue boats, are now quite common and are seen as cost effective, in non-passenger vessels. While operating systems have moved towards coxswain's wheel control instead of tiller control of the steering. Enclosed boats usually providing air tight, gas/tight internal spaces and hulls are protected by water sprinkler systems for tanker vessels.

Rescue boats, are designated to all foreign going vessels (Two are required for passenger vessels, one on each side), may be used as a lifeboat, but if so, they must be equipped with the additional rescue boat equipment. Semi-rigid inflatables are often employed as designated rescue boats especially in the offshore support sector.

Changes continue to take place with new ideas and new technology coming to the fore. More recently we have seen Marine Evacuation Systems (MES) and Marine Evacuation Chutes (MEC) allocated to passenger vessels and ferries, in addition to conventional lifeboats and liferafts. These fast methods of mass evacuation come with large inflatable liferafts with upto 150 man capacity.

Developments in evacuation methods continue alongside larger building projects. New passenger vessels are expecting to accommodate upto eight thousand persons in the near future. Such figures would require novel systems to cause total evacuation within the regulatory time periods. Alongside this necessity is a need for crowd control management training for seagoing personnel who are required to collate and monitor passenger evacuation.

**Launching Devices for Survival Craft**

*Figure 9.4    Overhead sliding Gravity Davit used for launching open boats. Operates with A Safe Working Load capacity of upto 5.7 tonnes, for the fibre glass constructed lifeboat. Many passenger ships operating in warm water, near coastal trades still carry open lifeboats, compared with the Tanker vessels which are fitted with Totally Enclosed Lifeboats, of one make or another.*

**Partially Enclosed Boat**

*Figure 9.5    A partially enclosed lifeboat stowed in gravity davits aboard a cross channel ferry vessel. The roll down covers seen deployed between the fore and aft fibre glass canopies, over the amidship's framework of the boat.*

## Free Fall Launch Systems

*Figure 9.6    The stern mounted launching slip of a free fall lifeboat system established at the aft part of the vessel. Boarding is achieved at the rear of the boat via a specifically constructed companionway from the embarkation deck to the lifeboat access position. These systems are also fitted with a davit or derrick operation to effect recovery of the boat once launched. The boat launching system is usually off centre, with the davit positioned on the opposite quarter.*

## Free Fall Launching Arrangements

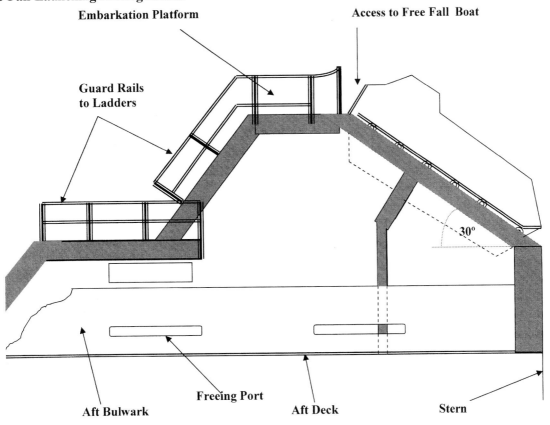

*Figure 9.7*

The freefall boat rests on side rollers secured to the steel launchway set at an angle of 30° to the horizontal. The number of rollers will vary with the length of boat. The launching framework is constructed in steel to accommodate the boat size, which will usually take upto an average complement of 40 persons. Different manufacturers customise the slip structure to suit the stern arrangement of the vessel.

Each system will provide four point securing harness fittings for the boats personnel and the boat is operated by a hydraulic release. Some designs incorporate a recovery davit into the support structure while others operate with a derrick or davit system close to the launch site.

**Boarding and Internal Views of: Free Fall Lifeboat**

*Figure 9.8    Boarding platform entrance into Free fall lifeboat.*

*Figure 9.9    Internal view of lifeboat: looking from forward towards the aft boarding access.*

## Launching Stations

*Figure 9.10   A typical station for the preparation and launch of survival craft seen aboard a Ro-Pax ferry. Crew embarkation position for gravity launched, partially enclosed lifeboat. The embarkation deck for passengers is situated below the lifeboat itself and carries a liferaft station aft of the boat embarkation point.*

**Fast Launching Operations**

Figure 9.11 *Several types of vessels have a need to be fitted with fast launch and recovery davits for operating Fast Rescue Craft. Such ships like anchor handling and the Offshore Supply vessels operating in the Oil and Gas sectors of the marine industry must have fast efficient means of launching. The "A" Frame Davit is a tilting davit system operating with a single hoist wire over a single sheave. Davit operation usually being limited upto 3 tonne Safe Working Load.*

## Radar and Communications Masts

Few modern day vessels are fitted with what used to be known as a conventional mast structure. Most vessels are now accommodated with the essential radar mast supporting two or more radar scanner aerials. Additionally they also support communication aerials, Sat-Coms domes, light signal lamps, signal halyards, etc., not to mention any structural support stays.

*Figure 9.12   The Radar/Communications mast of the tanker vessel, Motor Transport "Folegandros", seen mounted on the bridge deck, aft of the bridge housing.*

**Navigation Bridge Windows**

*Figure 9.13*

Bridge windows are manufactured in toughened glass and encased in the steel framework of the Bridge Front. The navigation bridge windows are usually fitted with wipers/washers and/or fast spinning clear view screens or a combination of both. They are often fitted with built in heater elements to reduce the risk of icing in cold weather, though many ships, only have selected heated windows.

The observed panorama is meant to provided an unrestricted view for the conning and observation duties, as required of ship's personnel. To this end, many bridge fronts are fitted with an external railed maintenance platform, to permit safe washing, painting, service of motors and heating elements as may be required from time to time.

## Window Arrangement for Integrated Navigation Bridge

*Figure 9.14    Bridge window arrangement all fitted with side moving wipers span the width of the navigation bridge. Side windows provide a virtual 360° all round viewing.*

## Window Wiper Construction/Operations

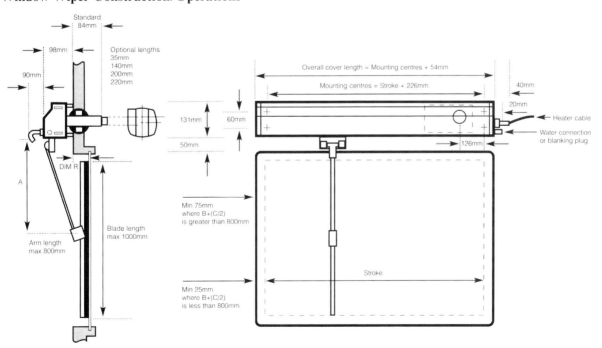

*Figure 9.15*

## Clear View Screens

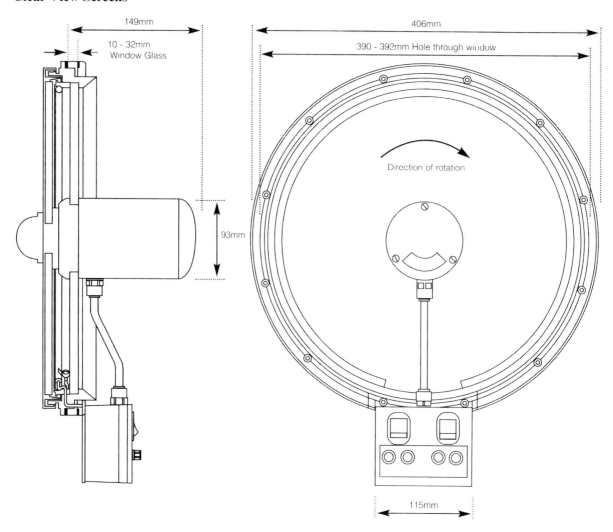

*Figure 9.16*

# ANNEX I

# Operation of the Shipyard

## Introduction

The very nature of the task of building a new ship or repairing an existing vessel requires certain obvious elements, not least a supply of steel. However, the process of turning that steel into a ship requires an infrastructure which is established around the shipyard, terminating with the launch of the vessel and the hull being placed on a fitting out berth.

Contractually, the shipyard will be committed to a hand over delivery date and as such can expect to process steel sections through all periods of the build time. The organisation of the shipyard must permit a flow from the design stage to the pattern stage, then onto a steel cutting shed, onwards through assembly and/or prefabrication to arrive at the paint shop prior to movement towards the building slip.

For this flow to take place without unnecessary hold ups, adequate facilities for steel delivery and storage are required. Assembly and prefabrication sheds must allow continuous working, in all weathers other wise the build programme will be compromised. Paint supply with a suitable labour force need to be managed to coat to a degree of quality and deliver coated sections as and when required for slip assembly.

Unless security is an issue as with say warships, most commercial vessels are now constructed in open air conditions. This is not always the case but the majority will prefabricate sections, building these inside internal workshops. Such an environment tends to protect against the weather and favours continuous work schedules. Movement of sections from one bay to another will be either by gantry mobile crane, or conveyor belt.

The small shipyard tends to cater for the smaller type vessel where as the larger, very often sprawling yard may cover many acres and have several new buildings underway at any one time. A combination of undercover working areas as well as exposed areas in close proximity to the building slip, is the norm. These would contain various facilities, inclusive of overhead crane facilities to move sections through the system.

Prefabrication has become the major element in ship building with sections often being manufactured away from the actual shipyard and being transported to the slip when required for assembly. Ground handling equipment has become very sophisticated and these low loader type transports are geared to moving the large and awkward assemblies with comparative ease. Conveyor belt movement of structures has geared the modern shipyard to high quality work and the meeting of required deadlines.

**Shipyard Organisation**

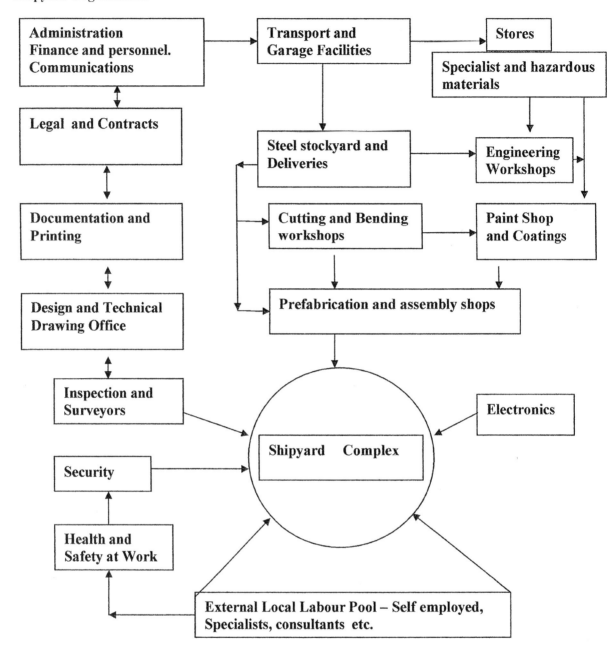

*Figure AI.1*

**Departmental Functions of Shipyard Operations**

**Legal Department** – A very busy department within a large shipyard complex. Although dealing with the intricacies of main line customer building contracts, its day to day business includes anything from accident litigation, to drawing up labour agreements. The department will vary in size dependant on the amount of business carried out by the yard. The smaller shipyard usually working with legal representatives from either a parent company or an off site specialists legal office. The large shipyard would most certainly have their own, "in house legal representatives" to carry out, company, contract and corporation legislation effecting the yards operations.

**Documentation and Printing** – An active department which features extensive copying facilities. It works closely with Legal and Administration sections employing secretarial, filing and clerical staff. Offices would normally contain large flat bed copy machines required for the reproduction of large ship plans, e.g. General arrangements, Shell expansion plans, Docking plans and the like. Day to day work would include invoice/order monitoring, duplicating contracts, word processes sing, etc.

**Design and technical Drawing Office** – Employing essentially "Naval Architects" with support staff. Generally engaged with design drawings and schematics of shipboard features. Large shipyards would employ in teams, rather than individuals, but all are essentially doing the same function. Day to day operations would probably be taken up by measuring and photographic operations of potential repairs then drawing up planned recommendations. Costing of materials is sometimes envisaged within design departments, though labour and man-hours is normally an item covered by finance.

**Inspection and Surveyors** – All large shipyards would carry on site classification surveyors. The smaller shipyard would use a buy in service and provide on site accommodation for as long as the work is in progress. Where a vessel is constructed under continuous survey it would be impractical not to have a surveyor permanently on call and especially so where several vessels are being constructed alongside each other. Inspection in new builds is involved from before the design stage and can expect to continue throughout the ship's life with individual vessel docking schedule.

**Security Department** – Since the ISPS has evolved (July 2004) port and dockyard security has become more high profile. Not that shipyard security was ever known to be slack. Gate access security officers are usually engaged in 24 hour shift work alongside shipboard security watchmen. Office and stores security are of concern to any large complex. A large labour force often means large cash sums in shipyards which are paid out in wages. Although the more developed establishments employing contractual personnel pay salaries directly into banks this is not always the case in third world countries. This section would vet potential employees and may have cause to work closely with the local police, they may or may not be equipped with their own transport.

**Shipyard Administration** – Procedures vary considerably when considering world wide practice. However, the developed yards administration procedures would tend to cover, the employment of staff, ordering of stores, including steel supplies and meeting the needs of the health and safety at work Act. The administration could also expect to work closely with associated sections including finance, legal and contracts, as well as design and architects departments. An attached personnel department taking account of wages/salaries, disbursements, social security, insurance, pensions, welfare, etc., is generally associated with administration.

**Transport and Garage Departments** – Even the small dockyards usually have their own transports, all be it limited in size depending on the site coverage. Small wagons, vans and the mobile crane units are usually maintained by this department. Personnel who are so attached are employed as drivers/mechanics, engineers, electricians and managerial staff. They are often engaged off site making or collecting, delivery parcels, or engaged in the servicing of dockyard transports. They would normally have a strong contact with the steel stockyard and any railhead delivery systems. Transport and delivery of large pre-fabricated structures, by land or sea to launching areas and/or lay-by berths would be expected.

*Figure AI.2   Pre-fabricated bridge and accommodation structure being delivered to a new build, Anchor Handling vessel by use of floating sheer legs. Such a move would be carried out with both the co-operation of transport and administration sectors of the shipyard.*

### New build – Principle of Concept through to Operation

The order of a new ship starts with the needs of the customer, usually influenced by the amount of trade, current and envisaged. The requirements of the customer form the detail of the contract, usually prior to going to design. All stages would have to be verified including the building stage. System integration would then follow prior to sea trials and then general operation.

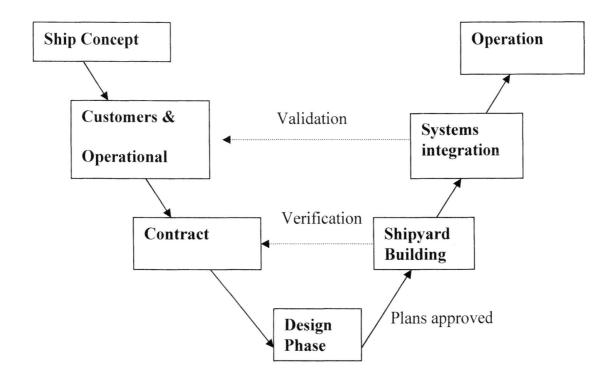

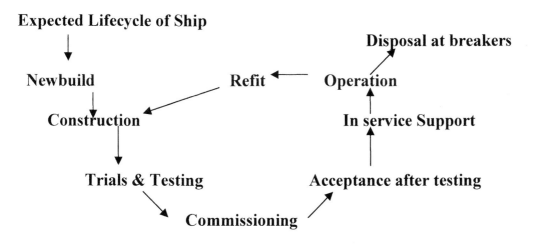

*Figure AI.3*

## Building Slip Operations

*Figure AI.4    A new build "Anchor Handling Vessel" (AHV) being assembled in a South Korean shipyard.*
*A tracked "Gantry Crane" straddles the building slip, seen aft of the vessel. While overside tasks are*
*handled via the array of staging and scaffolding which is set about the slip way against the hull sides.*

## Prefabrication

Virtually all ship building techniques these days are conducted with a greater or lesser degree of prefabrication. Large building halls are employed for what has become a conveyor belt system manufacturing hull sections and/or modular units, for adding to the gradual build of the vessel.

Prefabrication also lends to "Jumbo-isation" where large elements can be added quickly, so reducing time loss and subsequent freight loss while making changes to an existing vessel's structure.

*Figure AI.5    Examples of prefabrication can be seen with the bow section being manufactured ashore in the assembly shed and lifted as a complete unit for welding to the fore end of a vessel in MHI's shipyard, at Nagasaki, Japan.*

**Prefabrication Examples**

*Figure AI.6    A complete prefabricated bridge module, fully coated and prepared, seen being transported by an overhead gantry crane towards the building slip.*

*Figure AI.7    A prefabricated bridge/accommodation module, still being worked in open aspect, having been assembled but not yet coated, inside a building hall.*

## Essential Elements of Prefabrication Methods

Modern practice shows that prefabrication methods are widely employed in the worlds shipyards, but such methods must be supported by essential elements to permit the methods to succeed. The manufactured modules are often large and very heavy when assembled. As such the transport of completed units to the building dock or slip, must be an early consideration.

The size and weight of any modular unit must be within the capacity of the yards assembly sheds and in house gantry cranes. Where work is contracted outside the limits of the shipyard is when costs start to escalate. Manoeuvring modular units to a building position, requires extensive planning, specialised transporters in most cases and experienced technical staff. Such activity would normally only be undertaken when a task for one reason or another falls outside the capabilities of the shipyard. This would be rare in the case of a large shipbuilding complex.

The manufacture of small sections can be undertaken in building halls and while still comparatively small in overall size can be coated, prior to adding to the modular structure. The benefits of the assembly halls are that they are undercover and unaffected by inclement weather. Work can therefore continue on a twenty four hour basis if required. Better quality can be achieved, as opposed to working in awkward situations as can happen when modules are assembled. Units are capable of being turned over and turned around, while inside the assembly halls as these building sheds are equipped with overhead travelling cranage.

*Figure AI.8    A Double Bottom section being worked and manufactured inside an assembly shed at a Korean shipyard. All essential facilities are to hand, inside the covered area.*

## Conveyor Belt Construction

The movement flow of prefabricated modules is now a common practice. Tracked mobile transporter platforms are run directly into the assembly halls where units can be lifted by the internal overhead cranes. The movement of the transport platform is led directly to the building slip or into a crane accessible pick-up area.

Large gantry cranes range the build/assembly areas and straddle the building dock or building slips. By joint engagement of transporter platform and gantry lift, the module can be lifted to position and held, to permit final assembly to the hull form.

*Figure AI.9    The prefabricated stern unit of an anchor handling vessel is transported from the assembly hall via the paint shop, to a position of securing to the hull form. The Gantry crane supports are seen either side while the lifting purchase is manually prepared to take the modules weight, prior to final positioning.*

### The Practice of Welding

Welding is a method for the fusion of two metals together. It superseded riveting as a means of joining plate metal together and has distinct advantages to the shipping industry and shipbuilding practice. These have been seen more recently with innovations with the use of aluminium and friction stir welding methods. Electric arc welding and submerged arc welding has allowed high quality fusion welding to develop within the industry for both new builds and repair activity.

Welding advantages include:—

(a) Time saving in building practice especially where prefabrication methods are employed.
(b) A smooth surface is achieved reducing "hull roughness".
(c) A greater saving in weight is achieved and allows an increased deadweight of between 7.5% to 12.5%.
(d) Reduced maintenance goes with welding methods compared to riveted systems.
(e) Effective watertight and oil tight integrity is achieved with welded structures.
(f) Welding methods tend to be stronger than riveted joints.

(g) Repairs can generally be completed with more ease and usually *in situ*.

(h) Professional welders are now more readily available.

Manual or semi automatic welding employing the use of ceramic backing strips allows a faster progress and provides a smoother reverse surface to the weld run. Back gouging to the weld is not usually required and levels of porosity are greatly reduced.

Welding operations although favoured throughout the industry does have some dis-advantages and these are:—

(a) Hot welding methods may possibly lock in stresses effecting the materials.

(b) Heat applications may incur distortion in structures unless great care is used.

(c) High cost of electrodes and skilled labour is involved.

(d) Faults may go undetected in spite of stringent testing procedures.

(e) Panel strength may be reduced due to the lack of plate landings.

f) Methods may not arrest cracks, such as brittle fractures and consequently "crack arrestors" may be required.

(g) Structures may be inflexible, so it may be necessary to avoid sharp corners.

## Welding and Steel Cutting

*Figure AI.10   Welding and cutting operations ongoing inside a prefabrication shop on an external part of a ship's hull. One of the building phases, prior to coating and assembly, in the business of ship construction. A large area of a body shop allows the continued section building to take place, inside weather protected enclosed conditions. Overhead track cranes allow section movement, to provide ideal access for manual welding operations to upper and lower areas of assemblies.*

**Welding Practice – Plate Edge Preparations for Welding**

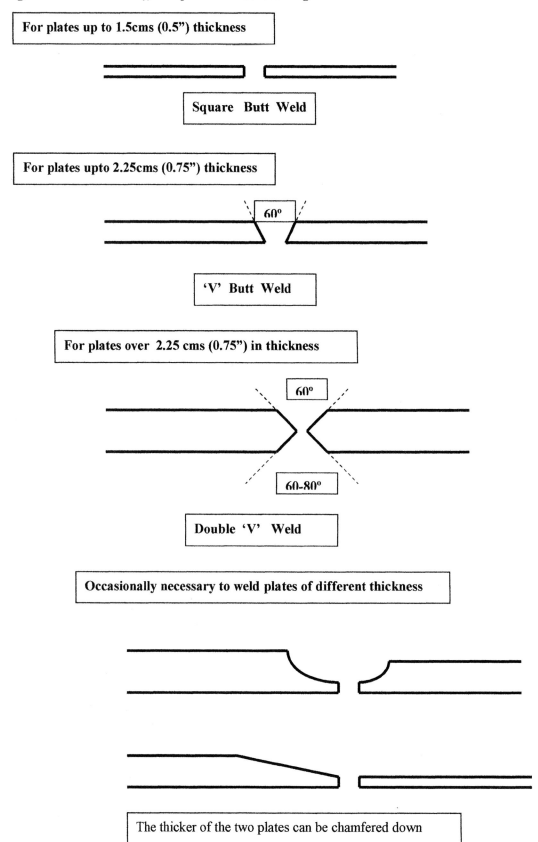

For plates up to 1.5cms (0.5") thickness

Square Butt Weld

For plates upto 2.25cms (0.75") thickness

60°

'V' Butt Weld

For plates over 2.25 cms (0.75") in thickness

60°

60-80°

Double 'V' Weld

Occasionally necessary to weld plates of different thickness

The thicker of the two plates can be chamfered down

*Figure AI.11*

**Weld Faults**

**Undercutting** – caused by the current being too high and burning the edge of the plate.

**Porosity** – caused by air bubbles trapped inside the weld.

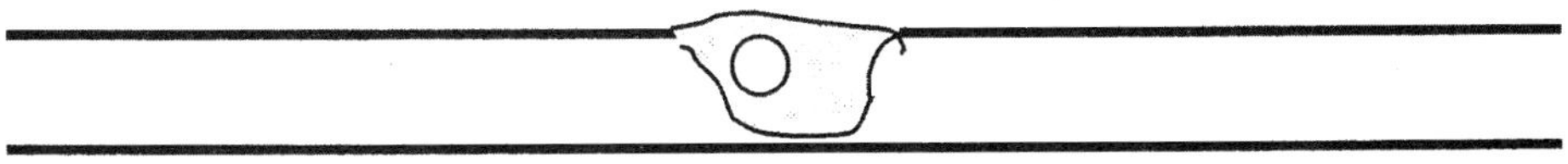

**Overlap** – caused by too much filler weld metal being used.

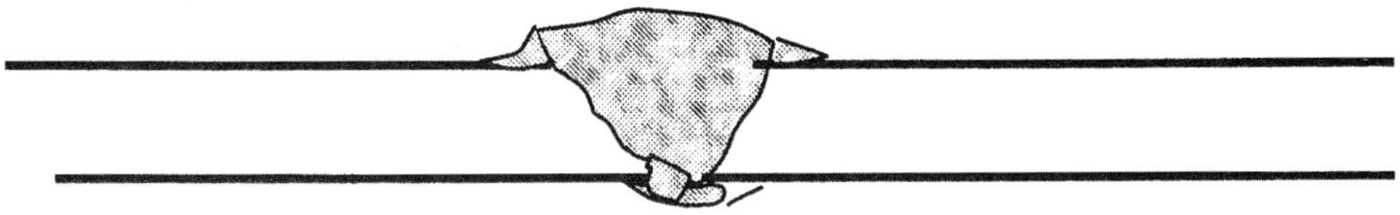

**Lack of Penetration** – caused by the wrong type of weld rod being used and inadequate plate preparation.

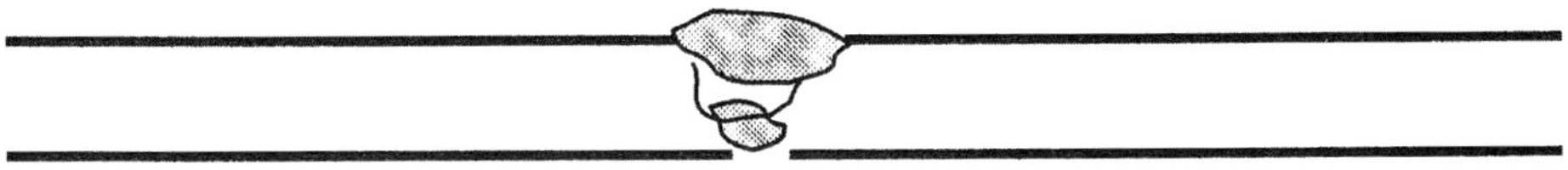

**Cracks** – caused by unequal cooling.

**Lack of Fusion** – caused by inadequate plate preparation and use of the wrong type of rod. This is considered very dangerous because it could run the length of the weld.

**Slag Inclusions** – caused by all slag not being chipped clear.

*Figure AI.12*

**Weld Tests**

Welds are tested first by visual inspection and then by:—

Dye application to show surface flaws. Achieved by washing the casting, if the dye remains after the wash flaws are present.

Radiographic testing has become increasingly popular by use of X-Ray or gamma rays and photographed for detection of flaws.

Magnetic particle testing to detect cracks in the weld. Where a casting is magnetized the spreading of a fluid of magnetic particles in paraffin which have a tendency to concentrate at a surface crack.

Ultrasonic testing where waves are reflected from the surface of flaws which are revealed on a cathode tube monitor.*

Compartments would normally be pressure tested with air, to just above a maximum static head level. Soapy water test to the weld seams would show any faults as a bubble stream.

*Figure AI.13   Deck stringers welded together seen on an exposed open deck next to a welded pipe section passing through the deck plate.*

* When testing for class purposes, testing processes must be carried out by a certified operator using approved type equipment (e.g. Vacuum boxes).

**Example Types of Weld**

Welded structures feature many alternatives welds to suit the steelwork and the specific design of the vessel. Some, like the "continuous fillet weld" are more common than say the "chain intermittent weld" but the alternative methods are worthy of note.

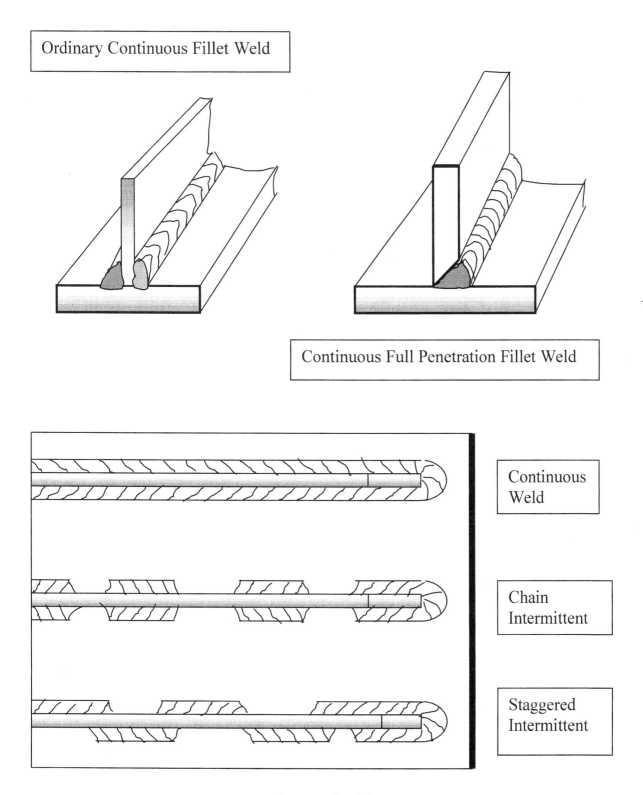

*Figure AI.14    Plan View of steel plate connections.*

## Tack Welding

Tack welding is a process of small welds at placed intervals, used in steel construction, to hold steel components together before completing a welded joint. By holding the components firmly in position, the process reduces the risk of heat distortion from the continuous welding process.

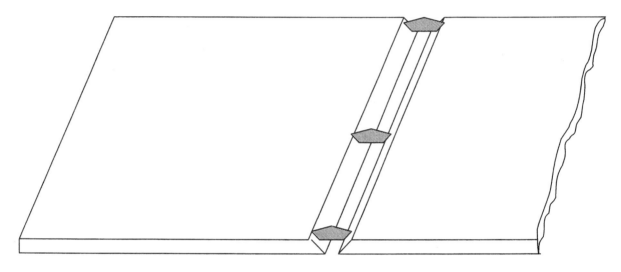

*Figure AI.15*

## Types of Welding

### Shielded Metal – Arc Welding

Probably the most common welding practice sometimes referred to as "Stick welding" or "covered electrode welding". This system places a bonding wire on the metal to be welded and the electrode. The electrode is charged so that when it is drawn into contact with the bonded metal, it arcs and generates heat. This heat melts both the edges of the material being joined. The weld (rod) electrode, which has a flux cover, also melts, filling in any gap between the material metals. The flux melts away during the process and forms a gas and slag area around the arc and the molten weld. As the weld cools the slag deposit solidifies and forms a "crust" on the surface of the weld which is removed by hammering prior to finishing or welding on top.

### Gas Metal – Arc Welding

Gas metal arc welding is more often referred to as MIG welding. This process is based on the basic principle of arc welding but employs the weld electrode being continually fed from a spool and a flux is not used. The flux being replaced by a bubble of inert gas, usually argon or $CO_2$ surrounding the weld pool. The gas bubble acts as a shield to the arc and causes a smoother transfer of metal from the weld wire.

This system is common to the welding of stainless steel or aluminium and titanium, all of which require an inert atmosphere to achieve a successful welding process. Where "argon gas" is used the speed of the welding is increased and slag is prevented from forming.

### Flux Core Welding

A system of welding which employs similar principles to "gas metal arc welding" but which employs a flux, hence the name of "flux core welding". This system allows a greater depth of weld to be achieved. However, a surface slag would be generated and this would have to be removed as the weld is built to completion.

**Example Connections**

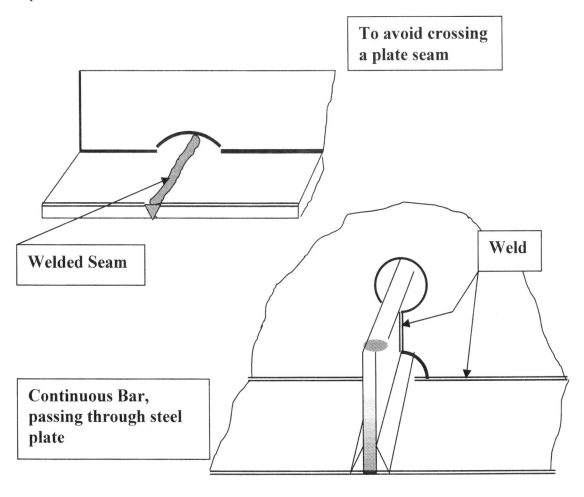

To avoid crossing
a plate seam

Welded Seam

Weld

Continuous Bar,
passing through steel
plate

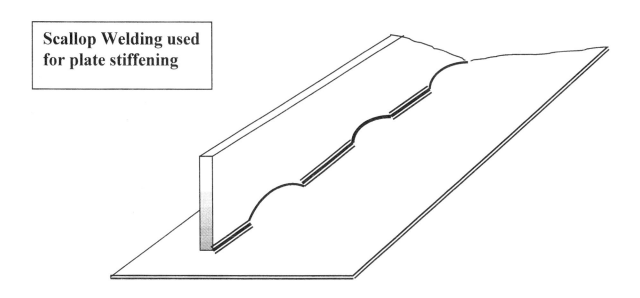

Scallop Welding used
for plate stiffening

*Figure AI.16*

## Gas Tungsten – Arc Welding

A system of welding which is often employed for pipe joints where a high standard of integrity is required. It may be used with or without a weld filler and produces a high quality welded joint. An arc is formed in a similar manner as with "gas metal arc welding" where an inert gas is passed through the welding torch causing a shield about the electrode and the molten weld pool. A non-consumable tungsten electrode is used and the weld metal itself to form the joint.

## Welding Example

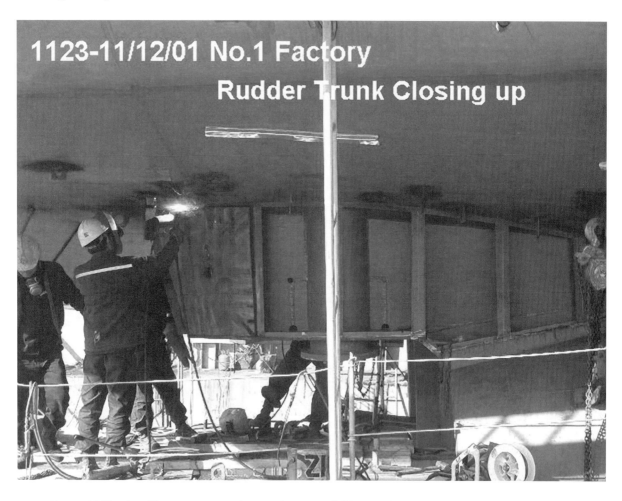

*Figure AI.17    A welding operation underway, from a scaffolding platform to close up the rudder trunk on a new build. Once completed, the trunk area would be coated. This is one of the final tasks undertaken, prior to hanging the rudder and testing the movement, in conjunction with the steering system.*

**Welding Methods**

**Electric Arc Welding**

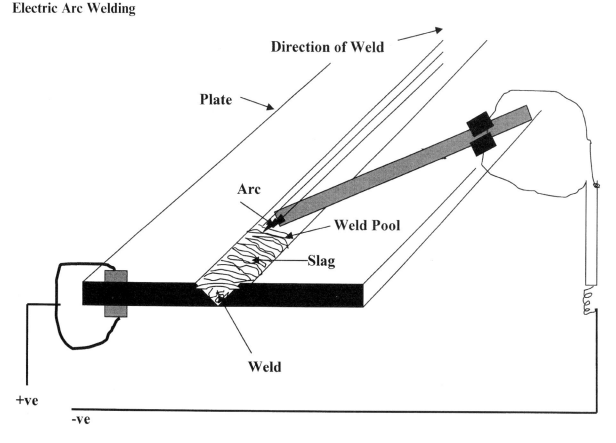

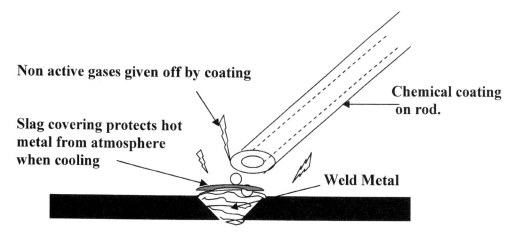

*Figure AI.18   Electric Arc Welding.*

Electric arc welding is a method of joining metals together by means of an electrode of a suitable composition, being fused under extreme temperature. The method employs an electric current of low voltage and high amps. It is the high amperage that generates the heat required. The current passes between the main material and the electrode in the form of an electric arc effect. (hence the name) The arc generated is heat intensive and melts the parent metal and the tip of the electrode.

The action causes globules of the electrode metal, to drop towards the weld pool of molten material of the base metal, filling any gap between the two prepared plates. As the length of the weld is progressed the molten pool solidifies and forms a join between the two plates.

It should be stated that the type of electrode used, must be compatible to fuse with the two base metal materials intended for joining. This electrode could be used in its base form, but practice has shown that better results are achieved by combining the electrode with a silicate "flux" coating. This effectively cools at a different rate to the weld metal and so forms a protective sealant against the atmosphere and keeps impurities in the air away from the weld as it cools.

The non-active gases given off in the process also provide an added protective shield in the atmosphere for the globules of metal in the arc. The chemical coating of the electrode contains a flux which cleans the join and leaves a slag deposit on top of the weld as it is progressed. This reduces the extent of any oxidisation taking place. The slag coating is finally chipped and cleaned away from the cooled, weld, before starting another weld run.

Effective welding is achieved by using a starting voltage of about 70 volts by just touching the base metal. Once contact is established between the electrode tip it can be withdrawn to a short distance off, which will cause the arc to generate and allow the weld to be progressed. The voltage can subsequently be reduced to about 30 volts, once the arc has been established. Current used will generally vary between 15 to 300 amps, depending on the density of heavy or light work being carried out.

**Submerged Arc Welding**

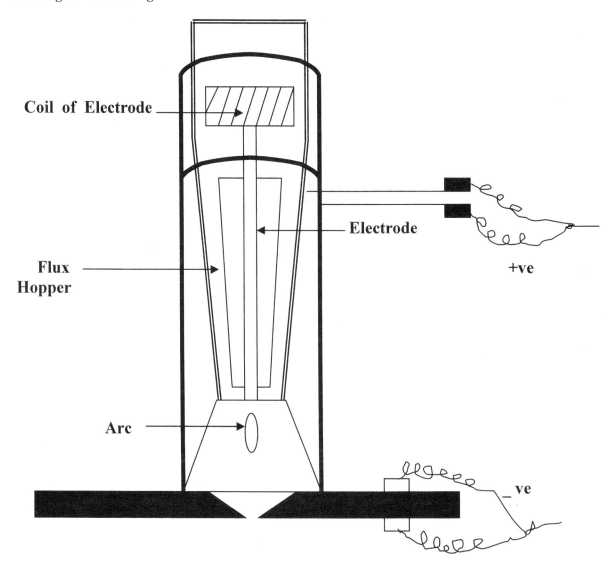

*Figure AI.19*

### Principle of Submerged Arc Welding Operations

This is a form of machine welding which delivers a powdered flux into the gap of the weld, followed by a consumable wire electrode fed via a roller from a coil. The electrode is buried into the molten flux giving good penetration and fusion. Submerged arc welding tends to be used extensively in the steel plate shops to perform on production line panels destined for prefabrication.

### Friction Stir Welding

The use of aluminium has increased considerably since the mid 90's mainly because of the use of Friction Stir Welding (FSW) processes. It was previously well used in the smaller fast craft sector of the industry but remained unpopular with the larger vessels.

However, the product is in plentiful supply and has increased strength and can now be more easily welded by FSW.

A low heat input is required which results in minimum residual stresses occurring in work pieces. Small sections can be interlinked to larger units effectively reducing welding time and costs. A massive weight saving can be achieved with improved sealing with void free and leak proof joints being an end product.

Effectively a rotational tool is plunged into the joint line, and moved along the joint length. Flux nor filler material is used in any way. The rotating tool produces severe plastic deformation under high pressure, during which the weld interfaces are stirred together and a homogenous structure is formed. This method produces a high quality join, which has greater strength than fusion welded joints.

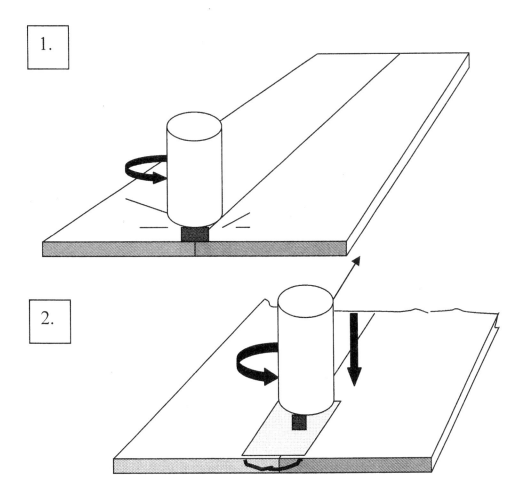

*Figure AI.20*

### Aluminium/Friction Stir Welding

The obvious advantages of low weight and corrosion resistance, with the use of aluminium are well known, but other factors are now making aluminium attractive to many more shipyards. Larger extrusions can now be built (upto 25 metres length in a single undivided piece) resulting in less welding taking place. This in itself brings down welding costs considerably. Also with less welding there is a significant lessening of heat effected zones which reduces fatigue in the structure.

Friction Stir Welding (FSW) has produced further advantages. It is a major cost reduction to the ship builder, who has now also benefited by the production of larger panels being used with larger extrusion presses. This has meant that large extrusions can be married to large panels without incurring residual stresses. This has ultimately reduced the prefabrication process and respective costings. The completed panel units meeting the criteria of several classification societies including: DNV, RINI, GL and LR.

However, the transport of such large extrusions to assembly yards can also generate associated problems because many roads do not have the capability of accepting such wide/long transports. To this end prefabrication plant located near to the sea can effectively eliminate many of the recognized road transport problems.

FSW was an original process developed by The Welding Institute (TWI) in England, and patented in 1991. Since then several companies around the world have adopted the process which produces the following advantages:—

(a) Higher strength than a corresponding fusion weld.
(b) Entirely non-porous joints.
(c) Minimal thermal distortion, resulting in flat surfaces.
(d) Allows wide thin gauge production in aluminium, previously thought impossible.
(e) Welds are homogenous and free of defects producing leak proof design.
(f) Uniform level of performance quality and narrow tolerances.
(g) The process is environmentally friendly.

Many yards are currently offering aluminium construction, inclusive of: Incat, NQEA, Austal, Afai, Fjellstrand, Alston Marine and Fincantieri.

**NB.** The most common ratio between steel and aluminium being, 1-1.5. This means that for every 1 mm of steel it could be replaced by 1.5 mm of aluminium. The overall reduction in weight in the build would then be 50%. Prefabricated profiles in aluminium reduces material handling, producing less shipyard welding and shortens assembly lines, generating cost effective savings.

### Aluminium Welding Procedures

Where aluminium alloy is to be welded, additional requirements are required by the regulations over and above the requirements for welding steel sections:—

(a) Aluminium alloys are to be welded by the metal inert gas or tungsten inert gas processes. Where other welding methods are proposed, the details of the alternative process must be submitted to the authority for approval.
(b) The edges of the material to be welded must be clean and free from grease, chemical, or solvent cleaners. The joint edges are to be scratch brushed, preferably immediately prior to the welding taking place, in order to remove oxide or films of dirt, filings, etc.

Conventional welding methods are generally unsuitable for welding stainless steel and aluminium because the flux would impair the weld owing to its corrosive properties.

Combined with the heat generated, excessive distortion and burning the base metal can also occur.

**Aluminium to Steel Connections**

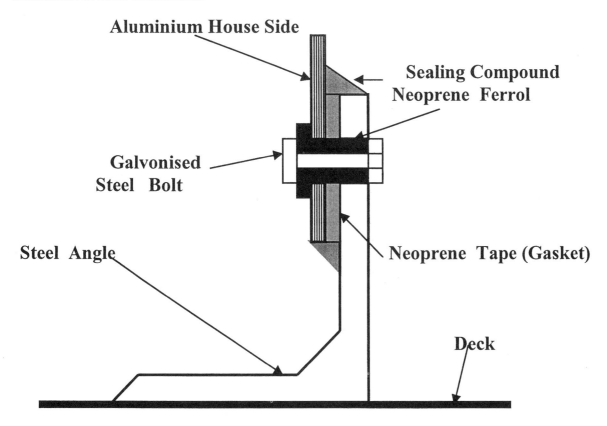

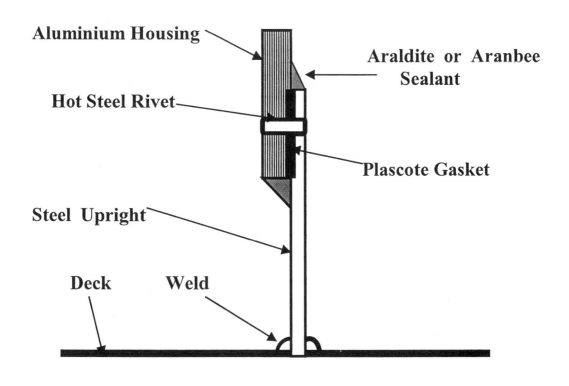

*Figure AI.21*

### Robotic Welding Systems

Several shipyards have looked to develop ship construction and building techniques employing "Robotics" to enhance production processes. Industrial Automation Systems have developed a vision based robotic system to increase efficiency in welding, cutting and grinding operations. High resolution cameras are employed by an operator who is left to approve the tracked movement and welding programme. The welding robot is a track mounted travelling gantry, mounted overhead of the steel work to be welded. The gantry, carrying both the welding robot and the vision cameras is automatic but manual operation can also be applied.

Current use is employing a two dimensional operational system, but a third dimension of depth can also be programmed into the system. The use of robotic welding practice is expected to reduce costs when compared with non automated operations. Certain limitations exist with early systems where the geometry of work pieces are complex. However, the future should be enhanced with improved quality work and increased production for lower cost.

### Semi-Automatic Welding Methods

Manual arc welding, although comparatively cheap requires a level of skill. Its main advantages being it is not complex, it is portable all be it somewhat slow. Consequently other semi-automatic systems have evolved and become popular, like Submerged Arc Welding.

Other examples include:—

**Tungsten Inert Gas (T.I.G.)** which employs a water cooled non consumable tungsten electrode, surrounded by a flow of inert argon gas. It is widely used in the welding of Aluminium and other non-ferrous metals which react with corrosive chemical fluxes.

The Argon gas prevents oxidation of the weld. Penetration tends to be poor so its use has limited plate thickness.

**Metal Inert Gas (M.I.G.)** – This method uses a consumable, cooled wire electrode and is useful for welding non-ferrous metals. The electrode is surrounded by an inert gas, usually $CO_2$ It has good penetration and is used to weld plate thickness upto 75 mm.

### Oxy-Acetylene Welding and Cutting

A cutting torch is supplied with two gases, oxygen and acetylene which when ignited generate a flame capable of melting sheet metal upto about 6 mm thick. Additional metal may be supplied from a hand held rod with or without a flux coating. Oxidation is reduced with the flux coating. This welding method has poor penetration. It is slow and lacks control.

When cutting the torch head provides a central high pressure oxygen stream which causes a rapid blasting away of the hot metal, once it has been pre-heated by the oxy-acetylene flame around the oxygen stream.

*Figure AI.22   On going welding and cutting operations on a section of a ship's double bottom. An enclosed assembly shop area, allows continuous working. Once completed overhead carriage cranage (Not shown) causes the prefabricated module to be moved forward for coating onto the next production phase.*

**Classification Societies (IACS The International Association of Classification Societies)**

An International Classification Society can be defined as an independent organization which develops and updates published rules, regulations and standards for the safe design, construction and maintenance of ships capable of international trade. They are a world wide organization which employs its own exclusive staff to inspect and assist the shipping industry to meet required standards. They set technical standards for the building of ships and provide design advice, oil analysis and quality accreditation.

American Bureau of Shipping (ABS)
Bureau Veritas (BV) (The largest organisation for classification)
China Classification Society (CCS)
Det Norske Veritas (DNV)
Germanischer Lloyd (GL)
Lloyds Register (LR)
Nippon Kaiji Kyokai (NK) (Largest Class Society in the world)
Registro Italiano Navale (RINA)
Russian Maritime Register of Shipping (RS)
Korean Register of Shipping (KR).

Additional Classification Organisations:—

Hellenic Register (Greece) (Recognised only in their own country)
Indian Register of Shipping (Associate of IACS)
Marshall Islands Registry
Polski Rejestr Statków (PRS) (Recognised only in their own country).
Croation Register of Shipping (Associate member of IACS).

## The Work Of the Classification Societies

Although not compulsory for ships to be "classed" the vast majority are Registered with one or other of the Societies. Registration brings with it many advantages for the ship owners. The Registers provides a reliable reference which supports the construction and repair to recognised standards, for their ships. Without the organisation of Classification Societies, many organisations such as underwriters, bankers, shippers and charter brokers would have great difficulty in conducting their businesses.

The work of the Classification Societies includes, but is not limited to, the following:—

(a)  The Classification and survey of ships and floating structures.
(b)  Classification of nuclear ships.
(c)  The Classification of "Ice Breakers" and of ice strengthened ships.
(d)  ISM and ISPS certification.
(e)  The survey of container units.
(f)  Certification of Training Centres.
(g)  Carrying out Risk Assessments.
(h)  Consultation services.
(i)  Conducting international seminars on maritime affairs.
(j)  ISO certification.
(k)  Human element studies.
(l)  Provision of expertise for Mobile Offshore Drilling Units (MODU).
(m) Provision of expertise for Floating Production, Storage and Offloading Systems (FPSO's).

Lloyds Register (LR) is the oldest of the Classification Societies and was established in a coffee house in London c.1688. A publication, originally known as the Underwriters Register or the "Green Book" catalogued the construction and characteristics of individual ships, first published in 1760.

**NB.** This publication has now been published by a separate organisation of Lloyds since 1834.

Lloyds Register of Shipping should not be confused with the Corporation of Lloyds Underwriters (known as "Lloyds of London").

## Conditions for Classification

Ships which are constructed in accordance with the Rules and Regulations of the Classification Society will be assigned a class in the Register Book. They will continue to retain this class provided they are found by examination and survey, to be maintained in accordance with the rules. Compliance with conditions for the ship's hull and machinery is a condition for classification. Any damage or defect occurring to the vessel which could invalidate the conditions of the issue of class, must be reported to the Society.

## Types of Ship Survey

- **Initial Survey** – A complete Inspection of all items relating to the particular certificate before the ship enters service to ensure that it is in a satisfactory condition for the intended service.
- **Periodical Survey** – An inspection of items which relate to a particular certificate to ensure that the items are in a satisfactory condition and fit for the intended service.
- **Renewal Survey** – As for the periodical survey, but leads to the renewal of the certificate.

- **Annual Survey – (+/– 3 months)** – A general inspection of the items which relate to a particular certificate to ensure that those items have been maintained and remain in a satisfactory condition for the service the ship is intended for.
- **Additional Survey** – An inspection either general or partial according to the circumstances, to be made after a repair resulting from a casualty, or whenever any important repairs or renewals are made.

## Certificates Required by Harmonized Survey System

- Passenger Ship Safety Certificate (Includes "record of inspection").
- Cargo Ship Safety Construction Certificate.
- Cargo Ship Safety Radio Certificate.
- Cargo Ship Safety Equipment Certificate.
- International Load Line Certificate.
- International Load Line Exemption Certificate.
- International Oil Pollution Prevention Certificate.
- International Pollution Prevention Certificate for the carriage of Noxious Liquid Substances in Bulk.
- International Certificate of Fitness for the carriage of Dangerous Chemicals in Bulk.
- International Certificate of Fitness for the carriage of Liquefied Gases in Bulk.
- Certificate of Fitness for the Carriage of Dangerous Chemicals in Bulk.

## Interim Certificate of Class

Lloyds may issue a provisional (interim) certificate to allow a ship to sail on the proviso that the ship is in a fit and proper condition. An example of such use may be following an accident to a vessel where damage has been sustained. Temporary repairs are made to ensure the immediate safety of the vessel. The interim certificate would be issued following satisfactory inspection, to allow the vessel to sail towards a recognised permanent repair facility, in order to return the ship to its previous level of seaworthiness. A local marine surveyor from Lloyds or from another reputable classification society would be designated to inspect the temporary repairs, on behalf of Lloyds, before the issue of the interim certificate. In the event that an approved surveyor was not available, the inspection could still be carried out by two British Masters, but this would not lead to the issue of an interim certificate of class, but a Seaworthy Certificate.

## Notice of Survey

It is the responsibility of the ship's owners to ensure that all surveys are carried out at the correct times. Notice of survey, is issued by Lloyds Register, by letter or computer print out.

## Suspension or Withdrawal of Class

There are several reasons why the classification of a ship could be withdrawn or suspended. Where an infringement of the Rules and Regulations is incurred, class may be withdrawn. Where a vessel sails overloaded or with incorrectly marked loadlines, class may be suspended. If a ship operates in waters for which she was not classed, then automatic suspension of class could be the result.

## Document File

The ship owner must maintain a Document File on board the vessel effecting its service history. This file would have an index and contain the following:—

Survey Reports to include,

(a) A report of structural survey.
(b) A condition evaluation of the hull.
(c) A thickness measurement report.
(d) Survey planning documents.

Supporting Documents to include,

   (a) Main structural plans of tank disposition.
   (b) A record of cargo and ballast history.
   (c) A defect and repair history.
   (d) A record of inert gas, tank cleaning and crude oil washing (COW) programme.
   (e) A record of inspections and activities of ship's staff.
   (f) Additional information.

## Hydrolift Docking Systems

In December, 2000, the "Lisnave Shipyard" at Setúbal, in Portugal opened a platform hydrolift, docking system for ships. This new concept allowed for the docking of three Panamax, sized ships simultaneously.

The system works in conjunction with a wet basin which is entered via a caisson at the seaward end. Once the inward bound ship is established in the basin, the outer caisson is closed. The water level is then increased in both the basin and the designated platform dock by pump operation. The platform dock can alternatively be filled by gravity from the basin area.

Once the basin is full and level with the dock space, the ship will have been elevated sufficiently to clear the sill of the platform dock. This position allows the dock caisson to open and permit the transfer of the vessel from the basin to the dock platform. The dock caisson is subsequently closed and draining of the dock is then allowed by gravity.

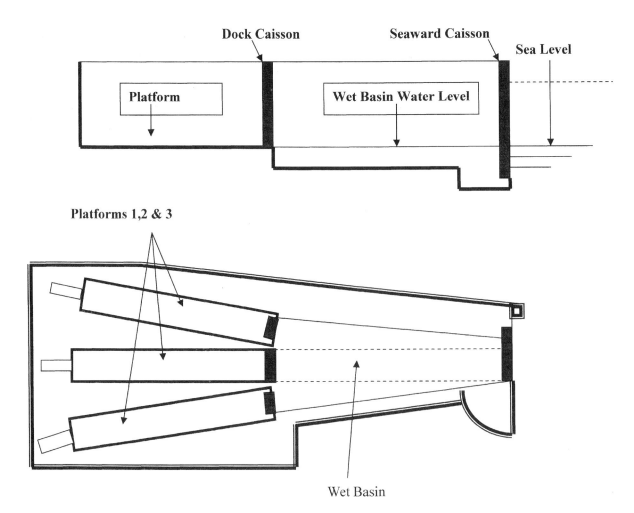

*Figure AI.23   Hydro Lift System.*

**Inward and Outward Procedures for Hydrolift Docking Systems**

The docking method by means of the hydrolift system operates in a similar fashion to a vessel passing through locks. A prime example of which is seen in the Panama Canal passage, when vessels pass from the Caribbean Sea through to the Pacific Ocean.

The example hydro lift at "Lisnave" has the advantage of being able to dock three large vessels at any one time, and not be restricted by time constraints on clearing the docking area. Such a method could no doubt be designed to accommodate more docks, being serviced by a single and wider hydrostatic wet basin to permit vessel manoeuvrability.

The time period of flooding large wet basin areas and docking platform areas can be lengthy and the pumping machinery would need regular maintenance and service, to keep the docking system operational.

*Figure AI.24    View of the Hydro-lift Dock, at the Lisnave Shipyard, showing the flooded "wet basin" and the left hand platform dock ready to receive the incoming vessel. The centre platform dock is seen caisson in place, dry with a tanker vessel in situation.*

**Launching of New and Docked Vessels**

Ship builders the world over must remain competitive or suffer the consequences of closure. To this end, once the contract to build has been commissioned, the need to complete the hull construction and effect the launch becomes all important. This will effectively clear the building slip/dock and make resources available to take on new business.

The launching of the newly constructed vessel in few cases brings the work load down.

On the contrary, man hours can expect to increase as the hull is moved to a fitting out berth. Although the prefabrication and much of the heavy steel work of the building yard has already been completed the future stages of making the vessel habitable and operational becomes task orientated. Workshops will still be engaged, but the new ship has moved on to a different construction level.

The design stage has been and gone, with the exception of modifications to ongoing construction. The specialist task and skills come into play, with the fitting out of transmission and control systems. Machinery drive operations, cargo handling gear, Sanitation and water systems, refrigeration and store facilities. Electrics, hydraulic and pneumatic systems need to be installed, while internal décor and hotel services generally become the final application before conducting the vessels acceptance trials.

The method of launch can vary from the conventional end slip, to side launching, where water width restrictions may exist. Employing a building dock where the dock can be flooded and the vessel allowed to become waterborne is probably the easiest of methods, but each system has merits and drawbacks.

Once successfully launched and the fitting out of the ship is virtually complete, a trials period would be anticipated where technician staff carry out fine tuning under operational conditions. Ship's staff would also probably be involved at this stage, as well as Shipping Company observers and a variety of approval specialists, prior to accepting ownership of the build.

## Launching

The early days of ship building generally employed an astern end slip style of launching, after the vessel had been constructed at right angles to the waters edge. More recently, with the increase in ship size, modular building methods and available water areas in the vicinity of shipyards, more innovative methods have been employed.

Side launching, module launching and float off methods have evolved alongside the conventional slip launchway. The side launch method tends to be a practical option and follows the ship being built in a parallel direction to the waterfront. Launching usually taking place into rivers, canals or similar areas of limited water access.

An alternative to a slip or side launch is to construct in an enclosed building area that can be flooded, like a floating building dock. The ship is constructed in the enclosed area and when completed it is directly floated off the building blocks, employing the same principle as when re-floating a vessel after a routine dry docking.

A more recent method employed has been the Skid-Launching System (SLS), as used by the Jinhae Shipyard of STX. This employs transfer of the build to a submersible barge. When floated clear of the building area the barge is submerged using a similar principle as the "Heavy Lift Vessel" and the new construction is allowed to float off.

## Slip Launching

The conventional method of launching a vessel, or module of a vessel, is achieved by transferring the weight of the ship or section from the building blocks onto a cradle arrangement. The cradle and vessel are then moved onto groundways leading into the water. The cradle and its load are then allowed to move seaward, down the angled groundways. The groundways are well lubricated and movement is achieved by gravity from the land side, towards and into the waters edge, to such an extent that utilizes the greatest depth of water. The groundways are usually made of heavy duty timbers and are laid at an angle of inclination to take account of the length of keel line and the declivity of the ground level. The ratio being a variable between sites, but is generally about 1 : 24. This effectively reduces the stresses on the end of the slip as the vessel enters the water. If maximum water depth is not available to allow the buoyancy forces to take full effect, the end groundways may have to be strengthened to reduce the risk of damage. Some shoring may also be needed in and around the fore-end of the vessel as the ship is affected by the buoyancy forces astern and starts to pivot about the fore end.

Other launching slip operations employ sliding ways on top of the groundways, in place of the cradle arrangement.

Launching usually takes place stern first, but can be carried out bow first. However, a bow first launch operation, is unusual and are few in number. As the vessel enters the water the hull will experience an increasing momentum as well as the pivotal action about the region of the forward poppets. The buoyancy forces will start to counter the movement down the slip and can be further checked by drag chains or even moorings, or a combination of both, to arrest the vessels astern motion down to the water.

Modern day launching operations generally employ the use of tugs to first encourage a downward movement on the slip, but then as a check on the hulls momentum once afloat.

After clearing the slip and the groundways, the tugs can effectively instigate control of the hull.

## Building Slips

Many ships are now directly constructed on building blocks which take the weight of the new vessel during construction. Groundways are then built up between the line of keel blocks and the bilge blocks, either side of the keel. The ship's weight is then transferred to the launch cradle or sliding ways on top of the fixed groundways. Weight transfer is effected by removing the keel and bilge block lines. This is usually achieved by taking the wedges away from the building blocks and systematically withdrawing them, to leave the ship sitting on the sliding ways. Involuntary movement is checked by the trigger device or "dagger shores" which prevent the sliding ways moving until the desired time of launching. Once the trigger is removed, the new build will move due to gravitational forces and some initial force by hydraulic jacks on the fore end groundways causing the sliding ways to overcome any frictional resistance.

## Building Block and Shore Arrangements

## Showing Launching Way Positions

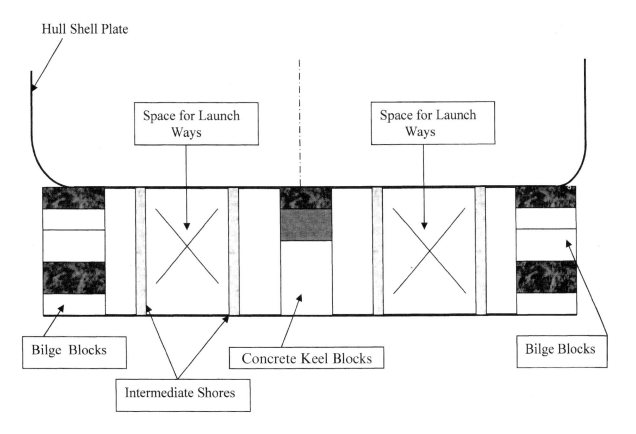

*Figure AI.25*

## Effecting Launching

Slip launching is achieved by "ramming" up the launch blocks after driving wedges in, to raise the building blocks. The procedure is labour intensive and employs a' ramming pole'. Two days prior to launch the shores are removed and some of the keel blocks are cleared leaving only an effective number to support the ship's length. About an hour before launch, the remaining building blocks are removed, transferring the weight onto the launch ways and the triggers.

The commonest way this is achieved, is to drive wedges into the launch cradle. This effectively lifts the ship and allows the building blocks to be removed. Some shipyards employ collapsible blocks which can be more easily removed. The ground ways on which the ship and cradle will slide are usually positioned at a distance apart which equates to about one third ($\frac{1}{3}$) of the ship's beam. In such a way that the pressure on the launch way tends not to exceed 20 t/m.

Lubricating grease is used between the sliding ways of the cradle and the ground ways to generate a smooth movement down the declivity of the groundways. The declivity of the ground way being such as to overcome the initial starting friction to allow the vessel to move under the influence of gravity. These days hydraulic rams are usually employed to provide the initial push to generate movement. Modern practice is to use an electrical or hydraulic trigger to initiate release.

Once movement has commenced it must be controlled and the speed of progress down the slip will be influenced by the camber of the ground ways and the declivity. The speed is further controlled by an arresting arrangement usually made up of drag chains secured to the hull of the vessel. These tend to reduce the momentum, as the vessel enters the water. Also the buoyancy forces effecting the hull as it enters the water will cause the ship to rise, reducing the frictional contact area on the slip.

Once the hull is afloat tugs and/or moorings can be used to manoeuvre and turn the vessel. While the purpose welded pad eyes can be removed and the drag chains recovered by the shipyard.

**Arresting Arrangements**

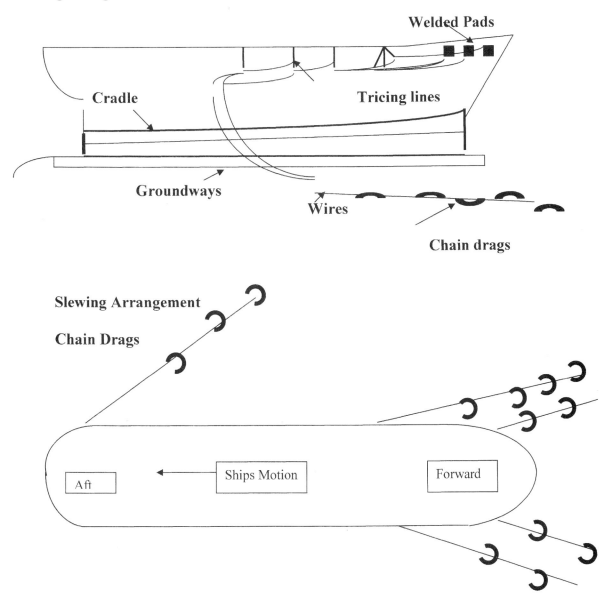

*Figure AI.26*

A requirement of launching, especially where the water area is restricted, is to arrest the launch by means of drag chains. The drag chains being arranged symmetrically on either side of the vessel. The chains being secured to wires which in themselves are shackled to temporary pad eyes welded to the hull, fit for purpose.

On occasions a vessel may need to be turned (slewed) on entering the water. This can be achieved by securing chain drags to the stern area to one side or another in order to achieve a turning action by the vessel as it leaves the slip end.

**Building and Launch**

Many vessels are now constructed in building docks and are launched by float off methods, by the subsequent flooding of the dock, once the hull perimeter is complete and watertight. The new build can then be moved to a fitting out berth. This allows further use of the building dock for another construction.

In a similar manner, where a new construction is built on a building slip, the requirement to launch as soon as the hull is complete is desirable by the shipyard. Once the slip is clear, further construction can be carried out.

*Figure AI.27    The Anchor Handling vessel "Pacific Retriever" being prepared for launch from the building slip. The hull length is complete and watertight but the superstructures have yet to be fitted.*

### Skid Launching System

This method is achieved by building the hull in two halves horizontally with a split division about the amidship's part. Once each section is complete it is jacked by hydraulics towards the seaward end and onto a specialised floating dock known as a skid-barge. The size of this barge being of a length about 200 m × 48 m in width. The two parts of the vessel are then welded together, the barge is towed clear from the berth and submerged in a similar way to a heavy lift ship The new vessel is then floated off and the barge is recovered for future launches.

### Load Out System

Several shipyards are now employing an alternative launch method following vessels constructed on dry land sites. Hyundai Heavy Industries, employs a hydraulic system to load outward the completed vessel onto semi-submersible barges. These take the ship into deep water and permits float off. The CIMAR shipyard employs 200 tonne low level transporters to lift hull sections onto semi-submersible barges to join sections together then establish float off. (Similar principle to the skid-launch operation.)

**Float Off, Float Out**

A system employed usually for the very large construction like passenger vessels, where the building takes place inside an enclosed dock area. Once the hull is water tight, the dock area is allowed to flood and the hull is usually towed outward towards a fitting out berth. The fitting out stage may take some considerable time to complete prior to carrying out ship trials. However, the removal of the hull early from the building dock allows the dock space to become available for a new build. The launch date and the commissioning date may very well be up to two years apart.

**Side Launching**

Side launching is a method which is employed when the width of the water is limited, but the water frontage is adequate for the ship's length. Construction of the ship takes place parallel to the water front. Launch ways are set at right angles to the ship's fore and aft line and extended into the water at a low incline. While the landward side blocks are jacked up, to angle the vessel off the centre line towards the waters edge.

The ship is encouraged to slide broadside down the launch ways, which are well lubricated prior to the launch time. Reaction moorings are often used to counter the roll and anti roll of the vessel as she takes the water. Prudent use of ballast weight, low down in the vessel can also influence the movement of the vessel once she is allowed to take the water.

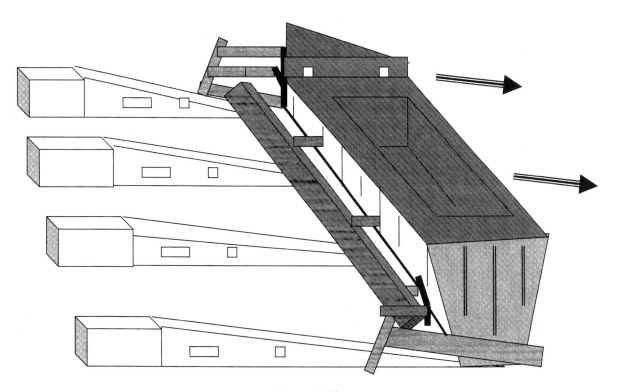

*Figure AI.28*

*Figure AI.29   The anchor handling vessel Pacific Retriever is positioned with a tug secured right aft prior to its launching debut.*

*Figure AI.30   The Pacific Retriever is launched clear of the building slip to become waterborne, prior to being moored to a fitting out lay-by berth.*

**Sectional Building and Launching**

*Figure AI.31    The midship's section of the "Norwegian Dream" cruise ship being launched prior to assembly to lengthen the vessel. The major operation to increase the vessels length taking place at the Lloyd Werft shipyard in Bremerhaven, Germany.*

Modern shipbuilding often involves ship's block sections being built in different shipyards, frequently many miles apart. Such practice may be planned for financial reasons or to deploy a labour or a skills base within additional company resources. Where sectional vessels are constructed they are often floated to a common assembly port where the final completion of the vessel can be achieved.

Such operations free up building yards more quickly while at the same time, keep personnel gainfully employed at different sites. Once the smaller sections are scheduled for construction these tend to have a wider appeal to the smaller shipyard anyway, while at the same time, allows their facilities to seek out new working commissions.

## Lengthening a Vessel by New Section

*Figure AI.32   The new amidship's section is manoeuvred between the bow and stern sections of the Norwegian Dream passenger vessel, prior to assembly of all three sections. Tugs are employed to manoeuvre the new additional section and the bow section, towards the in dock stern element. The width size of the dock must be sufficient to provide handling space for the tugs, once the sections start to close up for assembly.*

The option to lengthen a vessel is often viewed as an alternative to buying or even building new tonnage. Although an expensive operation in itself, it is cheaper than commissioning a new build to equate to the required size. The other option would be to charter an additional vessel to pick up the added trade, but such a move would normally only be made as a short term option.

## Launch Stresses

When a vessel is launched, it is a time when a variety of stress factors are generated. Historically most ships are built on building slips and launched stern first but some smaller vessel are launched sideways on, especially where the building yard has a restricted water area.

Although the ship is generally constructed on "keel blocks" and held in position by shores, such an arrangement cannot launch the vessel. Once building is completed. the keel blocks are sectionally removed and the weight of the vessel is taken by wooden launching cradles or slidingways, on top of groundways. Additionally, large ships are often fitted with a soft wood, cushion structure (forward poppets) to support the bow region when the after end of the vessel enters the water. At this moment of time the aft end being supported by the buoyancy of the water, while the wood cushion supports the forward end, which is still in contact with the slip.

To avoid undue frictional resistance on the groundways, these are coated with a thick grease. Drag chains are secured to the hull to slow the operation down and to reduce the vessels momentum, as the ship is allowed to slip to the waterline.

The launch time would take account of the state of the tide. If the tide is too low, the stern will not be fully supported and may be caused to "droop". If the tide is too high, hull distortion may occur as the aft end becomes waterborne while the rest of the vessels structural weight is taken on the launch ways at the forward end.

Some building yards use hydraulic rams to act as triggers to the launch generating the movement down the slip. Alternatively, tugs may be secured by long drift moorings under tension to generate a downward movement of the new vessel towards the water.

**NB.** By launching stern first, the risk of damage to the rudder and propellers from the drag chains is removed.

The angle of the groundways is such as to allow the effects of gravity to encourage movement of the vessel down the slip to the waterfront. The incline must be such that it will allow frictional forces to be overcome and allow the momentum to carry the vessel into the water. Though once buoyancy forces effect the hull the movement will experience some resistance. The drag chains will also act to slow the movement by generating additional resistance to the astern momentum.

# Shipbuilding Materials

In order to formulate shipyard practice it is essential to understand the materials that are employed within the basic concept of the modern shipyard. It is also a pre-requisite to understand the function of the shipyard in the first place.

Shipyards do not just build ships, they could not sustain themselves in the current economic climate, they must also become directly involved in the ship repair and also in some cases, civil engineering projects business. New contracts alone, for building or repair, are often heavily subsidised by a nations willingness to compete in the shipbuilding market and are rarely negotiated on a level playing field. The customer placing a new contract to build, is clearly looking for the best of deals to build a high quality vessel at the least cost. This similarly applies to repair contracts when and wherever possible.

Many factors are involved in completing a contract between customer and shipyard. Government subsidies could well be available to retain unemployment levels to an acceptable figure. While new development could well be supported by government loans at little or no interest to permit the growth of industry. How one nations shipyards establish and compete against another is clearly prominent in the industry.

Other factors such as the price of steel or importing costs to the building nation clearly influence the bottom line, to the eventual customer. While labour costs could well be the dominant feature of choice, as to where the customer places the final order. Once the letter of intent is placed and the contract signed it is then the time to build and deliver towards a completion date.

The build process incorporates the latest developments in planning and technology any industry has ever experienced. From design innovation, to the sophisticated welding practices of robotics and prefabrication techniques to the materials employed. The industry is awash with ideas of improvement to build bigger and better ships. Ships that will carry greater payloads, which will be environmentally friendly, which will be financially viable and above all, be safe.

### Shipyard Materials

**Steel, Steel and more Steel**, not any longer. Although steel remains the dominant material in shipbuilding, alloys, composites, plastics and ceramics are becoming ever popular in the building of ships' hulls, superstructures and machinery products.

In every case, the function and expectancy of each component must not only be practical but also cost effective in performance.

### Steel

Steel is basically an alloy which is made from a combination of elements namely, Iron, carbon and smaller elements from iron ore. The natural ore is mined and in its raw state contains several impurities, such as phosphorous, sulphur, manganese and silicon, all of which are removed in the manufacturing process.

The manufacturing process mixes iron ore with coal to provide the required carbon content. Limestone is then added, which causes the impurities to "bond" together which can later be removed in the form of a product known as "slag". The mixture is turned to a molten state inside a blast furnace where the "slag", lighter than the molten iron, floats to the top and can be skimmed off.

The molten iron is then drawn off from the Blast Furnace and known as "pig iron" which is then converted to steel. This is subsequently achieved by passing the liquid product through an oxygen furnace. This furnace is lined with magnesia bricks and pre-loaded with a percentage of scrap steel (approximately $\frac{1}{3}$ scrap to $\frac{2}{3}$ molten pig iron). Virtually pure oxygen is then blasted through at high pressure, using an "oxygen lance" causing the temperature to rise to approximately 1,500°C.

The mixture reacts to the extreme temperature rise and further impurities such as silica and metal emulsion form a further slag composite. Carbon monoxide gas is also produced in great quantity while the desired metal produced is a raw steel product, which can be drawn from the oxygen furnace.

It is at this stage that additives can be added to the manufacturing process to produce the many different grades and steel alloys required. The molten mix can then be finally cast into what is known as steel "billets". These are then reheated via another furnace and processed into plates, pipe products, roll off coils, rolled sheets, bars or structures, ready for industrial use.

### Grades and Types of Steel

**Alloy Steel** – This is a steel grade to which an alloy metal is added. A popular example of this is where aluminium is added, this produces a smooth and bright steel product with high tensile strength used extensively in the aircraft industry.

**Chromium Steel** – An alloy steel which is extensively employed in the automotive industry. It is easy to press and pre-form, yet retains strength and elasticity.

**High Carbon Steel** – This is the hardest form of steel and is used for the manufacture of cutting tools and engineering dies. It has great strength, but it is also very brittle and requires care in use. They contain free cementite ($Fe_3C$) which retains the sharpness in manufactured tools but reduces ductility and shock resistance of the metal.

**High Tensile Steels (HTS)** – is a steel grade which has a high resistance to stress, especially when employed in the longitudinal plane. It is predominant in the shipbuilding industry for all classes of vessel. Often used for decks, sides and bottom regions of tankers. It is usually selected because it has higher strength and allows thinner plates to be employed in order to comply with class standards. It also shows favourable fatigue properties when compared with mild steel. Some disadvantages are that thinner plates manufactured in HTS tend to flex more with wave motions. Such flexing can dislodge surface rust and scale exposing the bare metal. Such activity can cause rapid thickness loss of the steel plate.

**Medium or Low Carbon Steel** – The more common type of steel and in extensive use within the shipbuilding industry. They tend to contain between 0.3 to 0.7% carbon and are all heat treated. It is used for sheeting and structural applications. This grade of steel has an ease of use which lends to welding and tooling into refined products.

**Mild Steel** – A general term which does not actually denote a recognised steel grade. It usually refers to steels which have up to 0.25% carbon and which are hardened by a two stage heat treatment. Modern compositions have developed high tensile properties usually from precipitation hardening.

**Nickle-Chromium** – A well used grade of steelwork which has the high tensile properties of high carbon steel without possessing the brittleness associated with high carbon grade. It has high shock qualities and tends to be employed in the battle field vehicles for armoured plate protection.

**Stainless Steel** – This is a high quality grade of steel which contains more than 10% chromium together with additional elements to benefit the finished product. It has high anti-corrosive properties and retains a high strength capability even in high temperatures.

Although generally more expensive to produce once *in situ* it will require little maintenance. It is especially resistant to the corrosive actions of seawater but susceptible to galvanic corrosion and should be separated where possible from other metals.

**Steel Section Structures Common to Ship Repair and Building**

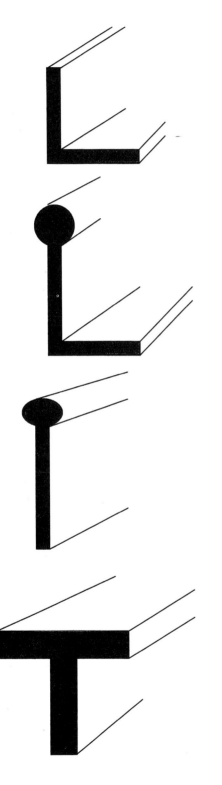

**Angle Bar** -  used for right angle stiffening,
Frames/stringer  and plate connections.

**Bulb Angle-** used for increased stiffening in both longitudinal, vertical  and athwartships directions.

**Bulb Plate** – Used for Bilge Keels, construction and stiffening.

**'T'  Girder** – Used for plate landings and   stiffening in both longitudinal and  athwartships directions.

*Figure AII.1*

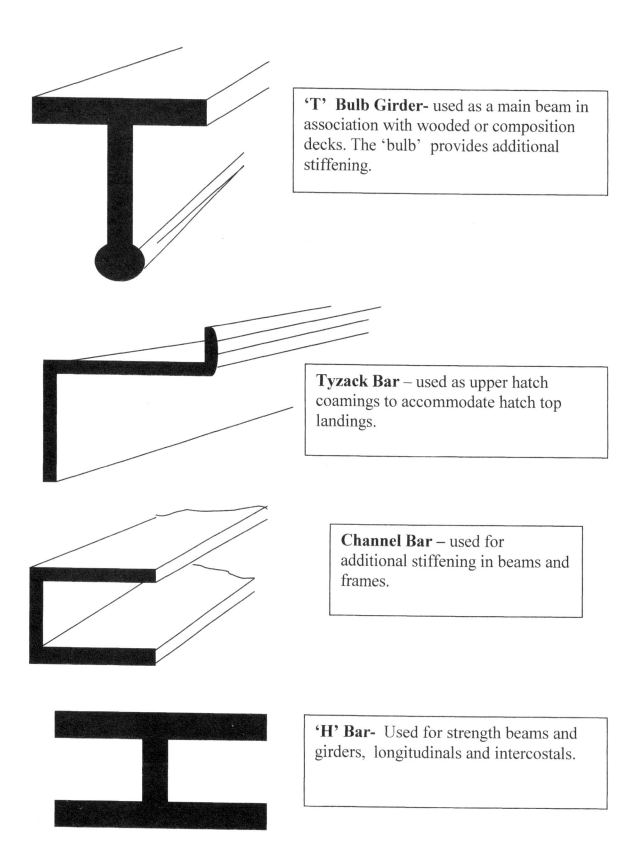

**'T' Bulb Girder-** used as a main beam in association with wooded or composition decks. The 'bulb' provides additional stiffening.

**Tyzack Bar** – used as upper hatch coamings to accommodate hatch top landings.

**Channel Bar** – used for additional stiffening in beams and frames.

**'H' Bar-** Used for strength beams and girders, longitudinals and intercostals.

*Figure AII.2*

**Pipe and Bar Sections**

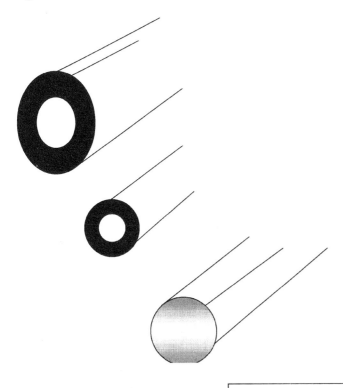

Pipe and Bar sections    -for the
construction of  hawse pipes,
spurling pipes, sounding and air
pipes.

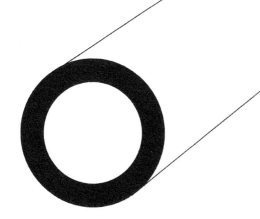

Tube section for fender bars, and rounded
gunwales popular in the building of anchor
handling vessels

*Figure AII.3*

**Corrugated Section Plate**

Cold formed steel, Corrugated
Sheeting provides rigidity and
Strength.

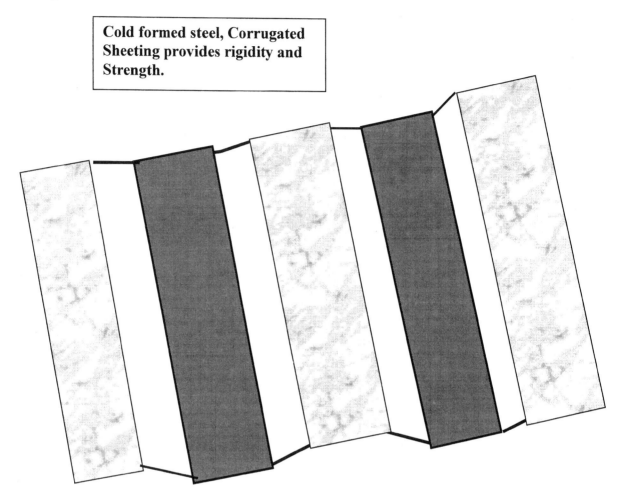

*Figure AII.4    Example in use, is found in corrugated bulkheads.*

**Design Factors to Minimise Corrosion**

1.  Any reduction in the use of dissimilar metals or different grades of steelwork, except where its is fundamentally required will reduce corrosion sources.
2.  Prudent use of sacrificial anodes, in ballast tanks directly attached to the hull can expect to retain steelwork quality.
3.  Suitable paint coatings applied to exposed hull areas or in cargo tanks, like deep tanks or chemical tanks will provide additional protection against corrosive effects.
4.  Adequate drainage features incorporated at the design stage, from decks, tanks, wells, etc., will reduce the possibility of an accumulation of slack water and associated corrosion effects.
5.  Use of corrosion resistant alloy steels, like with stainless steel bearings or valve seats, etc.
6.  Adequate insulation being deployed where extreme temperature ranges can expect to be experienced can expect to reduce brittle fractures.
7.  The fitting of rubbing strakes or doubling plates to absorb wear and tear can provide some structural protection.
8.  Removing mill scale from new steel work prior to fitting.
9.  The inclusion of measures to minimise the likelihood of fatigue caused by welding techniques, vibration and employing stress relieving methods.
10. The installation of an impressed current system for monitoring of corrosion cell activity. To include internal piping protection.

11. Use of insulating materials between dissimilar metals, e.g. like with aluminium/steel connections.
12. Taking advantage of an oxygen deficient atmosphere to reduce corrosive effects. As with the installation of high quality efficient scrubber,in an inert gas system

## Testing of Steelwork

All steelwork which is employed for shipbuilding purposes, must pass through a phase of testing to ensure that it meets the specifications of the Classification Societies. Testing is achieved by **non destructive test (NDT)** methods or by testing a sample to destruction, known as **destructive testing**.

**Destructive Testing** – Is where stresses are applied to steel samples until the sample fails. It includes tests for tensile strength and ductility. Impact tests are carried out for "Brittleness" and "Hardness".

Fatigue tests monitor the effect of stresses over a period of repeated cycles. Fatigue faults are insidious and will cause metal to crack and fail without warning.

A Creep Test is conducted for plastic deformation which may effect metals exposed to continuous high temperatures like steam pipes. A sample may fail the creep test at a lower stress level resulting in elongation. A result that would differ to that determined in a tensile test.

Tests are monitored and results obtained in a variety of ways. Tensile tests for example can be displayed graphically, Load (Stress) × Strain (Extension) to show the "Yield Point" and the "elastic limit" of the sample. Where as the brittleness is commonly ascertained by what is known as a **"Charpy Test"**. Here the sample is impacted by a swinging pendulum, the energy employed to break the sample is a measure of its brittleness. The lower the level of energy used, the more brittle the sample is considered to be.

**Non-Destructive Testing** – These are tests which do not deform or damage the material being tested. The function of this type of test is to detect faults or flaws in either the material or the bonding of that material, i.e. welds. There are numerous methods of non-destructive testing and a few of the more common ones are listed:—

**Magnetic Testing (MT)** – This is a method which is used to detect surface or near surface defects. Although it can also be employed to locate sub-surface flaws but tends to lose effectiveness with the increased depth of the material. It is based on the principle of magnetic lines of force being distorted by cracks or other similar flaws in the substance.

Iron particles can be applied wet or dry and location of flaws would be ascertained from any flux leakage.

**Penetration Test (PT)** – This method employs a coloured or fluorescent penetrating dye.

The objective is to reveal surface flaws by using the ability of a liquid to be drawn into a breaking flaw by capillary action. The excess surface liquid is then removed and a developer is applied. This developer causes the dye to be drawn from the flaw so revealing the defect. Fluorescent dyes need to be exposed in dark conditions with ultra-violet light.

**Ultrasonic Testing (UT)** – Employs high frequency, shortwave length, sound waves. A pulsed beam is transmitted by a transducer held next to the material for the test. A gel is used between the transducer and the material surface to ensure an air tight seal is achieved before commencing the test. Any returning sound (echo) back to the transducer can be screen displayed and the pulse amplitude and timing is measurable. The flaw size and distance from the surface can then be ascertained. This method can also be used to measure the thickness of a material.

**Visual Testing (VT)** – Probably the simplest and least expensive, of all test systems. It requires adequate illumination and good vision by the person doing the inspection. The inspector also needs the experience to know what to look for. Inspections can be enhanced by the use of low powered magnifying glasses to high powered electronic microscopes linked to camera and/or television receivers. It is one of the first tests applied to welded joints.

**Radiographic Testing (RT)** – employs x-radiography and gamma radiography. The x-rays or gamma rays are passed through the material at close range and captured on film. Once the film is processed a series of gray shades are achieved between the black and white image. Defects being visibly displayed on the film.

**NB.** Both x-ray and gamma rays are extremely dangerous to personnel and adequate protection must be made available to operators of such equipment.

## Treatment of Steel

### Cold Forming

Cold forming is a process which is often applied to varieties of steel alloy. It tends to offer many advantages, especially to the shipbuilding industry, including prefabrication methods A uniform quality and suitable for mass production operations. Such advantages leading to ease of handling, quick assembly and low weight products which are easier for transport.

The procedures require specialized equipment to achieve pre-forming, roll bending and steel presses being used to shape plate and sections of materials at room temperature. Such action will usually stretch the grain of the metal often leaving it subject to fracture and generally more brittle. However, annealing (heat treatment) can usually make the metal structure more workable. Although annealing can cause reduced tensile stress and reduces hardness, it will have a tendency to render steel more ductile.

*Figure AII.5    Steel Roll, Bending Machine, employed for shaping steel alloy sheeting and aluminium sections.*

### Hardening of Steel

Hardening of steelwork can be achieved by heat application then quickly providing rapid cooling. This process is known as "quenching", it is achieved by a brine bath coolant. More modern techniques employ, oils, fresh water or even freezing air.

Engaging such methods could expect to reduce the temperature of the steel by about 1,000°C per minute, while at the same time, producing probably the hardest of all steels. The disadvantage being, the metal is left in a very brittle state and would probably need tempering.

*The Annealing process is also a recognized method of hardening steelwork. Cooling after annealing, allows the molecular structure of the metal to re-crystallise and encourages grain growth, making the product more easy to work.

## Tempering

This is a process which is meant to render the steelwork less brittle and more manageable. It is a re-heating process which tends to hold the temperature to about 400°C for a variable period of time. It loses some of its hardness but it becomes a tougher product, which is less brittle and again, more easy to work.

## Pickling

A method of cleaning processed steelwork is achieved through "pickling". As hot rolled steel sheets or coils are cooled rust can form comparatively quickly. Pickling involves passing the steelwork through a series of hydrochloric acid baths. It is then washed and dried prior to being worked further. The process removes any impurities such as dirt rust or oil. Coatings are applied at an appropriate future stage to reduce the risk of corrosion attack later.

## Normalising

This is a term used to describe a heat treatment process, which relieves internal stresses within the steel sample. It is caused by heating the steelwork to about 800°C to 900°C, a variable that depends on the grade of steel. This temperature is retained for a specific time period then allowed to cool naturally (Not quenching as in other methods of hardening steel.)

Normalising refines the grain size and improves the mechanical properties of the steel.

It is of course easy to achieve with small welded sections, but is more difficult with large sections. To this end electrical strips are laid alongside weld runs to generate the required temperature so reducing the stress in areas of the steelwork that has been welded.

## Protection for Prefabricated Steelwork

*Figure AII.6    Steel section waiting to be cleaned by blasting, prior to coating and assembly.*

## Galvanizing

Galvanizing steelwork is a form of protection against corrosion and the process coats the steel in a thin layer of zinc. It is achieved in any of four ways:—

(a) by electro-galvanizing,
(b) by a cold zinc spray system,
(c) by the hot dip method, or
(d) by metalizing.

**Electro-galvanizing** – can be formed by passing negatively charged steelwork through positively charged zinc. The thickness of the coating can be controlled by increasing or reducing the electrical charge or by slowing the passage of the steelworks progress, through the procedure, causing the coating to thicken.

**Cold zinc spray** – this is a comparatively new method of galvanizing which requires an epoxy which the zinc adheres to in order to coat the steel surface. This process must have an absolute clean surface free of grease, dirt or corrosion. The spraying procedure being carried out inside well ventilated conditions. Although durable the expected life of this method is less than other procedures for galvanizing.

**Hot Dip method** – Probably the oldest method of galvanizing having been operational since the 1,800's. The finished steelwork is coated with a flux to aid the bonding process.

It is then immersed into a bath of molten zinc (98% pure maintained at about 450°C). Once the steelwork reaches the same temperature as the molten zinc solution they are slowly withdrawn. Excess zinc is drained off and the product is wiped down with an air jet to obtain uniform thickness of coverage.

**Metalizing** – this is another spray method which uses zinc or aluminium via a spray-gun. The spray gun may accept either a metal wire or a powder depending on type. Inside the gun the metal is melted by an electric arc and compressed air is used to blast the molten solution directly to the steel surface.

The steelwork is then allowed to cool and is left with a coating which is resistant to abrasion and wear and can expect to protect the steel for many years.

## Managing Steelwork

Once the processed steel is delivered to the stockyard, usually by rail or road transport, it enters the shipyards system towards the cutting rooms and trimmed to manageable sizes to suit customers needs. Original cutting procedures employed flame torches and manual transport systems to convey steel sections forward. More modern practice is for cutting to be carried out by plasma torches, which are much faster. Throughput of sections being handled by overhead mobile gantry cranes integral to the cutting sheds working in conjunction with a roller bed.

Different shipyards have alternative or combination systems of gantries and/or winches for moving steel sections forward. Where lifting is and was required plate clamps were common, but electro-magnets have become more popular.

**Operating Principal of Telescopic Magnetic Lifting Beam**

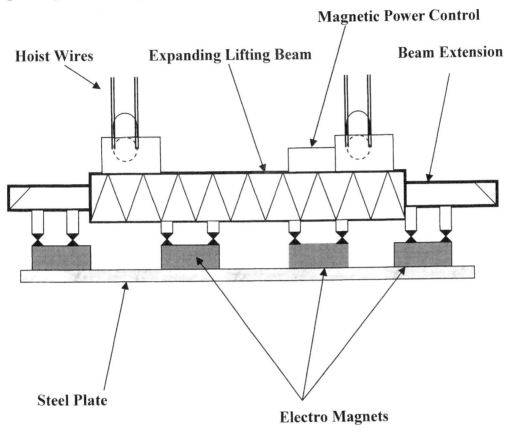

*Figure AII.7*

## Alternative Metals and Alloys

Historically, many choice metals have been employed within the ship construction industry, not least copper and more recently aluminium. Bearing in mind that alloys are a combination of two or more materials used to produce a specific metal, usually for a particular task, so many alloy products are also predominant.

The alloys tend to fall into two main categories as either ferrous alloys which have iron or steel as a base metal, or non-ferrous alloys like brass or the aluminium or copper alloys. They are often light weight, yet retain good strength qualities and have anti-corrosive properties. Aluminium being extensively used for upper structures aboard ships and in the fast ferry sector of the industry.

Modernization has allowed the development of welding methods to be adopted with virtually all of the alloy metals. They can also be heat treated, hardened and employed in areas which previously only engaged steel. Many of these alloys have the equivalent strength of steel and they can be handled better because of their lightweight properties.

*Figure AII.8    Aluminium alloy superstructure, prior to coating, being fitted to a Fast Ferry at NQEA Shipyard in Cairns, Australia.*

### Aluminium

Several companies now manufacture aluminium sections in profiles suitable to complement "Friction Stir Welding". These panels have some distinct advantages to both ship owner and shipbuilder. They are light and as such are easier to handle. They provide less weight for the ship allowing greater payload and faster speeds. Strength is retained by profiles which are custom designed for optimised dimensional tolerances.

**Example Profiles**

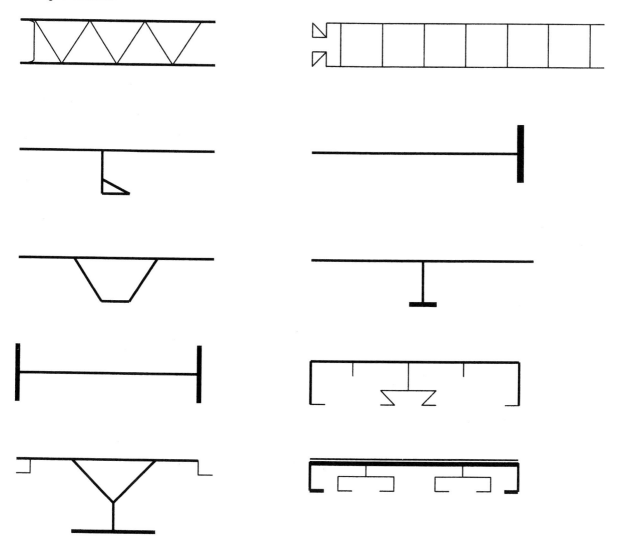

*Figure AII.9*

Supplied panels, can be delivered ready for use in the construction of hull sides, decks and superstructures and are used extensively in the High Speed Craft building sector.

## Use of Metals and Alloys

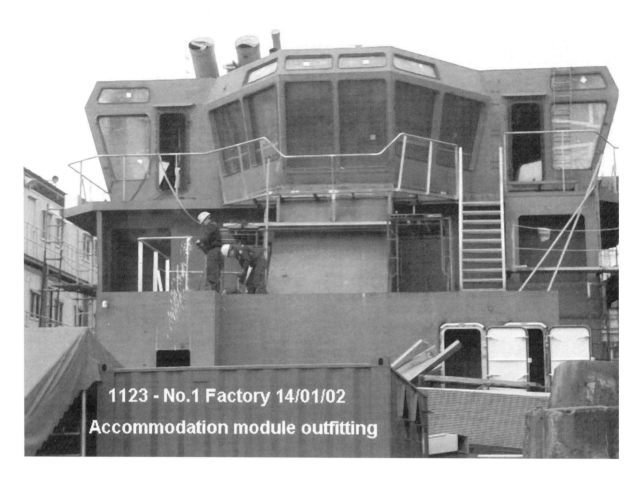

*Figure AII.10   Steel alloy Navigation Bridge and accommodation block structure being fitted out with galvanized steel rails, companionway and access doors to the prefabricated section.*

## Castings

Castings are work hardened structures used to take heavy duty bearings. They are used extensively for marine pumps, valve seatings, machinery bedplates, etc. Many are manufactured from gunmetal (88% copper, 10% tin, 2% zinc) or the bronze family of alloys. Propellers being an example which are generally made from "Manganese Bronze". This is of a hard construction which is corrosive resistant, and tends not to be too brittle. While drawn phosphor bronze (6% tin and upto 0.25% phosphorous) is used for shafts, valve spindles and similar turning components. All of which require corrosive resistant properties and a level of high strength. Phosphor bronze castings tend to contain 10-18% tin and upto 0.25% phosphorous with the remainder being copper.

*Figure AII.11   Twin cast bronze propellers attached to the pod propulsion units of the cruise ship "Amsterdam" seen positioned either side of a centre line skeg. Zinc sacrificial anodes are also seen, prolific on the upper steelwork of the rotary pod units.*

## Sandwich Plate System (SPS)

Sandwich Plate technology is probably one of the most modern and most influential construction changes to effect the industry. It has been granted approvals by most of the established Classification Societies, including Lloyds Register(LR), ABS, GL, Class NK, BV, and Det Norske Veritas. The system is currently being employed by Keppel, Pan United Lloyd Werft, Malta Shipyards and Pan United. Lloyds Register is expected to publish rules and regulations with additional notations to cover complete ship structures built with SPS.

This novel application is a structure made up of two metal plates with a continuous elastomer core, bonded between the two plates. Current development is ongoing with alternative and/or dissimilar metals for the panel faces. The sandwich panels being supplied direct to shipyard workshops and assembly lines.

When compared with conventional steel construction, closely spaced stiffeners used to resist buckling and local deformation are replaced by the elastomer core. This tends to make the Sandwich System stronger and lighter with obvious advantages to the new build. Additional advantages claimed for SPS include, simpler structure, reduced in service corrosion, increased fatigue resistance and lower through life costs. Other benefits of the system are being realized in the form of additional insulation and improved protection from noise and vibration effects. The manufactured panels are also approved to A60 standard without any additional insulation other than the elastomer core.

The system employs less stiffening and is expected to generate a fresh approach to structural design. Local strength requirements can be satisfied by tailoring the plate thickness to suit specific requirements while the inner core is not taken into consideration. The construction takes account of a precise separation between the two outer panels, achieved by welded spacers and the panel edges are sealed to ensure that none of the elastomer can escape during injection. Once injection of the elastomer has been completed it must be allowed to cure and this period of curing must be conducted at a specific temperature.

Considerable time saving is achieved by using this system against welding procedures employed for the welding needs for stiffeners on conventional construction. Its plane surface also favours easy coating applications. Such advantages are reducing construction costs potentially by upto 50% with reduced stiffening and welding applications, together with material savings in stainless steel tanks, where the inner face only is stainless steel.

Examples of SPS application already operating within the industry include:— Heli-deck Surface strengthening, Funnel casings, Hatch covers, Lightweight vehicle decks, tank top overlays and both transverse and longitudinal bulkheads.

(Also see Chemical Tank construction – Chapter 7.)

**Sandwich Plate System**

### Example SPS Panel                        16mm  Top Plate

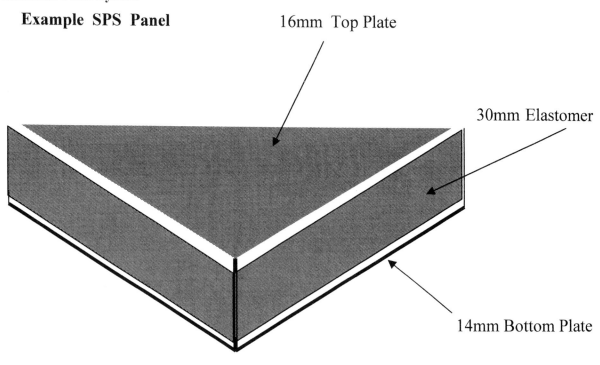

*Figure AII.12*

The top and bottom steel plates are bonded to a compact polyurethane elastomer core. This core is injected as a two part liquid into closed cavities formed by the steel plates edged with welded perimeter bars. (Perimeter bars not shown in diagram.)

Manufactures ensure that the plate surfaces are clean, dry and free of contaminates prior to injecting the elastomer. This is then allowed to cure over a period of time and the plate will then be designated as SPS 16-30-14, which denotes the thickness of the finished panel. Sizes can be varied to suit customer demands.

Panels can be employed for new builds or as overlay decking and tailored to give the required thickness ratio, desired strength and stiffness. It can be accepted and approved by classification societies as a permanent structural repair and/or a strengthening solution, in both the vertical or horizontal aspects.

Overlays can be established to worn and thinner plates quickly, without resorting to the need to crop and replace steelwork. Panels can be joined together by structural adhesives without the need for "hot work" making repairs *in situ* cost effective while the vessel remains operational.

SPS has distinct advantages for the shipyard in that building schedules can be improved considerably, because less stiffening is required and welding is reduced. Ship owners also gain from the lighter construction allowing the vessel to be able to carry more cargo.

Panels allow easy inspection and maintenance and are less prone to fatigue or failure.

(Information based on the product manufactured by Intelligent Engineering.)

## Plastics (Polymers)

Plastics have become an ever increasing commodity in the shipbuilding process. Fibre glass resin with a hardener has proved to be an effective construction element which is not only very strong, but also blessed with anti corrosive properties. Application of epoxy resin (two part) paint can be applied to suit specifications and reflects good adhesion properties with continuity of strength.

Good examples of polymers are seen in polypropylene ropes, lifeboat constructions, handrails and synthetic bearings. Additional fitments are seen in fire hoses to cabin furniture which are all seen as advertisements to the increased use of plastics to everyday applications.

Polymers can be segregated into two forms, namely, thermoplastics and thermosets. Thermoplastics are capable of being reheated after formation and being heated again to be reformed to suit an alternative image. Where as thermosets cannot be recycled and if reheating was attempted the material would be scorched.

Products can be enhanced by additives to increase hardness or by ultra violet light to protect plastics in exposed environments. They are seen to have substantial advantages by way of the following:—

(a) Polymers tend to project themselves as excellent thermal insulators, being used as accommodation modules for arctic conditions. They are also used in electrical flex, current bearing cables.
(b) They tend to be light to handle with inbuilt strength. Nylon washers and bearings being prime examples.
(c) They are also highly resistant to most chemicals and many cargo containers used for shipping chemicals are often packaged in plastic containers.
(d) Polymers are extremely versatile and can often be moulded in shape to carry liquids or used as insulation, like polystyrene. They are continually employed as tough binding strips and coverings for palletized packages.

Plastics have become very popular in all industries not just in ship building and shipping.

They have grown considerably since conception and have furnished world wide industry with some of its essential needs. (e.g. thermocouples, radio aerials, neophrene seals) Although the side effects are that it cannot be dumped and must be re-cycled to keep within current legislation. Disposal of plastics is therefore an expensive item and goes along with its general use.

Neither are they popular in the event of fire onboard (tests have shown that PVC produced six times as much smoke as Halogen Free wall panels. (Tests – Laboratorio Studie Ricerche Sul Fuoco, in Italy) As a result some calls have been made for reduced use, of PVC materials in shipboard applications.

Bearing the above in mind, acceptable alternative uses for composites are being sort, where the risk element from toxics is eliminated.

The US Navy have currently embarked on a project to determine the merits of composite propellers with Air Fertigung-Technologie in Luckow, Germany. The development is hoped to lead to reduced cavitation and vibration and subsequently reduced noise levels.

A reduced level of propeller fouling is also anticipated. A lighter propeller would be expected to increase acceleration by achieving top revolutions per minute more quickly than say a comparable conventional propeller. Maximum speed being generated at a lower engine performance, hence saving fuel as well as incurring lower vibrations.

Further advances have been made in the use of rudder bearings which have employed "Freeze Fitting". There are three acceptable methods of fitting rudder bearings: either by press fitting, resin chocking, or freeze fitting.

Freeze fitting is being used ever increasingly with composite, non-metallic bearings. The bearing being frozen usually by the use of Liquid Nitrogen. The more popular method being to engage a container, able to withstand $-197°C$ to accommodate the bearing and the freezing process. The diameter of the bearing being reduced to accommodate the fitting. The bearing is inserted into the rudder housing and normalization is allowed to take place so rounding the sleeve fit.

Both the propeller and bearing systems are seen to have value to the military, in their use of stealth submarine operations. While the ramifications of reduced vibrations for commercial vessels such as Passenger craft are seen as an equally acceptable by product.

### Examples of Plastics and Composites in Shipboard Use

(a) Radio whip aerials.
(b) Neoprene sleeves for aluminium steel connections.
(c) Panelling for cabin bulkheads.
(d) Furniture and sanitation fittings.
(e) Deck composition coatings.
(f) Lifeboat and liferaft constructions together with marine evacuation systems.
(g) Instrument control switches.
(h) Power cable insulating sheathing.
(i) Mooring ropes and flag halyards.
(j) Lifebuoys.
(k) Eye protection goggles.
(l) Immersion suits, lifejackets, lifebuoys.

### Ceramics

To understand ceramics it would seem important to know the benefits that they can provide and then adapt the usefulness to suitable applications.

Ceramic properties include:—

(a) Ceramic tiles provide excellent thermal insulation.
(b) They provide a hard wearing surface which is abrasive resistant.
(c) They can withstand extremely high and low temperatures.
(d) Ceramic products are durable in either strong acidic or alkaline conditions.
(e) They have electrical insulation properties.

With the knowledge of the benefits it is not hard to visualize the use of ceramics in furnace linings or as super conductors. But the question remains what are ceramics?

Ceramic products are made up from minute clay particles which are easily shaped when wet, but when heated to high temperatures, become rigidly hard. Adding sand or silica to the clay mixture is seen as an essential component of the hardness predicted for the product.

Ceramics have become an integral element within high temperature superconductors, replacing conventional copper coils in motors. This advance. established in 1987. led to reduced motor size which could generate a greater magnetic field but within a vastly reduced, physical space. Such an advance lent itself to pod propulsion systems and reducing engine room space subsequently increasing payload capacity. Extremely useful in the passenger vessel and ferry sectors of the industry.

### Examples of Ceramics in Shipboard Use

(a) Insulators for radio and power cables.
(b) Protective covers for thermocouple heat sensors.
(c) Furnace tiles.
(d) Galley deck tiles.
(e) Heat shield separators.
(f) Fresh water tank linings.

## Cement

Although some small boat manufactures have been successful with building "Cement boat hulls" they tend not to be a popular option, other mediums like wood and more lately fibre glass composites are more common. In commercial shipbuilding cement remains a useful commodity for emergency repairs like "cement box seals" and shipyards tend to remove these more often than putting them in place, usually prior to making permanent repairs.

Cement is hard wearing and can be moulded to a particular shape when in its liquid state.

Once hard and in its solid state it tends not to bend and is generally long lasting. Mixing cement is an important feature of the composition and air should not be trapped in the mix as this could lead to cracking and weakening effects.

Its prime use tends to be in the "offshore sector" when drilling operations are ongoing, where as on board ship it is used for emergency repairs to seal leaking pipes, cement washing of fresh water tanks, sealing the bottom of bilges, etc.

Additives to a cement mix can be used to accelerate hardness and make the cement quick drying. While inhibitors can be similarly added to reduce the rate of set and slow the fixing procedure down.

## Rubber Products

Rubber is widely used in ship construction other than just acting as a seal for ensuring joints are watertight. Its most common use is probably as a hard rubber packing around cargo hatch covers, or about watertight doors. Examples of large seals being achieved with hard rubber packing can also be seen where vehicle ramps/doors are closed up, on Roll On-Roll Off vessels. Ramps being normally lifted by hydraulics or mechanical methods and then cleated hard against the rubber sealant to achieve an acceptable level of water tight integrity. The hydraulic pressure being applied to the cleats creates a pressured seal around the perimeter of the vehicle access door.

It is also extensively used in providing anti-vibration mounts to machinery. Examples can be seen on thrust blocks, engine mountings, generator sets, pumps and compressors.

Other uses are found in seatings for light machinery parts or in the form of gaskets and washers. Especially so where vibration or noise is present and the rubber separation acts to absorb acoustic effects and reduce harmful vibrations.

The down side of rubber is that it can decay and deteriorate over time and such watertight seals that are in place, require regular inspection. Surveyors, if in doubt about the quality of a deck seal would most certainly carry out a "hose test" and a visual inspection. Any powdering or adverse distortion with or without discoloration of the rubber quality would usually carry a recommendation to renew the seal.

## Wood

Timber generated the earliest trends of ship construction. Although the Egyptians started with reed boats they employed branches as framing, as did the Britons with coracles. The Phoenicians, the Romans, the Vikings and the Greeks all built with wood as the main medium. The Bible tells of the citizens of Tyre making shipboards from fir trees, and the oaks of Bashan being used to manufacture oars. While ceder trees from Lebanon where taken to make masts. (Ref. Bible – Ezekiel XXVII.)

Wood construction also provided much of today's ship construction terminology. We still use the term "frames" from the timber frames (timbers), as they used to be known. We still refer to the garboard strake, and the sheer strake on modern steel construction, terms originating out of clinker and carvel small timber boat constructions. Wood was the beginning, in that it could be worked and managed comparatively easily, compared to the early development in iron. Carpentry became a skill and shipwrights made the transition from shore based work to the building of ships on all the major coastlines.

Wood is still used in the leisure industry for small boat building, but it is expensive when compared with the use of composites. While timber in Commercial Ship Building is now a rare sight. Up till recently the majority of Passenger vessels carried timber deck sheathing but even these are rapidly being replaced by composition deck products on top of steel surfaces. Some external doors are still employed, manufactured in timber but are becoming less popular because other products are cheaper and often stronger.

The sailing ship days, were all timber construction but as soon as the industrial revolution took hold and Brunel build the SS Great Britain (1843) steel dominated from 1880 and the use of timber declined to all but fittings.

Internal fittings, as with furniture, remain today but wooden decks have all but gone, as has, wood panelling, taff rails, wooden lifeboats, wood hatch covers, etc., Cargo ships still have cargo battens (spar ceiling) in wood and some ships are still fitted with wood tank top ceiling, but these are few and timber is now the exception rather than the norm.

\* Despite oil, coal, nuclear, solar, wave energy and the so called sources of modern power, wood remains the most widely used fuel in the world today.

## Management of Stress

From the outset of building and the laying of the ship's keel, stresses of one kind or another are going to occur in the structure. Where stress factors can be minimised, so much the better, especially when the ship is in a seaway. However, good building and design practice can effectively reduce stress effects and in some cases eliminate them for the future. Obviously, all stress elements cannot be permanently removed, as in the case of dry docking stress factors (see chapter 6), which will of course re-occur at each docking period.

Many stress elements can expect to be experienced by the working nature of the ship. Examples of these can be seen in point loading action, causing decks to be distorted due to sheer weight. While derricks and cranes suffer compression and shearing forces when in operation. Poor loading practice especially in bulk carriers and tankers can also expect to cause excessive bending and shear force moments.

Once at sea, the vessel can expect to encounter the well known expansion and compression forces of "hogging and sagging" as surface action tends to separately effect the centre and the extreme ends of the vessel. While the very long vessel must expect the additional effects of torsion stresses down its overall length.

Good design practice can provide continuity of strength and go some way to reducing operational stresses. Any corrosion reducing practices included in the build will leave steelwork with a better standing to resist detrimental external forces, causing increasing levels of stress factors.

Materials in the shipyard will form the vessels of the future. Correct scantling use and protection of steelwork both before and after installation into the build, will provide increased longevity with reduced corrosion effects and less structural fatigue.

## Fatigue

In 2000, fatigue assessments became mandatory for ships over 170 m in length. Fatigue calculations are now required for connections between longitudinals and transverse web frames, hopper knuckles, stringer connections and side shell connections to transverse bulkheads. Membrane type LNG tanks are also prone to fatigue, especially at the foot of cofferdam bulkheads and at the connections with superstructures.

## Building to counter: Stresses incurred in a Seaway

The Fore end structure, forward of the collision bulkhead, must be constructed to withstand panting and pounding stresses and is usually given specific features. The bow being shaped to reduce resistance to forward motion. The inclusion of a bulbous bow is considered very effective in achieving this, on many types of vessel. A flared side shell, in the bows deflects sea water and spray, while at the same time increases the fore deck mooring area.

Structural features like the stem bar, extends from the keel plate to the Load Water Line(LWL) and includes a solid round bar in its construction. The "Stem Plate" will extend from the LWL to the main deck and will be constructed in curved plates, stiffened by breasthooks.

The collision bulkhead is a transverse watertight bulkhead. It is stiffened to provide main line protection in the event of the vessel sustaining fore end damage. The position of the bulkhead will vary. However, in the case of vessels built with a bow-visor (Vehicle Ferries) SOLAS Regulations, chapter II, 1-10, require the ship to be fitted with a collision bulkhead at a set distance from the visor, when the ramp is not positioned at an adequate distance from the bow. to act as a collision bulkhead. An extra collision bulkhead must then be incorporated at a position not more than 5% of the ship's length, from the forward perpendicular.

## Panting

Panting is the in and outward movement of the ship's hull plates as the vessel pitches. The stress in the hull plates occurs in the bow section and is caused by the changing water pressure acting on the hull at differing depths, as the bow pitches deeper. The build of the ship allows a panting structure, incorporating "Panting Beams" and Stringers to be inter connected in the bow region, to resist such movement and reduce such incurred stresses.

Resistance to panting is achieved in the building stage by increasing the scantlings for 15% of the ship's length from forward. Panting stringers are established at 2 metre intervals while panting beams are installed at alternate frame spaces.

Additionally, intercostal side stringers are fitted abaft the collision bulkhead, in line with the fore peak side stringers to provide continuity of strength. Also partial wash bulkheads or a series of pillars are constructed on the centre line to provide extra support.

Some vessel are built with perforated flats to relieve internal liquid pressures. In the larger vessel, such flats would be placed not more than 2.5 m, apart.

## Pounding

The region effected by pounding is between 25%-30% of the ship's length measured from the forward perpendicular, the actual length being dependant on the block coefficient.

Pounding is caused by the ship's extremities slamming heavily onto the water surface with the pitching motion of the vessel when in a seaway. The action can happen at both the fore and after ends of the vessel, but is generally more common and experienced at the fore end.

The action is not an unusual occurrence in rough weather and is subsequently taken into account at the building stage. Frame space is reduced between the fore peak and the collision bulkhead to a maximum of 610 mm for 20% of the ship's length aft of the F.P.

The measure may be 610 mm or 700 mm being dependant on the ship's moulded depth.

Where a ship is fitted with transverse framing, solid plate floors are fitted to every frame space. If the ship is longitudinally framed then the plate floors are fitted at alternate frame spaces. Additionally intercostal side girders are positioned at a maximum of 2.2 metres apart with half height intercostal girders for transverse framed vessels, 2.1 metres apart for longitudinally framed vessels. The bottom shell plate to this region is also increased in thickness.

**NB.** Frame spacing is progressively reduced in the forward region where panting and pounding can be expected to occur.

**Critical Stress Areas**

**Double Hull Tanker Example**

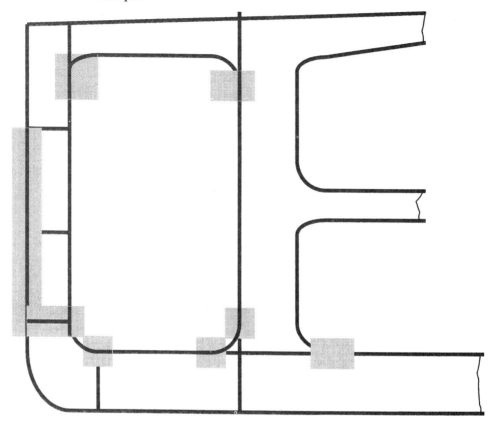

*Figure AII.13*

**Stress concentration areas**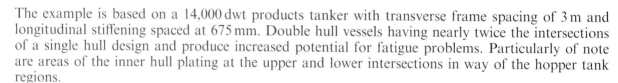

The example is based on a 14,000 dwt products tanker with transverse frame spacing of 3 m and longitudinal stiffening spaced at 675 mm. Double hull vessels having nearly twice the intersections of a single hull design and produce increased potential for fatigue problems. Particularly of note are areas of the inner hull plating at the upper and lower intersections in way of the hopper tank regions.

**Racking Stresses**

Caused by the ship rolling in a seaway is known to generate distortion at the upper deck level causing deformation of the fine lines of the hull.

**Water Pressure Distortion**

Water pressure acts at right angles to the surface of the hull and is an increasing pressure at greater depth. As with heavy pitching in a seaway, the movement inwards and outwards movement of the shell plate, takes place at greater or lesser depths. As in the case of "Panting" in the fore end additional structured strength members "Panting Beams" can provide compensation.

**Hogging and Sagging Stresses**

The design of modern vessels has always incorporated compensation for stress factors. With ships becoming wider beam and ever longer, the concerns regarding bending about the midship's point has become a major concern. The vessels performance when at sea must expect to be influenced by the forces of buoyancy as well as the forces of gravity and these forces combined will generate Hogging and Sagging actions over the ship's length. If the ship is considered as a long steel girder which is influenced at each end it would be expected to experience expansion and compression forces over the mid part section:—

## Hogging Stresses Effecting a Ship
## (Acting Like a Steel Girder)

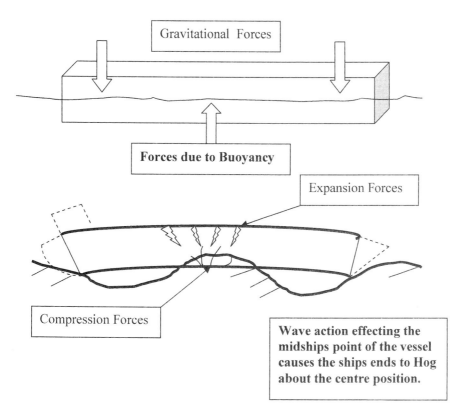

*Figure AII.14   Hogging Stresses effecting a Ship (acting like a steel girder).*

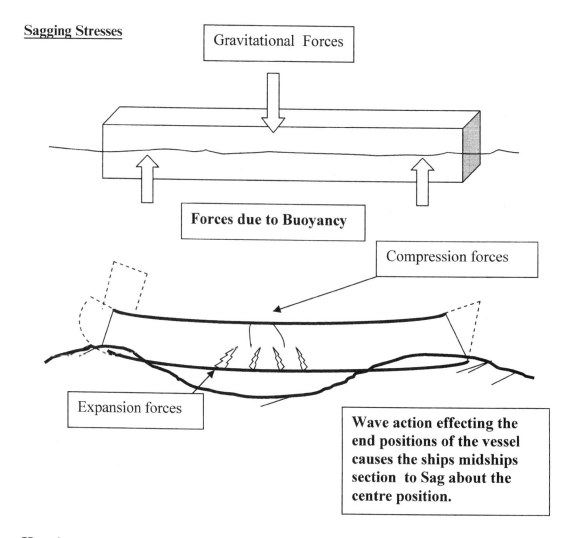

**Sagging Stresses**

Gravitational Forces

**Forces due to Buoyancy**

Compression forces

Expansion forces

Wave action effecting the
end positions of the vessel
causes the ships midships
section to Sag about the
centre position.

**Hogging**

Gravitational Forces      Buoyancy Force      Gravitational Forces

**Sagging**

Buoyancy      Gravitational Force      Buoyancy

*Figure AII.15*

Hogging and Sagging conditions are caused by incorrect loading of the ship and experienced when cargo has either been concentrated in the middle of the vessel causing the ship to sag in the middle (Sagging), or by concentrating the loads at the extremities of the vessel causing the ship to bend over its length (Hogging).

The conditions are accentuated when in a seaway and waves are encountered as illustrated causing suspension and pivot points respectively for the sagging and hogging conditions. Heavy bulk cargoes are loaded as per the ship's loading schedule so as to avoid these circumstances occurring.

Poor loading generating the above conditions can cause serious damage to the vessel even causing the vessel to break its back. They should be avoided at all costs bearing in mind that these stresses would be found alongside bending and shear forces, as well as torsion stresses throughout the ship's length.

**Torsional Stresses**

A twisting action down the length of the vessel can generate torsional stresses. The longitudinal strength members like the plate keel and intercostals can expect to experience such movement when the vessel is in rough sea conditions. The movement should not be confused with bending which is incurred with hogging and sagging type stresses. Torsional stresses are caused by sea action, causing a twist motion, along the central axis. They may be compared to a long ruler held fast at one end which is twisted out of its own plane. The stresses effecting the parallel middle body and particularly long structural members like the propeller shaft.

**Dry Dock Stresses**

Compression forces from the blocks in a dry dock cause the contact areas of the block to indent the ship's shell plate. The results of specific contact areas of the block or shore pushing the shell plate inward causes other areas of the shell in close proximity to be pushed outward in a bulge action.

**Ship Stresses from Lifting and Transporting Heavy Weights**

When loading heavy weights on deck or in the ship's hold there is a tendency to cause distortion to the structural features of the vessel. During the building of the vessel these distortions can be anticipated and can subsequently be compensated for by the addition of strength members, increased scantlings and extra stiffening on load bearing decks. However, despite the precautions taken up during the building stage some distortion must be expected to a greater or lesser degree.

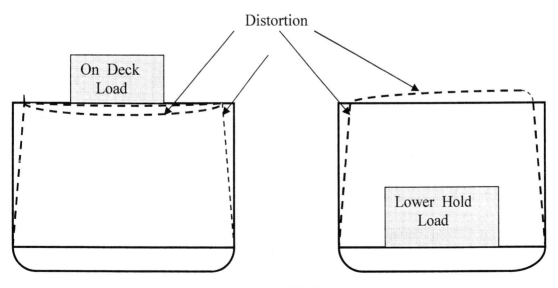

*Figure AII.16*

Regulations for the carriage of deck cargo are particularly relevant to General cargo type vessels and must be considered at the building stage. The deck load capacity must take account of the following:—

(a) The maximum loading on the deck must ensure that excessive stress is not caused Any single point loading must be distributed over adjacent parts of the ship's structure in order to avoid concentrated loads.

(b) The increased deck weight and consequence in the event of absorption, on the ship's "Centre of Gravity" and the resulting (KG), bearing in mind that the vessel will consume fuel and Fresh Water probably from lower parts of the vessel, which could also effect the movement of the ship's C of G.

(c) The height of any deck stow must not hinder or obscure the Navigational duties being carried out from the Bridge Deck. Neither should the stowage height generate a "wind moment" that may seriously alter the behaviour of the ship and cause a direct, detrimental influence on the ship's stability.

(d) The deck stowage must not cause an obstruction to gaining access to the working areas of the ship. Walk ways must be provided where appropriate, unless the vessel is fitted with underdeck passageways, e.g. Container vessels.

## Bending and Shear forces

When a vessel is badly loaded, namely by disproportioned cargo distribution, the vessel is likely to experience bending and shear forces in regions accommodating the limits of specific loads. This is why large bulk carriers and large tankers formulate a loading plan prior to commencing cargo operations. This plan provides an order of loading for specific compartments or tanks, with stated weights/capacity of cargo, without causing excessive bending moments to occur. Such an example is simplified by considering loading at the fore and aft extremities of the ship causing the vessel to bend about the amidship's position. Similarly, a fully loaded compartment next to an empty compartment could generate a shear force at that position where the two compartments join.

Today's operational vessels experience stress forces directly effecting the overall length. This is because a ship with its varied spaces is not homogeneous, i.e. it is not of the same density from forward to aft. This is particularly relevant to heavy lift vessels where disproportionate loading takes place. At some points on the vessels length, the buoyancy will exceed the weight, while at other points the weight will exceed the buoyancy. The difference between the buoyancy and weight at any point is called the LOAD and the following example illustrates how the buoyancy, weight and the load can be measured in tonne/metres.

Example

A box shaped, cargo barge measures 40 m long, 8 m wide and floats on even keel at a draught of 4.0 m in fresh water. The barge is constructed with four equal tanks down its length each 10 m long. No 1, and No 4, tanks are empty while No 2 and 3 tanks are both full each with 400 tonnes of bulk cargo trimmed level. Calculate the Load, the shear force and the bending moment curves along the length of the barge.

Total Displacement of Barge = Length × Breadth × Draught × R.D. of Water

$$= 40 \times 8 \times 4 \times 1 \qquad = 1{,}280 \text{ t}$$

Total weight of cargo $= 400 + 400 \qquad = \underline{800} \text{ t}$

Total weight of Barge $\qquad\qquad\qquad = 480 \text{ t}$

Buoyancy per metre $= \dfrac{\text{Displacement of Barge}}{\text{Length of Barge}} = \dfrac{1{,}280}{40} = 32 \text{ t/m}$

Weight of Barge per metre $= \dfrac{\text{Weight of Barge}}{\text{Length of Barge}} = \dfrac{480}{40} = 12 \text{ t/m}$

Weight of Cargo per metre $= \dfrac{\text{Weight of cargo}}{\text{Length of tank}} = \dfrac{400}{10} = 40 \text{ t/m}$

| Dist from A.P. | Buoyancy t/m | Weight Barge t/m | Weight Cargo t/m | Total Weight t/m | Load t/m |
|---|---|---|---|---|---|
| No 4 tank | 32 | 12 | 0 | 12 | +20 |
| No 3 tank | 32 | 12 | 40 | 52 | −20 |
| No 2 tank | 32 | 12 | 40 | 52 | −20 |
| No 1 tank | 32 | 12 | 0 | 12 | +20 |

An excess of weight over the buoyancy in the region of the middle two tanks exists. While an excess of buoyancy over weight exists at the end tanks.

This condition will tend to cause stress along the whole of the barge length.

**Example 4 Tank Barge**

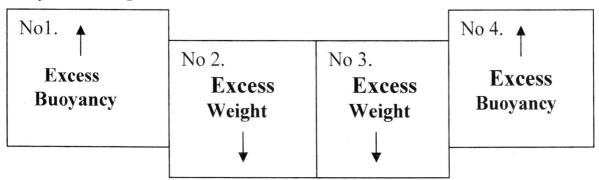

*Figure AII.17   The tendency towards shearing forces developing down the length of the barge is clearly evident, particularly between tanks 1 and 2, and 3 and 4. A bending moment will also be caused the barge to suffer a "Sagging" effect.*

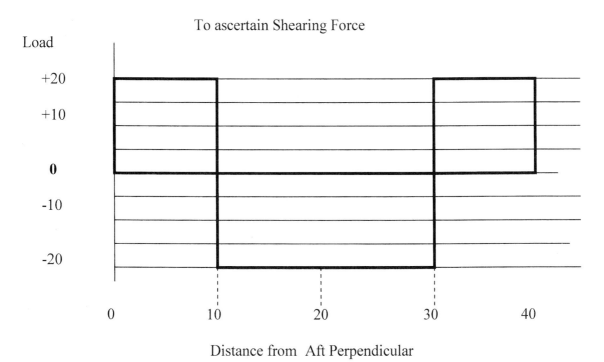

*Figure AII.18*

To calculate the shear force value at any point along the length of the barge it is necessary to find the area under the load curve at that point. Since the "Load Curve" is rectangular the area is the product of the distance along the base and the magnitude of the load.

For example: 5 m from the A.P., shear force equals $5 \times 20 = 100$ t

At    10 m from the A.P., shear force equals $10 \times 20 = 200$ t

At    15 m from the A.P., shear force equals $(10 \times 20) - (5 \times 20) = 100$ t.

| Distance from A.P. | Load T/m | Shear Force |
|:---:|:---:|:---:|
| 0 | $-20$ | 0 |
| $+5$ | $-20$ | 100 |
| $+10$ | $-20$ | 200 |
| $+15$ | $+20$ | 100 |
| $+20$ | $+20$ | 0 |
| $+25$ | $+20$ | $-100$ |
| $+30$ | $+20$ | $-200$ |
| $+35$ | $-20$ | $-100$ |
| $+40$ | $-20$ | 0 |

Such results can be graphically shown:—

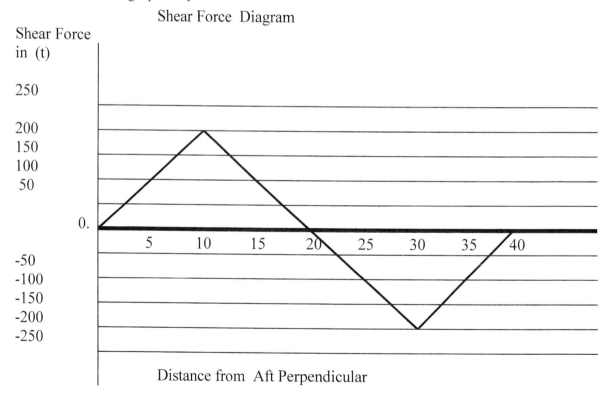

*Figure AII.19*

In this case the maximum shear force occurs at a position one quarter and three quarters of the length measured from the Aft perpendicular to the forward perpendicular and has a value of 200 tonnes.

**The Bending Moment Value**

The net area under the "shear force curve" to any point, provides the "Bending Moment" in tonnes/metres, at that point, therefore a bending moment curve can be produced for the same example barge. In the case provided, the shear force is a straight diagonal, therefore the area under the shear force curve is triangular:—

$$\text{Area} = \frac{\text{Base} \times \text{Height}}{2}.$$

From the previous shear force curve:—

Assuming a point of 10 metres from the aft perpendicular

$$\text{Bending Moment} = \frac{10 \times 200}{2} = 1,000 \text{ t/m}.$$

| Distance from A.P. | Shear Force Tonnes | Bending Moment T/m |
|:---:|:---:|:---:|
| 0 | 0 | 0 |
| +5 | 100 | 250 |
| +10 | 200 | 1,000 |
| +15 | 100 | 1,750 |
| +20 | 0 | 2,000 |
| +25 | −100 | 1,750 |
| +30 | −200 | 1,000 |
| +35 | −100 | 250 |
| +40 | 0 | 0 |

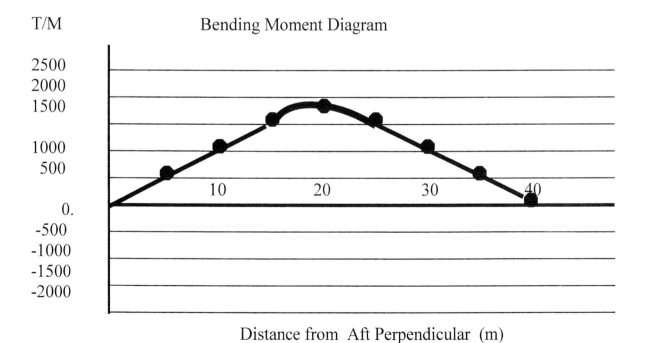

*Figure AII.20*

From the graph it can be seen that the Maximum Bending Moment occurs at the mid-length and has a value of 2,000 tonne/metres. In this case sagging is caused because the weight exceeds the buoyancy along the middle length of the barge.

### Ships' Structures – to withstand stress

**Shell Plating** – Compensates for all ships' stresses. Plating is thickened about the keel area in the garboard strake and in the sheer strake. It also is given increased thickness to combat localized stresses as would be expected in the region of shell door openings.

**Frames** – Compensate for water pressure, panting effects and dry docking stresses. They maybe compared to the ribs of the human body which stiffen the body overall. Ships may be constructed with longitudinal or athwartship's framing reinforcing the outer hull of the vessel.

**Longitudinal Girders** – Compensate for "Hogging and Sagging" influences. Dry docking and pounding stresses together with localized shearing influences.

**Beams** – Compensate for racking stresses and influences from water pressure. Also local stresses incurred from heavy weights.

**Pillars** – Extensively found in general cargo vessels in lower hold structures compensate for stresses caused by heavy weights, racking, dry docking and water pressure influences.

**Bulkheads** – Tend to compensate for most stresses, including racking, hogging and sagging, shearing dry docking and from heavy concentrated weights.

**Beam Knees** – Compensate for heavy weight and localized stresses as well as racking.

**Floors** – Compensate for pounding and vibration, dry dock stresses and localized stresses from water pressure, heavy weights and racking.

**Decks** – Compensate for hogging, sagging, shearing, bending and water pressure stresses. Decks and deck stringers, provide compensation to stresses incurred from heavy loading.

### Water Pressure Stresses

Water pressure acts at right angles to the ship's surface structure, and all forces are considered to act through the ship's "Centre of Buoyancy".

Fluctuations in water pressure are caused by the Pitch and roll motion of the vessel when in a seaway and cause the in and outward movement of the ship's plating, e.g. Panting.

*Greater depth greater pressure.*

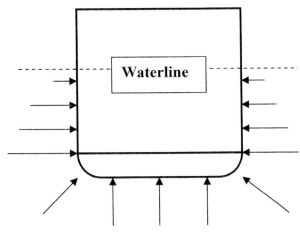

*Figure AII.21*

## Racking Stresses

Upper movement in a seaway to the upper part of the ship's parallel body. Some distortion may occur at deck edge and sheer strake areas in way of the camber.

Upper movement is more pronounced as the lower part is more contained by greater water pressure.

Structural members like athwartship's beams, beam knees, bulkheads and pillars tend to compensate for racking stresses and act to retain the ship's format.

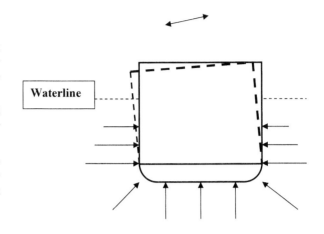

*Figure AII.22*

## Positioning of Shores and associated Docking Stresses

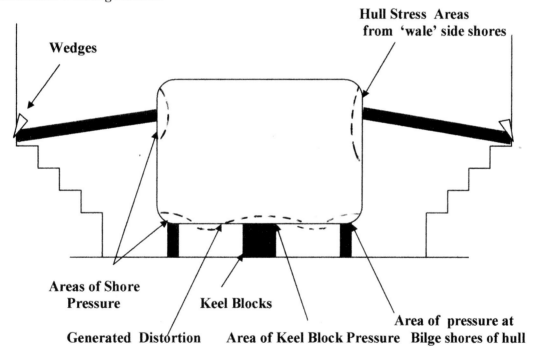

*Figure AII.23*

Shore positions should be placed with care and should ideally be placed in way of strength members like the intersection of "Deck Stringers and Frames". Bottom hull blocks, set for wide beam vessels especially, should be placed to coincide with intercostals and other similar longitudinal members to avoid "soft spots" which could lead to hull indentation of the shell plate.

Dry dock stresses occur because of the loss of support which is normally gained from the all round water pressure. The vessel will become subject to an upward thrust from below the keel position caused through the lower blocks on the floor of the dock. There will also be a tendency for the ship's weight to cause a downward and outward stress action to the vessel's sides while in the dock. Provided the ship is only docked for a short period of time, any permanent or extensive distortion through stress is unlikely and the ship should revert back to her normal lines once re-floating takes place.

# General Index

**A**

Abbreviation List  xi -xvii
Accommodation Block  xxxi
Accommodation Passengers  183-185
Active rudder  xviii
Access:
  Hatch  110/111
  Escape  116
  Companionway  116
Advance  xxx, xviii
"A" Frame  xviii
Aft peak  xxxi, 136
Aft peak bulkhead  136
Aft perpendicular  xviii, xxxi, 6, 13
Aft structure  31-69
Air cavity system  193
Air draught  6, 13
Air pipes  16, 111/112
Alloys  307
Alters  xviii, 6
Aluminium connections  140, 193,277-280, 307-309
Aluminium profiles  309
Amidships  xxvii, 6
Anchor:
  Cable  141
  Certificate  xviii
  Recess  141
  Shackle  xviii
  Slipping arrangement  150
Annealing  304/305
Anodes  xxvi
Apron  xviii
Ax-Bow  129
Axle loads  172
Azi-pods  xviii, 54/55, 60/61


**B**

Balanced rudder  xviii, 31/32
Bale space  6
Ballast pipes  83
Band brake (windlass)  141/142
Bar keel  70
Baseline  xviii, 6, 13
Beam:
  Extreme  6, 8, 11
  Half beam  xxxii, xviii, 92, 94
  Knees  91, 119

Bearing:
  Hanging  35
  Pintle  xviii
  Rudder  44-48
  Stern shaft  55
Becker Rudder  33
Bending moment  322-325
Bilge:
  Bay  75, 84
  Blocks  287
  Keel  85-89
  Pipe arrangement  83
  Pumping  84/85, 94
  Suctions  84/85
  Turn of  75/76, 84, 89
Bitter end  xviii, 127, 146, 149, 150
Block Coefficient  6/7, 15
Bollards (Bitts)  162
Bolster bar  49/50
Booby hatch  110
Boss:  xix, xxxiii, 44
  Plate  43, 51
Bottom structure  70-89
Bow:
  Arrangement  127
  Ax-bow  129
  Bulbous  xix, 128-132, 137, 141
  Conventional  129
  Doors  167-171
  Height  xxiv, 6
  Meirform  xxiv
  Rudder  xix, 138/139
  Section  (HSC)  140
  Section  (pre-fabricated)  263
  Shape  127/128
  Stem  126
  Stopper  141, 143/144
  Thrust  61, 131, 138/139, 151- 154
  Visor  141, 167-179, 317
  X-bow  130
Bracket  75,121, 135
Bracket floor  74
Breadth:  xxxii
  Extreme  8
  Over all  xix
Breaking strength  6
Breast hook  126,147, 155
Breast plate  xix
Bridge:  xxxi
  Front  123,186-189
  Windows  187/189, 254-256

Building materials 297-317
Building slip 262, 287
Bulbous bow xix, 128-132, 137, 141
Bulk carriers: 225-230
    Construction 226
    Design 227-230
Bulkhead: xix, 135
    Aft peak 136
    Collision xix, 127, 132-134, 146, 155
    Corrugated 93/94, 136, 226
    Deck 6, 10, 90, 136
    Draught 6
    Engine room 136
    Stiffening 136, 147, 155
    Watertight 132/133, 135
    Testing 37
Bull ring 128, 160
Bull wire 98
Bulwark: xxxiii, 156/157, 185/186
    Stay 19, 185/186
Buoyancy forces 319/320
Buoyancy reserve xxvii, 11


C

Camber xxxii, 6, 13
Cantilever frame xix, 118
Capstan xix, xxix
Car carrier 180-182
Cargo doors 167, 176-182
Carving note 16
Castings 43, 310
Catamarans 191-193
Caulking xix, 123/124
Cavitation 59
CCTV coverage 164, 171, 189
Ceiling xix, xxxii
Cell guides 237-239
Cement 315
Centre lead 128, 160
Ceramics 314
Certificates: 283
    Of fitness 224
    Of Registry xix
Chain lockers: xix, xxxi, 127, 132, 141, 146/150
Chain stoppers:
    AKD 160
    Compressor 143
    Guillotine 144
Check Wire 98
Chemical Carriers 4, 222-224
Class: 282/283
    Conditions 282
    Interim Certificate of 283
    Of ship 2-4
    Withdrawal 283
Classification of ships 2-4
Classification Societies 281-284
Coefficient:
    Block 7, 15
    Of expansion 28
    Of fineness 6
    Prismatic xxv, 7, 53/54

Coffin plate xx, 43/44
Cofferdam xix, 203
Cold forming 304
Collision bulkhead xix, 127, 132-134, 146, 155
Companionway 116
Compensated tonnage 21
Compressor 143
Construction waterline 7
Container: 225
    Capacity 7
    Cell Guide 237, 239, 242
    Construction 237-240
    Gantry 243
    Guides 237
    Hatch cover 238
    Support 240
    Vessel 237
Contra-rotating propellers xx, 66
Controllable Pitch propellers xx, 62/63
Control rod xxi
Conversion tables (weight & measure) 1/2
Corrosion 302/303
Corrugated bulkheads 94, 136, 226, 302
Cowl ventilator 109
Crack prevention 96
Cranes:
    Cargo lifting 99, 236
    Oil pipeline handling 215
Crippling pressure 7
Crop xx
Cruiser stern xx, 43
Curve of floodable length xx


D

Davit arrangements (Survival Craft) 247, 251/252
Deadlight xx, 113
Deadweight: 7
    Scale 22
    Loaded 10
Deck:
    House xxxiii
    Stringer xxviii, 185/185, 271
    water seal (IG) 214
Decks:
    Garage 108, 173/174
    Flush 75
    Fore 127, 156
    Forecastle xxxi, 90-96
    Helicopter 244-246
    Openings 104, 112-114
    Strength xx
    Tonnage xxviii
    Upper 90, 93
    Weather 90, 104
    Wood 122-125
Deep tanks xx, 104-106
Depth: xx, 7/8, 13
    Correction 15
Displacement 8
Docking plan 23
Doors:
    Sill 113

Doors (*continued*)
Watertight 113- 115
Sealing 171
Shell 189/190
Double Bottoms 135, 265
Double bottom tanks xx, xxxii, 70, 73-76, 80/81, 121, 135, 265
double hull design 199, 202
Doubling plate xx, 91, 94, 107, 145
Double hull design 199-203
Draught: 8, 13
Survey 8
Dry cargo vessels 225, 230-233
Dry docking: 284-286
Stresses 321, 327
Ducting (propellers) xx, 41/42
Duct keel xx, 72/73, 137, 230

**E**

Eductor 83
Electric Steering gear xx
Electro-hydraulic steering xxi
Emergency:
generating room 115
steering xxi
towing lead 160
Enclosed superstructures 14
Engine room: xxxi
Bottom plates 77
Bulkheads 136
Double bottom 78
Escape hatch 116
Floors 77/78
Seatings 79
Escutcheon plate xxi
Even keel xxi
Extreme:
Beam 8
Breadth 8
Depth 8
Length 10

**F**

Factor of sub-division 8
Fair xxi
Fairleads 156-159
Fashion plate xxi
Fatigue (in materials) 316
Ferry:
Transports 164-179
General arrangement 165/166
Fire fighting arrangement 24
Fish plate xxi
Flammable:
Limits 8
Liquid 8
Range 8
Flanging xxi
Flare, of bow 8
Flash point 8

Flettner rotor xxi, 34
Flipper fins xxi
Floating lever 8
Floodable length xxi, 8, 10
Floor:
Bracket xxi
Deep web 127
Plate xxiv, 73
Transverse 75
Flush decks 75
Fore end structure 147, 126-157
Fore & Aft line 6, 9
Fore foot xxi
Fore peak xxi,xxxi, 127, 147
Fore stay xxi
Forward perpendicular 9, 13
Forward mooring deck 156
Frames: xxi, xxxii,75/76, 91, 117-121, 226
Angle 117
Athwartships 135
Cantilever xix, 118
Longitudinal 120, 135
Spacing 138, 317
Stiffening 146
Web 121, 128
Freeboard: 9, 13, 17
Assignment 15
Conditions for assignment 16
Correction 15/16
Deck xxii, 14
Flush deck correction 15
Mean 9
Freefall boat arrangement 249/250
Free flow system 210/211
Freeing port 16, 185/186
Freeze fitting 313/314

**G**

Galvanising 306
Ganger length xxii, 143
Gantry crane 243
Garage decks 173/174
Garboard strake xxii, xxxii, 71
Gas carrier: 217-221
Cargo containment 219
General arrangement plan 24
General ships particulars 24
Girder (Half length) 73/74, 95/96
Grain capacity 9
Gross tonnage 9, 20
Guard rails xxii, 16
Gudgeons xxii
Guillotine bow stopper 144
Gunwale capping 185
Gusset plates xxii, xxxii, 76
Gypsy 143

**H**

Hallen derrick 231/232

Harmonized Survey system  283
Hat box  xxii, 106
Hatch:
    Cleating  100/101
    Coaming  92-94, 96, 99
    Covers  96,100, 102
    Direct pull  97/98
    Pontoons  92, 97, 100, 102, 238/239
    Sealing  97
    Side opening  228/229
    Top  xxxi, 92, 101
    Top loading  101
    Tween deck  102/103
    Wedges  98
Hatchways:  xxii, xxxi, 16, 93, 103
    Construction  16, 94/95, 144/145
    Covers  16, 96-103
    Deck surround  95
    Sealing  96/97
    Strength  94/95
Hawse pipe  xxii, 127, 141, 144/145
Heating coils  106
Heavy lift v/l's  232
Heeling tanks  166
Helicopter decks  244-246
High Speed Craft:
    categories  9, 190-196
    construction  140
Hogging  xix, 318-321
Hold arrangement  xxii, xxxi, xxxii, 105
Hopper tanks  xxii, 121, 226
Hose test  xxii
Hounds band  xxii, 235
Hull openings  163/164
Hull stress monitors  226
Hunting gear  xxii
Hydrofoils  194
Hydrolift Docking system  284/285
Hydrostatic curves  24


I

Ice:
    Class notations  5
    Classification  4/5
    Knife  xxii, xxxiii
    Light water line  xxii
    Load water line  xxii
Incling experiment  9
Inert Gas system:  212
    Alarms  213
    Deck water seal  214
Intercostals  xxi, xxii, xxxii
Interim Certificate of Class  283


J

Joggle plates  xxii
Jumbo-isation  262

K

Keel:  xxiii, 70-74
    Bar  70
    Blocks  xxiii
    Duct  72/73
    Laying  71/72
    Plate  xxxii, 70/71, 73/74
    Rake  xxiii, 9
Keelson  xxiii
Knee  91,119
Kort Nozzle  xxiii


L

Launch:  286
    Arresting  288/289
    Cradle  xxiii
    Lloyds  10
    Methods  288-295
    Slip  286-288
    Stations (boats)  250-252
    Stresses  294/295
    Ways  xxiii, 287
Leaching  xxiii
Leak test  xxiii
Length:  9, 13, 134
    Breadth ratio  xxiii
    Between perpendiculars  9, 13
    Depth ratio  xxiii
    On waterline  9, 12/13
    Overall  9
Letter of intent  297
Lifeboats  247-252
Life saving appliances  246-252
Light displacement  9
Lightening holes  xxiii, 82
Limbers  xxiii, 84
Liquid measurement (methods, examples)  27-30
Liquid Natural Gas  84
Lloyds Register  282
Load stress  321, 323-325
    Loadline:  10
        Assignment  14
        Certificate  18
        Rules  18
        Summer  13
        Survey  18
        Timber  19/20
Longitudinals  xxiii, 94
Longitudinal framing  204/205
Long ton  10
Lumber Loadline  17, 19/20


M

Magnetic lifting  307
Manholes  xxiii, 73
Manifold connections  208-210
Manoeuvring criteria  24
Margin:
    Line  xx, xxiii, 10

Margin (*continued*)
    Plate xxiv, xxxii, 73-76, 84
Mast house 233/234
Masts 232-235, 253
Measurement (marine) 1-30
Measurement Treaty xxiv
Membrane tank (Gas) 217, 220/221
Mooring:
    Decks 156/157
    Equipment 157- 162
    Leads 156-162
    Windlass 141-144
Moss tank 217/218
Moulded:
    Breadth 10, 13
    Dimensions 10
Mud box xxiv,127/128, 146,148

**N**

Net Tonnage 10
New ship build 261
Non return valve xxiv, 84
Non-skid surface, 173
Notice of Survey 283
Nozzle propeller 61

**O**

Oil fuel unit 10
Oil hose handling 215
Oil in Water separators 197
Oil tankers 197-211
Open boats 247/248
Oxter plate xxiv, xxxiii, 43

**P**

Panama Canal tonnage 21
Panama Lead xxiv, 159-161
Panting: 155, 317
    Arrangement 155, 317
    Beams xxiii, xxiv, 155
    Stringers xxiv, 128, 133, 147, 155
Parallel middle body 10
Parcel tanker 216, 224
Partially enclosed boat 248
Passenger ship: xxiv
    Bottom tank structure 82
    Vessel 183-196
Permeability 10
Permissible exposure limit 10
Permissible length 10
Perpendiculars 13
Pilgrim Nut 65
Pillars xxiv, xxxii, 94, 107/108, 318
Pintle xxiv, xxxiii, 32, 36/37, 41, 47/48
Pipeline systems 206-211
Pitch: xxiv, 24
    Angle 24/25
    Calculations 25/26

Measurement 24-27
Pivot Point 139
Plans of ship 24
Plastics 313/314
Plate:
    Keel 70/71
    Preparation 268
    rudder xxiv
Plimsoll marks 10/11, 17, 20
Plug plan 23/24
Plummer block xxiv, 67
Pontoon hatch 97, 100, 102, 238
Pounding 156
Pod propulsion xxv, 53/54
Pre-fabrication 262-266
Pressure vacuum valve 224
Proof load 11
Propeller: 59
    Bearing 55
    Blade 59, 63
    Boss xxv, 59
    Clearances 60
    Connection 64
    Contra rotating 66
    Controllable pitch 61-63
    Disc area 60
    Ducted 41/42
    Factors 60
    Hub xxv, 35, 63
    Materials 310
    Nozzle 61
    Rake 60
    Removal 65
    Securing 64
    Shaft xxv, xxxi, 63, 66/67
    Shaft support 50-52
    Tandem xxiv
Pump rooms 203, 206, 216

**Q**

Quadrant Steering xxv
Quarter vehicle ramps 179/180

**R**

Racking stresses 319, 327
Radar mast 253
Radar measure (tanks) 30
Rails 16
Ramps (vehicles) 172-182
Ranging cables xix
Reaction fins 41
Registered:
    Breadth 11
    Depth 11
    Length 11
    Ton 11
Relative density 28
Reserve buoyancy xxvii, 11
Rigging plan 24
Rise of floor xxv, 11, 13

Rising line  xxv
Rivet structure  xxv
Roller leads  156-159
Rope guard  158
Rope store  127
Ro-Ro transports  165-182
Rotary vane steering  xxv, 36, 68/69
Rubbing strake  xxv
Rudder:  31-50
  Angles  69
  Arrangement  45
  Axis  37, 41, 44
  Balanced:  32
    Semi-  xxvi, 32/33, 35
  Bearing  35, 38, 44, 47
  Becker:  33, 37
    Flap  37
    King  37
  Blade  xxv, 36
  Carrier  35, 37, 45/46, 69
  Construction  36/37
  Flap  33, 37
  Hanging  34/35
  Horn  xxv, 36
  Indicator  xxv
  Lifting tube  44
  Mariner  xxv, 35/36
  Parts of  37
  Pintles  32, 36, 41, 47/48
  Plate  xxii, xxv, 36
  Post  44
  Schilling  xxvi, 38-40
  Schottel  xxvvi
  Spade  xxvii
  Stock  xxix, 36, 45/47
  Stops  xxvi
  Suspended  xxviii, 34/35
  Trunk  xxvi, xxxi, xxxiii, 37, 45, 274
  Twin  49
  Types  32-40
  Vectwin  39/40
Rubber products  315
Run  11

**S**

Sacrificial anodes  xxvi, 34
Safe working load  11
Sagging  xix, 319/320
Samson post  231/232, 235
Sandwich plate system  xxvi, 311, 314
Scantlings  xxvi
Scarph  xxvi
Schilling rudder  xxvi, 33, 38-40
Scuppers  16, 90, 125
Scuttle  xxvii, 16, 112/113
Seams  xxvi
Sea trials  xxvi
Shackle length  11
Shaft:
  Propeller  xxv, xxx
  Rake  xxvi
  Tail end  xxix, 51, 64-66

Tunnel  xxvi, xxx, 105
Sheathed decks  124
Sheer:  11
  Correction  xxvii, 15
  Strake  xxvii, xxxii
Shell:
  Doors  189/190
  Expansion plan  24
  Plating  xxvii, xxxii, 94, 119
Ship Stresses:
  Bending moment  322-325
  Dry dock  321, 327
  Hogging  319/320
  Racking  319, 327
  Sagging  320
  Shear forces  322-325
  Torsional  321
  Water pressure  326
Ship markings  16
Ship plans  24
Ship types:  xxxiv
  Type A  14
  Type B  14
Shipyard operations  257-259
Shrouds  xxii, xxvii, xxix, 233
Skeg  xxvii, 53, 61
Slip:
  Apparent  26
  Calculated  27
  Propeller  26
  Real  26
Sole piece  xxvii, xxxii, 37, 41, 44
Sounding  28
Spade Rudder  xxvii, 38
Spar ceiling  xxvii
Spectacle frame  xxvii, 52
Speed formula (maximum)  192
Spider band  xxvii
Spider link  63
Spurling pipe  xxviii, xxxi, 127, 141
Stability criteria  24
Stabilizers:  xxviii, 85-89
  Control  87
  Fins  86/87
  Tanks  xxviii
Stays  xxii
Stealer plate  xxviii, 122
Steel:
  grades  297/298
  sections  299/300
  stainless  224
  testing  303/304
  treatment  304-306
Steelwork management  306
Steering Flat  xxviii, xxxi
Steering gear:  32
  Cut outs  32
Stem:
  Bar  126/127
  Rake  xxviii, 11, 126/127
Stern:
  Cruiser  xx
  Door  164, 172-175, 178-180
  Frame  xxviii, 43/44

Stern (*continued*)
  Gland 130
  Transom xxix
  Tube xxviii, 35, 56-58, 136
Stock xxviii, xxix, 31/32, 45-47, 69
Stocks xxviii
Stools 136, 227
Stowage factor 12
Strake:
  Garboard xxxii, xxxiii,71
  Sheer xxvii, xxxii
Strength deck xxviii
Stress 316-327
Stringer: xxviii, 122
Structure test xxviii
Strum box 84
Struts xxviii
Stuffing box xxvii, xxix
Subdivision 8, 12, 14/15
Suez tonnage 21
Summer loadline 12, 13
Sump space (engine) 78
Superstructure: xxvii, 14
  Correction 15
Survey 282/283
Survey (loadline) 18
Swifter xxix


**T**


Tabernacle xxix, 223/234
Tail end shaft 64/65
Tandem propellers xxix
Tank:
  Disposition 82, 216
  Lid 28
  Measurement 29/30
  Side bracket xxix, xxxii, 75/76
  Tops xxix, xxxii, 74 -76, 121
  Wing 239
Tanker: 197-224
  Operations 214-216
  Pipelines 206-211
  Requirements 206
  Safety 200
Tare weight 12
Telemotor xxix
Threshold limit 12
Thrust:
  Bearing xxix
  Block xxix, 42, 46, 66/67
  Surface xxix
Thrusters: 150- 156
  Azi pod 151
  Lub oil system 152
  Retractable 151, 154
  Tunnel 151
Tiller xxix
Timber Loadline 19/20
Tonnage: 20/21
  Coefficients 21
  Compensated 21
  Deck xxix

Gross 20
Measurement 20
Net 20
Panama 21
Suez 21
Tonne 12
Torsion box xxix
Torsion meter xxix
Torsional stresses 321
Transfer xxix
Transportable moisture limit 12
Transom post 44
Transom stern 43, 184, 242
Transverse thrust xxx, 59
Tread xxx
Triatic stay xxx
Tri-maran 193
Trim 12
Truck (mast) xxx
Tumblehome 12, 13
Tunnel xxx
Turning circle xxx
Turn of bilge xxxii, 84
Twin propellers 49/50
Twin rudders 49
Tween deck: xxxi, xxxii, 105, 135
  Covers 102/103
  Lower 105
Type "A" ship xxx, 14/15
  "B" ship xxx, 14/15
  "B-60" ship xxx, 15
  "B-100" ship xxx, 15


**U**


Ullage 12, 22, 28/29
Ultra Large Crude Carrier 204
Underdeck: 93, 95, 107, 121
  Beam 91. 95, 156
  Passage 239, 242
  Stiffening 107, 162
  tonnage 12, 121
Underwater body 12, 134
Upper most continuous deck 90


**V**


Valve chest 83
Vapour lines 224
Vapour pressure 12
Velle derrick 232, 236
Ventilators: 16, 109/110
  Battery room 110
  Cowl 109
  Mushroom 110
  Torpedo 109
Vertical fire safety zones 163
Very Large Crude Carrier 205
Vibration post 44
Voith Schneider propulsion xxx, 60
Volatile liquid 12

**W**

Wale shores  xxx
Wash Plate  146/147
Waterjets  193, 195/196
Waterline  13, 170
Water pressure  319
Watertight:  xxii, 14, 114
  Bulkhead  135-137
  Compartment  136
  Control  114
  Door  xxx, 14
  Flat  82
  Gland  xxx, 46, 56
  Sealing  167
  Sub-division  136/137
Weathertight  xxxi, 14
Weather deck  90, 104
  Doors  112, 115
Web frame  202
Welding:  266
  Aluminium  278
  Arc  272-274
  Electric arc  275/276
  Examples  271-273
  Faults  269
  Friction stir  277/278
  Flux core  272
  Gas  272
  Plate preparation  268

  Practice of  266-268
  Robotic  280
  Semi-auto  280
  Tack  272-274
  Tests  270
  Types  271-274
Whelps  xix
Whessoe tank gauge  29
Windlass:  xxxi, 127
  Bed  xxxi
  Brake  xxxi, 142/143
  Split  143/144
Windows:
  Bridge  254-256
Wing tank construction  202, 205, 216, 239
Winter North Atlantic  17
Wood decks  122-125
Wood hatch covers  18, 96
Wood, use  315


**X**

X- Bow  130


**Y**

Y mast structure  231, 236

# MARINE HEAVY LIFT & RIGGING OPERATIONS
## By DAVID J. HOUSE

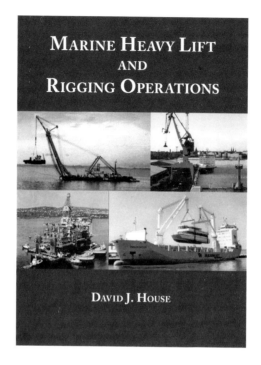

This publication covers the topic of Heavy Lifts within the marine industry. It is profusely illustrated and is directly aimed at the many industry sectors including: salvage operations, the offshore section, with the ship building and repair sectors, as well as the cargo aspects of the maritime environment.

The movement of bulk cargoes, both dry and liquid has expanded considerably alongside increased development in the third world. However, this expansion has not been limited to just bulk cargoes. Containerisation, roll on, roll off and designated project cargoes are all sectors which have seen increased activity in the field of heavy lifting practice.

The lifting and transportation of heavy weights has always been inherent with the maritime industries. The purpose of this work is designed to show not only some of the many routine lift operations aboard ships, but also the specialist movements of excessive loads, in a highly competitive commercial market.

The Offshore Industry in particular, generated probably the greatest interest in modular construction for oil and gas installations around the world. It is from the origins of the early floating cranes, which later developed the multi-purpose crane barges, floating sheer legs and salvage craft that has led to the massive activity and development in our coastline regions. Installations being constructed to mammoth proportions dominate the skylines of the world.

The rigging skills of personnel associated with a successful lift operation, should not be undermined. Their dedication to achieving what sometimes may appear as the impossible lift, is without equal. By the very nature of the task, the managers and operators have placed the safety of personnel and the protection of the environment at the forefront of the heavy-lift/transport industry. Nothing can expect to move without detailed 'Risk Assessment' and even then Project cargoes, heavy lift ships and major commercial operations all adhere to the first maritime principal for the Safety of Life at Sea.

**BROWN, SON & FERGUSON, LTD.**
**4-10 Darnley Street, Glasgow, G41 2SD**
website: www.skipper.co.uk  e-mail: info@skipper.co.uk